CAMBRIDGE TEXTS IN THE
HISTORY OF POLITICAL THOUGHT

JAMES HARRINGTON

The Commonwealth of Oceana
and *A System of Politics*

D1563851

CAMBRIDGE TEXTS IN THE
HISTORY OF POLITICAL THOUGHT

Series editors

RAYMOND GEUSS
Reader in Philosophy, University of Cambridge

QUENTIN SKINNER
Regius Professor of Modern History in the University of Cambridge

Cambridge Texts in the History of Political Thought is now firmly established as the major student textbook series in political theory. It aims to make available to students all the most important texts in the history of western political thought, from ancient Greece to the early twentieth century. All the familiar classic texts will be included, but the series seeks at the same time to enlarge the conventional canon by incorporating an extensive range of less well-known works, many of them never before available in a modern English edition. Wherever possible, texts are published in complete and unabridged form, and translations are specially commissioned for the series. Each volume contains a critical introduction together with chronologies, biographical sketches, a guide to further reading and any necessary glossaries and textual apparatus. When completed the series will aim to offer an outline of the entire evolution of western political thought.

For a list of titles published in the series, please see end of book

JAMES HARRINGTON

The Commonwealth of Oceana and A System of Politics

EDITED BY

J. G. A. POCOCK

Department of History
Johns Hopkins University, Baltimore, USA

CAMBRIDGE UNIVERSITY PRESS

PUBLISHED BY THE PRESS SYNDICATE OF THE UNIVERSITY OF CAMBRIDGE
The Pitt Building, Trumpington Street, Cambridge, United Kingdom

CAMBRIDGE UNIVERSITY PRESS
The Edinburgh Building, Cambridge CB2 2RU, UK
40 West 20th Street, New York, NY 10011–4211, USA
477 Williamstown Road, Port Melbourne, VIC 3207, Australia
Ruiz de Alarcón 13, 28014 Madrid, Spain
Dock House, The Waterfront, Cape Town 8001, South Africa

http://www.cambridge.org

First published 1992
Reprinted 1999, 2001, 2003

Printed in the United Kingdom at the University Press, Cambridge

A catalogue record for this book is available from the British Library

Library of Congress cataloguing in publication data

Harrington, James, 1611–1677.
[Commonwealth of Oceana]
The Commonwealth of Oceana and A system of politics / James
Harrington : edited and translated by J. G. A. Pocock.
p.   cm. – (Cambridge texts in the history of political thought)
Includes bibliographical references and index.
ISBN 0 521 41189 0 (hardcover). – ISBN 0 521 42329 5 (paper)
1. Utopias. 2. Political science – Early works to 1800.
I. Pocock, J. G. A. (John Greville Agard), 1924–
II. Harrinton, James, 1611–1677. System of politics. 1992.
III. Title   IV. Title: Commonwealth of Oceana.   V. Title: System of
politics.   VI. Series.
HX811 1656.H37   1992   91-23291 CIP
321'.07–dc20

ISBN 0 521 41189 0 hardback
ISBN 0 521 42329 5 paperback

WV/CP

Contents

Preface

This volume presents the texts of James Harrington's first and last political writings, *The Commonwealth of Oceana* (1656) and *A System of Politics* (written c. 1661 and published posthumously in 1700), as they were prepared by the present editor for *The Political Works of James Harrington* (Cambridge University Press, 1977).[1] The seventeenth-century spelling, punctuation and paragraph division of *The Commonwealth of Oceana* were modernized for that edition, as were those employed by John Toland and his printers for *The Oceana and Other Works of James Harrington* (1700), the edition in which *A System of Politics* appeared for the first time. In 1977 as now, the intention was to produce an edition for the eye of the modern reader, leaving detailed textual criticism (if thought necessary; none has been under-taken so far) to be performed upon the published originals. (No manuscripts by Harrington are known to exist.) The 1977 edition also contained an introductory and interpretative essay of 150 pages; this has been drawn upon in writing the introduction to the present volume, which is nevertheless a new piece of work.

JGAP

[1] Referred to in this volume as Harrington: 1977.

Introduction

Harrington's life and writings

Not much is known of James Harrington (1611–77) beyond what his published works tell us. There are next to no surviving personal papers or manuscripts of his various writings. Not all of these were published in his lifetime, however; a number of his works, including *A System of Politics*, are stated by John Toland (1670–1722) to have been preserved in manuscript by Harrington's sister Dorothy Bellingham and published by Toland in the first collected edition of 1700.[2] These manuscripts no longer seem to exist, and since we know that Toland extensively rewrote the memoirs of Edmund Ludlow before publishing them,[3] caution is in order. *The Commonwealth of Oceana*, on the other hand, was printed in 1656, and most of what we consider Harrington's major works between that year and 1660. In all these cases we can compare what he published with what Toland edited, and find the latter to have been no unreliable editor where printed originals already existed.

But we are also dependent on Toland – together with John Aubrey and Anthony Wood[4] – for most of our information about Harrington's personal life. He was a country gentleman, of an old family with Yorkist antecedents established in Northamptonshire and Lincoln-

---

[2] *The Oceana and other Works of James Harrington, with an Account of his Life by John Toland* (London, 1700; subsequent editions 1737 – enlarged by Thomas Birch – 1747, 1771).
[3] Blair Worden (ed.), *Edmund Ludlow: A Voyce from the Watchtower* (London, 1978).
[4] John Aubrey, *Brief Lives* (ed. Oliver Lawson Dick, London, 1958), pp. 124–27; Anthony Wood, *Athenae Oxonienses* (Oxford, 1848), vol. II, p. 389.

shire.[5] Notwithstanding his criticisms of primogeniture, he was an eldest son with younger brothers; but he remained unmarried until late in life and seems to have played no part in county or national politics, before or during the First Civil War. In 1647, probably at the instigation of his politically active cousin and namesake Sir James Harrington, he became a gentleman of the bedchamber to the captive Charles I, and remained with the King until shortly before the regicide of January 1649. During this period of twenty months, Harrington was personally involved in incidents which were certainly crucial in English history and may be thought significant in his life as a political author. He came face to face with Cornet Joyce when the latter arrived at Holmby House to take possession of the King's person for the Army; this experience did not make a Leveller of him,[6] though in *Oceana* he seems to accept an enlargement of the voting population as extensive as most Levellers desired.[7] Among Charles's first requests to Joyce was that he might have the company of Gilbert Sheldon and Henry Hammond, the two most active agents in ensuring the Church of England's survival during the Interregnum and its restoration after 1660; and when Harrington continued attending the King at Hampton Court and Carisbrooke Castle, he must have known of Charles's consultations with these and other divines of the episcopal allegiance – consultations of great significance for later Stuart and Hanoverian monarchy. But this encounter did not make Harrington an Anglican; rather, it must be seen in contrast with the virulent anticlericalism and religious heterodoxy of his writings in the late 1650s. It is curious to visit Carisbrooke and reflect that both *Eikon Basilike* and *The Commonwealth of Oceana* may have begun gestation there at the same time.

There is a story[8] that Charles used to discuss forms of government with Harrington, but would never endure to hear him speak of a republic. The tradition has a whiff of subsequent manufacture, but it is imaginable that they may have talked about Venice; Harrington had been there and admired it, while Charles was determined that a king must be something more than a doge. After Charles was removed from Carisbrooke, Harrington was separated from him by a commission of officers and ministers; there is a tradition that he was present

[5] Ian Grimble, *The Harrington Family* (London, 1957).
[6] Harrington: 1977, pp. 656–58.   [7] Below, pp. 75–76.
[8] Harrington: 1977, pp. 4–5.

on the scaffold at Whitehall, but the detailed account written by Edward Herbert, who had been Harrington's companion in attendance on the King, does not mention him. A further tradition states that Harrington had become personally devoted to Charles and suffered acute melancholy at his death.[9] This is wholly possible; Charles could exert personal charm, and the regicide was a traumatic shock to a great many individuals; but it is not reflected at all vividly in Harrington's writings. The value of all these stories is that they remind us how little evidence there is that Harrington or anyone else was a theoretical or doctrinaire republican before 1649. He wrote *Oceana* less to justify the fall of the English monarchy than to explain it, and this is why the work is important.

We hear nothing more of Harrington for seven years, until he published *The Commonwealth of Oceana* in September–November 1656, stating in a foreword that he had begun writing less than two years before. Its context then is not the revolutionary transition from monarchy to republic, but the discontents of the Cromwellian Protectorate; and if we think of it as related to the redefinition of the Protector's position by the Humble Petition and Advice and the election of a parliament during the summer of 1656, it falls into company[10] with Sir Henry Vane's *A Healing Question* and Marchmont Nedham's *The Excellency of a Free State*, which has a slightly better claim than *Oceana*'s to be considered the first programmatic statement of English classical republicanism. Vane was questioned by the Council of State for his writings, and Nedham may have apologized indirectly for his. Nothing links Harrington directly with either Vane or Nedham, and though he had some trouble getting his work printed – his foreword[11] mentions a "spaniel questing," presumably a government agent self-appointed or otherwise – the story that he had to appeal to Cromwell's daughter[12] has a strong flavour of fiction.

We have only one account of what led Harrington to compose *Oceana*. It occurs in a dialogue[13] printed by Toland under the title *The Examination of James Harrington* and purporting to be a conversation between Harrington and Lauderdale when he was a prisoner in the

[9] *Ibid.*
[10] Harrington: 1977, pp. 12–14; J. G. A. Pocock, "James Harrington and the Good Old Cause; a study of the ideological content of his writings," *Journal of British Studies*, x (1970), 1, pp. 30–48.   [11] Below, p. 2.
[12] Harrington: 1977, p. 8.   [13] Harrington: 1977, pp. 855–59.

Tower in 1662. Assuming it to be Harrington's work (which it probably is), it is still only his account of what he said to his inquisitors concerning events as many as eight years preceding the alleged conversation. In it he says that some of Cromwell's officers urged him to consider a commonwealth, and were told that they did not know what one was. This sounds like Cromwell, and in 1654 – two years before the publication of *Oceana* – Colonels Okey, Alured and Saunders complained of the Army's loss of status under the Protectorate and were dismissed from command. A lesser figure, Colonel John Streater, also lost his commission in 1654 and set up as a printer of literature on Greek and Roman republics. In 1656 he was to begin, and have some trouble completing, the printing of *Oceana*.[14] After Cromwell's rebuff of his officers, *The Examination of James Harrington* continues, "some sober men came to me and told me, if any man in England could show what a commonwealth was, it was myself."[15] These need not have been identical with the complaining officers, and the mind may turn to the group of Henry Neville, Henry Marten and Thomas Chaloner, who have been linked with Nedham as early as 1652, when he was writing what became *The Excellency of a Free State*. The phrase "some sober men" might inspire disrespectful chuckles, since Marten and Chaloner were supposed to be heavy drinkers and religious libertines, but Henry Neville was to be Harrington's close and devoted friend for the rest of the latter's life. It remains unknown to us, however, when or why Harrington acquired the republican learning of which *Oceana* is full, and there is nothing more (except the text itself) to tell us what he intended by publishing the work in 1656.

The Commonwealth of Oceana attracted attention and criticism, and during the next three and a half years Harrington published a number of further writings, of which *The Prerogative of Popular Government* (1657) and *The Art of Lawgiving* (1659) are the most ambitious.[16] They consist in part of a controversial defence against the most pertinacious of his critics – Matthew Wren, son of the Bishop of Ely[17] – and in part of elaborations of what his theories of government implied for religious authority, theology and philosophy. It is very possible that we have here the strongest force driving Harrington to write and

[14] Harrington: 1977, pp. 6–7, 9–10, 14.   [15] Harrington: 1977, p. 859.
[16] All are printed in full in Harrington: 1977.
[17] Harrington: 1977, pp. 83–89.

publish,[18] and these works should certainly be read together with those here introduced. In the last phase of his literary activity – between the accession of Richard Cromwell and the restoration of Charles II – Harrington's tracts and pamphlets reflect the death agonies of the English Commonwealth; he opposed Vane and Milton, who still hoped for a rule of the saints, but maintained that unless legislative reform could change the nature of English politics, a reversion to parliamentary monarchy was inevitable.[19]

He was left undisturbed in 1660, but at the end of 1661 was taken into custody, apparently in connexion with the Derwentwater Plot. (At this time Henry Neville left England for some years.) *The Examination of James Harrington* claims to belong to this episode, and Toland says that the manuscript of *A System of Politics* survived Harrington's arrest and passed into family keeping. In prison at Plymouth, he underwent a physical and mental collapse of some nature, and after his release lived in retirement at Westminster till he died in 1677. He wrote one essay, *The Mechanics of Nature*, on the medical and philosophical implications of his condition,[20] but apparently nothing more on politics. Nor do we know if he conversed on the subject with Neville or anyone else, though Neville lived till 1694 and in 1682 published *Plato Redivivus*, a work of some importance in carrying on what we know as the "commonwealth" or "neo-Harringtonian" style in English political discourse. So much for what the facts of Harrington's life may tell us about his authorship of the English republican classic. What it means to call *Oceana* that must next be considered.

Oceana and English republicanism

There is a real sense in which republican theories were a consequence, not a cause or even a precondition, of the execution of the King and the temporary abolition of the monarchy. If Louis XVI in 1793 was executed for being a king – for being a species of ruler which his condemners had come to consider illegitimate – Charles I

[18] Mark Goldie, "The civil religion of James Harrington," in Anthony Pagden (ed.), *The Languages of Political Theory in Early Modern Europe* (Cambridge, 1987), pp. 197–222.
[19] Harrington: 1977, pp. 100–18, 729, 744–45, 797–98; A. F. Woolrych, "The Good Old Cause and the fall of the protectorate," *Cambridge Historical Journal*, XIII, 2 (1957), pp. 133–61; (intro.), *Complete Prose Works of John Milton*, vol. VII (New Haven, 1980).
[20] Printed by Toland, but not in the 1977 edition.

in 1649 was executed for failing to be a king: for exercising his office in such a way as to reduce his subjects to a frenzy of frustration and those who condemned him to the conviction that he was the chief obstacle to the restitution of order and government. There is a level at which it is true that the King was put to death by men who still believed in the kingly office, but it was an appalling paradox that, for this reason, they could not judge the man without abolishing the office; the logic of resistance theory had pointed in this direction, but not all the way. How unwilling they were to act on this imperative is seen in the ordinance abolishing the monarchy which followed the King's execution;[21] it appeals only to fact, to the experience of history which is said to have revealed that monarchy does more to divide and destroy the nation than to unite and preserve it, that monarchy does not do what it is supposed to do. Therefore the people are to provide themselves with another form of government; this is not a liberating discovery of democratic principle, but a harsh and painful discovery of what at another moment in English history was to be called "utmost necessity."[22] The dissolution of government was an appeal to the *de facto* before the *de jure*; monarchy had failed *de facto*, a form of government *de facto* was to replace it, and the legal, ethical, political and religious problem now became for many that of by what right the subject might give obedience to a government *de facto* and not *de jure*, and by what right such a government might demand obedience.

What we now consider a classic body of English political theory took shape in the attempt to give answers to these questions,[23] but its contents have little to do with English republicanism and even less with the writings of James Harrington. It stated the problem, and attempted to solve it, in the language of natural and civil jurisprudence: of right, obligation and authority, and of property, nature and knowledge as these terms were defined by the vocabulary of natural and civil law. This language and vocabulary are rightly enough considered dominant and paradigmatic in the foundations of political

---

[21] *A Declaration of the Parliament of England, expressing the grounds of their late proceedings, and of setling the present government in the way of a free state* (1649). Harrington: 1977, p. 28.

[22] In 1688–89; see Keith Feiling, *History of the Tory Party, 1640–1714* (Oxford, 1924), pp. 235, 254, 285.

[23] Perez Zagorin, *A History of Political Thought in the English Revolution* (London, 1954); John M. Wallace, *Destiny His Choice: the Loyalism of Andrew Marvell* (Cambridge, 1968); Margaret Judson, *From Tradition to Political Reality: a study of the ideas set forth in support of the Commonwealth government in England, 1649–1653* (Hamden, Connecticut, 1980).

thought in early modern Europe;[24] but in order to understand Harrington, and perhaps republican theory as well, we have to recognize
that – to a degree very surprising in an educated Englishman of the
mid-seventeenth century – Harrington's text is devoid of the vocabulary of natural law, and (no less surprisingly) of common law as well.
He reverts almost unequivocally to an earlier vocabulary, one in which
the concepts of property and nature functioned as means of pro-
nouncing that man the political animal was by nature a citizen and not
a subject, a creature who used intelligence to define himself rather
than to acknowledge binding law. It was this which made Harrington
a republican and made it hard for him to be an orthodox Christian.
The premises on which such thinking rested were immensely
remote from those at the foundations of normal English political
thinking. This is why republican theories are hard to find in England
before 1649, and why there were none to which the regicide regime
could appeal. The only such theory currently known to scholars was
austere, aristocratic, based on a study of Plato's *Laws*, and very little
disseminated outside the family of Philip and Algernon Sidney.[25] We
shall see that Harrington's republicanism was of a very different
stripe, far more intimately connected with the advent of the *de facto*
problem.
  It is to be derived, along one of several lines, from that crucial
document, *His Majesty's Answer to the Nineteen Propositions of Parliament*, put into Charles's mouth in August 1642 by his advisers Falkland and Culpeper.[26] Falkland may have been touched by the Platonic
republicanism mentioned above, but what he here helped to frame
was a description of English parliamentary monarchy "republican" in
the sense that it was Polybian, the description of a mixed government

[24] Pagden (ed.), *The Languages of Political Theory*; Quentin Skinner, *The Foundations of
Modern Political Thought* (Cambridge, 1978); Richard Tuck, *Natural Rights Theories: their
origin and development* (Cambridge, 1980); James Tully, *A Discourse on Property: John
Locke and his adversaries* (Cambridge, 1980).
[25] Jonathan Scott, *Algernon Sidney and the English Republic, 1623–77* (Cambridge, 1988);
Blair Worden, "Classical republicanism and the Puritan Revolution," in Lloyd-Jones et
al. (eds.), *History and Imagination: essays in honour of H. R. Trevor-Roper* (Oxford, 1981),
and "The Commonwealth kidney of Algernon Sidney," *Journal of British Studies*, XXIV, 1
(1984), pp. 1–40.
[26] Corinne C. Weston, *English Constitutional Theory and the House of Lords* (London, 1965);
Corinne C. Weston and Janelle R. Greenburg, *Subjects and Sovereigns: the Grand Controversy over Legal Sovereignty in Stuart England* (Cambridge, 1981); Michael J. Mendle,
Dangerous Positions: Mixed Government, Estates and the Answer to the XIX Propositions
(Alabama, 1985).

in which monarchy, aristocracy and democracy combined to balance one another. Each of the three was imperfect – including monarchy, which is what was aberrant about *His Majesty's Answer* – having its characteristic vices as well as virtues, which must bring it to corruption if it attempted to function by itself; but the combination of all three would check the degenerative tendency of each. There were two major difficulties about this thesis. In the first place, theocracy was not of its essence; in the second, it did not really allow for the sovereignty of king in parliament, which the language of balance might reinforce but could not describe.

The *Answer to the Nineteen Propositions* was intended as a warning against civil war; by making king, lords and commons equal in government, it made them equally responsible for maintaining the balance of government. However, civil war did ensue, and the problem in which the *Answer* was instantly involved was that of ascertaining the subject's duty when two or more legitimate authorities were competing to claim his allegiance at the sword's point. Henry Parker, writing for the Parliament,[27] exploited the *Answer's* implicit reduction of the king to an estate within his own realm, and went on to argue that Parliament was more truly representative of the subject than the king was, and therefore had the better claim to allegiance. But a deeper insight was achieved by Philip Hunton in *A Treatise of Monarchy*, when he pointed out that should the components of a mixed government go to war among themselves, no one of them had authority to bind the other two, since if one had that authority, no balanced mixture of equal powers would have existed in the first place.[28] From this Hunton drew the conclusion that the individual was obliged to decide for himself; Sir Robert Filmer drew the conclusion of *The Anarchy of a Limited or Mixed Monarchy*.[29] But anarchy was the objective reality of a state of civil war, and Hunton had gone further than Filmer in anticipating the problem of *de facto* obedience. By 1650, when the Engagement to obey a kingless (and lordless) government had laid that problem in principle before every adult male, it was possible for Nedham to argue that a civil war between the

[27] Henry Parker, *Observations upon some of his Majesties late Answers and Expresses* (1642); *The Contra-Replicant his Complaint to his Majesty* (1643).
[28] Philip Hunton, *A Treatise of Monarchy* (1643), p. 69.
[29] Peter Laslett (ed.), *Patriarcha and Other Political Writings by Sir Robert Filmer* (Oxford, 1949).

components of a mixed government was an appeal to heaven, and that when heaven's judgment was known by the issue of the war, the victor enjoyed the authority of a conqueror over his former partners and the subject was enjoined to obey his sword by all the imperatives existing in the state of nature. Here Nedham took his stand upon juristic ground, and in *The Case of the Commonwealth of England Stated* (1650) made use of the writings so far published by Hobbes.[30] But his argument presupposed that a mixed government had existed in the first instance, without making it clear why a conqueror should use his unshared authority to restore or establish a form in which it would be limited by being shared with others. In 1651–52 his writings – editorials in *Mercurius Politicus* which he published in 1656 as *The Excellency of a Free State* – took a republican form[31] with the argument that England had been conquered by its democratic component, the Army acting with the authority of the representative Commons, which now enjoyed a power legislative like that of Lycurgus, to create a republic in which monarchy, aristocracy and democracy should balance one another more efficiently than they had under king, lords and commons. The hand of Neville, Marten and Chaloner has been detected in these editorials of 1652,[32] and the situation they presume to exist in England is that presumed by Harrington in the Second Part of the Preliminaries to *Oceana*, when he describes Olphaus Megaletor and his victorious army at a moment easier to recall in 1654 than in 1656.[33] He goes on to tell the tale of how these heroes met in council to shoulder the task of Lycurgus.

Harrington's republicanism is more Machiavellian than Platonic – the Florentine was an author he deeply admired – because of its concern with the *de facto*. He wanted to know how the English parliamentary monarchy, the government of king, lords and commons, had come to collapse, and he wanted to know what should replace it. He accepted the Polybian thesis that the aim in government was to maintain a balance between the one, few and many, and he accepted the dictum of 1649 that the historic monarchy had never been very good, and had got worse, at maintaining it. This was how he

---

[30] *The Case of the Commonwealth*, edited by Philip A. Knachel, was published in Charlottesville (1969). For its use of Hobbes, see Harrington: 1977, pp. 33–34, and the references there given.

[31] Harrington: 1977, pp. 34–37.

[32] Blair Worden, *The Rump Parliament, 1648–53* (Cambridge, 1974), p. 252.

[33] Below, pp. 66–67.

came to write a historicist republicanism, and he had access to resources for interpreting history which had been unavailable to Plato or even Machiavelli. There is, unsurprisingly, debate as to how far he achieved or attempted the description of a republic having the perfection of a Platonic idea. Perhaps his Oceana is only an imaginary historical construct, the product of a constellation of historic forces which can last no longer than they permit, and the actors in his story no more than inhabitants of Plato's cave. On the other hand, he seems to assert that, in passing out of the period of history he terms "Gothic," actors in the history of Oceana left behind "the goods of fortune" in which they were the servants of masters, and entered on "the goods of the mind" in which they were together free to be the masters of themselves.[34] We seem therefore to find in his text a mixture of history and utopia, the analysis of the rise and fall of social forms alternating with descriptions of a state of affairs in which humans can apply their intelligence in determining what they shall be, and are to that extent godlike. There is here a political philosophy in the strict classical sense; a study of how political association and human intellect can be perfectly combined. What is extraordinary in someone of Harrington's era, however, is less the persistence of philosophy than the innovative presence of a historical intelligence capable of synthesizing schemes of social change which set the *de facto* disorderliness of the English Civil Wars in a context of long-range and even universal historical processes.

Oceana and English history

Because *The Commonwealth of Oceana* employs the devices of fiction to portray the arrangements of an ideal state, it exhibits characteristics which we call utopian. And because it was the third such portrayal to become prominent in English literature – the others being Thomas More's *Utopia* and Francis Bacon's *The New Atlantis* – and because it was applied to a moment of deeply sensed and unwanted historical crisis, it helped form the notion of a utopian genre which could be condemned as absurd and unworldly. Practical politicians and their literary hangers-on began declaring that they had no part in "Platonic," "Utopian," "Atlantic" and "Oceanic" dreaming, and of

---

[34] Below, pp. 10–11, 18–19.

course have been doing so ever since. Matthew Wren,[35] an establishment man waiting in Oxford for the formation of a new establishment, was foremost in ridiculing Harrington as an armchair legislator, and Marchmont Nedham employed the same device in weaselling out of his own authorship of *The Excellency of a Free State*. Harrington was more sophisticated than they made him appear. He always referred to his portrayal of "Oceana" as a "model,"[36] a term he employed in very much its modern sense; and he pointed out that "state empirics" and "ministers of state" very often acted without understanding the springs of their own actions,[37] a way of behaving which could succeed only in a political system stable enough to survive them. The England of Charles I and Oliver Cromwell was not such a system, and practical politicians were by 1656 unknown.

There is a deeper reason why *Oceana* is not a utopia in More's, Bacon's or Campanella's sense.[38] It does not portray a no-place or *outopia*, an imaginary island in unknown seas, but a fictionalized yet instantly recognizable England (Harrington made only one minor use of the fiction in his subsequent writings). What is being idealized is not a commonwealth isolated from the history of mankind, but the immediate present or imminent future which Harrington presents England as occupying in history as he understands it. *Oceana* is not a utopia so much as an *occasione*, a moment of revolutionary opportunity at which old historical forms have destroyed themselves and there is a chance to construct new forms immune from the contingencies of history (known as *fortuna*). Harrington employed fiction to show what might be done, and satire because of the chances that it might not be done. At a deeper level, he was less a founder of the genre of historical utopia or futuristics than an important figure in the history of revolutionary theory; he does not use the modern term revolution, but it has come to denote a moment of historical exhaustion and opportunity, and this he explicitly does describe. We cannot understand *Oceana*'s character as utopia unless we first understand its character as history.

---

[35] He was one of the circle around Wilkins and Wallis, mathematicians and future latitudinarians.
[36] For the first occurrence of the term see below, p. 2, 7.
[37] Below, pp. 137, 292; Harrington: 1977, pp. 395, 709.
[38] For the state of "utopian" writing in England, see J. C. Davis, *Utopia and the Ideal Society: a study of English utopian writing, 1516–1700* (Cambridge, 1981).

The sense of history in early-modern England[39] was increasing, and drew on many sources. Ancient writers, Aristotle and Polybius, had been interested in political change and ways in which regimes undermined their own foundations. The successive rise and fall of the Roman republic and the Roman empire had enlarged this into a theme of universal history; but change, growth and decline were explained largely in moral and characterological, rather than institutional or material terms. Renaissance historiography had intensified its sense of the latter in two ways: first, through Machiavelli's stress on the association between arms and liberty, with republican Rome displaying arms in the hands of the citizen body, Rome of the Caesars placing them in those of the legions controlled by the emperors. Secondly, humanist legal scholarship had given a central role to the holding of land, and the rights it conferred, by tenures which entailed the right, and the duty, to bear arms. The association between the ideas of arms, rights and land did a great deal to give the concept of property its central role in early-modern Western thought.

West European and English scholars – John Selden prominent among the latter – had developed the image of the "Gothic" invaders of decadent legionary Rome settling everywhere according to allodial and later feudal tenures which preserved the association between arms, property and liberty for later refinement. Harrington was a keen reader of both Machiavelli and Selden, but he also perceived the history of "Gothic" Europe and England from its latter end. Bacon's *History of King Henry the Seventh*[40] supplied him with the image of that King emancipating feudal tenants from the control of their lords by means of his Statute of Retainers, and this he enlarged into the conviction that the English peerage, assembled in the House of Lords in 1642, had been unable to prevent the outbreak of civil war because they no longer controlled armies of their own followers.[41] Had he been told of recent research which has stressed the "baronial" component in aristocratic behaviour at this period,[42] Harrington could have replied that it was unsurprising that Essex, Warwick and Northumberland should have thought and behaved like barons, but a

[39] See Pocock, *The Machiavellian Moment: Florentine Political Thought and the Atlantic Republican Tradition* (Princeton, 1975), chs. 2 and 11.
[40] First published 1622; ed. F. J. Levy (Indianapolis, 1972).
[41] Below, pp. 54–56.
[42] E.g. J. S. A. Adamson, "The English nobility and the projected settlement of 1647," *Historical Journal*, XXX, 3 (1987), pp. 567–602.

basic reality that they no longer possessed baronial power; they were not the masters of armies. This was his explanation of the fall of the monarchy and the House of Lords; neither the king nor the peerage controlled armies because the sword had passed into the hands of independent proprietors, freeholders and gentlemen, who when assembled in armies necessarily behaved in ways which were revolutionary because neither monarchy nor nobility controlled them.

The central significance of *The Commonwealth of Oceana*, and the central reason for regarding its author as a creative genius, is not that it is utopian or republican, but that it confronts the problem of *de facto* authority by offering, for the first time in intellectual history, an explanation of the English Civil Wars as a revolution, produced by the erosion of one political structure and the substitution of another through processes of long-term social change. Against this interpretation recent historians have mounted a persistent and damaging offensive, but their need to do so indicates that Harrington is not a trivial but a pivotal figure in the history of English political thought and historiography. His explanation situates an English revolution in the context of European history as a whole, from the citizen armies of the ancient republics through the legions of the emperors and their replacement by settlements of Gothic mercenaries turned feudal tenants, to the reconquest of England by its own proprietors with swords in their hands and no task before them other than the institution of a well-ordered republic. At this point, however, we encounter two features of Harrington's vision of contemporary society which are crucial if we wish to situate it in history and see what became of it.

The first is that he had no conception of a standing army. The term indeed occurs in his writings,[43] but does not bear the meaning of an army maintained by a state possessing the financial and bureaucratic resources necessary to feed, arm and pay it. He did not think that the state (with the possible exception of the Dutch republic) possessed those resources,[44] and indeed the Cromwellian Army was a revolutionary force because it was less an army maintained by the state than an army in search of a state which could either maintain it or pay it off. The armies of his day were still hordes wandering on the face of the land, and if they were to become settled political societies the question was whether they would be the military colonists of an emperor,

---

[43] Below, pp. 251–52.   [44] Below, pp. 60, 286; Harrington: 1977, pp. 59, 404.

the feudal tenants of a "Gothic" king and nobility, or the armed citizens of a republic. He was hopeful that the English armies would act as the last-mentioned because he thought of them as already independent proprietors who had taken up arms. We reach the limits of his analysis when we see he thought there was no way of maintaining a military class other than settling it on the land. By the time he died, twenty years after *Oceana*, the state was developing the financial capacity to maintain permanent armies; twenty years later still, the growth of this capacity was becoming a key to a new historical analysis of politics.[45] Without Harrington, this analysis could not have taken shape; but the course of history left him as the author of the antithesis in a new historical dialectic, in which his heirs were spokesmen for the citizen as opposed to the professional army.

There is a second, and deeper, explanation of why he failed as a prophet and survived only as a critic of historical development. The discovery that the English peerage had once been a feudal and baronial aristocracy, but were so no longer, encouraged him to suppose that their power had consisted only in their control over feudal subtenants and had vanished with it. Because England was no longer a feudal society there could never again be a hereditary aristocracy or the kind of kingship that went with it; to restore the Stuart line – as by 1659 he clearly saw was about to happen[46] – would be to restore a monarchy even more unstable than the "Gothic" had been. We can see that he failed to perceive that the power of a courtly monarchy and a landed aristocracy was patronal as well as feudal, resting on that whole edifice of patron and client, interest and connexion, benefit and gratitude, service and office, association and affection, influence and deference, court and country, and so on and on, which was to hold England together and provide its cement of value for a very long time to come. It was this nexus of government which was restored in 1660, and then reinforced and modernized by Williamite and Hanoverian monarchy, so effectively as to permit the growth of the revisionist historiography which presents the Civil Wars and Interregnum not as the revolution Harrington thought them to be, but as a devastating series of contingencies and accidents. He was so far from giving patronage its due as to be very untypical of the gentry to which he belonged, all of whose members knew what a court was for, no matter

[45] Pocock, *Machiavellian Moment*, ch. 12.
[46] Harrington: 1977, pp. 762, 797–98.

how heartily they disliked its inhabitants. Eighteenth-century England was to be ruled by a combination of patronage and commerce; Harrington's heirs attacked this "court" in the name of "country" values.

Political philosophy and *A System of Politics*

The paradox of Harrington is that he went deeper into historical analysis than any English writer before him, with the intention of showing the way out of history and nearer to ideal freedom. Like Karl Marx, he thought that history was ending and history about to begin. His way of putting it was by saying that, with the collapse of feudal society and the return to property so widely distributed as to permit a republic of equals – this did not mean an equality of all males or all human beings – European men were leaving behind "the goods of fortune" and returning to "the goods of the mind." When there was so little power that those possessing it were preoccupied with maintaining their control over the lives of others, they were vulnerable to the contingencies of history and could not look beyond them. When power was widely distributed, a multitude of patriarchs (this is what they are) could occupy themselves with sharing and exercising the capacity of intellect to direct the lives of free men. This history of property moved men into and out of the dictatorship of fortune.

What is "utopian" about *Oceana* therefore arises from the confrontation between history and the freedom of political reason (which Harrington traces back to the Book of Exodus).[47] Freedom is to be attained by systematizing the exercise of intelligence among citizens associated in a commonwealth, republic or polis; a community as large as England is to have the form of a city state. The elaborate "orders" of Oceana are designed to involve all citizens in the process of political decision and to distribute the exercise of intelligence among them. These "orders" are very largely concerned with regulating the relations between a political aristocracy or "few," and a political democracy or "many"; partly for the class reason that Harrington thought government must be exercised by the leisured as well as the industrious, partly for the philosophical reason that he thought the mind's activity in reflection was sharply different from its activity in decision. A psychology of reason and passion lies behind this, and

[47] Below, pp. 28, 71–73, 198, 201.

xxi

therefore behind the "utopian" (in the sense of "impracticable") proposal to separate a reflective senate, which may distinguish but never decide between alternative courses of action, from a decisive popular assembly, which must decide between them by casting ballots in silence without ever debating. The comic character Epimonus here protests that ballotting Venetians are dehumanized automata, whereas in the old English parliament men might "know and be known" by conversing and learning from each other.[48] The question is how far the processes of reason may be systematized and separated from the individual as an intelligent personality.

We encounter here what is Platonic, and at the same time disputably Christian, about Harrington's thought: his equation of God with pure intelligence, and man as the vehicle of that intelligence's presence in the organic and material world. In orthodox Christianity the mode of that presence was Christ the incarnate Logos, but in Harrington it shows signs of becoming property – the means by which God establishes men in the earth and gives them the opportunity of knowing and ruling it and one another, thus becoming like him and sharing his nature.[49] Gerrard Winstanley shared this perception, but thought that when the land was held in common Christ would be incarnate in all humans alike.[50] The more aristocratically minded Harrington maintained differences of political functioning between the otherwise equal proprietors, and his community is therefore more political and more Platonic than Winstanley's; but Oceana is to be a collaborative perfection of human reason, which will make men like God and typify the return of Christ.

There is one theological problem here, and one philosophical. Does the republic substitute itself for Christ's kingdom, thus subverting the existence of any church distinct from political society? Both Hobbes and Harrington seem to have looked on Christ as returning to restore the theocracy God had exercised in Israel, thus raising the question whether the Son added anything to the Father.[51] For Hobbes the political form of this theocracy had been monarchy, but for Harrington it had been a republic, in origin as much Gentile as

---

[48] Below, pp. 114–15.

[49] Harrington: 1977, pp. 80–81, 90–96, 112–13, 391, 543–44, 566, 604.

[50] G. Winstanley, *The Law of Freedom in a Platform and other works* (ed. Hill, Cambridge, 1982).

[51] For the relation of Hobbes to Harrington, see Harrington: 1977, pp. 80–82, 90–96; Pocock, "Time, history and eschatology in the thought of Thomas Hobbes," *Politics,*

Israelite; there may have been something in Richard Baxter's suspicion that he aimed to restore "the religion of old Rome."[52] Philosophically, it has been argued by the most recent scholars that Harrington failed to sustain the position of an "ancient" political philosopher, for whom the republic was the perfection of political intelligence for the contemplation and government of human existence, and moved significantly towards becoming a "modern," for whom intelligence is incapable of knowing any ultimate reality and confined in politics to the adjustment of conflicts of interest between necessarily finite and imperfect human beings.[53] This view of politics was most energetically advanced by Harrington's critic Matthew Wren (who by the way wished to ground it on the supremacy of mobile property rather than land); is it to be unmasked in Harrington as well?

The problem should be pursued by studying what he has to say about "interest" and about "legislation." He tells us that "good orders will make us good men"[54]; does he mean that they will perfect our natures, giving us the Platonic "form" of political creatures which it is our nature to fulfil? Or does he mean merely (as he also says)[55] that good laws will manipulate us into acting well, whether our natures are good or not? Good laws will be attained when it is no one's "interest" to act against the "interest" of all; does this mean that the commonwealth is a coalition of morally finite interests, which the political intelligence must cajole into acting more or less in harmony? The question may be whether the intellect is capable of knowing final or only practical goods. In *A System of Politics*, where someone – the style suggests Harrington and not Toland – has set out to summarize (and thereby enlarge) Harrington's entire theory in aphoristic form, the Platonic note is struck very strongly indeed. "As the form of a man is the image of God, so the form of a government is the image of man"; in erecting a government men aim to act in the image of God

---

Language and Time (New York, 1971; Chicago, 1989), pp. 148–201, and "Contexts for the study of James Harrington," *Il Pensiero Politico*, XI, 1 (1978).

[52] William M. Lamont, *Richard Baxter and the Millennium* (London, 1979), p. 189. I differ from Lamont in holding that by "old Rome" Baxter meant pagan rather than papal Rome. Cf. p. 63 below.

[53] Scott, *Algernon Sidney and the English Republic*, pp. 15ff.; and J. C. Davis, "Pocock's Harrington; grace, nature and art in the classical republicanism of James Harrington," *Historical Journal*, XXIV, 3 (1981), pp. 683–97.

[54] Below, pp. 64 (*Oceana*) and 274 (*System*); Harrington: 1977, p. 763.

[55] Harrington: 1977, p. 753.

and to contemplate themselves doing so; "the contemplation of form is astonishing to man, and has a kind of trouble or impulse accompanying it, that exalts his soul to God."[56] This is a Platonic view of politics, and there is no way round it. But there are obstacles in a world imperfectly formed. In matters of religion, most men can be neither saints nor atheists; they need a religion but are not autonomous enough to furnish their own.[57] In matters of politics, there can be no republic of all mankind, and competing republics will practice "reason of state" to further their competing interests; they must never confuse this with the reason that maintains them as forms of government.[58] This is Machiavellian rather than Hobbesian; it depicts the imperfections of a Platonic cosmos. Harrington, so strangely indifferent to the philosophy of the seventeenth-century jurists and living at the last moment when it was possible to ignore the power of capital in the formation of states, contributed powerfully to the historical thinking of modernity, but did not step into it philosophically. This is his challenge to us as historians of political thought.

[56] Below, p. 273.   [57] Below, p. 283.   [58] Below, pp. 286–87.

Principal events in Harrington's life

1611   Born January 3, son of Sir Sapcote Harrington of Upton, Northamptonshire, and Rand, Lincolnshire.

1629   Gentleman commoner of Trinity College, Oxford. Studied with William Chillingworth.

1631   Admitted to the Middle Temple. Traveled in the Netherlands and Italy; visited Venice and Rome.

1639   Accompanied Charles I to Scotland.

1642   Outbreak of First Civil War.

1647   Becomes Groom of the Bedchamber to Charles I. In his household at Holmby, Carisbrooke and Hurst Castle.

1649   Removed from attendance on the King. Charles I executed on January 30. Harrington's movements unknown. The Engagement controversy begins.

1651 Thomas Hobbes publishes *Leviathan*. Battle of Worcester.

1652 Ejection of the Rump Parliament.

1653 The Parliament of Saints.

1654 Oliver Cromwell Lord Protector. Discontent of some officers. Possible commencement of Harrington's work on *Oceana*.

1656 Publication of Hobbes's *Six Lessons to the Professors of Mathematics*, Nedham's *The Excellency of a Free State*, Vane's *A Healing Question*, and (between September and November) *The Commonwealth of Oceana*.

1657 Matthew Wren's *Considerations upon Mr. Harrington's Commonwealth of Oceana*. Harrington's *The Prerogative of Popular Government* bought for the Thomason collection.

1658 Death of Oliver Cromwell.

1659 Harrington's *The Art of Lawgiving* and other writings. Richard Baxter's *A Holy Commonwealth*. Meetings of the Rota Club.

1660 Milton's *The Ready and Easy Way to Establish a Free Commonwealth*. Restoration of Charles II.

1661 Probably working on *A System of Politics*. Arrested December 28.

1662 Released after physical and nervous collapse. Resides in Westminster.

1677 Dies September 11.

1681 Henry Neville's *Plato Redivivus*.

1698 Andrew Fletcher's *Discourse of Government with Relation to Militias*.

1700 John Toland publishes *The Oceana and Other Works of James Harrington*.

Further reading

There is a modern edition, *The Political Works of James Harrington*, *edited with an introduction by J. G. A. Pocock* (Cambridge, 1977). Other twentieth-century studies are H. F. Russell Smith, *Harrington and his Oceana* (Cambridge, 1914); S. B. Liljegren (ed.), *James Harrington's "Oceana"* (Lund and Heidelberg, 1924); Charles Blitzer, *An Immortal Commonwealth: the Political Thought of James Harrington* (New Haven, 1960); Jurgen Gebhardt (ed.), *James Harrington: Politische Schriften* (Munich, 1973); Giuseppe Schiavone (ed.), *La Repubblica di Oceana, di James Harrington* (Milan, 1985).

For the political thought of the English Interregnum, see Perez Zagorin, *A History of Political Thought in the English Revolution* (London, 1954); J. G. A. Pocock, *The Ancient Constitution and the Feudal Law* (Cambridge, 1957, 1987); John M. Wallace, *Destiny His Choice: the Loyalism of Andrew Marvell* (Cambridge, 1968); Andrew Sharp, *Political Ideas of the English Civil Wars, 1641–49* (London, 1983).

For Harrington and the context of republican thought, see Z. S. Fink, *The Classical Republicans* (Evanston, 1945); Caroline Robbins, *The Eighteenth-Century Commonwealthman* (Cambridge, MA, 1957); J. G. A. Pocock, *The Machiavellian Moment* (Princeton, 1975) and *Virtue, Commerce and History* (Cambridge, 1985); J. C. Davis, *Utopia and the Ideal Society: a Study of English Utopian Writing, 1516–1700* (Cambridge, 1980); Jonathan Scott, *Algernon Sidney and the English Republic, 1623–1677* (Cambridge, 1988) and *Algernon Sidney and the Restoration Crisis, 1677–1683* (Cambridge, 1991); Anna Maria Strumia, *L'Immaginazione Repubblicana: Sparta ed Israele nel dibattito filosofico-politico dell' età di Cromwell* (Turin, 1991).

THE
Commonwealth
OF
Oceana

Tantalus a labris sitiens fugientia captat
Flumina: quid rides? mutato nomine, de te
Fabula narratur.

Horace

Dedicated
to His Highness
The
LORD PROTECTOR
of
The Commonwealth of England,
Scotland and Ireland

By JAMES HARRINGTON

[This title page is a composite. Two editions appeared simultaneously in 1656, one bearing the name of Livewell Chapman as bookseller, the other that of Daniel Pakeman (referred to in notes as 'C' and 'P'). In both editions, there is a first title page consisting of the title, the lines from Horace, the name of the bookseller and (in 'Chapman') the printer; and (in both) a second title page, repeating the title and adding the dedication.]

Epistle to the Reader

Sir,

If this writing be not acceptable, here is already enough, and too much of it; but if it be, it is but a rough draft, for I have not been yet two years about it, nor ever saw all or half my papers together. And now, in the bringing them to light, they have been dispersed into three presses where, because I could not be present at them all, I was present at none, by which means the weakness of my performance hath been so strangely managed for the worse, that I am quite out of countenance at my work, which, the ensuing errors mended, will not be perfect, but not mended, is not to be understood. Wherefore let me entreat you, before you cast away the time in beginning to read, that you mend the faults according unto the ensuing corrections, which done, I dare promise you that if I have not made you a good flight, I have sprung you the best quarry; for though the discourses be full of crudities, the model hath had perfect concoction.

[Three pages of errata follow. They include the 'spaniel' message discussed on pp. 7–10 of Harrington: 1977.]

The Introduction or Order of the Work

Oceana is saluted by the panegyrist after this manner:

O the most blessed and fortunate of all countries Oceana! How deservedly hath Nature with the bounties of heaven and earth endowed thee, the ever fruitful womb not closed with ice, nor dissolved by the raging star; where Ceres and Bacchus are perpetual twins. Thy woods are not the harbour of devouring beasts, nor thy continual verdure the ambush of serpents, but the food of innumerable herds and flocks, presenting thee their shepherdess with distended dugs or golden fleeces. The wings of thy night involve thee not in the horror of darkness, but have still some white feather, and thy day is that for which we esteem life, the longest.

But this ecstasy of Pliny's (as is observed by Bertius)[1] seemeth to allude as well unto Marpesia and Panopea, now provinces of this commonwealth, as unto Oceana herself.

To speak of the people in each of these countries, this of Oceana, for so soft an one, is the most martial in the whole world.

Let states that aim at greatness (saith Verulamius) take heed how their nobility and gentlemen do multiply too fast, for that maketh

---

[1] On this passage Liljegren's note should be consulted (S. B. Liljegren, *James Harrington's Oceana*, Lund and Heidelberg, 1924, pp. 227–31). It is not by either Pliny, but occurs in *Panegyricus Constantino Augusto dictus*, probably by Eumenius and found in *C. Plinii Secundi Epistolarum libri XX . . . cum variis lectionibus et notis Henrici Stephani, Isaac Casauboni, Gasp. Barthii, Augusti Buchneri* (Jena, 1650). It had been several times quoted by Camden, Selden and other English authors of the seventeenth century. Liljegren was unable to find any allusion to it in the works of Pierre Bertius, professor of geography at Leyden (1565–1629); perhaps H had Barthius in mind.

3

the common subject grow to be a peasant and base swain, driven out of heart and in effect but a gentleman's labourer. Even as you may see in coppice woods, if you leave the staddles too thick, you shall never have clean underwood, but shrubs and bushes; so in countries, if the gentlemen be too many, the commons will be base, and you will bring it to that, that not the hundredth poll will be fit for an helmet, especially as to the infantry which is the nerve of an army; and so there will be great population and little strength. This which I speak of hath been nowhere better seen than by comparing of Oceana and France, whereof Oceana though far less in territory and population hath been nevertheless an overmatch; in regard the middle people of Oceana make good soldiers, which the peasants in France do not.

In which words,[2] Verulamius (as Machiavel hath done before him) harps much upon a string which he hath not perfectly tuned, and that is the balance of dominion or property; as it followeth more plainly in his praise of

> the profound and admirable device of Panurgus King of Oceana, in making farms and houses of husbandry of a standard; that is, maintained with such a proportion of land unto them as may breed a subject to live in convenient plenty and no servile condition, and to keep the plough in the hands of the owners and not mere hirelings; and thus indeed (saith he) you shall attain unto Virgil's character which he gives of ancient Italy: *terra potens armis atque ubere glebae.*[3]

But the tillage, bringing up a good soldiery, bringeth up a good commonwealth, which the author in the praise of Panurgus did not mind, nor Panurgus in deserving that praise; for where the owner of the plough comes to have the sword too, he will use it in defence of his own, whence it hath happened that the people of Oceana, in

---

[2] This and the following quotation are adapted (with the substitution of fictitious for historical names) from a single passage of Bacon's essay 'Of the True Greatness of Kingdoms and Estates' (Spedding, *The Works of Francis Bacon*, vol. VI, London, 1890, pp. 446–7). A Latin version is in *De Augmentis Scientiarum*, VIII, iii, 3. See also *The History of King Henry VII*, *Works*, vol. VI, pp. 94–5.

[3] H breaks off his quotation from Bacon at the point where the author goes on to note as 'almost peculiar to England, and hardly to be found anywhere else, except it be perhaps in Poland . . . the state of free servants and attendants upon noblemen and gentlemen; which are no ways inferior unto the yeomanry for arms'. Bacon thought these 'retinues' highly conducive to military greatness, but this opinion would have conflicted with H's Machiavellism. Nor can it have seemed at all convincing in Cromwellian England.

proportion to their property, have been always free, and the genius of this nation hath ever had some resemblance with that of ancient Italy, which was wholly addicted unto commonwealths, and where Rome came to make the greatest account of her rustic tribes and to call her consuls from the plough. For in the way of parliaments, which was the government of this realm, men of country lives have been still entrusted with the greatest affairs and the people have constantly had an aversion from the ways of the court. Ambition, loving to be gay and to fawn, hath been a gallantry looked upon as having something of the livery, and husbandry or the country way of life, though of a grosser spinning, as the best stuff of a commonwealth, according unto Aristotle, *agricolarum democratica respublica optima*; such an one being the most obstinate assertress of her liberty and the least subject unto innovation or turbulency.[4] Wherefore, till the foundations (as will be hereafter shown) were removed, this people was observed to be the least subject unto shakings and turbulency of any; whereas commonwealths upon which the city life hath had the stronger influence, as Athens, have seldom or never been quiet, but at the best are found to have injured their own business by overdoing it. Whence the urban tribes of Rome, consisting of the *turba forensis*, libertines that had received their freedom by manumission, were of no reputation in comparison of the rustics. It is true that with Venice it may seem to be otherwise, in regard the gentlemen (for so are all such called as have right unto that government) are wholly addicted unto the city life; but then the *turba forensis*, the secretaries, *cittadini*, with the rest of the populacy, are wholly excluded. Otherwise a commonwealth consisting but of one city would doubtless be stormy, in regard that ambition would be every man's trade: but where it consisteth of a country, the plough in the hands of the owner findeth him a better calling, and produceth the most innocent and steady genius of a commonwealth, such as is that of Oceana.

Marpesia, being the northern part of the same island, is the dry nurse of a populous and hardy people, but where the staddles have been formerly too thick; whence their courage answered not unto their hardiness, except in the nobility, who governed that country

---

[4] Cf. Aristotle, *Politics*, VI iv, where, however, the emphasis is more heavily on an agrarian democracy's aversion to innovation, and the deference of its masses to the magistrates, than on its liberty-loving or martial qualities. The former characteristics are also those stressed in H's succeeding sentences.

much after the manner of Poland, save that the king was not elective, till the people received their liberty, the yoke of the nobility being broken by the commonwealth of Oceana; which in grateful return is thereby provided with an inexhaustible magazine of auxiliaries. Panopea, the soft mother of a slothful and pusillanimous people, is a neighbour island, anciently subjected by the arms of Oceana; since almost depopulated for shaking the yoke, and at length replanted with a new race. But (through what virtues of the soil, or vice of the air soever it be) they come still to degenerate; wherefore seeing it is neither likely to yield men fit for arms, nor necessary it should, it had been the interest of Oceana so to have disposed of this province, being both rich in the nature of the soil and full of commodious ports for trade, that it might have been ordered for the best in relation unto her purse. Which in my opinion (if it had been thought upon in time) might have been best done by planting it with Jews, allowing them their own rites and laws, for that would have brought them suddenly from all parts of the world, and in sufficient numbers; and though the Jews be now altogether for merchandise, yet in the land of Canaan (since their exile from whence they have not been landlords) they were altogether for agriculture; and there is no cause why a man should doubt but, having a fruitful country and good ports too, they would be good at both. Panopea well peopled would be worth a matter of four millions dry rents, that is besides the advantage of the agriculture and trade, which with a nation of that industry comes at least unto as much more. Wherefore Panopea, being farmed out unto the Jews and their heirs forever, for the pay of a provincial army to protect them during the term of seven years, and for two millions annual revenue from that time forward – besides the customs, which would pay the provincial army – would have been a bargain of such advantage, both unto them and this commonwealth, as is not to be found otherwise by either. To receive the Jews after any other manner into a commonwealth were to maim it; for they of all nations never incorporate but, taking up the room of a limb, are of no use or office unto the body, while they suck the nourishment which would sustain a natural and useful member.

If Panopea had been so disposed of, that knapsack, with the Marpesian auxiliary, had been an inestimable treasure; the situation of these countries, being islands (as appears by Venice how advantageous such an one is to the like government), seemeth to have been designed by God for a commonwealth. And yet that, through the straitness of the place and defect of proper arms, can be no more than a commonwealth for preservation; whereas this, reduced unto the like government, is a commonwealth for increase, and upon the mightiest foundation that any hath been laid from the beginning of the world unto this day.

> *Illam arcta capiens Neptunus compede stringit:*
> *Hanc autem glaucis captus complectitur ulnis.*[5]

The sea giveth law unto the growth of Venice, but the growth of Oceana giveth law unto the sea.

These countries, having been anciently distinct and hostile kingdoms, came by Morpheus the Marpesian, who succeeded by hereditary right unto the crown of Oceana, not only to be joined under one head, but to be cast, as it were by a charm, into that profound sleep which, broken at the length by the trumpet of civil war, hath produced those effects that have given the occasion unto the ensuing discourse, divided into four parts:

1. The Preliminaries, showing the principles of government.
2. The Council of Legislators, showing the art of making a commonwealth.
3. The Model of the Commonwealth of Oceana, showing the effect of such art.
4. The Corollary, showing some consequences of such a government.

---

[5] Liljegren declared himself unable to trace this quotation.

7

The Preliminaries, showing the Principles of Government[1]

Giannotti, the most excellent describer of the commonwealth of Venice, divideth the whole series of government into two times or periods.[2] The one ending with the liberty of Rome, which was the course or empire, as I may call it, of ancient prudence, first discovered unto mankind by God himself in the fabric of the commonwealth of Israel, and afterward picked out of his footsteps in nature and unanimously followed by the Greeks and Romans. The other beginning with the arms of Caesar which, extinguishing liberty, were the transition of ancient into modern prudence, introduced by those inundations of Huns, Goths, Vandals, Lombards, Saxons which, breaking the Roman Empire, deformed the whole face of the world with those ill features of government which at this time are become far worse in these western parts, except Venice which, escaping the hands of the barbarians by virtue of her impregnable situation, hath had her eye fixed upon ancient prudence and is attained to a perfection even beyond her copy.

Relation being had unto these two times, government (to define it *de jure* or according to ancient prudence) is an art whereby a civil society of men is instituted and preserved upon the foundation of common right or interest, or (to follow Aristotle and Livy) it is the empire of laws and not of men.

---

[1] The Preliminaries are in fact divided into two parts or chapters, of which the second begins on p. 43 below.
[2] Donato Giannotti, *Libro della repubblica de' Viniziani*, in *Opere* (Pisa, 1819), 1, p. 15. Giannotti's division applies to the history of Italy, not that of government in general, and the thought of the sentences ensuing above is very much H's own.

And government (to define it *de facto* or according unto modern prudence) is an art whereby some man, or some few men, subject a city or a nation, and rule it according unto his or their private interest; which, because the laws in such cases are made according to the interest of a man or of some few families, may be said to be the empire of men and not of laws.

The former kind is that which Machiavel (whose books are neglected) is the only politician that hath gone about to retrieve, and that Leviathan (who would have his book imposed upon the universities)[3] goes about to destroy. For it is (saith he)

> another error of Aristotle's *Politics*, that in a well-ordered commonwealth, not men should govern but the laws. What man that hath his natural senses, though he can neither write nor read, does not find himself governed by them he fears, and believes can kill or hurt him when he obeyeth not? Or who believes that the law can hurt him, which is but words and paper without the hands and swords of men?[4]

I confess that *magistratus est lex armata*; the magistrate upon his bench is that unto the law, which a gunner upon his platform is unto his cannon. Nevertheless I should not dare to argue with a man of any ingenuity after this manner. An whole army, though they can neither write nor read, are not afraid of a platform, which they know is but earth or stone, nor of a cannon which, without a hand to give fire unto it, is but cold iron; therefore a whole army is afraid of one man. But of this kind is the ratiocination of Leviathan (as I shall show in divers places that come in my way) throughout his whole politics, or worse; as where he saith of Aristotle and of Cicero, of the Greeks and of the Romans, who lived under popular states, that they 'derived those rights not from the principles of nature, but transcribed them into their books out of the practice of their own commonwealths, as grammarians describe the rules of language out of poets'.[5] Which is as if a man should tell famous Harvey that he transcribed his circulation of the blood not out of the principles of nature, but out of the anatomy of this or that body.

[3] Hobbes, *Leviathan*, 'A Review and Conclusion' (Tuck ed., Cambridge Texts in the History of Political Thought, 1991, p. 127): also part II, ch. 30 (Tuck, p. 237). H had read Hobbes's vindication of himself upon this point; see p. 38, n. 32, below.

[4] *Leviathan*, IV, 40 (Tuck, p. 471).

[5] *Leviathan*, II, 21 (Tuck, pp. 149–50). The concluding words should read: 'out of the practice of the time; or the rules of poetry out of the poems of Homer and Virgil'.

To go on therefore with this preliminary discourse, I shall divide it, according unto the two definitions of government relating unto Giannotti's two times, into two parts: the first treating of the principles of government in general, and according to the ancients; the second treating of the late governments of Oceana in particular, and in that of modern prudence.

Government, according to the ancients and their learned disciple Machiavel, the only politician of later ages, is of three kinds: the government of one man, or of the better sort, or of the whole people; which by their more learned names are called monarchy, aristocracy, and democracy. These they hold, through their proneness to degenerate, to be all evil. For whereas they that govern should govern according to reason, if they govern according unto passion, they do that which they should not do. Wherefore, as reason and passion are two things, so government by reason is one thing and the corruption of government by passion is another thing, but not always another government: as a body that is alive is one thing, and a body that is dead is another thing, but not always another creature, though the corruption of one come at length unto the generation of another. The corruption then of monarchy is called tyranny; that of aristocracy, oligarchy; and that of democracy, anarchy. But legislators, having found these three governments at the best to be naught, have invented another consisting of a mixture of them all, which only is good. This is the doctrine of the ancients.

But Leviathan is positive that they are all deceived, and that there is no other government in nature than one of the three, as also that the flesh of them cannot stink, the names of their corruptions being but the names of men's fancies; which will be understood when we are shown which of them was *senatus populusque Romanus*.

To go mine own way, and yet to follow the ancients, the principles of governments are twofold: internal, or the goods of the mind, and external, or the goods of fortune. The goods of the mind are natural or acquired virtues, as wisdom, prudence and courage, etc. The goods of fortune are riches. There be goods also of the body, as health, beauty, strength, but these are not to be brought into account upon this score, because if a man or an army acquire victory or empire, it is more from their discipline, arms, and courage, than from their natural health, beauty, or strength, in regard that a people conquered may have more of natural strength, beauty and health, and yet find little remedy. The principles of government then are in the goods of the mind, or in the goods of fortune. To the goods of the mind answers authority; to the goods of fortune, power or empire. Wherefore Leviathan, though he be right where he saith that 'riches are power', is mistaken where he saith that 'prudence, or the reputation of prudence, is power'.[6] For the learning or prudence of a man is no more power than the learning or prudence of a book or author, which is properly authority. A learned writer may have authority, though he have no power; and a foolish magistrate may have power, though he have otherwise no esteem or authority. The difference of these two is observed by Livy in Evander, of whom saith he: *regebat magis auctoritate quam imperio*; he ruled rather by authority than power.[7]

To begin with riches, in regard that men are hung upon these, not of choice as upon the other, but of necessity and by the teeth: for as much as he who wanteth bread is his servant that will feed him, if a man thus feed an whole people, they are under his empire.

Empire is of two kinds, domestic and national, or foreign and provincial.

Domestic empire is founded upon dominion.

Dominion is property real or personal; that is to say in lands, or in money and goods.

Lands, or the parts and parcels of a territory, are held by the proprietor or proprietors, lord or lords of it, in some proportion; and such (except it be in a city that hath little or no land, and whose revenue is in trade) as is the proportion or balance of dominion or property in land, such is the nature of the empire.

If one man be sole landlord of a territory, or overbalance the people, for example, three parts in four, he is grand signor, for so the Turk is called from his property; and his empire is absolute monarchy.

If the few or a nobility, or a nobility with the clergy, be landlords, or overbalance the people unto the like proportion, it makes the Gothic

---

[6] *Leviathan*, I, 10 (Tuck, pp. 62–3): 'riches joined with liberality is power; because it procureth friends, and servants: without liberality, not so; because in this case they defend not; but expose men to envy, as a prey. . . . Reputation of prudence in the conduct of peace or war, is power; because to prudent men, we commit the government of ourselves, more willingly than to others.'

[7] Livy, *Historiarum*, I, vii.

balance (to be shown at large in the second part of this discourse) and the empire is mixed monarchy, as that of Spain, Poland, and late of Oceana.

And if the whole people be landlords, or hold the lands so divided among them, that no one man, or number of men, within the compass of the few or aristocracy, overbalance them, the empire (without the interposition of force) is a commonwealth.

If force be interposed in any of these three cases, it must either frame the government unto the foundation, or the foundation unto the government, or, holding the government not according unto the balance, it is not natural but violent; and therefore, if it be at the devotion of a prince, it is tyranny; if at the devotion of the few, oligarchy; or if in the power of the people, anarchy; each of which confusions, the balance standing otherwise, is but of short continuance, because against the nature of the balance which, not destroyed, destroyeth that which opposeth it.

But there be certain other confusions which, being rooted in the balance, are of longer continuance and of greater horror: as first, where a nobility holdeth half the property, or about that proportion, and the people the other half; in which case, without altering the balance, there is no remedy but the one must eat out the other, as the people did the nobility in Athens, and the nobility the people in Rome. Secondly, when a prince holdeth about half the dominion, and the people the other half – which was the case of the Roman emperors, planted partly upon their military colonies and partly upon the senate and the people – the government becometh a very shambles both of the princes and the people. Somewhat of this nature are certain governments at this day, which are said to subsist by confusion. In this case to fix the balance is to entail misery; but in the three former not to fix it is to lose the government. Wherefore, it being unlawful in Turkey that any should possess land but the grand signor, the balance is fixed by the law, and that empire firm. Nor, though the kings often fell, was the throne of Oceana known to shake, until the statute of alienations broke the pillars, by giving way unto the nobility to sell their estates. *Si terra recedat, Ionium Aegaeo frangat mare.*[8] Lacedaemon, while she held unto her division of land made by Lycurgus, was immovable, but breaking that, could stand no longer.

[8] Lucan, *Pharsalia*, I, lines 102–3.

12

This kind of law fixing the balance in lands is called agrarian, and was first introduced by God himself, who divided the land of Canaan unto his people by lots, and is of such virtue that, wherever it hath held, that government hath not altered, except by consent; as in that unparalleled example of the people of Israel, when being in liberty they would needs choose a king. But without an agrarian, government, whether monarchical, aristocratical or popular, hath no long lease.

For dominion personal or in money, it may now and then stir up a Melius or a Manlius, which, if the commonwealth be not provided with some kind of dictatorian power, may be dangerous, though it have been seldom or never successful; because unto property producing empire, it is required that it should have some certain root or foothold, which, except in land, it cannot have, being otherwise as it were upon the wing.

Nevertheless, in such cities as subsist most by trade and have little or no land, as Holland and Genoa, the balance of treasure may be equal unto that of land in the cases mentioned.

But Leviathan, though he seems to skew at antiquity, following his furious master Carneades, hath caught hold of the public sword, unto which he reduceth all manner and matter of government; as where he affirms 'the opinion that any monarch receiveth his power by covenant, that is to say upon condition, to proceed from want of understanding this easy truth, that covenants, being but words and breath, have no force to oblige, contain, constrain or protect any man, but what they have from the public sword'.[9] But as he said of the law that without this sword it is but paper, so he might have thought of this sword that without an hand it is but cold iron. The hand which holdeth this sword is the militia of a nation; and the militia of a nation is either an army in the field, or ready for the field upon occasion. But an army is a beast that hath a great belly and must be fed; wherefore this will come unto what pastures you have, and what pastures you have will come unto the balance of property, without which the public sword is but a name or mere spitfrog. Wherefore, to set that which Leviathan saith of arms and of contracts a little straighter: he that can graze this beast with the great belly, as the Turk doth his timariots,

---

[9] *Leviathan*, II, 18 (Tuck, pp. 123–4). In the last clause H has correctly emended 'it has' to read 'they have'.

may well deride him that imagines he received his power by covenant, or is obliged unto any such toy: it being in this case only that covenants are but words and breath. But if the property of the nobility stocked with their tenants and retainers be the pasture of that beast, the ox knows his master's crib; and it is impossible for a king in such a constitution to reign otherwise than by covenant; or if he break it, it is words that come to blows.

'But', saith he, 'when an assembly of men is made sovereign, then no man imagineth any such covenant to have passed in the institution.' But what was that by Publicola, of appeal unto the people, or that whereby the people had their tribunes? Fie, saith he, 'nobody is so dull as to say that the people of Rome made a covenant with the Romans, to hold the sovereignty on such or such conditions; which not performed, the Romans might depose the Roman people'.[10] In which there be remarkable things; for he holdeth the commonwealth of Rome to have consisted of one assembly, whereas it consisted of the senate and the people. That they were not upon covenant, whereas every law enacted by them was a covenant between them. That the one assembly was made sovereign, whereas the people, who only were sovereign, were such from the beginning, as appears by the ancient style of their covenants or laws: *censuere patres, jussit populus.* That a council, being made sovereign, cannot be made such upon conditions; whereas the *decemviri*, being a council that was made sovereign, was made such upon conditions. That all conditions or covenants making a sovereign, the sovereign being made, are void; whence it must follow, that the decemvirs, being made, were ever after the lawful government of Rome, and that it was unlawful for the commonwealth of Rome to depose the decemvirs; as also that Cicero, if he writ otherwise out of his commonwealth, did not write out of nature. But to come unto others that see more of this balance.

You have Aristotle full of it in divers places, especially where he saith that

> Immoderate wealth, as where one man or the few have greater possessions than equality or the frame of the commonwealth will bear, is an occasion of sedition, which ends for the greater part in monarchy; and that for this cause the ostracism hath been received in divers places, as in Argos and Athens. But it were

[10] *Ibid.*

14

better to prevent the growth in the beginning, than, when it hath gotten head, to seek the remedy of such an evil.[11]

Machiavel hath missed it very narrowly and more dangerously; for not fully perceiving that if a commonwealth be galled by the gentry, it is by their overbalance, he speaks of the gentry as hostile to popular governments, and of popular governments as hostile unto the gentry, and makes us believe, that the people in such are so enraged against them, that where they meet a gentleman they kill him; which can never be proved by any one example, unless in civil war, seeing that even in Switz the gentry are not only safe, but in honour. But the balance as I have laid it down, though unseen by Machiavel, is that which interpreteth him, and that which he confirmeth by his judgment in many other as well as in this place, where he concludes that

> he who will go about to make a commonwealth where there be many gentlemen, unless he first destroy them, undertakes an impossibility: and he who goes about to introduce monarchy where the condition of the people is equal shall never bring it to pass, unless he cull out such of them as are the most turbulent and ambitious, and make them gentlemen or noblemen, not in name but in effect, that is by enriching them with lands, castles, and treasures, that may gain them power amongst the rest and bring in the rest unto dependence upon themselves, to the end that, they maintaining their ambition by the prince, the prince may maintain his power by them.[12]

Wherefore, as in this place I agree with Machiavel that a nobility or gentry, overbalancing a popular government, is the utter bane and destruction of it; so I shall show in another that a nobility or gentry in a popular government, not overbalancing it, is the very life and soul of it.

supports existence of nobility

By what hath been said, it should seem that we may lay aside

[11] Aristotle, *Politics*, v, iii. Sir Ernest Barker's translation (*The Politics of Aristotle*, Oxford, 1946, p. 208) runs: 'The presence of some form of superiority becomes an occasion for sedition when a person, or body of persons, is in a position of strength which is too great for the state and more than a match for the strength of the general body of citizens. Such a position usually results in a monarchy, or in a "dynastic" oligarchy. It is for this reason that, in a number of states, a policy of ostracism comes to be used. Argos and Athens are examples. But it is a better policy to begin by ensuring that there shall be no such persons of outstanding eminence, than first to allow them to arise and then to attempt a remedy afterwards.'

[12] Machiavelli, *Discorsi sopra la prima deca di Tito Livio*, I, 55.

15

farther disputes of the public sword, or of the right of the militia, which, be the government what it will or let it change how it can, is inseparable from the overbalance in dominion, nor, if otherwise stated by law or custom – as in the commonwealth of Rome (*consules sine lege curiata rem militarem attingere non potuerunt*)[13] where, the people having the sword, the nobility came to have the overbalance – availeth it to other end than destruction; for as a building swaying from the foundation must fall, so the law swaying from reason, and the militia from the balance of dominion. And so much for the balance of national or domestic empire, which is in dominion.

The balance of foreign or provincial empire is of a contrary nature. A man may as well say that it is unlawful for him who hath made a fair and honest purchase to have tenants as for a government that hath made a just progress and enlargement of itself to have provinces. But how a province may be justly acquired appertaineth to another place. In this I am to show no more than how or upon what kind of balance it is to be held; in order whereunto, I shall first show upon what kind of balance it is not to be held. It hath been said that national or independent empire, of what kind soever, is to be exercised by them that have the proper balance of dominion in the nation; wherefore provincial or dependent empire is not to be exercised by them that have the balance of dominion in the province, because that would bring the government from provincial and dependent to national and independent. Absolute monarchy, as that of the Turk, neither planteth her people at home nor abroad, otherwise than as tenants for life or at will, wherefore her national and her provincial government is all one. But in governments that admit the citizen or subject unto dominion in lands, the richest are they that share most of the power at home, whereas the richest among the provincials, though native subjects or citizens that have been transplanted, are least admitted to the government abroad; for men, like flowers or roots, being transplanted take after the soil wherein they grow. Wherefore the commonwealth of Rome, by planting colonies of her citizens within the bound of Italy, took the best way of propagating herself and naturalising the country; whereas if she had planted such colonies without the bounds of Italy, it would have aliened the citizens and given a root to liberty abroad, that might have sprung up foreign or savage and hostile to

---

[13] Cicero, *Oratio de lege agraria*, II, xii, 30 (*M. Tullii Ciceronis Orationes*, ed. A. C. Clark, Oxford, 1909): 'consuli, si legem curiatam non habet, attingere rem militarem non licet'.

her; wherefore she never made any such dispersion of herself and her strength until she was under the yoke of her emperors who, disburdening themselves of the people as having less apprehension of what they could do abroad than at home, took a contrary course.

The Mamelukes[14] (which, till any man show me the contrary, I shall presume to have been a commonwealth consisting of an army, whereof the common soldier was the people, the commission-officer the senate, and the general the prince) were foreigners, and by nation Circassians, that governed Egypt; wherefore these never durst plant themselves upon dominion, which, growing naturally up into the national interest, must have dissolved the foreign yoke in that province.

The like in some sort may be said of Venice, the government whereof is usually mistaken; for Venice, though she do not take in the people, never excluded them. This commonwealth, the orders whereof are the most democratical or popular of all others, in regard of the exquisite rotation of the senate, at the first institution took in the whole people; they that now live under the government without participation of it are such as have since either voluntarily chosen so to do, or were subdued by arms. Wherefore the subject of Venice is governed by provinces, and the balance of dominion not standing, as hath been said, with provincial government – as the Mamelukes durst not cast their government upon this balance in their provinces, lest the national interest should have rooted out the foreign – so neither dare the Venetians take in their subjects upon this balance, lest the foreign interest should root out the national, which is that of the three thousand now governing, and by diffusing the commonwealth throughout her territories, lose the advantage of her situation, by which in a great part she subsisteth. And such also is the government of the Spaniard in the Indies, unto which he deputeth natives of his own country, not admitting the Creolios unto the government of those provinces though descended from Spaniards.

But if a prince or a commonwealth may hold a territory that is foreign in this, it may be asked why he may not hold one that is native in like manner? To which I answer: because he can hold a foreign by a native territory, but not a native by a foreign; and as hitherto I have shown what is not the provincial balance, so by this answer it may

---

[14] 'Mamalucs' in both first editions.

appear what it is, namely the overbalance of a native territory to a foreign; for as one country balanceth itself by the distribution of property according unto the proportion of the same, so one country overbalanceth another by advantage of divers kinds. For example, the commonwealth of Rome overbalanced her provinces by the vigour of a more excellent government opposed unto a crazier, or by a more exquisite militia opposed unto one inferior in courage or discipline. The like was that of the Mamelukes, being an hardy, unto the Egyptians that were a soft people. And the balance of a situation is in this kind of wonderful effect, seeing the king of Denmark, being none of the most potent princes, is able at the Sound to take toll of the greatest; and as this king by the advantage of the land can make the sea tributary, so Venice, by the advantage of the sea, in whose arms she is impregnable, can make the land to feed her gulf. For the colonies in the Indies, they are yet babes that cannot live without sucking the breasts of their mother-cities, but such as I mistake, if when they come of age they do not wean themselves; which causeth me to wonder at princes that delight to be exhausted in that way. And so much for the principles of power, whether national or provincial, domestic or foreign; being such as are external, and founded in the goods of fortune.

I come unto the principles of authority, which are internal and founded upon the goods of the mind. These the legislator that can unite in his government with those of fortune, cometh nearest unto the work of God, whose government consisteth of heaven and earth; which was said by Plato, though in different words, as 'when princes should be philosophers, or philosophers princes, the world would be happy'; and saith Solomon, *There is an evil which I have seen under the sun, which proceedeth from the ruler. Enimvero neque nobilem, neque ingenuum, nec libertinum quidem armis praeponere regia utilitas est. Folly is set in great dignity and the rich* (either in virtue and wisdom, in the goods of the mind, or those of fortune, upon that balance which giveth them a sense of the national interest) *sit in low places. I have seen servants upon horses, and princes walking as servants upon the earth.*[15] Sad complaints, that the principles of power and authority, the goods of

---

[15] The biblical passages are from Ecclesiastes, 10: 5–7; the Latin insertion from Tacitus, *Germania*, 44, quoted by Grotius in his *Annotationes in Vetus Testamentum* with reference to this very passage from Ecclesiastes. Liljegren in his note considers this highly revealing of H's methods of composition. He does, however, cite Grotius's name in the margin

the mind and of fortune, do not meet and twine in the wreath or crown of empire! Wherefore if we have anything of piety or of prudence, let us raise ourselves out of the mire of private interest unto the contemplation of virtue, and put an hand unto the removal of this evil from under the sun: this evil against which no government that is not secured can be good; this evil from which the government that is secure must be perfect. Solomon tells us that the cause of it is from the ruler: from those principles of power which, balanced upon earthly trash, exclude the heavenly treasures of virtue, and that influence of it upon government which is authority. We have wandered the earth to find out the balance of power; but to find out that of authority we must ascend, as I said, nearer heaven, or to the image of God which is the soul of man.

The soul of man (whose life or motion is perpetual contemplation or thought) is the mistress of two potent rivals, the one reason, the other passion, that are in continual suit; and according as she gives up her will to these or either of them, is the felicity or misery which man partakes in this mortal life.

For as whatever was passion in the contemplation of a man, being brought forth by his will into action, is vice and the bondage of sin; so whatever was reason in the contemplation of a man, being brought forth by his will into action, is virtue and the freedom of soul.

Again, as those actions of a man that were sin, acquire unto himself repentance or shame, and affect others with scorn or pity; so those actions of a man that are virtue, acquire unto himself honour, and upon others authority.

Now government is no other than the soul of a nation or city; wherefore that which was reason in the debate of a commonwealth, being brought forth by the result,[16] must be virtue; and for as much as the soul of a city or nation is the sovereign power,[17] her virtue must be law. But the government whose law is virtue, and whose virtue is law, is the same whose empire is authority, and whose authority is empire.

Again, if the liberty of a man consist in the empire of his reason, the absence whereof would betray him unto the bondage of his passions; then the liberty of a commonwealth consisteth in the empire of her *laws;*

at this point (1656, both C and P, p. 10), and perhaps the crucial point is that Grotius introduced the reference to arms and that H's eye singled it out.

[16] The words 'debate' and 'result' first occur here.

[17] Cf. *Leviathan*, II, 21 (Tuck, pp. 152–3).

the absence whereof would betray her unto the lusts of tyrants.

19

laws, the absence whereof would betray her unto the lusts of tyrants; and these I conceive to be the principles upon which Aristotle and Livy (injuriously accused by Leviathan for not writing out of nature) have grounded their assertion that a commonwealth is an empire of laws and not of men. But they must not carry it so. For, saith he, 'the liberty whereof there is so frequent and honourable mention in the histories and philosophy of the ancient Greeks and Romans, and the writings and discourses of those that from them have received all their learning in the politics, is not the liberty of particular men, but the liberty of the commonwealth'.[18] He might as well have said that the estates of particular men in a commonwealth are not the riches of particular men, but the riches of the commonwealth; for equality of estates causeth equality of power, and equality of power is the liberty not only of the commonwealth, but of every man. But sure a man would never be thus irreverent with the great authors, and positive against all antiquity, without some certain demonstration of truth; and what is it? Why, 'there is written on the turrets of the city of Lucca in great characters at this day the word LIBERTAS, yet no man can thence infer, that a particular man hath more liberty or immunity from the service of the commonwealth there, than in Constantinople. Whether a commonwealth be monarchical or popular, the freedom is the same.'[19] The mountain hath brought forth, and we have a little equivocation! For to say that a Lucchese hath no more liberty or immunity from the laws of Lucca than a Turk hath from those of Constantinople, and to say that a Lucchese hath no more liberty or immunity by the laws of Lucca than a Turk hath by those of Constantinople, are pretty different speeches. The first may be said of all governments alike, the second scarce of any two; much less of these, seeing it is known that whereas the greatest bashaw is a tenant, as well of his head as of his estate, at the will of his lord, the meanest Lucchese that hath land is a freeholder of both, and not to be controlled but by the law; and that framed by every private man unto no other end (or they may thank themselves) than to protect the liberty of every private man, which by that means comes to be the liberty of the commonwealth.

But seeing they that make the laws in commonwealths are but men, the main question seems to be how a commonwealth comes to be an

---

[18] *Leviathan*, II, 21 (Tuck, p. 149).   [19] *Ibid.*

empire of laws and not of men? or how the debate or result of a commonwealth is so sure to be according unto reason, seeing they who debate and they who resolve be but men. And 'as often as reason is against a man, so often will a man be against reason'.[20]

This is thought to be a shrewd saying, but will do no harm; for be it so that reason is nothing but interest, there be divers interests, and so divers reasons.

As first, there is private reason, which is the interest of a private man.

Secondly, there is reason of state, which is the interest (or error, as was said by Solomon) of the ruler or rulers, that is to say of the prince, of the nobility, or of the people.

Thirdly, there is that reason which is the interest of mankind or of the whole.

Now if we see even in those natural agents that want sense, that as in themselves they have a law which directeth them, in the means whereby they tend to their own perfection, so likewise that another law there is, which toucheth them as they are sociable parts united into one body, a law which bindeth them each to serve unto others' good, and all to prefer the good of the whole, before whatsoever their own particular; as when stones or heavy things forsake their ordinary wont or centre, and fly upwards, as if they heard themselves commanded to let go the good they privately wish, and to relieve the present distress of nature in common.[21]

There is a common right, law of nature, or interest of the whole, which is more excellent, and so acknowledged to be by the agents themselves, than the right or interest of the parts only.

Wherefore though it may be truly said that the creatures are naturally carried forth unto their proper utility or profit, that ought not to be taken in too general a sense; seeing divers of them abstain from their own profit, either in regard of those of the same kind, or at the least of their young.[22]

---

[20] These words are italicized, as if H had meant them to be read as a quotation. They have a Hobbesian flavour.

[21] Hooker, *The Laws of Ecclesiastical Polity*, i, iii, 5.

[22] Grotius, *De Jure Belli ac Pacis*, Prolegomena (Amsterdam, 1646) fo. 4r.: 'Quod ergo dicitur natura quodque animal ad suas tantum utilitates ferri, ita universe sumtum

Mankind then must either be less just than the creature, or acknowledge also his common interest to be common right. And if reason be nothing else but interest, and the interest of mankind be the right interest, then the reason of mankind must be right reason. Now compute well, for if the interest of popular government come the nearest unto the interest of mankind, then the reason of popular government must come the nearest unto right reason.

But it may be said that the difficulty remains yet; for be the interest of popular government right reason, a man doth not look upon reason as it is right or wrong in itself, but as it makes for him or against him; wherefore unless you can show such orders of a government as, like those of God in nature, shall be able to constrain this or that creature to shake off that inclination which is more peculiar unto it and take up that which regards the common good or interest, all this is to no more end than to persuade every man in a popular government not to carve himself of that which he desires most, but to be mannerly at the public table, and give the best from himself unto decency and the common interest. But that such orders may be established as may, nay must, give the upper hand in all cases unto common right or interest, notwithstanding the nearness of that which sticks unto every man in private, and this in a way of equal certainty and facility, is known even unto girls, being no other than those that are of common practice with them in divers cases. For example, two of them have a cake yet undivided, which was given between them. That each of them therefore may have that which is due, 'Divide', says one unto the other, 'and I will choose; or let me divide, and you shall choose.' If this be but once agreed upon, it is enough; for the divident dividing unequally loses, in regard that the other takes the better half; wherefore she divides equally, and so both have right. *O the depth of the wisdom of God!* and yet *by the mouths of babes and sucklings hath he set forth his strength.* That which great philosophers are disputing upon in vain is brought unto light by two silly girls: even the whole mystery of a commonwealth, which lies only in dividing and choosing; nor hath God (if his works in nature be understood) left so much unto mankind

concedi non debet. Nam & caeterarum animantium quaedam utilitatum suarum studium, partim foetuum suorum, partim aliorum sibi congenerum, respectu aliquatenus temperant: quod in illis quidem procedere credimus, ex principio aliquo intelligente extrinseco, quia circa actus alios, istis neutiquam difficiliores, par intelligentia in illis non apparet.'

to dispute upon as who shall divide and who choose, but distributed them for ever into two orders, whereof the one hath the natural right of dividing, and the other of choosing. For example:

A commonwealth is but a civil society of men. Let us take any number of men, as twenty, and forthwith make a commonwealth. Twenty men, if they be not all idiots – perhaps if they be – can never come so together, but there will be such difference in them that about a third will be wiser, or at least less foolish, than all the rest. These upon acquaintance, though it be but small, will be discovered and (as stags that have the largest heads) lead the herd; for while the six, discoursing and arguing one with another, show the eminence of their parts, the fourteen discover things that they never thought on, or are cleared in divers truths which had formerly perplexed them; wherefore in matter of common concernment, difficulty or danger, they hang upon their lips as children upon their fathers, and the influence thus acquired by the six, the eminence of whose parts is found to be a stay and comfort to the fourteen, is *auctoritas patrum*, the authority of the fathers. Wherefore this can be no other than a natural aristocracy diffused by God throughout the whole body of mankind to this end and purpose, and therefore such as the people have not only a natural but a positive obligation to make use of as their guides; as where the people of Israel are commanded to *take wise men and understanding and known among their tribes, to be made rulers over them.*[23] The six then approved of, as in the present case, are the senate, not by hereditary right, nor in regard of the greatness of their estates only, which would tend unto such power as might force or draw the people, but by election for their excellent parts, which tendeth unto the advancement of the influence of their virtue or authority that leads the people. Wherefore the office of the senate is not to be commanders but counsellors of the people; and that which is proper unto counsellors is first to debate the business whereupon they are to give advice, and afterward to give advice in the business whereupon they have debated; whence the decrees of the senate are never laws, nor so called, but *senatusconsulta*, and these, being maturely framed, it is their duty *ferre ad populum*, to propose in the case unto the people. Wherefore the senate is no more than the debate of the commonwealth. But to debate is to discern, or put a difference between things that being

---

[23] Deuteronomy, 1: 13. This is the first appearance of H's favourite scriptural citation.

alike are not the same, or it is separating and weighing this reason against that and that reason against this, which is dividing.

The senate then having divided, who shall choose? Ask the girls; for if she that divided must have chosen also, it had been little worse for the other, in case she had not divided at all, but kept the whole cake unto herself, in regard that being to choose too, she divided accordingly. Wherefore if the senate have any further power than to divide, the commonwealth can never be equal. But in a commonwealth consisting of a single council, there is no other to choose than that which divided; whence it is, that such a council faileth not to scramble, that is to be factious, there being no other dividing of the cake in that case but among themselves.

Nor is there any remedy but to have another council to choose. The wisdom of the few may be the light of mankind, but the interest of the few is not the profit of mankind, nor of a commonwealth; wherefore, seeing we have granted interest to be reason, they must not choose, lest it put out their light; but as the council dividing consisteth of the wisdom of the commonwealth, so the assembly or council choosing should consist of the interest of the commonwealth. As the wisdom of the commonwealth is in the aristocracy, so the interest of the commonwealth is in the whole body of the people, and whereas this, in case the commonwealth consist of an whole nation, is too unwieldy a body to be assembled, this council is to consist of such a representative as may be equal, and so constituted as can never contract any other interest than that of the whole people; the manner whereof, being such as is best shown by exemplification, I remit unto the model. But in the present case, the six dividing, and the fourteen choosing, must of necessity take in the whole interest of the twenty.

Dividing and choosing, in the language of a commonwealth, is debating and resolving; and whatsoever upon debate of the senate is proposed unto the people, and resolved by them, is enacted *auctoritate patrum et jussu populi*, by the authority of the fathers and the power of the people, which concurring make a law.

But the law being made, saith Leviathan, 'is but words and paper without the hands and swords of men';[24] wherefore as those two orders of a commonwealth, namely the senate and the people, are

---

[24] This seems to be paraphrase, rather than quotation, of the passage quoted above, p. 13, n. 9.

legislative, so of necessity there must be a third to be executive of the laws made, and this is the magistracy; in which order with the rest, being wrought up by art, the commonwealth consisteth of the senate proposing, the people resolving, and the magistracy executing, whereby partaking of the aristocracy as in the senate, of the democracy as in the people, and of monarchy as in the magistracy, it is complete. Now there being no other commonwealth but this in art or nature, it is no wonder if Machiavel have showed us that the ancients held this only to be good. But it seemeth strange to me, that they should hold that there could be any other; for if there be such a thing as pure monarchy, yet that there should be such an one as pure aristocracy or pure democracy is not to my understanding. But the magistracy, both in number and function, is different in different commonwealths; nevertheless there is one condition of it that must be the same in every one, or it dissolves the commonwealth where it is wanting. And this is no less than that, as the hand of the magistrate is the executive power of the law, so the head of the magistrate is answerable unto the people that his execution be according unto the law; by which Leviathan may see that the hand or sword that executeth the law is in it, and not above it.

Now whether I have rightly transcribed these principles of a commonwealth out of nature, I shall appeal unto God and to the world. Unto God in the fabric of the commonwealth of Israel, and unto the world in the universal series of ancient prudence. But in regard the same commonwealths will be opened at large in the council of legislators, I shall touch them for the present but slightly, beginning with that of Israel.

The commonwealth of Israel consisted of the senate, the people, and the magistracy.

The people by their first division, which was genealogical, were contained under their ten tribes, houses or families, whereof the firstborn in each was prince of his tribe and had the leading of it (Numbers, 1); the tribe of Levi only, being set apart to serve at the altar, had no other prince but the high priest. In their second division they were divided locally by their agrarian (Joshua, c. 13 to c. 42), or the distribution of the land of Canaan unto them by lot, the tithe of all remaining unto Levi; whence according unto their local division, the tribes are reckoned but twelve.

The assemblies of the people thus divided were methodically

gathered by trumpets (Numbers, 10: 7) unto the congregation, which was it should seem of two sorts. For if it were called by one trumpet only, the princes of the tribe and the elders only assembled (Numbers, 10: 4), but if it were called with two, the whole people gathered themselves unto the congregation (Numbers, 10: 3), for so it is rendered by the English; but in the Greek it is called *ecclesia*, or the Church of God (Judges, 20: 2), and by the Talmudists, *synagoga magna*. The word *ecclesia* was also anciently and properly used for the civil congregations or assemblies of the people in Athens, Lacedaemon and Ephesus, where it is so called in Scripture (Acts, 19: 23), though it be otherwise rendered by the translators, not much as I conceive to their commendations; seeing by that means they have lost us a good lesson, the apostles borrowing that name for their spiritual congregations, to the end that we might see they intended the government of the church to be democratical or popular, as is also plain in the rest of their constitutions.

The church or congregation of the people of Israel assembled in a military manner (Judges, 20: 2), and had the result of the commonwealth, or the power of confirming all their laws, though proposed even by God himself, as where they make him king (Exodus, 19). And where they reject or depose him as civil magistrate and elect Saul (1 Samuel, 8: 8), it is manifest that he giveth no such example unto a legislator in a popular government as to deny or evade the power of the people, which were a contradiction; but, though he deservedly blame the ingratitude of the people in that action, commandeth Samuel, being next under himself supreme magistrate, to hearken unto their voice (for where the suffrage of the people goes for nothing, it is no commonwealth) and comforteth him, saying: *They have not rejected thee, but they have rejected me, that I should not reign over them.* But to reject him, that he should not reign over them, was as civil magistrate to depose him. The power therefore which the people had to depose even God himself as he was civil magistrate, leaveth little doubt, but that they had power to have rejected any of those laws confirmed by them throughout the Scripture, which (to omit the several parcels) are generally contained (Deuteronomy, 29) under two heads, those that were made by covenant with the people in the land of Moab, and those which were made by covenant with the people in Horeb – which two, I think, amount unto the whole body of the Israelitish laws – but if all and every one of the laws of Israel, being proposed by God, were no otherwise enacted than by covenant with the people, then that only which was resolved by the people of Israel was their law; and so the result of that commonwealth was in the people. Nor had the people the result only in matter of law: but the power in some cases of judicature (Joshua, 7: 16; Judges, 20: 8, 9, 10), as also the right of levying war (Judges, 20: 8, 9, 10; I Samuel, 7: 6, 7, 8), cognizance in matter of religion (I Chronicles, 13: 2; II Chronicles, 30: 4), and the election of their magistrates, as the judge or dictator (Judges, 11: 11), the king (I Samuel, 10: 17), the prince (I Maccabees, 14), which functions were exercised by the *synagoga magna*, or congregation of Israel, not always in one manner; for sometimes they were performed by the suffrage of the people, *viva voce* (Exodus, 9: 3, 4, 5), sometimes by the lot only (Joshua, 7; I Samuel, 10), and all others by the ballot, or by a mixture of the lot with the suffrage, as in the case of Eldad and Medad, which I shall open with the senate.

The senate of Israel, called in the Old Testament the seventy elders and in the New the Sanhedrim, which word is usually translated the Council, was appointed by God and consisted of seventy elders besides Moses (Numbers, 11), which were at the first elected by the people (Deuteronomy, 1), but in what manner is rather intimated (Numbers, 11) than shown. Nevertheless, because I cannot otherwise understand the passage concerning Eldad and Medad, of whom it is said that *they were of them that were written, but went not up unto the Tabernacle*, then with the Talmudists I conceive that Eldad and Medad had the suffrage of the tribes, and so were written as competitors for magistracy; but, coming afterwards unto the lot, failed of it and therefore went not up unto the Tabernacle, or place of confirmation by God, or to the session house of the senate with the seventy upon whom the lot fell to be senators; for the session house of the Sanhedrim was first in the court of the Tabernacle, and afterwards in that of the Temple, where it came to be called the stone chamber or pavement. If this were the ballot of Israel, that of Venice is the same transposed; for in Venice the competitor is chosen as it were by the lot, in regard that the electors are so made, and the magistrate is chosen by the suffrage of the great council or assembly of the people. But the Sanhedrim of Israel being thus constituted, Moses for his time, and after him his successor, sat in the midst of it as prince or archon, and at his left hand the orator or father of the senate; the rest of the bench, coming round with either horn like a crescent, had a scribe attending upon the tip of it.

This senate, in regard that the legislator of Israel was infallible, and the laws given by God such as were not fit to be altered by men, is much different in the exercise of their power from all other senates, except that of the Areopagites in Athens, which also was little more than a supreme judicatory; for it will hardly, as I conceive, be found that the Sanhedrim proposed unto the people, till the return of the children of Israel out of captivity under Esdras, at which time there was a new law made: namely for a kind of excommunication, or rather banishment, which had never been before in Israel. Nevertheless it is not to be thought that the Sanhedrim had not always that right, which from the time of Esdras it more frequently exercised, of proposing unto the people, but that they forbare it in regard of the fulness and infallibility of the law already made, whereby it was needless. Wherefore the function of this council, which is very rare in a senate, was executive, and consisted in the administration of the law made (Deuteronomy, 17: 9, 10, 11); and whereas the council itself is often understood in Scripture by the priest and the Levite, there is no more in that, save only that the priests and the Levites, who otherwise had no power at all, being in the younger years of this commonwealth those that were best studied in the laws, were the most frequently elected into the Sanhedrim. For the courts, consisting of three and twenty elders sitting in the gates of every city, and the triumvirates of judges constituted almost in every village, which were parts of the executive magistracy subordinate unto the Sanhedrim, I shall take them at better leisure, and in the larger discourse; but these, being that part of this commonwealth which was instituted by Moses upon the advice of Jethro the priest of Midian (Exodus, 18), as I conceive an heathen, are unto me a sufficient warrant, even from God himself who confirmed them, to make further use of humane prudence wherever I find it bearing a testimony unto itself, whether in heathen commonwealths or others. And the rather because so it is, that we who have the holy Scriptures, and in them the original of a commonwealth made by the same hand that made the world, are either altogether blind or negligent of it, while the heathens have all written theirs, as if they had had no other copy. As, to be more brief in the present account of that which you shall have more at large hereafter:

Athens consisted of the senate of the bean proposing, of the church or assembly of the people resolving and too often debating – which was the ruin of it – as also of the senate of the Areopagites, the nine archons, with divers other magistrates, executing.

Lacedaemon consisted of the senate proposing, of the church or congregation of the people resolving only, and never debating – which was the long life of it – and of the two kings, the court of the ephors, with divers other magistrates, executing.

Carthage consisted of the senate proposing and sometimes resolving too, of the people resolving and sometimes debating too, for which fault she was reprehended by Aristotle; and she had her suffetes, and her hundred men, with other magistrates, executing.

Rome consisted of the senate proposing, the *concio* or people resolving and too often debating, which caused her storms; as also of the consuls, censors, aediles, tribunes, praetors, quaestors, and other magistrates executing.

Venice consisteth of the senate or *pregati* proposing, and sometimes resolving too, of the great council or assembly of the people, in whom the result is constitutively; as also of the Doge, the signory, the censors, the *dieci*, the quaranties, and other magistrates executing.

The proceeding of the commonwealths of Switzerland[25] and Holland is of a like nature, though after a more obscure manner; for the sovereignties, whether cantons, provinces or cities, which are the people, send their deputies commissioned and instructed by themselves (wherein they reserve the result in their own power) unto the provincial or general convention or senate, where the deputies debate, but have no other power of result than what was conferred upon them by the people, or is farther conferred by the same upon farther occasion. And for the executive part they have magistrates or judges in every canton, province or city; besides those which are more public and relate unto the league, as for controversies between one canton, province or city, and another, or the like between such persons as are not of the same canton, province or city.

But that we may observe a little farther how the heathen politicians have written, not only out of nature, but as it were out of Scripture: as in the commonwealth of Israel, God is said to have been king, so the commonwealth where the law is king is said by Aristotle to be the kingdom of God. And where, by the lusts or passions of men, a power

---

[25] *Sic,* for once; 'Switz' is the usual rendering.

is set above that of the law, deriving from reason which is the dictate of God, God in that sense is rejected or deposed that he should not reign over them, as he was in Israel. And yet Leviathan will have it, that by reading of these Greek and Latin (he might as well in this sense have said Hebrew) authors,

> young men and all others that are unprovided of the antidote of solid reason, receiving a strong and delightful impression of the great exploits of war achieved by the conductors of their armies, receive withal a pleasing idea of all they have done besides; and imagine their great prosperity not to have proceeded from the emulation of particular men, but from the virtue of their popular form of government: not considering the frequent seditions and civil wars produced by the imperfection of their policy.[26]

Where first, the blame he lays to the heathen authors is, in his sense, laid unto the Scripture; and whereas he holds them to be young men, or men of no antidote, that are of like opinions, it should seem that Machiavel, the sole retriever of this ancient prudence, is to his solid reason a beardless boy that hath newly read Livy. And how solid his reason is may appear where he grants the great prosperity of ancient commonwealths, which is to give up the controversy, for such an effect must have some adequate cause; which to evade, he insinuates that it was nothing else but the emulation of particular men; as if so great an emulation could have been generated without as great virtue, so great virtue without the best education, the best education without the best laws, or the best laws any otherwise than by the excellency of their policy.[27]

But if some of these commonwealths, as being less perfect in their policy than others, have been more seditious, it is not more an argument of the infirmity of this or that commonwealth in particular, than of the excellency of that kind of policy in general, which if they that have not altogether reached, have nevertheless had greater prosperity, what would befall them that should reach?

In answer to which question, let me invite Leviathan, who of all other governments giveth the advantage unto monarchy for perfection, to a better disquisition of it, by these three assertions:

The first, that the perfection of government lieth upon such a

---

[26] *Leviathan*, II, 29 (Tuck, pp. 225–6).
[27] A Machiavellian echo; *Discorsi*, I, 4.

libration in the frame of it, that no man or men, in or under it, can have the interest or, having the interest, can have the power to disturb it with sedition.

The second, that monarchy, reaching the perfection of the kind, reacheth not unto the perfection of government, but must have some dangerous flaw in it.

The third, that popular government, reaching the perfection of the kind, reacheth the perfection of government and hath no flaw in it.

The first assertion requireth no proof.

For the proof of the second, monarchy, as hath been shown, is of two kinds, the one by arms, the other by a nobility, and there is no other kind in art or nature; for if there have been anciently some governments called kingdoms – as one of the Goths in Spain, and another of the Vandals in Africa – where the king ruled without a nobility, and by a council of the people only, it is expressly said by the authors that mention them that the kings were but the captains, and that the people not only gave them laws, but deposed them as often as they pleased; nor is it possible in reason that it should be otherwise in like cases, wherefore these were either no monarchies, or had greater flaws in them than any other.

But for a monarchy by arms, as that of the Turk (which of all models that ever were cometh up unto the perfection of the kind), it is not in the wit or power of man to cure it of this dangerous flaw, that the janissaries have frequent interest and perpetual power to raise sedition, and to tear the magistrates, even the prince himself, in pieces. Therefore the monarchy of Turkey is no perfect government.

And for a monarchy by a nobility, as of late in Oceana (which of all other models before the declination of it came up to the perfection in that kind), it was not in the power or wit of man to cure it of that dangerous flaw, that the nobility had frequent interest and perpetual power by their retainers and tenants to raise sedition and (whereas the janissaries occasion this kind of calamity no sooner than they make an end of it) to levy a lasting war unto the vast effusion of blood, and that even upon occasions wherein the people, but for their dependence upon their lords, had no concernment, as in the feud of the Red and White. The like hath been frequent in Spain, France, Germany and other monarchies of this kind; wherefore monarchy by a nobility is no perfect government.

For the proof of the third assertion, Leviathan yieldeth it unto me

31

that there is no other commonwealth but monarchical or popular; wherefore if no monarchy be a perfect government, then either there is no perfect government or it must be popular; for which kind of constitution I have something more to say than Leviathan hath said or ever will be able to say for monarchy; as:

1. That it is the government that was never conquered by any monarch, from the beginning of the world unto this day; for if the commonwealth of Greece came under the yoke of the kings of Macedon, they were first broken by themselves.

2. That it is the government that hath frequently led mighty monarchs in triumph.

3. That it is the government which if it have been seditious, it hath not been from any imperfection in the kind, but in the particular constitution; which wherever the like hath happened must have been unequal.

4. That it is the government which, if it have been anything near equal, was never seditious; or let him show me what sedition hath happened in Lacedaemon or Venice.

5. That it is the government which, attaining unto perfect equality, hath such a libration in the frame of it, that no man living can show which way any man or men in or under it can contract any such interest or power as should be able to disturb the commonwealth with sedition; wherefore an equal commonwealth is that only which is without flaw and containeth in it the full perfection of government. But to return.

By what hath been shown in reason and experience it may appear that though commonwealths in general be governments of the senate proposing, the people resolving, and the magistracy executing, yet some are not so good at these orders as others, through some impediment or defect in the frame, balance, or capacity of them, according unto which they are of divers kinds.

The first division of them is into such as are single, as Israel, Athens, Lacedaemon, etc., and such as are by leagues, as those of the Achaeans, Aetolians, Lycians, Switz and Hollanders.

The second (being Machiavel's) is unto such as are for preservation, as Lacedaemon and Venice, and such as are for increase, as Athens and Rome; in which I can see no more than that the former

32

taketh in no more citizens than are necessary for defence, and the latter so many as are capable of increase.

The third division (unseen hitherto) is into equal and unequal, and this is the main point especially as to domestic peace and tranquillity; for to make a commonwealth unequal is to divide it into parties, which setteth them at perpetual variance, the one party endeavouring to preserve their eminence and inequality, and the other to attain unto equality, whence the people of Rome derived their perpetual strife with the nobility or senate: but in an equal commonwealth, there can be no more strife than there can be overbalance in equal weights, wherefore the commonwealth of Venice, being that which of all others is the most equal in the constitution, is that wherein there never happened any strife between the senate and the people.

An equal commonwealth is such an one as is equal both in the balance or foundation and in the superstructures, that is to say in her agrarian law and in her rotation.

An equal agrarian is a perpetual law establishing and preserving the balance of dominion, by such a distribution that no one man or number of men within the compass of the few or aristocracy can come to overpower the whole people by their possessions in lands.

As the agrarian answereth unto the foundation, so doth rotation unto the superstructures.

Equal rotation is equal vicissitude in government, or succession unto magistracy conferred for such convenient terms, enjoying equal vacations, as take in the whole body by parts, succeeding others through the free election or suffrage of the people.

The contrary whereunto is prolongation of magistracy which, trashing the wheel of rotation, destroys the life or natural motion of a commonwealth.

The election or suffrage of the people is freest where it is made or given in such a manner that it can neither oblige (*qui beneficium accepit libertatem vendidit*)[28] nor disoblige another, or through fear of an enemy, or bashfulness towards a friend, impair a man's liberty.

Wherefore saith Cicero: *Grata populo est tabella qua frontes aperit hominum, mentes tegit, datque eam libertatem ut quod velint faciant;*[29] the tablet or ballot of the people of Rome, who gave their votes by

---

[28] Publilius Syrus, *Sententiae*, 58; 'Beneficium accipere libertatem est vendere.'
[29] Cicero, *Oratio pro Cn. Plancio*, VI, 16.

throwing tablets or little pieces of wood secretly into urns marked for the negative or affirmative, was a welcome constitution unto the people, as that which, not impairing the assurance of their brows, increased the freedom of their judgment. I have not stood upon a more particular description of this ballot, because that of Venice, exemplified in the model, is of all others the most perfect.

An equal commonwealth (by that which hath been said) is a government established upon an equal agrarian, arising into the superstructures or three orders, the senate debating and proposing, the people resolving, and the magistracy executing by an equal rotation through the suffrage of the people given by the ballot. For though rotation may be without the ballot, and the ballot without rotation, yet the ballot not only as to the ensuing model includeth both, but is by far the most equal way; for which cause under the name of the ballot I shall hereafter understand both that and rotation too.

Now, having reasoned the principles of an equal commonwealth, I should come to give an instance of such an one in experience, if I could find it; but if this work be of any value, it lieth in that it is the first example of a commonwealth that is perfectly equal. For Venice, though she come the nearest, yet is a commonwealth for preservation; and such an one, considering the paucity of citizens taken in and the number not taken in, is externally unequal; and though every commonwealth that holdeth provinces must in that regard be such, yet not unto that degree. Nevertheless Venice internally and for her capacity is by far the most equal, though she hath not in my judgment arrived at the full perfection of equality; both because her laws, supplying the defect of an agrarian, are not so clear nor effectual at the foundation, nor her superstructures by the virtue of her ballot or rotation exactly librated, in regard that through the paucity of her citizens, her greater magistracies are continually wheeled through a few hands. As is confessed by Giannotti, where he saith that if a gentleman come once to be *savio di terra ferma*, it seldom happens that he faileth from thenceforward to be adorned with some one of the greater magistracies, as *savi di mare, savi di terra ferma, savi grandi*, counsellors, those of the decemvirate or dictatorian council, the *avvocatori*, or censors, which require no vacation or interval.[30] Wherefore if this in Venice, or

---

[30] Giannoti, *Libro della repubblica de' Viniziani*, p. 124. Both C and P have '*aurogatori*' in

that in Lacedaemon, where the kings were hereditary, and the senators (though elected by the people) for life, cause no inequality (which is hard to be conceived) in a commonwealth for preservation, or such an one as consisteth of a few citizens; yet is it manifest that it would cause a very great one in a commonwealth for increase, or consisting of the many, which by the engrossing the magistracies in a few hands would be obstructed in their rotation.

But there be that say (and think it a strong objection): let a commonwealth be as equal as you can imagine, two or three men when all is done will govern it; and there is that in it, which notwithstanding the pretended sufficiency of a popular state, amounteth unto a plain confession of the imbecility of that policy, and of the prerogative of monarchy; for as much as popular governments in difficult cases have had recourse unto dictatorian power, as in Rome.

To which I answer, that as truth is a spark whereunto objections are like bellows, so in this our commonwealth shines; for the eminence acquired by suffrage of the people in a commonwealth, especially if it be popular and equal, can be ascended by no other steps than the universal acknowledgement of virtue, and where men excel in virtue, the commonwealth is stupid and unjust if accordingly they do not excel in authority: wherefore this is both the advantage of virtue, which hath her due encouragement, and the commonwealth, which hath her due services. These are the philosophers which Plato would have to be princes, the princes which Solomon would have to be mounted, and their steeds are those of authority, not empire; or, if they be buckled to the chariot of empire, as that of the dictatorian power, like the chariot of the sun it is glorious for terms and vacations or intervals. And as a commonwealth is a government of laws and not of men, so is this the principality of the virtue and not of the man; if that fail or set in one, it riseth in another, which is created his immediate successor.

> *Uno avulso non deficit alter,*
> *Aureus et simili frondescit virga metallo.*[31]

And this taketh away that *vanity from under the sun*, which is an error

mistake for *avvocatori*, and the suggestion that these are identical with the censors should be inadvertent.

[31] Slightly adapted from *Aeneid*, VI, 143–4.

proceeding more or less from all other rulers under heaven but an equal commonwealth.

These things considered, it will be convenient in this place to speak a word unto such as go about to insinuate to the nobility or gentry a fear of the people, or into the people a fear of the nobility or gentry, as if their interests were each destructive unto other; when in truth an army may as well consist of soldiers without officers, or of officers without soldiers, as a commonwealth (especially such an one as is capable of greatness) of a people without a gentry, or of a gentry without a people. Wherefore this (though not always so intended, as may appear by Machiavel, who else would be guilty) is a pernicious error. There is something first in the making of a commonwealth, then in the governing of her, and last of all in the leading of her armies, which, though there be great divines, great lawyers, great men in all professions, seems to be peculiar unto the genius of a gentleman. For so it is in the universal series of story, that if any man have founded a commonwealth, he was first a gentleman. Moses had his education by the daughter of Pharaoh; Theseus and Solon, of noble birth, were held by the Athenians worthy to be kings; Lycurgus was of the blood-royal, Romulus and Numa princes, Brutus and Publicola patricians; the Gracchi, that lost their lives for the people of Rome and the restitution of that commonwealth, were the sons of a father adorned with two triumphs and of Cornelia, the daughter of Scipio, who, being sought in marriage by King Ptolemy, disdained to be the Queen of Egypt. And the most renowned Olphaus Megaletor, sole legislator (as you will see) of the commonwealth of Oceana, was derived from a noble family; nor will it be any occasion of scruple in this case that Leviathan affirms the politics to be no ancienter than his book *De Cive*. Such also as have gotten any fame in the civil government of a commonwealth, or by the leading of her armies, have been gentlemen; for so in all other respects were those plebeian magistrates elected by the people of Rome, being of known descents and of equal virtues, save only that they were excluded from the name by the usurpation of the patricians. Holland, through this defect at home, hath borrowed princes for her generals and gentlemen for her commanders, of divers nations: and Switz, if she have defect in this kind, rather lendeth her people unto the colours of other princes than maketh that noble use of them herself which should assert the liberty of mankind. For where there is not a nobility to bolt out the people, they are slothful, regardless of the world and the public interest of liberty, as even that of Rome had been without her gentry; wherefore let the people embrace the gentry, in peace as the light of their eyes, and in war as the trophy of their arms. And if Cornelia disdained to be Queen of Egypt, if a Roman consul looked down from his tribunal upon the greatest king; let the nobility love and cherish the people that afford them a throne so much higher in a commonwealth, and in the acknowledgement of their virtue, than the crowns of monarchs.

But if the equality of a commonwealth consist in the equality first of the agrarian, and next of the rotation, then the inequality of a commonwealth must consist in the absence or inequality of the agrarian, or of the rotation, or of both.

Israel and Lacedaemon, which commonwealths (as the people of this, in Josephus, claims kindred of that) have great resemblance, were each of them equal in their agrarian and unequal in their rotation, especially Israel, where the Sanhedrim or senate, first elected by the people, as appeareth by the words of Moses, took upon them thenceforth without any precept of God to substitute their successors by ordination; which having been there of civil use, as excommunication, community of goods, and other customs of the Essenes, who were many of them converted, came afterwards to be introduced into the Christian church. And the election of the judge, *suffes*, or dictator was irregular, both for the occasion, the term, and the vacation of that magistracy; as you find in the book of Judges, where it is often repeated that in those days there was no king in Israel, that is no judge, and in the first of Samuel, where Eli judged Israel forty years, and Samuel all his life. In Lacedaemon the election of the senate, being by suffrage of the people, though for life was not altogether so unequal; but the hereditary right of kings, but for the agrarian, had ruined her.

Athens and Rome were unequal as to their agrarian, that of Athens being infirm, and that of Rome none at all; for if it were more anciently carried, it was never kept. Whence by the time of Tiberius Gracchus the nobility had almost eaten the people quite out of their lands, which they held in the occupation of tenants and servants; whereupon the remedy being too late and too vehemently applied, that commonwealth was ruined.

These also were unequal in their rotation, but in a contrary manner: Athens in regard that the senate, chosen at once by lot, not by suffrage, and changed every year not in part but the whole, consisted not of the natural aristocracy nor, sitting long enough to understand or be perfect in their office, had sufficient authority to withhold the people from that perpetual turbulence in the way which was ruin in the end, in despite of Nicias, who did what a man could do to help it. But as Athens by the headiness of the people, so Rome fell by the ambition of the nobility, through the want of an equal rotation, which if the people had had into the senate, and timely into the magistracies (whereof the former was always usurped by the patricians, and the latter for the most part), they had both carried and held their agrarian, and that had rendered that commonwealth immovable.

But let a commonwealth be equal or unequal, it must consist, as hath been shown by reason and all experience, of the three general orders, that is to say, of the senate debating and proposing, of the people resolving and of the magistracy executing; wherefore I can never wonder enough at Leviathan, who without any reason or example will have it that a commonwealth consisteth of a single person, or of a single assembly; nor sufficiently pity that 'thousand gentlemen whose minds, which otherwise would have wavered, he hath framed', as is affirmed by himself, 'unto a conscientious obedience,' for so he is pleased to call it, 'of such a government'.[32]

But to finish this part of the discourse, which I intend for as complete an epitome of ancient prudence, and in that of the whole art of the politics, as I am able to frame in so short a time:

The two first orders, that is to say the senate and the people, are legislative, whereunto answers that part of this science which by politicians is entitled *de legibus*, or of laws; and the third order is executive, to which answers that part of the same science which is styled *de judiciis*, or of the frame and course of courts or judicatories. A word unto each of these will be necessary.

And firstly for laws; they are either ecclesiastical or civil, such as concern religion or government.[33]

---

[32] This is a rare example of H's citing a work of Hobbes other than *Leviathan*. The allusion is to *Six Lessons to the Professors of the Mathematics . . . in the Chairs set up by the Noble and Learned Sir Henry Savile in the University of Oxford* (*English Works*, ed. Molesworth, vol. VII, London, 1845, pp. 335–6 and 343–7), where Hobbes defends himself against an accusation of seeking to impose his book upon the Universities. The dedication to this work is dated 10 June 1656, and H can therefore have had little enough time to include this reference in *Oceana*.

[33] Here (p. 27 in the first edition) C has, but P omits, the parenthesis: 'Somebody blushes, but I will do no harm.'

Laws ecclesiastical, or such as concern religion, according unto the universal course of ancient prudence, are in the power of the magistrate; according unto the common practice of modern prudence since the Papacy, torn out of his hands.

But as a government pretending unto liberty, and suppressing the liberty of conscience, which (because religion not according to a man's conscience can as to him be none at all) is the main, must be a contradiction; so a man that, pleading for the liberty of private conscience, refuseth liberty unto the national conscience, must be absurd.

A commonwealth is nothing else but the national conscience. And if the conviction of a man's private conscience produce his private religion, the conviction of the national conscience must produce a national religion. Whether this be well reasoned, as also whether these two may stand together, will best be shown by the examples of the ancient commonwealths taken in their order.

In that of Israel the government of the national religion appertained not unto the priests and Levites, otherwise than as they happened to be of the Sanhedrim[34] or senate, to which they had no right at all but by election. It is in this capacity therefore that the people are commanded under pain of death *to hearken unto them, and to do according to the sentence of the law which they should teach,*[35] but in Israel the law ecclesiastical and civil was the same; therefore the Sanhedrim, having the power of one, had the power of both. But as the national religion appertained unto the jurisdiction of the Sanhedrim, so the liberty of conscience appertained from the same date and by the same right unto the prophets and their disciples; as where it is said, *I will raise up a prophet . . . and whosoever will not hearken unto my words which he shall speak in my name, I will require it of him.*[36] The words relate unto prophetic right, which was above all the orders of this commonwealth, whence Elijah not only refused to obey the king, but destroyed his messengers with fire.[37] And whereas it was not lawful by the national religion to sacrifice in any other place than the temple, a prophet was his own temple, and might sacrifice where he would, as Elijah did in Mount Carmel.[38] By this right John the Baptist and our Saviour, unto whom it more particularly related, had their disciples, and taught the

---

[34] C: 'otherwise then as to the *Sanhedrim*'. A few minor variants in addition.
[35] Deuteronomy, 17: 10.   [36] Deuteronomy, 18: 10.
[37] II Kings, 1.   [38] I Kings, 18.

people, whence is derived our present right of *Gathered Congregations.*[39] Wherefore the Christian religion grew up according unto the orders of the commonwealth of Israel, and not against them. Nor was liberty of conscience infringed by this government till the civil liberty of the same was lost, as under Herod, Pilate and Tiberius, a three-piled tyranny.

To proceed, Athens preserved her religion, by the testimony of Paul, with great superstition. If Alcibiades, that atheistical fellow, had not showed them a pair of heels, they had shaven off his head for shaving their Mercuries, and making their gods look ridiculously upon them without beards. Nevertheless, if Paul reasoned with them, they loved news, for which he was the more welcome; and if he converted Dionysius the Areopagite, that is one of the senators, there followed neither any hurt unto him nor loss of honour to Dionysius. And for Rome, if Cicero in his most excellent book, *De natura deorum*, overthrew the national religion of that commonwealth, he was never the farther from being consul. But there is a meanness and poorness in modern prudence, not only unto the damage of civil government, but of religion itself; for to make a man in matter of religion, which admitteth not of sensible demonstration, *jurare in verba magistri*, engage to believe no otherwise than is believed by my lord Bishop or Goodman Presbyter, is a pedantism that hath made the sword to be a rod in the hands of schoolmasters; by which means,[40] whereas Christian religion is the farthest of any from countenancing war, there never was a war of religion but since Christianity. For which we are beholding unto the *Pope*;[41] for the Pope not giving liberty of conscience unto princes and commonwealths, they cannot give that unto their subjects which they have not, whence both princes and subjects, either through his instigation or disputes among themselves, have introduced that execrable custom, never known in the world before, of fighting for religion and denying the magistrate to have any jurisdiction over it; whereas the magistrate, losing the power of religion, loseth the liberty of conscience which in that case hath nothing to protect it. But if the people be otherwise taught, it concerns them to

---

[39] H capitalises these words, a thing he rarely does.

[40] C: 'not only unto the damage of *Civil Government*, but of *Religion* itself: for whereas . . .' This is one of the largest differences between the two printings.

[41] 'Pope' capitalised in both printings.

look about, and distinguish between the shrieking of the lapwing and the voice of the turtle.

To come unto civil laws: if they stand one way and the balance another, it is the case of a government which of necessity must be new modelled; wherefore your lawyers, advising you upon like occasions to fit your government unto their laws, are no more to be regarded than your tailor if he should desire you to fit your body unto his doublet. There is also danger in the plausible pretence of reforming the law, except the government be first good, in which case it is a good tree and (trouble not yourselves overmuch) bringeth not forth evil fruit. Otherwise, if the tree be evil, you can never reform the fruit; or, if a root that is naught bring forth fruit of this kind that seemeth to be good, take the more heed, for it is the ranker poison. It was no wise probable, if Augustus had not[42] made excellent laws, that the bowels of Rome could have come to be so miserably eaten out by the tyranny of Tiberius and his successors.[43] The best rule as to your laws in general is that they be few. Rome, by the testimony of Cicero, was best governed under those of the twelve tables; and by that of Tacitus, *plurimae leges, corruptissima respublica*. You will be told that where the laws be few, they leave much unto arbitrary power; but where they be many, they leave more, the laws in this case, according to Justinian and the best lawyers, being as litigious as the suitors. Solon made few, Lycurgus fewer laws; commonwealths have fewest at this day of all other governments. And to conclude this part with a word *de judiciis*, or of the constitution or course of courts, it is a discourse not otherwise capable of being well managed but by particular examples, both the constitution and course of courts being divers in different governments, but best beyond compare in Venice, where they regard not so much the arbitrary power of their courts, as the constitution of them; whereby that arbitrary power, being altogether unable to retard or do hurt unto business, produceth and must produce the quickest dispatch and the most righteous dictates of justice that are perhaps in

---

[42] The sense is unclear and the passage has been altered from that appearing in C (see next note). The point of the sentence should be that even if Augustus made good laws, he still founded a government that permitted tyranny under Tiberius.

[43] The passage runs in C: 'in which case it is a good tree, and bringeth not forth evil fruit; otherwise, if the Tree be evill, you can never reform the fruit; begin (*sc.* not?) with reformation of the *Government* by the *Lawes*, but first begin with reformation of the *Lawes* by the *Government*'.

human nature.[44] The manner I shall not stand in this place to describe, because it is exemplified at large in the judicature of the people of Oceana. And thus much of ancient prudence, and the first branch of this preliminary discourse.

[44] C: 'And to conclude this part with a word *de Judiciis*, or the *constitution or course of Courts*; it is such in *Venice*, as the *arbitrary power* of them can never retard or do hurt unto *businesse*, but produceth the *quickest dispatch*, and the most *righteous dictates of Justice* that are perhaps in *humane nature*.'

The Second Part of the Preliminaries

In the second part I shall endeavour to show the rise, progress and declination of modern prudence.

The date of this kind of policy is to be computed, as was shown, from those inundations of Goths, Vandals, Huns and Lombards that overwhelmed the Roman Empire. But as there is no appearance in the bulk or constitution of modern prudence that she should ever have been able to come up and grapple with the ancient, so something of necessity must have interposed, whereby this came to be enervated and that to receive strength and encouragement. And this was the execrable reign of the Roman emperors, taking rise from that *felix scelus*, the arms of Caesar, in which storm the ship of the Roman commonwealth was forced to disburthen herself of that precious freight, which never since could emerge or raise the head but in the Gulf of Venice.

It is said in Scripture, *thy evil is of thyself, O Israel!* to which answers that of the moralists, *nemo nocetur nisi ex se*, as also the whole matter of the politics: at present this example of the Romans who, through a negligence committed in their agrarian laws, let in the sink of luxury, and forfeited the inestimable treasure of liberty for themselves and posterity.

Their agrarian laws were such[1] whereby their lands ought to have been divided among the people, either without mention of a colony, in which case they were not obliged to change their abode; or with

---

[1] 'Sigonius De Ant. Ro.' – H's note. Carolus Sigonius, *De antiquo jure civium Romanorum*, Frankfort, 1593.

mention and upon condition of a colony, in which case they were to change their abode and, leaving the city, to plant themselves upon the lands so assigned. The lands assigned, or that ought to have been assigned, in either of these ways were of three kinds. Such as were taken from the enemy and distributed unto the people; or such as were taken from the enemy and, under colour of being reserved unto the public use, were by stealth possessed by the nobility; or such as were bought with the public money to be distributed. Of the laws offered in these cases, those which divided the lands taken from the enemy, or purchased with the public money, never occasioned any dispute; but such as drove at dispossessing the nobility of their usurpations, and dividing the common purchase of the sword among the people, were never touched but they caused earthquakes, nor could ever be obtained by the people or, being obtained, be observed by the nobility, who not only preserved their prey but, growing vastly rich upon it, bought the people be degrees quite out of those shares that had been conferred upon them. This the Gracchi coming too late to perceive, found the balance of the commonwealth to be lost; but putting the people (when they had least force) by forcible means unto the recovery of it, did ill, seeing it neither could nor did tend unto any more than to show them, by worse effects, that what the wisdom of their leaders had discovered was true. For (quite contrary unto what hath happened in Oceana, where the balance falling unto the people, they have overthrown the nobility) the nobility of Rome, under the conduct of Sulla, overthrew the people and the commonwealth; seeing Sulla first introduced that new balance, which was the foundation of the succeeding monarchy, in the plantation of military colonies, instituted by his distribution of the conquered lands – not now of enemies, but of citizens – unto forty-seven legions of his soldiers; so that how he came to be *dictator perpetuus*, or other magistrates to succeed him in like power, is no miracle.

These military colonies, in which manner succeeding emperors continued (as Augustus by the distribution of the veterans, whereby he had overcome Brutus and Cassius) to plant their soldiery, consisted of such as I conceive were they that are called *milites beneficiarii*; in regard that the tenure of their lands was by way of benefices, that is, for life and upon condition of duty or service in the war, upon their own charge. These benefices Alexander Severus granted unto the heirs of the incumbents, but upon the same conditions; and such was the dominion by which the Roman emperors gave their balance. But to the beneficiaries, as was no less than necessary for the safety of the prince, a matter of eight thousand, by the example of Augustus, were added, which departed not from his sides, but were his perpetual guard, called praetorian bands; though these, according to the incurable flaw already observed in this kind of government, became the most frequent butchers of their lords that are to be found in story. Thus far the Roman monarchy is so much the same with that at this day in Turkey – consisting of a camp and an horse-quarter: a camp in regard of her spahis and janissaries, the perpetual guard of the prince, except they also chance to be liquorish after his blood; and an horse-quarter in regard of the distribution of his whole land unto tenants for life, upon condition of continual service or as often as they shall be commanded, at their own charge, by *timars* (being a word which they say signifies benefices) – that it shall save me a labour of opening the government.

But the fame of Mahomet and his prudence is especially founded in this: that whereas the Roman monarchy (except that of Israel) was the most imperfect, the Turkish is the most perfect that ever was. Which happened in that the Roman (as the Israelitish of the Sanhedrim and the congregation) had a mixture of the senate and the people, and the Turkish is pure; and that this was pure, and the other mixed, happened not through the wisdom of the legislators, but the different genius of the nations, the people of the eastern parts, except the Israelites (which is to be attributed to their agrarian), having been such as scarce ever knew any other condition than that of slavery; and these of the western having ever had such a relish of liberty, as through what despair soever could never be brought to stand still while the yoke was putting on their necks, but by being fed with some hopes of reserving unto themselves some part of their freedom.

Wherefore Julius Caesar, saith Suetonius, *comitia cum populo sortitus est*; contented himself, in naming half the magistrates, to leave the rest unto the suffrage of the people. And Maecenas, though he would not have Augustus to give the people their liberty, would not have him take it away for, saith he, *neque id existimare debes auctorem me tibi esse, ut tyrannidem in S. P. Q. R. in servitutem redactum teneas; quod neque dicere meum, neque facere tuum est.*[2] Whence this empire, being neither hawk nor buzzard, made a flight accordingly; and having the avarice of the soldiery on this hand to satisfy upon the people, and the

[2] 'Dion' – H's note. Liljegren (p. 265) gives the reference for this Latin version as Dio Cassius, *Historiae Romanae*, 52, 14ff., ed. Hanau, 1606, 474.

senate and the people on the other to be defended from the soldiery, the prince, being perpetually tossed, seldom died any other death than by one horn of this dilemma, as is noted more at large by Machiavel. But the praetorian bands, those bestial executioners of their captain's tyranny upon others, and of their own upon him, having continued from the time of Augustus, were by Constantine the Great (incensed against them for taking part with his adversary Maxentius) removed from their strong garrison which they held in Rome, and distributed into divers provinces. The benefices of the soldiers, that were hitherto held for life and upon duty, were by the prince made hereditary, so that the whole foundation whereupon this empire was first built, being now removed, showeth plainly that the emperors must long before this have found out some other way of support, and this was by stipendiating the Goths, a people that, deriving their roots from the northern parts of Germany, or out of Sweden, had (through their victories obtained against Domitian) long since spread their branches unto so near neighbourhood with the Roman territories, that they began to overshade them; for the emperors, making use of them in their arms (as the French do at this day of the Switz), gave them that, under the notion of stipend, which they received as tribute, coming (if there were any default in the payments) so often to distrain for it, that in the time of Honorius they sacked Rome and possessed themselves of Italy. And such was the transition of ancient into modern prudence, or that breach which, being followed in every part of the Roman Empire with inundations of Vandals, Huns, Lombards, Franks, Saxons, overwhelmed ancient languages, learning, prudence, manners, cities, changing the names of rivers, countries, seas, mountains and men; Camillus, Caesar and Pompey being come to Edmund, Richard and Geoffrey.[3]

To open the ground-work or balance of these new politicians: *feudum*, saith Calvine the lawyer, is a Gothic word of divers significations; for it is taken either for war, or for a 'possession of conquered lands, distributed by the victor unto such of his captains and soldiers as had merited in his wars, upon condition to acknowledge

[3] 'Machiavil' – H's note. *History of Florence*, Book I: 'Hanno oltre di questo variato il nome non solamente le provincie, ma i laghi, i fiumi, i mari, e gli uomini; perchè la Francia, l'Italia, e la Spagna sono ripiene di nomi nuovi, ed al tutto dagli antichi alieni; come si vede, lasciandone indietro molti altri, che il Po, Garda, l'Arcipelago sono per nome disformi agli antichi nominati; gli uomini ancora di Cesari e Pompei, Pieri, Giovanni e Mattei diventarono.' The reference to 'prudence' is H's own. Note that his 'new names' have a more feudal flavour than Machiavelli's.

him to be their perpetual lord, and themselves to be his subjects'.[4]

Of these there were three kinds or orders: the first, of nobility, distinguished by the titles of dukes, marquesses and earls; and these being gratified with cities, castles and villages of the conquered Italians, their feuds participated of royal dignity, and were called *regalia*, by which they had right to coin money, create magistrates, take toll, customs, confiscations and the like.

Feuds of the second order were such as with the consent of the king were bestowed by these feudatory princes upon men of inferior quality, called their barons, on condition that next unto the king they should defend the dignities and fortunes of their lords in arms.

The lowest order of feuds were such as being conferred by those of the second order upon private men whether noble or not noble, obliged them in the like duty unto their superiors; these were called *vavasors*. And this is the Gothic balance, by which all the kingdoms this day in Christendom were at first erected, for which cause, if I had time, I should open in this place the empire of Germany and the kingdoms of France, Spain and Poland; but so much as hath been said being sufficient for the discovery of the principles of modern prudence in general, I shall divide the remainder of my discourse, which is more particular, into three parts:

The first showing the constitution of the late monarchy of Oceana.

The second the dissolution of the same.

And the third the generation of the present commonwealth.

The constitution of the late monarchy of Oceana is to be considered in relation unto the different nations, by whom it hath been successively subdued and governed. The first of these were the Romans, the second the Teutons, the third the Scandians, and the fourth the Neustrians.[5]

---

[4] 'Calvine the lawyer' is Johann Kahl or Calvinus; *Lexicon juridicum juris Romani*, Frankfort, 1600 (many later eds.), s.v. 'feudum'.

[5] H here resumes the practice of using easily recognisable fictitious equivalents for proper names from English history (cf. the references to 'Panurgus', 'Morpheus', 'Marpesia', 'Panopea', pp. 3–6, above). A short list of equivalents may be given here.

Adoxus	John	Panurgus	Henry VII
Coraunus	Henry VIII	Parthenia	Elizabeth I
Dicotome	Richard II	Scandians	Danes
Morpheus	James I	Teutons	Saxons
Neustrians	Normans	Turbo	William I

Other fictions, referring either to countries, topographical features or contemporary authors, are explained where necessary as they occur.

The government of the Romans, who held it as a province, I shall omit because I am to speak of their provincial government in another place; only it is to be remembered in this that if we have given over running up and down naked and with dappled hides, learned to write and read, to be instructed with good arts, for all these we are beholding to the Romans either immediately, or mediately by the Teutons; for that the Teutons had the arts from no other hand is plain enough by their language, which hath yet no word to signify either writing or reading but what is derived from the Latin. Furthermore, by the help of these arts so learned, we have been capable of that religion which we have long since received; wherefore it seemeth unto me that we ought not to detract from the memory of the Romans, by whose means we are as it were of beasts become men, and by whose means we might yet of obscure and ignorant men (if we thought not too well of ourselves) become a wise and a great people.

The Romans having governed Oceana provincially, the Teutons were the first that introduced the form of the late monarchy; to these succeeded the Scandians, of whom (because their reign was short, as also because they made little alteration in the government as to the form) I shall take no notice. But the Teutons, going to work upon the Gothic balance, divided the whole nation into three sorts of feuds; that of ealdorman, that of king's thane, and that of middle thane.[6]

When the kingdom was first divided into precincts will be as hard to show as when it began first to be governed; it being impossible that there should be any government without some division. The division that was in use with the Teutons was by counties, and every county had either its ealdorman, or high reeve. The title of ealdorman came in time to eorl, or erle, and that of high reeve to high sheriff.

Earl of the shire or county denoted the king's thane, or tenant by grand serjeantry, or knight's service in chief or *in capite*; his possessions were sometimes the whole territory, from whence he had his denomination, that is the whole country, sometimes more than one county and sometimes less, the remaining part being in the crown. He had also sometimes a third, or some other customary part of the profits of certain cities, boroughs or other places within his earldom. For an example of the possessions of earls in ancient times, Ethelred

---

[6] H here gives a reference to his principal source for English feudal history, John Selden's *Titles of Honour* (second and enlarged edition, 1631), part II, ch v, pp. 593–837.

had unto him and his heirs the whole kingdom of Mercia, containing three or four counties; and there were others that had little less.

'King's thane' was also an honorary title, unto which he was qualified that had five hides of land held immediately of the king by service of personal attendance; insomuch that if a churl or country man had thriven unto this proportion, having a church, a kitchen, a bell house (that is a hall with a bell in it to call his family to dinner), a borough gate with a seat (that is a porch) of his own, and any distinct office in the king's court, then was he the king's thane. But the proportion of an hide land, otherwise called *caruca*, or a ploughland, is difficult to be understood, because it was not certain; nevertheless it is generally conceived to be so much as may be managed with one plough, and would yield the maintenance of the same with the appurtenances in all kinds.

The middle thane was feudal, but not honorary; he was also called a vavasor, and his lands a vavasory, which held of some mesne lord, and not immediately of the king.

Possessions and their tenures, being of this nature, show the balance of the Teuton monarchy; wherein the riches of earls were so vast, that to arise from the balance of their dominion unto their power, they were not only called *reguli* or little kings, but were such indeed, their jurisdiction being of two sorts, either that which was exercised by them in the court of their counties, or in the high court of the kingdom.

In the territory denominating an earl, if it were all his own, the courts held, and the profits of that jurisdiction, were to his own use and benefit. But if he had but some part of his county, this his jurisdiction and courts (saving perhaps in those possessions that were his own) were held by him to the king's use and benefit; that is, he commonly supplied the office which the sheriffs regularly executed in countries that had no earls, and whence they came to be called *vicecomites*. The court of the county that had an earl was held by the earl and the bishop of the diocese, after the manner of the sheriff's tourns unto this day, by which means both the ecclesiastical and temporal laws were given in charge together unto the country; the causes of vavasors or vavasories appertained to the cognisance of this court, where wills were proved, judgment and execution given, cases criminal and civil determined.

The king's thanes had like jurisdiction in their thane-lands as lords in their manors, where they also kept courts.

Besides these in particular, both the earls and king's thanes, together with the bishops, abbots, and vavasors or middle thanes, had in the high court or parliament[7] of the kingdom a more public jurisdiction, consisting, first, of deliberative power for advising upon and assenting unto new laws; secondly, of giving counsel in matters of state; and thirdly, of judicature upon suits and complaints. I shall not omit to enlighten the obscurity of these times, in which there is little to be found of a methodical constitution of this high court, by the addition of an argument which I conceive to bear a strong testimony unto itself, though taken out of a late writing that conceals the author.

> It is well known (saith he) that in every quarter of the realm a great many boroughs do yet send burgesses unto the parliament, which nevertheless be so anciently and so long since decayed and gone to naught, that they cannot be shown to have been of any reputation since the Conquest, much less to have obtained any such privilege by the grant of any succeeding king; wherefore these must have had this right by more ancient usage, and before the Conquest; they being unable now to show whence they derived it.[8]

This argument (though there be more) I shall pitch upon as sufficient to prove, first, that the lower sort of the people had right unto session in parliament during the time of the Teutons. Secondly, that they were qualified unto the same by election in their boroughs and, if knights of the shire (as no doubt they are) be as ancient, in the counties.[9] Thirdly, if it be a good argument to say that the commons during the reign of the Teutons were elected into parliament, because they are so now and no man can show when this custom began, I see not which way it should be an ill one to say that the commons during the reign of the Teutons constituted also a distinct house, because they do so now; unless any man can show that they did ever sit in the same house with the lords. Wherefore, to conclude this part, I conceive, for these and other reasons to be mentioned hereafter, that the

[7] 'Weidenagamoots' – H's note.
[8] Liljegren identified this quotation as coming from Συλλογολογία, or a Historical Discourse of Parliaments in their originall before the Conquest and continuance since, by 'J.S.', purchased by Thomason on 14 June 1656. It is possible that the author was John Streater. [9] Both C and P have 'countries'; H's normal usage is 'counties'.

parliament of the Teutons consisted of the king, the lords spiritual and temporal, and the commons of the nation, notwithstanding the style of divers acts of parliament which runs, as that of Magna Carta, in the king's name only, seeing the same was nevertheless enacted by the king, peers and commons of the land, as is testified in those words by a subsequent act.[10]

The monarchy of the Teutons had stood in this posture about two hundred and twenty years, when Turbo, Duke of Neustria, making his claim to the crown of one of their kings that died childless, followed it with successful arms and, being possessed of the kingdom, used it as conquered, distributing the earldoms, thane-lands, bishoprics and prelacies of the whole realm amongst his Neustrians. From this time the earl came to be called *comes, consul* and *dux* (though *consul* and *dux* grew afterward out of use). The king's thanes came to be called barons and their lands baronies; the middle thane, holding still of a mesne lord, retained the name of vavasor.

The earl or *comes* continued to have the third part of the pleas of the county paid unto him by the sheriff or *vice-comes*, now a distinct office in every county depending upon the king, saving that such earls as had their counties to their own use were now counts palatine, and had under the king regal jurisdiction, insomuch that they constituted their own sheriffs, granted pardons, and issued writs in their own names; nor did king's writ of ordinary justice run in their dominions, till a late statute whereby much of this privilege was taken away.[11]

For barons, they came from henceforth to be in different times of three kinds: barons by their estates and tenures, barons by writ, and barons created by letters patents. From Turbo the first to Adoxus the seventh king from the conquest, barons had their denomination from their possessions and tenures, and these were either spiritual or temporal; for not only the thane-lands, but the possessions of bishops, as also of some twenty-six abbots and two priors, were now erected into baronies, whence the lords spiritual, that had suffrage in the Teuton parliament as spiritual lords, came to have it in the Neustrian parliament as barons, and were made subject (which they had not formerly been) unto knight's service in chief. Barony coming henceforth to signify all honorary possessions, as well of earls as barons, and baronage to denote all kinds of lords, as well spiritual as temporal,

----

[10] '25 Edw. 3, cap. 1' – H's note.   [11] '27 H. 8' – H's note.

having right to sit in parliament, the baronies in this sense were sometimes more and sometimes fewer, but commonly about two hundred or two hundred and fifty, containing in them a matter of sixty thousand *feuda militum*, or knights' fees, whereof some twenty-eight thousand were in the clergy. It is ill luck that no man can tell what the land of a knight's fee (reckoned in some writs at 40 £. a year, and in others at 10) was certainly worth, for by such an help we might have exactly demonstrated the balance of this government. But says Coke,[12] it contained twelve plough-lands, and that was thought to be the most certain account; but this again is extremely uncertain, for one plough out of some land that was fruitful might work more than ten out of some other that was barren. Nevertheless, seeing it appeareth by Bracton that of earldoms and baronies it was wont to be said that the whole kingdom was composed, as also that these, consisting of 60,000 knight's fees, furnished 60,000 men for the king's service (being the whole militia of this monarchy), it cannot be imagined that the vavasories or freeholds in the people amounted to any considerable proportion. Wherefore the balance and foundation of this government was in the 60,000 knight's fees and, these being possessed by the two hundred and fifty lords, it was a government of the few, or of the nobility, wherein the people might also assemble, but could have no more than a mere name. And the clergy holding a third of[13] the whole nation, as is plain by the parliament roll, it is an absurdity – seeing the clergy of France came first through their riches to be a state of that kingdom – to acknowledge the people to have been a state of this realm and not to allow it unto the clergy, who were so much more weighty in the balance,[14] which is that of all other whence a state or order in a government is denominated; wherefore this monarchy consisted of the king and of the three *ordines regni* or estates: the lords spiritual and temporal, and the commons. It consisted of these, I say, as to the balance, though during the reign of some of these kings not as to the administration.

For the ambition of Turbo, and some of those that more immediately succeeded him, to be absolute princes, strove against the nature of their foundation and, inasmuch as he had divided almost the whole

[12] 'Coke, II Inst. pag. 596' – H's note. He would have used the edition of 1641.
[13] Emended; H has 'a third to the whole'.
[14] '4 Rich. 2. Num. 13' – H's note. Liljegren identifies the reference as *Rotul Parl.* IV Rich. II, 13: 'le clergie que occupe la tierce partie del Roialme'.

realm among his Neustrians, with some encouragement for a while. But the Neustrians – while they were but foreign plants, having no security against the natives but in growing up by their prince's sides – were no sooner well rooted in their vast dominions than they came up according to the infallible consequences of the balance domestic and, contracting the national interest of the baronage, grew as fierce in the vindication of the ancient rights and liberties of the same as if they had been always natives; whence, the kings being as obstinate on the one side for their absolute power as these on the other for their immunities, grew certain wars which took their denomination from the barons.

This fire about the middle of the reign of Adoxus began to break out; and whereas the predecessors of this king had diverse times been forced to summon councils resembling those of the Teutons, unto which the lords only that were barons by dominion and tenure had hitherto repaired, Adoxus, seeing the effects of such dominion, began first, not to call such as were barons by writs, for that was according to the practice of ancient times, but to call such by writs as were otherwise no barons, by which means, striving to avoid the consequence of the balance, in coming unwillingly to set the government straight, he was the first that set it awry. For the barons in his reign and his successor's, having vindicated their ancient authority, restored the parliament with all the rights and privileges of the same, saving that from thenceforth the kings had found out a way whereby to help themselves against the mighty;[15] creatures of their own, and such as had no other support but by their favour. By which means this government, being indeed the masterpiece of modern prudence, hath been cried up to the skies as the only invention whereby at once to maintain the sovereignty of a prince and the liberty of the people; whereas indeed it hath been no other than a wrestling match, wherein the nobility, as they have been stronger, have thrown the king, or the king, if he have been stronger, hath thrown the nobility; or the king, where he hath had a nobility and could bring them to his party, hath thrown the people, as in France and Spain; or the people, where they have had no nobility, or could get them to be of their party, have thrown the king, as in Holland and of latter times in Oceana. But they

---

[15] H's errata direct a semi-colon at 'mighty'. He might have emended the passage to read: 'against the mighty: namely, by raising up creatures of their own . . .'.

came not to this strength but by such approaches and degrees, as remain to be further opened. For whereas the barons by writs (as the sixty-four abbots and thirty-six priors that were so called) were but *pro tempore*, Dicotome,[16] being the twelfth king from the conquest, began to make barons by letters patent, with the addition of honorary pensions for the maintenance of their dignities to them and their heirs; so that they were hands in the king's purse, and had no shoulders for his throne. Of these when the house of peers came once to be full, as will be seen hereafter, there was nothing more empty. But for the present, the throne having other supports, they did not hurt that so much has they did the king; for the old barons, taking Dicotome's prodigality to such creatures so ill that they deposed him, got the trick of it, and never gave over setting up and pulling down of their kings, according to their various interests and that faction of the white and red into which they had been thenceforth divided, till Panurgus, the eighteenth king from the conquest, was more by their favour than his right advanced unto the crown.[17]

This king, through his natural subtlety, reflecting at once upon the greatness of their power, and the inconstancy of their favour, began to find another flaw in this kind of government, which is also noted by Machiavel: namely, that a throne supported by a nobility is not so hard to be ascended, as kept warm.[18] Wherefore his secret jealousy lest the dissension of the nobility, as it brought him in, might throw him out, travelled in ways undiscovered by them unto ends as little foreseen by himself, while to establish his own safety he, by mixing water with their wine, first began to open those sluices that have since overwhelmed not the king only, but the throne; for whereas a nobility striketh not at the throne, without which they cannot subsist, but at some king that they do not like, popular power striketh through the king at the throne, as that which is incompatible with it. Now that Panurgus, in abating the power of the nobility, was the cause whence

---

[16] In his account of the institution of barons by writ (by John) and by letters patent (by Richard II), H is following Selden, *Titles of Honour*, ch. v, sections xxi–xxii, xxxvii–xxxviii, pp. 708–20, 744–51.

[17] 'Dissolution of the late Monarchy of *Oceana*' – H's note, not specifically attached to these words but occurring in the margin at this point. The hint that the medieval kings ruled by corruption – i.e., by adulterating the baronage with placemen – seems not to have been followed up in his other writings.

[18] The reference (not given by H) is to ch. IV of *Il Principe*. H cites this work much less frequently than the *Discorsi*.

it came to fall into the hands of the people, appears by those several statutes that were made in his reign; as that for population, those against retainers, and that for alienations.

By the statute of population, all houses of husbandry that were used with twenty acres of ground and upwards were to be maintained and kept up for ever, with a competent proportion of land laid to them and in no wise, as appears by a subsequent statute, to be severed. By which means the houses being kept up, did of necessity enforce dwellers; and the proportion of land to be tilled being kept up, did of necessity enforce the dweller not to be a beggar or cottager, but a man of some substance, that might keep friends and servants and set the plough on going. This did mightily concern (saith the historian of that prince)[19] the might and manhood of the kingdom, and in effect amortize a great part of the lands unto the hold and possession of the yeomanry, or middle people, who, living not in a servile or indigent fashion, were much unlinked from dependence upon their lords and, living in a free and plentiful manner, became a more excellent infantry, but such an one upon which the lords had so little power, that from henceforth they may be computed to have been disarmed.

And as they lost their infantry after this manner, so their cavalry and commanders were cut off by the statute of retainers; for whereas it was the custom of the nobility to have younger brothers of good houses, mettled fellows and such as were knowing in the feats of arms, about them, they who were longer followed with so dangerous a train escaped not such punishment as made them take up.

Henceforth the country lives and great tables of the nobility, which no longer nourished veins that would bleed for them, were fruitless and loathsome till they changed the air, and of princes became courtiers, where their revenues, never to have been exhausted by beef and mutton, were found narrow, whence followed rackings of rents and at length sale of lands, the riddance through the statute of alienations being rendered far more quick and facile than formerly it had been, by the new invention of entails.[20]

To this it happened that Coraunus, the successor of that king,

---

[19] The whole paragraph above is a close copy of Bacon, *History of King Henry VII*, vol. VI (London, 1890), pp. 94–5.

[20] Bacon, 'Of the True Greatness of Kingdoms and Estates', had commented on Henry's legislation making it easier to break entails, so that the phrase 'new invention of entails' seems strained. Nor had Bacon suggested that this statute was of radical importance.

dissolving the abbeys, brought with the declining estate of the nobility so vast a prey unto the industry of the people, that the balance of the commonwealth was too apparently in the popular party to be unseen by the wise council of Queen Parthenia who, converting her reign through the perpetual love tricks that passed between her and her people into a kind of romance, wholly neglected the nobility. And by these degrees came the house of commons to raise that head, which since hath been so high and formidable unto their princes that they have looked pale upon those assemblies. Nor was there anything now wanting unto the destruction of the throne but that the people, not apt to see their own strength, should be put to feel it, when a prince, as stiff in disputes as the nerve of monarchy was grown slack, received that unhappy encouragement from his clergy which became his utter ruin; while, trusting more unto their logic than the rough philosophy of his parliament, it came unto an irreparable breach; for the house of peers, which alone had stood in this gap, now sinking down between the king and the commons, showed that Crassus was dead and Isthmus broken.[21] But a monarchy divested of her nobility hath no refuge under heaven but an army. *Wherefore the dissolution of this government caused the war, not the war the dissolution of this government.*[22]

Of the king's success with his arms it is not necessary to give any further account, than that they proved as ineffectual as his nobility. But without a nobility or an army (as hath been shown) there can be no monarchy. Wherefore what is there in nature that can arise out of these ashes but a popular government, or a new monarchy to be erected by the victorious army?

To erect a monarchy, be it ever so new, unless like Leviathan you can hang it (as the country fellow speaks) by geometry (for what else is it to say that every other man must give up his will unto the will of this one man without any other foundation?),[23] it must stand upon old principles, that is upon nobility or an army planted upon a due balance of dominion. *Aut viam inveniam aut faciam* was an adage of

---

[21] The reference is to Lucan, *Pharsalia*, I, 99–106, where it is said that Crassus formed a link, by holding the balance, between his colleagues in the First Triumvirate, and that his death made war between Pompey and Caesar certain.

[22] H's italics.

[23] The idiom here is obscure, though the sense is fairly plain. The phrase 'hang it' has not been traced, though the meaning is presumably 'prove it' or 'argue it'. Hobbes's fondness for geometry is well known, but why unilateral surrender of rights should be geometrical is not so clear.

Caesar's; and there is no standing for a monarchy unless she finds this balance or make it. If she finds it, her work's done unto her hand; for where there is inequality of estates, there must be inequality of power, and where there is inequality of power, there can be no commonwealth. To make it, her sword must extirpate out of dominion all other roots of power, and plant her army upon that ground. An army may be planted nationally or provincially. To plant it nationally, it must be in one of the four ways mentioned: that is, either monarchically in part, as the Roman *beneficiarii*; or monarchically in the whole, as the Turkish timariots; aristocratically, that is, by earls and barons, as the Neustrians were planted by Turbo: or democratically, that is by equal lots, as the Israelitish army in the land of Canaan by Joshua. In every one of these ways there must not only be confiscations, but confiscations unto such a proportion as may answer to the work intended.

Confiscation of a people that never fought against you, but whose arms you have borne, and in which you have been victorious, and this upon premeditation and in cool blood, I should have thought to be against any example in human nature, but for those alleged by Machiavel of Agathocles and Oliverotto da Fermo; the former whereof, being captain general of the Syracusans, upon a day assembled the senate and the people, as if he had something to communicate with them, when at a sign given he cut the senators in pieces to a man, and all the richest of the people, by which means he came to be king. The proceedings of Oliverotto in making himself prince of Fermo, were somewhat different in circumstances, but of the same nature. Nevertheless Catiline, who had a spirit equal to any of these in his intended mischief, could never bring the like to pass in Rome. The head of a small commonwealth, such an one as was that of Syracuse or Fermo, is easily brought unto the block; but that a populous nation such as Rome had not such an one was the grief of Nero.[24] If Sulla or Caesar attained to be princes it was by civil war, and such civil war as yielded rich spoils, there being a vast nobility to be confiscated; which also was the case in Oceana, when it yielded earth by earldoms and baronies to the Neustrian, for the plantation of his new potentates. Where a conqueror finds the riches of a land in the hands of the few, the forfeitures are easy, and amount to vast

---

[24] It was Caligula, not Nero, who wished that the Roman people had only one neck.

advantage; but where the people have equal shares, the confiscation of many comes to little, and is not only dangerous but fruitless.

The Romans in one of their defeats of the Volsci found among the captives certain Tusculans, who upon examination confessed that the arms they bore were by command of their state, whereupon, information being given to the senate by the general Camillus, he was forthwith commanded to march against Tusculum; which doing accordingly he found the Tusculan fields full of husbandmen that stirred not otherwise from the plough, than to furnish his army with all kinds of accommodations and victuals. Drawing near to the city, he saw the gates wide open, the magistrates coming out in their gowns to salute and bid him welcome; entering, the shops were all at work and open, the streets sounded with the noise of schoolboys at their books, there was no face of war. Whereupon Camillus, causing the senate to assemble, told them that though the art was understood, yet had they at length found out the true arms whereby the Romans were most undoubtedly to be conquered, for which cause he would not anticipate the senate, unto which he desired them forthwith to send, which they did accordingly; and their dictator with the rest of their ambassadors being found by the Roman senators, as they went into the house, standing sadly at the door, were sent for in as friends and not as enemies. Where, the dictator having said 'if we have offended, the fault was not so great as is our penitence and your virtue', the senate gave them peace forthwith and soon after made the Tusculans citizens of Rome.

But putting the case, of which the world is not able to show an example, that the forfeiture of a populous nation, not conquered, but friends, and in cool blood, might be taken, your army must be planted in one of the ways mentioned. To plant it in the way of absolute monarchy – that is upon feuds for life, such as the timars – a country as large and fruitful as that of Greece would afford you but sixteen thousand timariots, for that is the most the Turk (being the best husband that ever was of this kind) makes of it at this day. And if Oceana, which is less in fruitfulness by one half and in extent by three parts, should have no greater a force, whoever breaketh her in one battle may be sure she shall never rise, for such (as was noted by Machiavel) is the nature of the Turkish monarchy: if you break her in two battles you have destroyed her whole militia, and the rest being all slavès you hold her without any further resistance. Wherefore the erection of an absolute monarchy in Oceana, or in any other country that is no larger, without making it a certain prey unto the first invader, is altogether impossible.

To plant by halves, as the Roman emperors did their beneficiaries or military colonies, it must be either for life, and this an army of Oceaners in their own country (especially having estates of inheritance) will never bear, because such an army so planted is as well confiscated as the people – nor had the Mamelukes been contented with such usage in Egypt but that they were foreigners and, daring not to mix with the natives, it was of absolute necessity to their being – or, planting them upon inheritance, whether aristocratically as the Neustrians or democratically as the Israelites, they grow up by certain consequence into the national interest, and this, if they be planted popularly, comes unto a commonwealth; if by way of nobility, unto a mixed monarchy, which of all other will be found to be the only kind of monarchy of which this nation, or any other that is of no greater extent, hath been or can be capable. For if the Israelites, though their democratical balance, being fixed by their agrarian, stood firm, be yet found to have elected kings, it was because, their territory lying open, they were perpetually invaded, and being perpetually invaded turned themselves to anything which, through the want of experience, they thought might be a remedy; whence their mistake in election of their kings (under whom they gained nothing but to the contrary lost all they had acquired by their commonwealth, both estates and liberties) is not only apparent, but without parallel. And if there have been (as was shown) a kingdom of the Goths in Spain, and of the Vandals in Africa, consisting of a single person and a parliament (taking a parliament to be a council of the people only, without a nobility), it is expressly said of those councils that they deposed their kings as often as them pleased; nor can there be other consequence of such a government, seeing where there is a council of the people, they do never receive laws but give them, and, a council giving laws unto a single person, he hath no means in the world whereby to be any more than a subordinate magistrate, but force; in which case, he is not a single person and a parliament, but a single person and an army, which army again must be planted as hath been shown, or can be of no long continuance.

It is true that, the provincial balance being in nature quite contrary unto the national, you are no ways to plant a provincial army upon dominion. But then you must have a native territory in strength, situation or government able to overbalance the foreign, or you can never hold it. That an army should in any other case be long supported by a mere tax is a mere fancy, as void of all reason and experience as if a man should think to maintain such an one by robbing of orchards; for a mere tax is but pulling of plumtrees, the roots whereof are in other men's grounds, who, suffering perpetual violence, come to hate the author of it. And it is a maxim that no prince that is hated by his people can be safe. Arms planted upon dominion extirpate enemies and make friends, but, maintained by a mere tax, have enemies that have roots and friends that have none.

To conclude: Oceana, or any other nation of no greater extent, must have a competent nobility, or is altogether incapable of monarchy. For where there is equality of estates, there must be equality of power; and where there is equality of power, there can be no monarchy.

To come then to the generation of the commonwealth, it hath been shown how, through the ways and means used by Panurgus to abase the nobility, and so to mend the flaw which we have asserted to be incurable in this kind of constitution, he suffered the balance to fall into the power of the people and so broke the government; but the balance being in the people, the commonwealth (though they do not see it) is already in the nature of them. *Cornua nota prius vitulo quam frontibus extant.* There wanteth nothing else but time (which is slow and dangerous) or art (which would be more quick and secure) for the bringing those native arms — wherewithal they are found already to resist, they know not how, everything that opposeth them — unto such maturity as may fix them upon their own strength and bottom.

But whereas this art is prudence, and that part of prudence which regards the present work is nothing else but the skill of raising such superstructures of government as are natural to the known foundations, they never mind the foundation but, through certain animosities (wherewith by striving one against another they are infected), or through certain freaks by which, not regarding the course of things nor how they conduce unto their purpose, they are given to building in the air, come to be divided and subdivided into endless parties and factions, both civil and ecclesiastical; which briefly to open, I shall first speak of the people in general, and then of their divisions.

A people (saith Machiavel) that is corrupt is not capable of a commonwealth; but in showing what a corrupt people is, he hath either involved himself or me, nor can I otherwise come out of the labyrinth than by saying that, the balance altering, a people, as to the foregoing government, must of necessity be corrupt; but corruption in this sense signifieth no more than that the corruption of one government (as in natural bodies) is the generation of another; wherefore, if the balance alter from monarchy, the corruption of the people in this case is that which maketh them capable of a commonwealth. But whereas I am not ignorant that the corruption which he meaneth is in manners, this also is from the balance. For the balance, swaying from monarchical into popular, abateth the luxury of the nobility and, enriching the people, bringeth the government from a more private unto a more public interest, which, coming nearer, as hath been shown, unto justice and right reason, the people upon a like alteration is so far from such corruption of manners as should render them incapable of a commonwealth, that of necessity they must thereby contract such reformation of manners as will bear no other kind of government. On the other side, where the balance changeth from popular to oligarchical or monarchical, the public interest, with the reason and justice included in the same, becometh more private; luxury is introduced in the place of temperance and servitude in that of freedom, which causeth such a corruption of manners both in the nobility and the people as, by the example of Rome in the time of the Triumvirs, is more at large discovered by the author to have been altogether incapable of a commonwealth.

But the balance of Oceana changing quite contrary to that of Rome, the manners of the people were not thereby corrupted, but on the contrary fitted for a commonwealth. For differences of opinion in a people not rightly informed of their balance, or division into parties while there is not any common ligament of power sufficient to reconcile or hold them, is no sufficient proof of corruption in a people. Nevertheless, seeing this must needs be matter of scandal and danger, it will not be amiss, in showing what were the parties, to show what were their errors.

The parties into which this nation was divided were temporal or spiritual; and the temporal parties were especially two, the one the royalists, the other commonwealthsmen, each of which asserted their different causes, either out of prudence or ignorance, out of interest or conscience.

For prudence, either that of the ancients is inferior unto the modern (which we have hitherto been setting face to face, that any one may judge), or that of the royalists must be inferior unto that prudence of the commonwealthsman; and for interest, taking the commonwealthsman to have really intended the public (for otherwise he is an hypocrite, and the worst of men), that of the royalist must of necessity have been more private; wherefore the whole dispute will come upon matter of conscience, and this, whether it be urged by the right of kings, the obligation of former laws, or of the oath of allegiance, is absolved by the balance.

For if the right of kings were as immediately derived from the breath of God as the life of man, yet this excludeth not death and dissolution. But that the dissolution of the late monarchy was as natural as the death of a man hath been already shown; wherefore it remains with the royalists to discover by what reason or experience it is possible for a monarchy to stand upon a popular balance; or, the balance being popular, as well the oath of allegiance as all other monarchical laws imply an impossibility, and are therefore void.

To the commonwealthsman I have no more to say but that if he exclude any party, he is not truly such, nor shall ever found a commonwealth upon the natural principle of the same, which is justice; and the royalist, for having opposed a commonwealth in Oceana (where the laws were so ambiguous that they might be eternally disputed and never reconciled), can neither be justly for that cause excluded from his full and equal share in the government, nor prudently for this, that a commonwealth consisting of a party will be in perpetual labour of her own destruction; whence it was that the Romans, having conquered the Albans, incorporated them with equal right into the commonwealth, and if the royalists be flesh of your flesh, and nearer of blood than were the Albans to the Romans, you are also Christians. Nevertheless there is no reason that a commonwealth should any more favour a party remaining in fixed opposition against her than Brutus did his sons.[25] But if she fix them upon that opposition, it is her fault, not theirs, and this is done by excluding them. Men that have equal possessions and the same security of their estates and of their liberties that you have, have the same cause with you to defend; but if you will be trampling, they fight for liberty,

---

[25] Brutus, executing his sons for conspiring to restore the Tarquins, had been raised to symbolic importance by Machiavelli in *Discorsi*, III, 3.

though for monarchy, and you for tyranny, though under the name of a commonwealth; the nature of orders in a commonwealth rightly instituted being void of all jealousy, because, let the parties which she embraceth be what they will, her orders are such as they neither would resist if they could, nor could if they would, as hath in part been already shown, and will appear more at large by the ensuing model.

The parties that are spiritual are of more kinds than I need mention: some for a national religion and others for liberty of conscience, with such animosity on both sides as if these two did not consist; of which I have already sufficiently spoken to show that the one cannot well consist without the other. But they of all the rest are the most dangerous who, holding that the saints must govern, go about to reduce the commonwealth unto a party; as well for the reasons already shown, as that their pretences are against Scripture, where the saints are commanded to submit unto the higher powers, and be subject unto the ordinance of man. And that men pretending under the notion of saints or religion unto civil power have hitherto never failed to dishonour that profession, the world is full of examples, whereof I shall confine myself at the present unto two, the one of old, the other of new Rome.

In old Rome the patricians or nobility, pretending to be the godly party, were questioned by the people for engrossing all the magistracies of that commonwealth, and had nothing to say why they did so, but *quod nemo plebeius auspicia haberet*; that magistracy required a kind of holiness which was not in the people. *Plebs ad id maxima indignatione exarsit, quod auspicari tanquam invisi diis immortalibus negarentur posse*;[26] at which the people were filled with such indignation as had come to cutting of throats, if the nobility had not forthwith laid by the insolency of that plea, which nevertheless when they had done, the people for a long time after continued to elect none other than patrician magistrates.

The example of new Rome in the rise and practice of the hierarchy (too well known to require any further illustration) is far more immodest.

This hath been the course of nature; and when it hath pleased or shall please God to introduce anything that is above the course of nature, he will, as he hath always done, confirm it by miracle; for so in

[26] Livy, IV, vi.

63

his prophecy of the reign of Christ upon earth, he expressly promiseth, seeing that the souls of them that were beheaded for Jesus shall be seen to live and reign with him, which will be an object of sense; the rather because the rest of the dead are not to live again until the thousand years be finished. And it is not lawful for men to persuade us that a thing is, though there be no such object of our sense, which God hath told us shall not be until it be an object of our sense.[27]

The saintship of a people as to government consisteth in the election of magistrates fearing God and hating covetousness, and not in their confining themselves or being confined unto men of this or that party or profession. It consisteth in making the most prudent and religious choice that they can, but not in trusting unto men but, next God, in their orders. 'Give us good men and they will make us good laws' is the maxim of a demagogue, and (through the alteration which is commonly perceivable in men, when they have power to work their own wills) exceeding fallible. But 'give us good orders, and they will make us good men' is the maxim of a legislator and the most infallible in the politics.

But these divisions (however there be some good men that look sadly on them) are trivial things: first (as to the civil concernment) because the government whereof this nation is capable,[28] once seen, taketh in all interests. And secondly (as to the spiritual) because, as pretence of religion hath always been turbulent in broken government, so where the government hath been sound and steady, religion hath never shown herself with any other face than that of her natural sweetness and tranquillity, nor is there any reason why she should; wherefore the errors of the people are occasioned by their governors. If they be doubtful of the way or wander from it, it is because their guides misled them; and the guides of the people are never so well qualified for leading by any virtue of their own, as by that of the government.

The government of Oceana (as it stood at the time whereof we discourse) consisting of one single council of the people, to the exclu-

---

[27] Revelation, 20: 4–5. The eschatological materialism of H's interpretation should be compared with that of Hobbes, *Leviathan*, III, 38 and IV, 44 (Tuck, pp. 306–20 and 417–40). Like Hobbes, he is denying the present existence of a Church Triumphant, on the grounds that the saved are not to live again before a point in future time. There is in fact no promise in the King James text that the souls 'shall be seen' to live.

[28] 'the Errors of the people are from their Governours' – H's marginal note. The words are repeated below, but an asterisk draws attention to them at this point.

sion of the king and of the lords, was called a parliament; howbeit the parliaments of the Teutons and of the Neustrians consisted, as hath been shown, of the king, lords and commons, wherefore this under an old name was a new thing: a parliament consisting of a single assembly, elected by the people and invested with the whole power of government, without any covenants, conditions, or orders whatsoever. So new a thing that neither ancient nor modern prudence can show any avowed example of the like; and there is scarce anything that seemeth unto me so strange as that (whereas there was nothing more familiar with these counsellors than to bring the Scripture to the House) there should not be a man of them that so much as offered to bring the House unto the Scripture, wherein, as hath been shown, is contained that original whereof all the rest of the commonwealths seem to be copies. Certainly if Leviathan (who is surer of nothing than that a popular commonwealth consisteth but of one council) transcribed his doctrine out of this assembly, for him to except against Aristotle and Cicero for writing out of their own commonwealths was not so fair play; or if the parliament transcribed out of him, it had been an honour better due unto Moses. But where one of them should have an example but from the other, I cannot imagine; there being nothing of this kind that I can find in story but the oligarchy of Athens, the thirty tyrants of the same, and the Roman decemvirs.

For the oligarchy, Thucydides tells us that it was a senate or council of four hundred, pretending to a balancing council of the people consisting of five thousand, but not producing them;[29] wherein you have the definition of an oligarchy, which is a single council both debating and resolving, dividing and choosing; and what that must come to was shown by the example of the girls, and is apparent through all experience. Wherefore the thirty set up by the Lacedaemonians when they had conquered Athens are called tyrants by all authors, Leviathan only excepted, who will have them against all the world to have been an aristocracy, but for what reason I cannot imagine, these also as void of any balance having been void of that which is essential to every commonwealth, whether aristocratical or popular; except he be pleased with them in that, by the testimony of Xenophon, they killed more men in eight months than the

---

[29] Thucydides, *History of the Peloponnesian War*, VIII, 66. The words 'pretending' and 'producing' apparently mean that the Four Hundred alleged its responsibility to the Five Thousand, but took no steps to ensure that the latter ever met.

Lacedaemonians had done in ten years, oppressing the people (to use Sir Walter Ralegh's words) with all base and intolerable slavery.[30]

The usurped government of the decemvirs in Rome was of the same kind. Wherefore in the fear of God let Christian legislators, setting the pattern given in the Mount on the one side, and these execrable examples on the other, know the right hand from the left, and so much the rather because those things which do not conduce to the good of the governed are fallacious if they appear to be good for the governors. God in chastising a people is accustomed to burn his rod. The empire of these oligarchies was not so violent as short, nor did they fall upon the people but in their own immediate ruin. A council without a balance is not a commonwealth, but an oligarchy; and every oligarchy, except she be put to the defence of her wickedness or power against some outward danger, is factious. Wherefore, the errors of the people being from their government (which maxim in the politics, bearing a sufficient testimony unto itself, is also proved by Machiavel),[31] if the people of Oceana have been factious the cause is apparent. But what remedy?

In answer to this question, I come now to the army, of which the most victorious captain and incomparable patriot Olphaus Megaletor was now general; who, being a much greater master of that art whereof I have made a rough draft in these preliminaries, had so sad reflections upon the ways and proceedings of the parliament as cast him upon books and all other means of diversion, among which he happened upon this place of Machiavel. 'Thrice happy is that people which chances to have a man able to give them such a government at once, as without alteration may secure them of their liberties; seeing it is certain that Lacedaemon, in observing the laws of Lycurgus, continued about eight hundred years without any dangerous tumult or corruption.'[32] My lord general (as it is said of Themistocles that he could not sleep for the glory obtained by Miltiades at the battle of Marathon) took so new and deep impression at these words of the much greater glory of Lycurgus that, being on this side assaulted with the emulation of his illustrious object, on the other with the misery of the nation, which seemed (as it were ruined by his victory) to cast herself at his feet, he was almost wholly deprived of his natural rest, until the debate he had within himself came to a firm resolution: that

---

[30] Ralegh, *History of the World*, III, 8, 12.
[31] Machiavelli, *Discorsi*, III, 29.   [32] *Discorsi*, I, 2.

the greatest advantages of a commonwealth are, first, that the legislator should be one man, and secondly that the government should be made altogether, or at once. For the first, it is certain, saith Machiavel, that a commonwealth is seldom or never well turned or constituted, except it have been the work of one man; for which cause a wise legislator, and one whose mind is firmly set not upon private but the public interest, not upon his posterity but upon his country, may justly endeavour to get the sovereign power into his own hands, nor shall any man that is master of reason blame such extraordinary means as in that case shall be necessary, the end proving no other than the constitution of a well-ordered commonwealth.[33] The reason of this is demonstrable; for the ordinary means not failing, the commonwealth hath no need of a legislator, but the ordinary means failing, there is no recourse to be had but to such as are extraordinary. And whereas a book or a building hath not been known to attain perfection, if it had not had a sole author or architect, a commonwealth, as to the fabric of it, is of the like nature. And thus it may be made at once, in which there be great advantages: for a commonwealth made at once taketh her security at the same time she lendeth her money, trusteth not herself to the faith of men but launcheth immediately forth into the empire of laws and, being set straight, bringeth the manners of her citizens unto her rule; whence followed that uprightness which was in Lacedaemon. But manners that are rooted in men bow the tenderness of a commonwealth, coming up by twigs unto their bent; whence followed the obliquity that was in Rome, and those perpetual repairs by the consuls' axes and tribunes' hammers, which could never finish that commonwealth but in destruction.

My lord general, being clear in these points and the necessity of some other course than would be thought upon by the parliament, appointed a rendezvous of the army, where he spoke his sense agreeable to these preliminaries, with such success unto the soldiery that the parliament was soon after deposed; and himself, in the great hall of the Pantheon or Palace of Justice situated in Emporium the capital city,[34] created, by the universal suffrage of the army, Lord Archon, or sole legislator of Oceana; upon which theatre you have, to conclude this piece, a person introduced whose fame shall never draw his curtain.

[33] *Discorsi*, I, 9.   [34] 'Emporium' is London.

The Lord Archon being created, fifty select persons to assist him by labouring in the mines of ancient prudence, and bringing her hidden treasures unto new light, were added, with the style also of legislators; and sat as a council, whereof he was the sole director and president.

The Council of Legislators

Of this piece, being the greater half of the whole work, I shall be able at this time to give no farther account than very briefly to show at what it aims.

My Lord Archon, in opening the council of legislators, made it appear how unsafe a thing it is to follow fancy in the fabric of a commonwealth,[1] and how necessary that the archives of ancient prudence should be ransacked before any counsellor should presume to offer any other matter in order to the work in hand, or towards the consideration to be had by the council upon a model of government. Wherefore he caused an urn to be brought, and every one of the counsellors to draw a lot.

By the lots as they were drawn, the commonwealth of Israel fell unto Phosphorus de Auge; that of Athens unto Navarchus de Paralo; that of Lacedaemon unto Laco de Scytale; that of Carthage unto Mago de Syrtibus; that of the Achaeans, Aetolians and Lycians unto Aratus de Isthmo; that of the Swiss unto Alpester de Fulmine; that of Holland and the United Provinces unto Glaucus de Ulna; that of Rome unto Dolabella de Enyo; that of Venice unto Lynceus de Stella.[2]

These, containing in them all those excellencies whereof a commonwealth is capable (so that to have added more had been to no

---

[1] H has 'Phansie'. There is no modern equivalent which carries the full load of implications born by words such as 'fancy', 'phansie', 'phantasy', in Renaissance English.

[2] The names of republics and the counsellors who report on them are arranged in an elaborate tabulation, here re-converted into continuous prose. It is the first sign of H's love of schematising the imaginary setting. The name of the rapporteur for Holland recalls the Latin couplet on p. 7 above.

purpose), upon time given unto the counsellors, by their own studies and those of their friends to prepare themselves, were opened in the order and by the persons mentioned at the council of legislators, and afterwards by order of the same were repeated at the council of the prytans unto the people; for in drawing of the lots, there were a matter of a dozen of them inscribed with the letter P, which the counsellors that drew became prytans.

The prytans were a committee or council sitting in the great hall of Pantheon, to whom it was lawful for any man to offer anything in order to the fabric of the commonwealth, for which cause, that they might not be oppressed by the throng, there was a rail about the table where they sat, and on each side of the same a pulpit; that on the right hand for any man that would propose anything and that on the left for any other that would oppose him; and all parties (being indemnified by proclamation of the Archon) were invited to dispute their own interests, or propose whatever they thought fit in order to the future government, to the council of the prytans, who (having a guard of a matter of two or three hundred men, lest the heat of the dispute might break the peace) had the right of moderators, and were to report from time to time such propositions or occurrences as they thought fit to the council of legislators, sitting more privately in the palace called Alma.[3]

This was that which made the people (who were neither safely to be admitted unto, nor conveniently to be excluded from the framing of their commonwealth) verily believe when it came forth that it was no other than that whereof they themselves had been the makers.

Moreover, this council sat divers months after the publishing, and during the promulgation of the model unto the people, by which means there is scarce anything was said or written for or against the said model, but you shall have it with the next impression of this work,[4] by way of oration addressed unto and moderated by the prytans.

By this means the council of legislators had their necessary solitude and due aim in their greater work, as being acquainted from time to

---

[3] 'Pantheon' is presumably Westminster Hall, and 'Alma' Whitehall.
[4] It is unclear whether H contemplated a further edition of *Oceana*, or was momentarily assuming the *persona* of a correspondent writing from that imaginary land, on the model of Boccalini in his *Ragguagli di Parnasso*. The orations which follow in the book are all addressed to the council of legislators, not the prytans. Cf. p. 242 below.

time with the pulse of the people, and yet without any manner of interruption or disturbance.

Wherefore, every commonwealth in her place having been opened by her due method – that is, first by the people, secondly by the senate and thirdly by the magistracy – the council upon mature debate took such results or orders out of each one, and out of each part of each one of them, as upon opening the same they thought fit; which being put from time to time in writing by the clerk or secretary, there remained no more in the conclusion than, putting the orders so taken together, to view and examine them with a diligent eye, to the end that it might be clearly discovered whether they did interfere, or could anywise come to interfere or jostle one the other. For as such orders, jostling or coming to jostle one another, are the certain dissolution of the commonwealth, so, taken upon the proof of like experience, and neither jostling nor showing which way they can possibly come to jostle one another,[5] make a perfect and (for ought that in human prudence can be foreseen) an immortal commonwealth.

And such was the art whereby my Lord Archon, taking counsel of the commonwealth of Israel as of Moses, and of the rest of the commonwealths as of Jethro, framed the model of the commonwealth of Oceana.

[5] 'They', inserted here, would make for better syntax.

The Model of the Commonwealth of Oceana

Whereas my Lord Archon – being, from Moses and Lycurgus, the first legislator that hitherto is found in story to have introduced or erected an entire commonwealth at once – happened, like them also, to be more intent upon putting the same into execution or action than into writing, by which means the model came to be promulgated or published with more brevity and less illustration than is necessary for their understanding, who have not been acquainted with the whole proceedings of the council of legislators and of the prytans, where it was asserted and cleared from all objections and doubts; unto the end that I may supply what was wanting in the promulgated epitome unto a more full and perfect narrative of the whole, I shall rather take the commonwealth practically and as she hath now given account of herself in some years' revolutions (as Dicaearchus is said to have done that of Lacedaemon, first transcribed by his hand some three or four hundred years after the institution), yet not omitting to add for proof unto every order such debates and speeches of the legislators in their council, or at, least such parts of them, as may best discover the reason of the government, nor such ways and means as were used in the institution or rise of the building, not to be so well conceived without some knowledge given of the engines wherewithal the mighty weight was moved. But through the entire omission of the council of legislators, or workmen that squared every stone unto this structure in the quarries of ancient prudence, the proof of the first part of this discourse will be lame except I insert, as well for illustration as to avoid frequent repetition, three remarkable testimonies in this place.

The first is taken out of the commonwealth of Israel. *So Moses hearkened unto the voice of (Jethro) his father-in-law, and did all that he had said. And Moses chose able men out of all Israel, and made them heads over the people;* tribunes as it is in the vulgar Latin, or phylarchs, that is princes of the tribes, sitting *sellis curulibus,* saith Grotius, upon twelve thrones, and judging the twelve tribes of Israel; and next unto these he chose *rulers of thousands, rulers of hundreds, rulers of fifties, and rulers of tens,*[1] which were the steps or rise of this commonwealth, from her foundation or root unto her proper elevation or accomplishment in the Sanhedrim and the congregation, already opened in the Preliminaries.

The second is taken out of Lacedaemon, as Lycurgus (for the greater impression of his institutions upon the minds of his citizens) pretended to have received the model of that commonwealth from the oracle of Apollo at Delphos, the words whereof are thus recorded by Plutarch in the life of that famous legislator:

> when thou shalt have divided the people into tribes (which were six) and *obai* (which were five in every tribe), thou shalt constitute the senate, consisting with the two kings of thirty counsellors who, according as occasion requireth, shall cause the congregation to be assembled between the bridge and the river Gnacion, where the senate shall propose unto the people and dismiss them, without suffering them to debate.[2]

The *obai* were lineages into which every tribe was divided, and in each tribe there was one other division containing all those of the same that were of military age, which, being called the *mora,* was subdivided into troops and companies that were held in perpetual discipline under the command of a magistrate called the polemarch.

The third is taken out of the commonwealth of Rome, or those parts of it which are comprised in the first and second books of Livy: where the people, according to the institution by Romulus, are first divided into thirty *curiae* or parishes, whereof he elected (by three out of each *curia*) the senate, which from his reign on to that of Servius Tullius proposed unto the parishes or parochial congregations. And these, being called the *comitia curiata,* had the election of the kings

---

[1] 'Exo. 18: 24. Numb. 1: 16. Math.' – H's note. The reference 'Math.' is to Grotius. *Annotationes in Evangelium secundum Mathaeum,* 19, 28 (Liljegren, p. 289), where Grotius uses the strictly Roman phrase 'sellis curulibus' in connexion with 'sit upon twelve thrones, judging the twelve tribes of Israel'.

[2] Plutarch, *Lycurgus,* VI.

(*Quirites, regem create; ita patribus visum est;*[3] again, *Tullium Hostilium regem populus jussit, patres auctores facti*),[4] the confirmation of their laws (*ut ab Romulo traditum, suffragium viritim eadem vi, eademque jure omnibus datum est*),[5] and the last appeal in matters of judicature, as appears in the case of Horatius that killed his sister, till in the reign of Servius, *non enim ut ab Romulo traditum caeteri servaverunt reges*.[6] The people being grown somewhat, the power of the *curiata* was for the greater part translated unto the *centuriata comitia* instituted by this king, which distributed the people, according to the cense or valuation of their estates, unto six *classes*, every one containing about forty centuries, divided into youth and elders; the youth for field service, the elders for the defence of their territory, all armed and under continual discipline, in which they assembled both upon military and civil occasions. But when the senate proposed unto the people, the horse only, whereof there were twelve centuries, consisting of the richest sort over and above those of the foot enumerated, were called with the first *classis* of the foot unto the suffrage; or if these accorded not, then the second *classis* was called to them, but seldom or never any of the rest. Wherefore the people after the expulsion of the kings, growing impatient of this inequality, rested not till they had reduced the suffrage, as it had been in the *comitia curiata*, to the whole people again; but in another way, that is to say by the *comitia tributa* which thereupon were instituted, being a council where the people in exigencies made laws without the senate, which laws were called *plebiscita*. This council is that in regard whereof Cicero and other great wits so frequently inveigh against the people, and sometimes even Livy, as at the institution: *hunc annum insignem maxime comitia tributa efficiunt; res major victoria suscepti certaminis quam usu, plus enim dignitatis comitiis ipsis detractum est, patribus ex concilio submovendis, quam virium aut plebi additum aut demptum patribus*.[7] To say truth, it was a kind of anarchy, whereof the people could not be excusable, if there had not, through the course taken by the senate, been otherwise a necessity that they must have seen the commonwealth run into oligarchy.

---

[3] Livy, I, xvii. [4] Livy, I, xxii. [5] Livy, I, xliii. [6] *Ibid.*

[7] Livy, II, lvi; Cicero, *De Legibus*, III, 19. Liljegren (p. 292) was of opinion that, while regularly citing Livy, H relied rather on Sigonius for his account of the primitive Roman constitution. The marginal reference 'Sigonius' appears against the opening lines of the next paragraph.

The manner how the *comitia curiata*, *centuriata* or *tributa* were called, during the time of the commonwealth, to the suffrage was by lot: the *curia*, century or tribe whereon the first lot fell being styled *principium*, or the prerogative; and the other *curiae*, centuries or tribes, whereon the second, third, fourth lots, etc. fell, the *jure vocatae*; from henceforth not the first *classis*, as in the times of Servius, but the prerogative, whether *curia*, century or tribe, came first to the suffrage, whose vote was called *omen praerogativum*, and seldom failed to be leading unto the rest of the tribes. The *jure vocatae* in the order of their lots came next. The manner of giving suffrage was by casting wooden tablets marked for the affirmative or the negative into certain urns standing upon a scaffold, as they marched over it in files, which for the resemblance it bore was called the bridge. The candidate or competitor who had most suffrages in a *curia*, century or tribe, was said to have that *curia*, century or tribe; and he who had most of the *curiae*, centuries or tribes carried the magistracy.

These three places being premised as such upon which there will be frequent reflection, I come unto the narrative, divided into two parts, the first containing the institution, the second the constitution of the commonwealth; in each whereof I shall distinguish the orders, as those which contain the whole model, from the rest of the discourse, which tendeth only unto the explanation or proof of them.

In the institution or building of a commonwealth, the first work (as that of builders) can be no other than fitting and distributing the materials.

The materials of a commonwealth are the people; and the people of Oceana were distributed by casting them into certain divisions, regarding their quality, their ages, their wealth, and the places of their residence or habitation, which was done by the ensuing orders.

> *The first* distributing the people into freemen or citizens, and servants, while such; for if they attain unto liberty, that is to live of themselves, they are freemen or citizens.

This order needeth no proof, in regard of the nature of servitude, which is inconsistent with freedom or participation of government in a commonwealth.

> *The second order* distributeth citizens into youth and elders (such as are from 18 years of age to 30 being accounted youth, and such as are of 30 and upwards elders) and establisheth that

75

the youth shall be the marching armies, and the elders the standing garrisons of this nation.

A commonwealth whose arms are in the hands of the servants had need be situated, as is elegantly said of Venice by Contarini, *lontana dalla fede degli huomini,*[8] out of the reach of such clutches; witness the danger run by that of Carthage in the rebellion of Spendius and Matho. But though a city (if one swallow make a summer) may thus chance to be safe, yet shall she never be great; for if Carthage or Venice acquired any fame in their arms, it is known to have happened through the mere virtue of their captains, and not of their orders; wherefore Israel, Lacedaemon and Rome entailed their arms upon the prime of their citizens, divided (at least in Lacedaemon and Rome) into youth and elders, the youth for the field and the elders for defence of the territory.

> *The third order* distributeth the citizens into horse and foot by the cense or valuation of their estates; they who have above one hundred pounds a year in lands, goods or monies, being obliged to be of the horse, and they who have under to be of the foot. But if a man have prodigally wasted and spent his patrimony, he is neither capable of magistracy, office nor suffrage in the commonwealth.

Citizens are not only to defend the commonwealth, but according to their abilities; as the Romans under Servius Tullius (regard had unto their estates) were some enrolled in the horse centuries, and other of the foot, with arms enjoined accordingly; nor could it be otherwise in the rest of the commonwealths, though out of remains that are so much darker it be not so clearly proveable. And the necessary prerogative, to be given by a commonwealth unto estates in some measure, is in the nature of industry, and the use of it to the public.

Populus Romanus (saith Julius Exuperantius) *per classes divisus erat, et pro patrimonii facultate censebantur; ex iis, omnes quibus res erat, ad militiam ducebantur; diligenter enim pro victoria laborabant qui ex libertate bona patriam defendebant. Illi autem quibus nullae opes erant, caput suum, quod solum possidebant, censebantur et belli tempore in moenibus residebant; facile enim poterant existere proditores, quia egestas haud facile habetur sine damno. Hos igitur Marius, quibus non fuerat respublica committenda, duxit ad bellum,*[9]

---

[8] Gasparo Contarini, *La Republica e i Magistrati di Vinegia* (Venice, 1548), p. iii *bis*.

[9] According to Liljegren (p. 294), this passage may more conveniently be found in Sallust.

and his success was accordingly. There is a mean in things: as exorbitant riches overthrow the balance of a commonwealth, so extreme poverty cannot hold it nor is by any means to be trusted with it. The clause in the order concerning the prodigal is Athenian, and a very laudable one; for he that could not live upon his patrimony, if he come to touch the public money makes a commonwealth bankrupt.

The fourth order distributeth the people, according unto the places of their habitation, unto parishes, hundreds and tribes.

For except the people be methodically distributed, they cannot be methodically collected, but the being of a commonwealth consisteth in the methodical collection of the people; wherefore you have the Israelite divisions into rulers of thousands, of hundreds, of fifties, and of tens, and of the whole commonwealth into tribes; the Laconic into *obai, morai* and tribes; the Roman into tribes, centuries, and *classes*; and something there must of necessity be in every government of like nature, as that in the late monarchy by counties. But this, being the only institution in Oceana (except that of the agrarian) which required any charge or included any difficulty, engageth me unto a more particular description of the manner how it was performed, as followeth.

One thousand surveyors commissioned and instructed by the Lord Archon and the council, being divided into two equal numbers, each under the inspection of two surveyors general, were distributed into the northern and southern parts of the territory, divided by the river Hemisua,[10] the whole whereof containeth about ten thousand parishes, some ten of those being assigned unto each surveyor. For as to this matter there needed no great exactness, it tending only, by showing whither everyone was to repair and whereabout to begin, unto the more orderly carrying on of the work; the nature of their instructions otherwise regarding rather the number of the inhabitants than of the parishes. The surveyors therefore, being every one furnished with a proportion convenient of urns, balls and balloting boxes (in the use whereof they had been formerly exercised), and now arriving each at his respective parishes, began with the people by teaching them their first lesson, which was the ballot; and albeit they found them in the beginning somewhat froward, as at toys, with

[10] Presumably the Trent.

77

which, while they were in expectation of greater matters from a council of legislators, they conceived themselves to be abused, they came within a while to think them pretty sport, and at length such as might very soberly be used in good earnest; whereupon the surveyors began the institution included in

The fifth order: requiring that upon the first Monday next ensuing the last of December, the bigger bell in every parish throughout the nation be rung at eight of the clock in the morning, and continue ringing for the space of one hour; and that all the elders of the parish respectively repair unto the church before the bell have done ringing, where, dividing themselves unto five equal numbers, or as near equal as may be, they shall take their places according to their dignities, if they be of divers qualities, and according to their seniority, if they be of the same, the one half on the one side and the other half on the other, in the body of the church; which done, they shall make oath unto the overseers of the parish for the time being (*instead of these the surveyors were to officiate at the institution or first assembly*), by holding up their hands, to make a fair election, receiving according unto the laws of the ballot, as they be hereafter explained, of such persons amounting unto a fifth part of their whole number, to be their deputies and to exercise their power in manner hereafter explained, as they shall think in their consciences to be fitted for that trust, and will acquit themselves of it to the best advantage of the commonwealth. And, oath being thus made, they shall proceed unto election, if the elders of the parish amount unto one thousand, by the ballot of the tribe (as it is in due place explained); and if the elders of the parish amount unto fifty or upwards, but within the number of one thousand, by the ballot of the hundred (as it is in the due place explained). But if the elders amount not unto fifty, then they shall proceed unto the ballot of the parish, as it is in this place and after this manner explained. The two overseers for the time being shall seat themselves at the upper end of the middle alley, with a table before them, their faces being towards the congregation. And the constable for the time being shall set an urn before the table, into which he shall put so many balls as there be elders present, whereof there shall be one that is gilded, the rest being white; and when the constable hath shaken the urn sufficiently to mix the balls, the overseers shall call the elders unto the urn, who from each side of the church shall come up the middle alley in two files, every man

78

passing by the urn and drawing one ball, which if it be silver, he shall cast into a bowl standing at the foot of the urn, and return by the outward alley on his side unto his place. But he who draweth the gold ball is the proposer, and shall be seated between the overseers, where he shall begin in what order he pleaseth, and name such as (upon his oath already taken) he conceiveth fittest to be chosen, one by one unto the elders; and the party named shall withdraw, while the congregation is in balloting of his name by the double box or boxes, appointed and marked on the outward part, to show which side is affirmative and which negative, being carried by a boy or boys appointed by the overseers unto every one of the elders, who shall hold up a pellet made of linen rags between his finger and his thumb and put it after such a manner into the box, as though no man can see into which side he putteth it, yet any man may see that he puts in but one pellet or suffrage; and the suffrage of the congregation, being thus given, shall be returned with the box or boxes unto the overseers, who opening the same shall pour the affirmative balls into a white bowl standing upon the table on the right hand, to be numbered by the first overseer, and the negative into a green bowl standing on the left hand, to be numbered by the second overseer; and the suffrages being numbered, he who hath the major part in the affirmative, is one of the deputies of the parish; and when so many deputies are chosen as amounts unto a full fifth part of the whole number of the elders, the ballot for that time shall cease. The deputies being chosen are to be listed by the overseers in order as they were chosen, save only that such as are horse are to be listed in the first place with the rest proportionably to the number of the congregation, after this manner:

Anno Dom.

The List of the First Mover.

A.A. *ord eq.*	1st Dep.	of the parish of—— in the hundred of—— and the
B.B.	2nd Dep.	tribe of——, which parish at the present election
C.C.	3rd Dep.	containeth 20 elders, whereof one of the horse or
D.D.	4th Dep.	equestrian order.
E.E.	5th Dep.	

The first and second in the list are overseers by consequence; the third is the constable, and the fourth and fifth are church-wardens; the persons so chosen are deputies of the parish for the space of one year from their election and no longer, nor may they be elected two years together. This list, being the *primum mobile* or first mover of the commonwealth, is to be registered in a book,

79

diligently kept and preserved by the overseers, who are responsible in their places for these and other duties to be hereafter mentioned unto the censors of the tribe, and the congregation is to observe the present order, as they will answer the contrary unto the phylarch, or prerogative troop of the tribe; which, in case of failure in the whole or any part of it, have power to fine them or any of them, at discretion, but under an appeal unto the parliament.

For proof of this order in reason: it is with all politicians past dispute that paternal power is in the right of nature, and this is no other than the derivation of power from fathers of families, as the natural root of a commonwealth; and for experience, if it be otherwise in that of Holland, I know no other example of like kind. In Israel, the sovereign power came clearly from the natural root, the elders of the whole people, and Rome was born *comitiis curiatis*, in her parochial congregations, out of which Romulus first raised her senate, then all the rest of the orders of that commonwealth which rose so high. For the depth of a commonwealth is the just height of it.

> *Ipsa haeret scopulis et tantum vertice ad auras*
> *Aethereas, quantum radice ad tartara tendit.*[11]

> She raises up her head unto the skies,
> Near as her root unto the centre lies.

And if the commonwealth of Rome were born of thirty parishes, this of Oceana was born of ten thousand. But whereas mention in the birth of this is made of an equestrian order, it may startle such as know that the division of the people of Rome at the institution of that commonwealth into orders was the occasion of her ruin. The distinction of the patrician as an hereditary order from the very institution, engrossing all the magistracies, was indeed the destruction of Rome; but to a knight or one of the equestrian order, saith Horace:

> *Si quadringentis sex septem millia defunt*
> *Plebs eris.*[12]

By which it should seem that this order was no otherwise hereditary than a man's estate, nor gave it any claim to magistracy; wherefore you shall never find that it disquieted the commonwealth, nor doth the

---

[11] *Aeneid*, IV, 445f.   [12] Horace, *Epistles*, I, i, 57f.

name denote any more in Oceana than the duty of such a man's estate unto the public.

But the surveyors both in this place and in others, for as much as they could not observe all the circumstances of this order, especially that of the time of election, did for the first as well as they could and, the elections being made and registered, took each of them copies of those lists which were within their allotments; which done, they produced

The sixth order, directing, in case a parson or vicar of a parish come to be removed by death or by the censors, that the congregation of the parish assemble and depute one or two elders of the ballot, who upon the charge of the parish shall repair unto one of the universities of this nation with a certificate signed by the overseers, and addressed unto the vice-chancellor; which certificate giving notice of the death or removal of the parson or vicar, of the value of the parsonage or vicarage, and of the desire of the congregation to receive a probationer from that university, the vice-chancellor upon the receipt thereof shall call a convocation and, having made choice of a fit person, shall return him in due time unto the parish, where the person so returned shall receive the full fruits of the benefice or vicarage, and do the duty of the parson or vicar for the space of one year, as probationer; and the space of one year being expired, the congregation of the elders shall put their probationer to the ballot and if he attain not unto two parts in three of the suffrage affirmative, he shall take his leave of the parish, and they shall send in like manner for another probationer: but if their probationer attain unto two parts in three of the suffrage affirmative, he is the pastor of that parish. And the pastor of the parish shall pray with the congregation, preach the word and administer the sacraments unto the same, according unto the directory to be hereafter appointed by the parliament. Nevertheless such as are of gathered congregations, or from time to time shall join with any of them, are in no wise obliged to this way of electing their teachers, or to give their votes in this case, but wholly left unto the liberty of their conscience, and unto that way of worship which they shall choose, being not Popish, Jewish, nor idolatrous; and to the end that they may be the better protected by the state in the free exercise of the same, they are desired to make choice, in such manner as they best like, of certain magistrates in every one of their congregations, which we could wish might be four in each of them, to be auditors in cases of differences or distaste, if any through variety of opinions, that may be grievous or injurious unto them, should fall out. And such auditors or magistrates shall have power to examine the matter and inform themselves to the end that if they think it of sufficient weight they may acquaint the phylarch, or introduce it into the council of religion; where all such causes as such magistrates shall introduce shall from time to time be heard and determined according unto such laws as are or shall hereafter be provided by the parliament for the just defence of the liberty of conscience.

This order consisteth of three parts, the first restoring the power of ordination unto the people, which that it originally appertaineth unto them is clear, though not in English, yet in Scripture, where the apostles *ordained elders by the holding up of hands in every congregation,*[13] that is by the suffrage of the people, which was also given in some of those cities by the ballot; and though it may be shown that the apostles ordained some by the laying on of hands, it will not be shown that they did so in every congregation.

Excommunication, as not clearly provable out of Scripture, being omitted, the second part of the order implies and establisheth a national religion. For there be degrees of knowledge in divine things; true religion is not to be attained unto without searching the Scriptures; the Scriptures cannot be searched by us unless we have them to search; and if we have nothing else or (which is all one) understand nothing else but a translation, we may be (as in the place alleged we have been) beguiled or misled by the translation, while we should be searching the true sense of the Scripture, which cannot be attained unto in a natural way (and a commonwealth is not to presume upon that which is supernatural) but by the knowledge of the original and of antiquity, acquired by our own studies or those of some other, for even faith cometh by hearing.[14] Wherefore a commonwealth, not making provision of men from time to time knowing in the original languages wherein the Scriptures were written, and versed in those antiquities whereunto they so frequently relate that the true sense of them dependeth in a great part upon that knowledge, can never be

---

[13] Acts, 14: 23. As Liljegren observes, the reference must be to the Greek text, where the vital word χειροτονήσαντες occurs, and not to the Authorised Version, where 'the holding up of hands' does not.

[14] Romans, 10: 17. Cf. *Leviathan*, III, 29 and 43 (Tuck, pp. 223–4 and 405–6). H's use of the Pauline text is very like Hobbes's.

secure that she shall not lose the Scripture and by consequence her religion, which to preserve she must institute some method of this knowledge, and some use of such as have acquired it, which amounteth unto a national religion.

The commonwealth, having thus performed her duty towards God as a rational creature, by the best application of her reason unto Scripture, for the preservation of religion in the purity of the same, yet pretendeth not unto infallibility; but comes in the third part of the order, establishing liberty of conscience according to the instructions given unto her council of religion, to raise up her hands to heaven for further light, in which proceeding she followeth that (as was shown in the preliminaries) of Israel, who, though her national religion were evermore a part of her civil law, gave unto her prophets the upper hand of all her orders.

But the surveyors, having now done with the parishes, took their leaves so: *A parish is the first division of land occasioned by the first collection of the people of Oceana, whose function proper unto that place is comprised in the six foregoing orders.*[15]

The next step in the progress of the surveyors was to a meeting of the nearest of them, as their work lay, by twenties where, conferring their lists and computing the deputies contained therein, as the number of them in parishes, being nearest neighbours, amounted unto one hundred, or as even as might conveniently be brought with that account, they cast them and those parishes into the precinct which (be the deputies ever since more or fewer) is still called the hundred, and unto every one of these precincts they appointed a certain place, being the most convenient town within the same, for the annual rendezvous; which done, each surveyor returning unto his hundred and summoning the deputies contained in his lists unto the rendezvous, they appeared and received

> *The seventh order*, requiring that upon the first Monday next ensuing the last of January, the deputies of every parish annually assemble in arms at the rendezvous of the hundred, and there elect out of their number one justice of the peace, one juryman, one captain, one ensign of their troop or century, each of these out of the horse, and one juryman, one crowner, one high constable, out of the foot; the election to be made by the ballot in this

---

[15] H's italics, possibly indicating that these words are a decree by the legislators.

manner: the jurymen for the time being are to be overseers of the ballot (*instead of these the surveyors are to officiate at the first assembly*) and to look unto the performance of the same according to what was directed in the ballot of the parishes, save that the high constable setting forth the urn shall have five several suits of gold balls, and one dozen of every suit, whereof the first shall be marked with the letter A, the second with the letter B, the third with C, the fourth with D, and the fifth with E. And of each of these suits he shall cast one ball into his hat or into a little urn and, shaking the balls together, present them unto the first overseer, who shall draw one, and the suit which is so drawn by the overseer shall be of use for that day, and none other: for example, if the overseer drew an A, the high constable shall put seven gold balls marked with the letter A into the urn, with so many silver ones as shall bring them even with the number of the deputies who, being sworn as before, at the ballot of the parish, to make a fair election, shall be called unto the urn; and every man coming in manner as was there showed shall draw one ball which if it be silver, he shall cast it into a bowl standing at the foot of the urn, and return unto his place; but the first that draweth a gold ball (showing it unto the overseers who, if it have not the letter of the present ballot, have power to apprehend and punish him) is the first elector; the second the second elector, and so to the seventh, which order they are to observe in their function. The electors as they are drawn shall be placed upon the bench by the overseers, till the whole number be complete, and then be conducted with the list of the officers to be chosen into a place apart where, being private, the first elector shall name a person unto the first office in the list; and if the person so named, being balloted by the rest of the electors, attain not unto the better half of the suffrages in the affirmative, the first elector shall continue nominating others, until one of them so nominated by him attain unto the plurality of the suffrages in the affirmative, and be written first competitor to the first office. This done, the second elector shall observe in his turn the like order, and so the rest of the electors, naming competitors each unto his respective office in the list, till one competitor be chosen unto every office: and when one competitor is chosen unto every office, the first elector shall begin again to name a second competitor unto the first office, and the rest successively shall name unto the rest of the offices till two competitors be chosen unto every office; the like shall be repeated till three competitors be chosen to every office. And when three competitors be chosen to every office, the list shall be returned unto the overseers, or such as the overseers, in case they or either of them happened to be electors, have substituted in his or their place or places; and the overseers or substitutes, having caused the list to be read unto the congregation, shall put the competitors in order as they are written unto the ballot of the congregation; and the rest of the proceedings being carried on in the manner directed in the fifth order, that competitor of the three written unto each office who hath most of the suffrages above half in the affirmative, is the officer. The list, being after this manner completed, shall be entered into a register, to be kept at the rendezvous of the hundred, under inspection of the magistrates of the same, after this manner:

Anno Domini

The List of the Nebulosa

A.A. *ord. eq.*, Justice of the peace

of the hundred of——

B.B. *ord. eq.*, First juryman

in the tribe of——

C.C. *ord. eq.*, Captain of the hundred

which hundred consisteth

D.D. *ord. eq.*, Ensign

at this election of 105 deputies.

E.E.   Second juryman
F.F.   High constable
G.G.   Crowner

The list being entered, the high constable shall take three copies of the same, whereof he shall forthwith return one unto the lord high sheriff of the tribe, a second unto the lord custos rotulorum, and a third unto the censors (or these, through the want of such magistrates at the first muster, may be returned unto the orator to be appointed for that tribe). To the observation of all and every part of this order, the officers and deputies of the hundred are all and every of them obliged, as they will answer it to the phylarch, who hath power, in case of failure in the whole or any part, to fine all or any of them so failing at discretion, or according unto such laws as shall hereafter be provided in that base; but under an appeal unto the parliament.

There is little in this order worthy of any further account, than that it answers unto the rulers of hundreds in Israel, to the *mora* or military

85

part of the tribe in Lacedaemon, and to the century in Rome. The jurymen, being two in a hundred, and so forty in a tribe, give the latitude allowed by the law for exceptions. And whereas the gold balls at this ballot begin to be marked with letters, whereof one is to be drawn immediately before it begin, this is to the end that, the letter being unknown, men may be frustrated of tricks or foul play, whereas otherwise a man might bring a gold ball with him and make as if he had drawn it out of the urn. The surveyors, when they had taken copies of these lists, had accomplished their work in the hundreds.

So, *an hundred is the second division of land occasioned by the second collection of the people, whose civil and military functions proper unto this place are comprised in the foregoing order.*[16] Having stated the hundreds, they met once again by twenties, where there was nothing more easy than to cast every twenty hundreds, as they lay most conveniently together, into one tribe; so the whole territory of Oceana, consisting of about ten thousand parishes, came to be cast into one thousand hundreds, and into fifty tribes. In every tribe, at the place appointed for the annual rendezvous of the same, were then, or soon after, put in hand those buildings which are now called pavilions, each of them standing with one open side, upon fair columns like the porch of some ancient temple, and looking into a field capable of the muster of some four thousand men. Before each pavilion stand three pillars sustaining urns for the ballot: that on the right hand, equal in height to the brow of an horseman, being called the horse urn, that on the left hand, with bridges on either side to bring it equal in height with the brow of a footman, being called the foot urn; and the middle urn, with a bridge on the side towards the foot urn, the other side, as left for the horse, being without one. And here ended the whole work of the surveyors, who returned unto the Lord Archon with this

Account of the Charge

	£	s.
Imprimis, urns, balls, and balloting boxes for ten thousand parishes, the same being wooden ware	20,000	0
Item, Provisions of like kind for a thousand hundreds	3,000	0
Item, urns and balls of metal, with balloting boxes for fifty tribes	2,000	0
Item, for erecting of fifty pavilions	60,000	0

[16] H's italics, as above.

Item, wages for four surveyors general at 1000£
a man   4,000–0
Item, wages for the rest of the surveyors,
being 1000, at 250£ a man   250,000–0

sum total, 339,000 – – – – – 0

No great matter of charge for the building of a commonwealth, in regard that it hath cost (which was pleaded by the surveyors) as much to rig a few ships. Nevertheless that proveth not them to be honest, not their account to be just; but they had their money for once, though their reckoning be plainly guilty of a crime[17] to cost him his neck that commits it another time – it being impossible for a commonwealth, without an exact provision that she be not abused in this kind, to subsist, if it were not in regard of the charge (though that may go deep), yet in regard of the debauchery and corruption whereunto, by negligence in her accounts, she infallibly exposeth her citizens, and thereby slackeneth the public faith which is the nerve and ligament of government.[18] But the surveyors being dispatched, the Lord Archon was very curious in giving names unto his tribes, which having caused to be written in scrolls cast unto an urn and presented unto the counsellors, each of them drew one, and was accordingly sent unto the tribe in his lot as orators of the same, a magistracy no otherwise instituted than for once and *pro tempore*, to the end that the council, upon so great an occasion, might both congratulate with the tribes and assist at the first muster, in some things of necessity to be differently carried from the established administration and future course of the commonwealth.

The orators, being arrived, every one as soon as might be, at the rendezvous of his tribe, gave notice to the hundreds and summoned the muster, which appeared for the most part upon good horses and already indifferently well armed; as, to instance in one for all, the tribe of Nubia, where Hermes de Caduceo, lord orator of the same, after a short salutation and an hearty welcome, applied himself unto his business, which began with

---

[17] The 'crime' of the surveyors is apparently that of charging too much for their services, unless it be significant that a balloting box for a hundred costs £3, as against £2 for a parish. H may have intended to intimate that the Machiavellian thought that the foundation of a commonwealth is a moment peculiarly hard to keep free from misdeeds (the most famous instance being Romulus's murder of his brother).

[18] Toland here added the words 'ought to be prevented' (p. 85 in 1771 edition), evidently thinking that H had neglected to complete the sentence.

The eighth order: requiring that the lord high sheriff as commander in chief, and the lord custos rotulorum as muster-master of the tribe (or the orator for the first muster), upon reception of the lists of their hundreds returned unto them by the high constables of the same, forthwith cause them to be cast up, dividing the horse from the foot and listing the horse by their names in troops, each troop containing about a hundred in number, to be inscribed first, second or third troop, etc., according to the order agreed upon by the said magistrates; which done, they shall list the foot in like manner, and inscribe the companies in like order. These lists upon the eve of the muster shall be delivered unto certain trumpeters and drummers, whereof there shall be fifteen of each sort (as well for the present as other uses to be hereafter mentioned), stipendiated by the tribe, and the trumpeters and drummers shall be in the field before the pavilion upon the day of the muster, so soon as it is light, where they shall stand everyone with his list in his hand, at a due distance, placed according unto the order of the list; the trumpeters with the lists of the horse on the right hand, and the drummers with the lists of the foot on the left hand; where having sounded a while, each of them shall begin to call, and continue calling, the names of the deputies as they come into the field, till both the horse and foot be gathered by that means into their due order. The horse and foot being in order, the lord lieutenant of the tribe shall cast so many gold balls marked with the figures 1, 2, 3, 4, etc., as there be troops of horse in the field, together with so many silver balls as there be companies, marked in the same manner, into a little urn, whereunto he shall call the captains; and the captains drawing the gold balls shall command the horse, and those that draw the silver the foot, each in the order of his lot. The like shall be done by the conductor at the same time for the ensigns, at another urn; and they that draw the gold balls shall be cornets, the rest ensigns.

This order may trash the reader, but tends unto a wonderful speed of the muster, to which it would be a great matter to lose a day in ranging and marshalling, whereas by virtue of this the tribe is no sooner in the field than in battalia, nor sooner in battalia than called unto the urns, or the ballot, by virtue of

The ninth order: whereby the censors (or the orator for the first muster) upon reception of the lists of the hundred from the high constables, according as is directed by the seventh order, are to make their notes for the urns beforehand, with regard had unto the lists of the magistrates to be elected by the ensuing orders; that is to say, by the first list called the prime magnitude, six, and by the second called the galaxy, nine. Wherefore the censors are to put into the middle urn for the election of the first list twenty-four gold balls with twenty-six blanks or silver balls, in all sixty [*sic*]; and into the side urns sixty gold balls divided unto each according unto the different number of the horse and the foot; that is to say, if the horse and the foot be equal, equally, and if the horse and the foot be unequal unequally, by an arithmetical proportion. The like shall be done the second day of the muster, for the second list, save that the censors shall put into the middle urn thirty-six gold balls with twenty-four blanks, in all sixty, and sixty gold balls into the urns, divided respectively unto the number of the horse and the foot; and the gold balls in the side urns at either ballot are by the addition of blanks to be brought even with the number of the ballottants at either urn respectively. The censors having prepared their notes, as hath been shown, and being come at the day into the field, shall present a little urn unto the lord high sheriff, who is to draw twice for the letters to be used that day, the one at the side urns and the other at the middle. And the censors, having fitted the urns accordingly, shall place themselves in certain moveable seats or pulpits (to be kept for that use in the pavilion), the first censor before the horse urn, the second before the foot urn, the lord lieutenant doing the office of censor *pro tempore* at the middle urn; where all and every one of them shall cause the laws of the ballot to be diligently observed, taking a special care that no man be suffered to come above once unto the urn (whereof it more particularly concerns the sub-censors, that is to say, the overseers of every parish, to be careful, they being each in this regard responsible for their respective parishes), or to draw above one ball, which if it be gold, he is to present unto the censor, who shall look upon the letter; and if it be not that of the day and of the respective urn, apprehend the party, who for this or any other like disorder is obnoxious unto the phylarch.

This order being observed by the censors, it is not possible for the people, if they can but draw the balls, though they understand nothing at all of the ballot, to be out. To philosophise further upon this art, though there be nothing more rational, were not worth the while, because in writing it will be perplexed and the first practice of it gives the demonstration; whence it came to pass that the orator, after some needless pains in the explanation of the two foregoing orders, betaking himself to exemplify the same, found the work done unto his hand; for the tribe, as eager upon a business of this nature, had retained one of the surveyors, out of whom (before the orator arrived) they had gotten the whole mystery by a stolen muster, at which, in order unto the ballot, they had made certain magistrates *pro tempore*; wherefore he found not only the pavilion (for this time a tent) erected, with three posts supplying the place of pillars unto the urns, but the urns, being prepared with a just number of balls for the first ballot, to become the field and the occasion very gallantly, with their covers made in the manner of helmets, open at either ear to give passage unto the hands of the ballottants, and slanting with noble plumes to direct the march of the people; wherefore he proceeded to

> *The tenth order:* requiring of the deputies of the parishes that upon every Monday next ensuing the last of February, they make their personal appearance, horse and foot in arms accordingly, at the rendezvous of the tribe where, being in discipline, the horse upon the right and the foot upon the left before the pavilion, and having made oath, by holding up their hands upon the tender of it by the lord high sheriff, to make election without favour, and of such only as they shall judge fittest for the commonwealth, the conductor shall take 3 balls, the one inscribed with these words 'outward files', another with these words 'inward files', and the third with these 'middle files', which balls shall be cast into a little urn, and present it to the lord high sheriff who, drawing one, shall give the words of command as they are thereupon inscribed, and the ballot shall begin accordingly. For example, if the ball be inscribed 'middle files', the ballot shall begin by the middle: that is, the two files that are middle to the horse shall draw out first to the horse urn, and the two files that are middle to the foot shall draw out first to the foot urn, and be followed by all the rest of the files as they are next unto them in order. The like shall be done by the inward, or by the outward files, in case they be first called. And the files, as every man hath drawn his ball, if it be silver, shall begin at the urn to counter-march unto their places; but he that hath drawn a gold ball at a side urn, shall proceed unto the middle urn where, if the ball he draweth be silver, he also shall countermarch. But if it be gold, he shall take his place upon a form set across the pavilion, with his face toward the lord high sheriff, who shall be seated in the middle of the pavilion with certain clerks by him, one of which shall write down the names of

every elector, that is of every one that drew a gold ball at the middle urn, and in the order his ball was drawn, till the electors amount unto six in number; and the first six electors, horse and foot promiscuously, are the first order of electors; the second six (still accounting them as they are drawn) the second order; the third six, the third order; and the fourth six, the fourth order of electors: every elector having place in his order, according unto the order wherein he was drawn. But so soon as the first order of electors is complete, the lord high sheriff shall send them with a copy of the following list, and a clerk that understands the ballot, forthwith unto a little tent standing before the pavilion in his eye, whereunto no other person but themselves during the election shall approach: the list shall be written in this manner:

Anno Domini
The List of the Prime Magnitude
or first day's election of magistrates.

1. The lord high sherriff, commander-in-chief
2. Lord lieutenant
3. Lord custos rotulorum, muster-
   master general
4. The conductor, being
   quartermaster-general
5. The first censor
6. The second censor

of the tribe of Nubia, containing at this present muster 700 horse, and 1500 foot, in all 1200 deputies.

And the electors of the first hand or order, being six, shall each of them name unto his respective magistracy in the list[19] such as are not already elected in the hundreds, till one competitor be chosen unto every magistracy in the list by the ballot of the electors of the first order; which done, the list with the competitors thereunto annexed shall be returned unto the lord high sheriff by the clerk attending that order; but the electors shall keep their places, for they have already given their suffrage and may not enter into the ballot of the tribe. If there arise any dispute in an order of electors, one of the censors, or sub-censors appointed by them in case they be electors, shall enter into the tent of that order, and that order shall stand unto his judgment in the decision of the controversy. The like shall be done exactly by each other order of electors, being sent as they are drawn, each

---

[19] C and P have 'left'.

with another copy of the same list, into a distinct tent, till there be returned unto the lord high sheriff four competitors unto every magistracy in the list, that is to say, one competitor elected unto every office in every one of the four orders; which competitors the lord high sheriff shall cause to be pronounced or read by a cryer unto the congregation and, the congregation having heard the whole list repeated, the names shall be put by the lord high sheriff unto the tribe, one by one, beginning with the first competitor in the first order, thence proceeding to the first competitor in the second order, and so the first in the third and fourth orders; and the suffrages, being taken in boxes by boys (as hath been already shown), shall be poured into the bowls standing before the censors, who shall be seated at each end of the table in the pavilion, the one numbering the affirmatives, and the other the negatives; and he of the four competitors to the first magistracy, that hath most above half the suffrages of the tribe in the affirmative, is the first magistrate. The like is to be done successively by the rest of the competitors in their order. But because soon after the boxes sent out for the first name, there be others sent out for the second, and so for the third, etc., by which means divers names are successively at one and the same time in balloting, the boy that carries a box shall sing or repeat continually the name of the competitor for whom that box is carrying, with that also of the magistracy unto which he is proposed. A magistrate of the tribe, happening to be an elector, may substitute any one of his own order to execute his other function; the magistrates of the prime magnitude, being thus elected, shall receive the present charge of the tribe.

If it be objected against this order that the magistrates to be elected by it will be men of more inferior rank than those of the hundreds, in regard that those are chosen first, it may be remembered that so were the burgesses in the former government; nevertheless the knights of the shire were men of greater quality. And the election at the hundred is made by a council of electors of whom less cannot be expected than the discretion of naming persons fittest for those capacities, with an eye upon these to be elected at the tribe. For what may be objected in the point of difficulty, it is demonstrable by the foregoing orders that a man might bring ten thousand men (if there were occasion) with as much ease, and as suddenly to perform the ballot, as he can make five thousand men (drawing them out by double files) to march a quarter of a mile; but because at this ballot, to go up and down the field, distributing the linen pellets unto every man with which he is to ballot or give suffrage, would lose a great deal of time, therefore a man's wife, his daughters or others make him his provision of pellets before the ballot, and he cometh into the field with a matter of a score of them in his pocket. And now I have as good as done with the sport. The next is

> *The eleventh order:* explaining the duties and functions of the magistrates contained in the list of the prime magnitude, and those of the hundreds, beginning with the lord high sheriff, who over and above his more ancient offices and those added by the former order, is the first magistrate of the phylarch, or prerogative troop. The lord lieutenant, over and above his duty mentioned, is commander in chief of the musters of the youth, and second magistrate of the phylarch; the custos rotulorum is to return the yearly muster-rolls of the tribe, as well that of the youth as of the electors, unto the rolls in Emporium, and is the third magistrate of the phylarch. The censors by themselves, and their sub-censors, that is the overseers of the parishes, are to see that the respective laws of the ballot be observed in all the popular assemblies of the tribe; they have power also to put such national ministers, as in preaching shall intermeddle with the matter of government, out of their livings, except the party appeal unto the phylarch or unto the council of religion, where in that case the censors shall prosecute all and every one of these magistrates, together with the justices of peace; and the jurymen of the hundreds, amounting in the whole number unto three score and six, are the prerogative troop or phylarch of the tribe.

The function of the phylarch or prerogative troop is five-fold. First, they are the council of the tribe, and as such to govern the musters of the same according to the foregoing orders, having cognizance of what hath passed in the congregations or elections made in the parishes or the hundreds, with power to punish any undue practices or variation from their respective rules and orders, under an appeal to the parliament. A marriage legitimately is to be pronounced by the parochial congregation, the muster of the hundred, or the phylarch; and if a tribe have a desire (which they are to express at the muster by their captains, every troop by his own) to petition the parliament, the phylarch as the council shall frame the petition in the pavilion, and propose it by clauses unto the ballot of the whole tribe; and the clauses that shall be affirmed by the ballot of the tribe, and be signed by the hands of the six magistrates of the prime magnitude, shall be received and esteemed by the parliament as the petition of the tribe, and no other.

Secondly, the phylarch hath power to call unto their assistance what other troops of the tribe they please (be they elders or youth, whose discipline will be hereafter directed) and with these to receive the judges itinerant in their circuits, whom the magistrates of the phylarch shall assist upon the bench, and the juries elsewhere in their proper functions according unto the more ancient laws and customs of this nation.

Thirdly, the phylarch shall hold the court called the quarter-sessions according unto the ancient custom, and therein shall also hear causes in order unto the protection of liberty of conscience, by such rules as are or shall hereafter be appointed by the parliament.

Fourthly, all commissions issued into the tribes by the parliament, or by the chancery, are to be directed unto the phylarch, or some of that troop, and executed by the same respectively.

Fifthly, in the case of levies of money the parliament shall tax the phylarchs, the phylarchs shall tax the hundreds, the hundreds the parishes, and the parishes shall levy it upon themselves. The parishes, having levied the tax money, accordingly shall return it unto the officers of the hundreds, the hundreds unto the phylarchs, and the phylarchs unto the exchequer. But if a man have ten children living, he shall pay no taxes; if he have five living, he shall pay but half taxes; if he have been married three years, or be above twenty-five years of age, and have no child or children lawfully begotten, he shall pay double taxes. And if there happen to grow any dispute upon these or such other orders as shall or may hereunto be added hereafter, the phylarchs shall judge the tribes, and the parliament shall judge the phylarchs. For the rest, if any man shall go about to introduce the right or power of debate into any popular council or congregation of this nation, the phylarch, or any magistrate of the hundred or of the tribe, shall cause him forthwith to be sent in custody unto the council of war.

The part of the order relating unto the rolls in Emporium, being of singular use, is not unworthy to be somewhat better opened. In what manner the lists of the parishes, hundreds and tribes are made hath been shown in their respective orders, where, after the parties elected, they give account of the whole number of the elders or deputies in their respective assemblies or musters. The like for this part exactly is done by the youth in their discipline (to be hereafter shown), wherefore the lists of the parishes, youth and elders, being summed up, give the whole number of the people able to bear arms; and the lists of the tribes, youth and elders, being summed up, give the whole number of the people bearing arms. This account, being annually recorded by the master of the rolls, is called the Pillar of Nilus, because the people, being the riches of the commonwealth, as they are found to rise or fall by the degrees of this pillar, like that river, give account of the public harvest.

This much for the description of the first day's work at the muster, which happened, as hath been shown, to be done as soon as said; for as in practice it is of small difficulty, so requires it not much of time, seeing the great council of Venice, consisting of a like number, begins at twelve of the clock, and elects nine magistrates in one afternoon. But the tribe, being dismissed for this night, repaired unto their quarters under the conduct of their new magistrates. The next morning, returning into the field very early, the orator proceeded to

The twelfth order: directing the muster of the tribe in the second day's election, being that of the list called the galaxy, in which the censors shall prepare the urns according to the directions given in the ninth order for the second ballot, that is to say, with thirty-six gold balls in the middle urn, making four orders, and nine electors in every order according unto the number of the magistrates in the list of the galaxy, which is as followeth:

1st Knight	To be chosen out of the horse.
2nd Knight	
3rd Deputy	
4th Deputy	To be chosen out of the horse.
5th Deputy	
6th Deputy	
7th Deputy	To be chosen out of the foot.
8th Deputy	
9th Deputy	

The rest of the ballot shall proceed exactly according unto that of the first day. But for as much as the commonwealth demandeth as well the fruits of a man's body as of his mind, he that hath not been married shall not be capable of these magistracies until he be married.[20] If a deputy, already chosen to be an officer in the

---

[20] H was a bachelor at the time of writing.

parish, in the hundred or in the tribe, be afterwards chosen of the galaxy, it shall be lawful for him to delegate his office in the parish, in the hundred or in the tribe, unto any one of his own order being not already chosen into office. The knights and deputies being chosen, shall be brought unto the head of the tribe by the lord high sheriff, who shall administer unto them this oath: 'Ye shall well and truly observe and keep the orders and customs of this commonwealth which the people have chosen.' And if any of them shall refuse the oath, he shall be rejected, and that competitor which had the most voices next shall be called in his place, who, if he take the oath, shall be entered in the list; but if he also refuse the oath, he who had most voices next shall be called, and so until the number of nine out of those competitors which had most voices be sworn knights and deputies of the galaxy. (This clause, in regard of the late divisions, and to the end that no violence be offered unto any man's conscience, to be of force but for the first three years only.) The knights of the galaxy, being elected and sworn, are to repair, by the Monday next ensuing the last of March, unto the Pantheon or palace of justice situated in the metropolis of this commonwealth (except the parliament, through sickness or some other occasion, have adjourned unto some other part of the nation), where they are to take their places in the senate, and continue in full power and commission as senators for the full term of three years next ensuing the date of their election. The deputies of the galaxy are to repair by the same day (except as before excepted) unto the hall situated in Emporium, where they are to be listed of the prerogative tribe or equal representative of the people, and to continue in full power and commission as their deputies for the full term of three years next ensuing their election. But for as much as the term of every magistracy or office in this commonwealth requireth an equal vacation, a knight, a deputy of the galaxy, having fulfilled his term of three years, shall not be re-elected unto the same or any other tribe, till he have also fulfilled his three years' vacation.

Whoever shall rightly consider the foregoing orders, will be as little able to find how it is possible that a worshipful knight should declare himself in ale and beef worthy to serve his country, as how my lord high sheriff's honour, in case he were protected from the law, could play the knave. But though the foregoing orders so far as they regard the constitution of the senate and the people, requiring no more as to an ordinary election than is therein explained (that is but one third part of their knights and deputies), are perfect, yet must we in this place, and as to the institution, of necessity erect a scaffold. For the commonwealth, to the first creation of her councils in full number, required thrice as many as are eligible by the foregoing orders; wherefore the orator, whose aid in this place was most necessary, rightly informing the people of the reason, stayed them two days longer at the muster, and took this course. One list, containing two knights and seven deputies, he caused to be chosen upon the second day, which list, being called the first galaxy, qualified the parties elected of it, with power for the term of one year and no longer; another list containing two knights and seven deputies more, he caused to be chosen the third day, which list, being called the second galaxy, qualified the parties elected of it with power for the term of two years and no longer. And upon the fourth day he chose the third galaxy according as it is directed by the order, empowered for three years, which lists successively falling (like the signs or constellations of one hemisphere that setting cause those of the other to rise) cast the great orbs of this commonwealth into an annual, triennial and perpetual revolution.

The business of the muster being thus happily finished, Hermes de Caduceo, lord orator of the tribe of Nubia, being now put into her first rapture, caused one of the censors' pulpits to be planted in front of the squadron and, ascending into the same, spake after this manner:

My lords the magistrates, and the people of the tribe of Nubia:

We have this day solemnised the happy nuptials of the two greatest princes that are upon the earth or in nature: arms and councils, in the mutual embraces whereof consisteth your whole commonwealth; whose councils upon their perpetual wheelings, marches and countermarches, create her armies, and whose armies with the golden volleys of the ballot at once create and salute her councils. There be (such is the world nowadays) that think it ridiculous to see a nation exercising her civil functions in military discipline, while they, committing their buff unto their servants, come themselves to hold trenchers. For what availeth it, such as are unarmed (or, which is all one, whose education acquainteth them not with the proper use of their swords) to be

97

called citizens? What were two or three thousand of you, well
affected to your country but naked, unto one troop of mercenary
soldiers? If they should come upon the field and say, 'Gentlemen,
it is thought fit that such and such men should be chosen by you',
where were your liberty? Or, 'Gentlemen, parliaments are exceeding good, but you are to have a little patience; these times are not
so fit for them', where were your commonwealth? What causeth
the monarchy of the Turks but servants in arms? What was it that
begot the glorious commonwealth of Rome, but the sword in the
hands of her citizens? Wherefore my glad eyes salute the serenity
and brightness of this day with a shower that shall not cloud it.
Behold the army of Israel become a commonwealth, and the commonwealth of Israel remaining an army; with her rulers of tens and
of fifties, her rulers of hundreds and her rulers of thousands,
drawing near (as this day throughout our happy fields) unto the lot
by her tribes, increased above threefold, and led up by her
phylarchs or princes, to sit *sellis curulibus* upon fifty thrones, judging the fifty tribes of Oceana. Or is it Athens, breaking from her
iron sepulchre, where she hath been so long trampled upon by
hosts of janissaries? For certainly that – *nec vox hominem sonat* – is
the voice of Theseus, having gathered his scattered Athenians into
one city.

> *Haec juris sui*
> *Parere domino civitas uni negat:*
> *Rex ipse populus annuas mandat vices*
> *Honoris huic illive.*[21]

This free-born nation liveth not upon the dole or bounty of one
man but, distributing her annual magistracies and honours with
her own hand, is herself King People. . . .

At which the orator was a while interrupted with shouts, but at length
proceeded:

Is it grave Lacedaemon in her armed tribe, divided by her *obai*
and her *morai*, which appears to chide me that I teach the people to
talk, or conceive such language as is dressed like a woman to be a

---

[21] Liljegren (p. 296) found these verses in Grotius, *De Jure Belli ac Pacis*, I, iii, 8, and
identified them as a rendering of Euripides, Ἱκέται, 401 ff.

fit usher of the joys of liberty into the hearts of men? Is it Rome in her victorious arms (for so she held her *concio* or congregation) that congratulateth with us for finding out that which she could not hit on, and binding up her *comitia curiata*, *centuriata* and *tributa* in one inviolable league of union? Or is it the great council of incomparable Venice, bowling forth by the self-same ballot her immortal commonwealth? For neither by reason nor by her experience is it impossible that a commonwealth should be immortal, seeing the people, being the materials, never dies, and the form, which is motion, must without opposition be endless. The bowl which is thrown from your hand, if there be no rub, no impediment, shall never cease; for which cause the glorious luminaries that are the bowls of God were once thrown forever, and next these, those of Venice. But certainly, my lords, whatever these great examples may have shown us, we are the first that have shown unto the world a commonwealth established in her rise upon fifty such towers, and so garrisoned, as are the tribes of Oceana, containing one hundred thousand elders upon the annual list, and yet but an outguard; besides her marching armies, to be equal in the discipline and in the number of her youth.

And for as much as sovereign powers[22] is a necessary but a formidable creature, not unlike the powder which (as you are soldiers) is at once your safety and your danger, being subject to take fire against you as for you; how well and securely is she by your galaxies so collected as to be in full force and vigour, and yet so distributed that it is impossible you should be blown up by your own magazine. Let them who will have it that power if she be confined cannot be sovereign tell us whether our rivers do not enjoy a more secure and fruitful reign within their proper banks, than if it were lawful for them, in ravishing our harvests, to spill themselves? Whether souls not confined unto their peculiar bodies do govern them any more than those of witches in their trances? Whether power not confined unto the bounds of reason and virtue have any other bounds than those of vice and passion? Or if vice and passion be boundless, and reason and virtue have certain limits, on which of these thrones holy men should anoint their sovereign? But to blow away this dust, the sovereign power of a

---

[22] 'powers' in both C and P.

commonwealth is no more bounded, that is to say, straitened, than that of a monarch, but is balanced. The eagle mounteth not unto her proper pitch if she be bounded, nor if she be not balanced. And lest a monarch should think that he can reach farther with his sceptre, the Roman eagle upon her balance spread her wings from the ocean to Euphrates. Receive the sovereign power; you have received her; hold her fast, embrace her forever in your shining arms. The virtue of the loadstone is not impaired or limited, but receiveth strength and nourishment, by being bound in iron. And so giving your lordships much joy, I take my leave of this tribe.

The orator, descending, had the period of his speech made with a vast applause and exultation by the whole tribe, attending him for that night unto his quarter; as the phylarch, with some commanded troops, did the next day unto the frontiers of the tribe, where leave was taken on both sides with more tears than grief.

So, *a tribe is the third division of land occasioned by the third collection of the people, whose functions proper unto that place are contained in the five foregoing orders.*

The institution of the commonwealth was such as needed those props and scaffolds, which may have troubled the reader; but I shall here take them away and come unto the constitution, which stands by itself and yields a clearer prospect.

The motions, by what hath been already shown, are spherical, and spherical motions have their proper centre; for which cause (ere I proceed further) it will be necessary, for the better understanding of the whole, that I discover the centre whereupon the motions of this commonwealth are formed.

The centre or basis of every government is no other than the fundamental laws of the same.

Fundamental laws are such as state what it is that a man may call his own, that is to say property, and what the means be whereby a man may enjoy his own, that is to say protection; the first is also called dominion, and the second empire or sovereign power, whereof this (as hath been shown) is the natural product of the former, for such as is the balance of the dominion in a nation, such is the nature of her empire.

Wherefore the fundamental laws of Oceana, or the centre of this commonwealth, are the agrarian and the ballot: the agrarian by the balance of dominion preserving equality in the root, and the ballot by an equal rotation conveying it into the branch, or exercise of sovereign power; as, to begin with the former, appeareth by:

> *The thirteenth order:* constituting the agrarian laws of Oceana, Marpesia and Panopea; whereby it is ordained, first, for all such lands as are lying and being within the proper territories of Oceana, that every man who is at present possessed, or shall hereafter be possessed, of an estate in land exceeding the revenue of five thousand pounds a year, and having more than one son, shall leave his lands either equally divided among them, in case the lands amount unto above 2000 £ a year unto each, or so near equally, in case they come under, that the greater part or portion of the same remaining unto the eldest exceed not the value of two thousand pounds revenue. And no man, not in present possession of lands above the value of two thousand pounds by the year, shall receive, enjoy (except by lawful inheritance), acquire or purchase unto himself lands within the said territories amounting, with those already in his possession, above the said revenue. And if a man have a daughter or daughters, except she be an heir or they be heirs, he shall not leave or give unto any one of them in marriage, or otherwise for her portion, above the value of one thousand five hundred pounds in lands, goods and monies. Nor shall any friend, kinsman, or kinswoman add unto her or their portion or portions that are so provided for, to make any one of them greater; nor shall any man demand or have more in marriage with any woman. Nevertheless an heir shall enjoy her lawful inheritance, and a widow whatsoever the bounty or affection of her husband shall bequeath unto her, to be divided in the first generation wherein it is divisible, according as hath been shown.
>
> Secondly, for lands lying and being within the territories of Marpesia, the agrarian shall hold in all parts as it is established in Oceana, save only in the standard or proportion of estates in land, which shall be set for Marpesia at five hundred pounds.
>
> And thirdly, for Panopea, the agrarian shall hold in all parts as in Oceana. And whosoever, possessing above the proportion allowed by these laws, shall be lawfully convicted of the same, shall forfeit the overplus unto the use of the state.

Agrarian laws of all others have ever been the greatest bugbears, and so in the institution were these; at which time it was ridiculous to see how strange a fear appeared in everybody of that which, being good for all, could hurt nobody. But instead of the proof of this order,

I shall out of those many debates that happened ere it could be passed, insert two speeches that were made at the council of legislators, the first by the right honourable Philautus de Garbo, a young man, being heir apparent unto a very noble family, and one of the councillors, who expressed himself as followeth:

May it please your highness, my Lord Archon of Oceana:
If I did not (to my capacity) know from how profound a counsellor I dissent, it would certainly be no hard task to make it as light as the day, first, that an agrarian is altogether unnecessary; secondly, that it is dangerous unto a commonwealth; thirdly, that it is insufficient to keep out monarchy; fourthly, that it destroys families; fifthly, that it destroys industry; and last of all, that, though it were indeed of any good use, it will be a matter of such difficulty to introduce in this nation, and so to settle that it may be lasting, as is altogether invincible.

First, that an agrarian is unnecessary unto a commonwealth, what clearer testimony can there be, than that the commonwealths which are our contemporaries (Venice, whereunto your highness giveth the upper hand of all antiquity, being one) have no such thing? And there can be no reason why they have it now, seeing it is in the sovereign power at any time to establish such an order, but that they need it not; wherefore no wonder if Aristotle, who pretends to be a good commonwealthsman, have long since derided Phaleas, to whom it was attributed by the Greeks, for this invention.

Secondly, that an agrarian is dangerous unto a commonwealth is affirmed upon no slight authority, seeing Machiavel is positive that it was the dissension which happened about the agrarian that caused the destruction of Rome. Nor do I think that it did much better in Lacedaemon, as I shall show anon.

Thirdly, that it is insufficient to keep out monarchy cannot without impiety be denied, the holy Scriptures bearing witness that the commonwealth of Israel, notwithstanding her agrarian, submitted her neck unto the arbitrary yoke of her princes.

Wherefore, to come unto my fourth assertion, that it is destructive unto families; this also is so apparent that it needeth pity rather than proof. Why, alas, do you bind a nobility, which no generation shall deny to have been the first that freely sacrificed her blood unto the ancient liberties of this people, upon an unholy altar? Why are the people taught, that their liberty, which, except our noble ancestors had been born, must have long since been buried, cannot now be born except we be buried? A commonwealth should have the innocence of the dove. Let us leave this purchase of her birth unto the serpent, which eateth herself out of the womb of her mother.

But it may be said perhaps that we are fallen from our first love, become proud and idle. It is certain, my lords, that the hand of God is not upon us for nothing; but take heed how you admit of such assaults and sallies upon men's estates as may slacken the nerve of labour, and give others also reason to believe that their sweat is vain. Or whatsoever be pretended, your agrarian (which is my fourth assertion) must indeed destroy industry. For that so it did in Lacedaemon is most apparent, as also that it could do no otherwise, where every man, having his forty quarters of barley, with wine proportional, supplied him out of his own lot by his labourer or helot, and being confined in that unto the scantling above which he might not live, there was not any such thing as a trade or other art, save that of war, in exercise. Wherefore a Spartan, if he were not in arms, must sit and play with his fingers, whence ensued perpetual war; and, the estate of the citizen being as little capable of increase as that of the commonwealth, her inevitable ruin.

Now what better ends you can propose unto yourselves in like ways, I do not so well see as that there may be worse. For Lacedaemon yet was free from civil war, but if you employ your citizens no better than she did, I cannot promise you that you shall fare so well, because both they are still desirous of war that hope it may be profitable unto them, and the strongest security you can give of peace is to make it gainful. Otherwise men will rather choose that whereby they may break your laws, than that whereby your laws may break them; which I do not speak so much in relation unto the nobility, or such as would be holding, as to the people, or them that would be getting, the passion in these being of so much the more strength as a man's felicity is weaker in the fruition of things than in the prosecution and increase of them.

Truly, my lords, it is my fear that, by taking off more hands, and the best, from industry, you will farther endamage it than can be

repaired by laying on a few, and the worst; while the nobility must
be forced to send their sons unto the plough, and, as if this were
not enough, to marry their daughters also unto farmers.

But I do not see (to come unto the last point) how it is possible
that this thing should be brought about, to your good I mean,
though it may unto the destruction of many. For that the agrarian
of Israel or that of Lacedaemon might stand is no such miracle, the
lands, without any consideration of the former proprietor, being
surveyed and cast into equal lots, which could neither be bought,
nor sold, nor multiplied, so that they knew whereabouts to have a
man; but in this nation no such division can be introduced, the
lands being already in the hands of proprietors, and such whose
estates lie very rarely together, but mixed one with another, being
also of tenures in nature so different that, as there is no experience
that an agrarian was ever introduced in such a case, so there is no
appearance how, or reason why, it should: but that which is against
reason and experience is impossible.

The case of my lord Philautus was the most concerned in the whole
nation; for he had four younger brothers, his father being yet living,
unto whom he was heir of ten thousand pounds a year. Wherefore,
being a man both of good parts and esteem, his words wrought both
upon men's reason and passions, and had borne a stroke at the head
of the business, if my Lord Archon had not interposed the buckler in
this oration:

My lords, the legislators of Oceana:
My lord Philautus hath made a thing which is easy to seem hard;
if he owed the thanks unto his eloquence, it would be worthy of
less praise than that he oweth it unto his merit and the love he hath
most deservedly purchased of all men; nor is it rationally to be
feared that he who is so much beforehand in his private, should be
in arrear in his public capacity. Wherefore, my lord's tenderness
throughout his speech arising from no other principle than his
solicitude lest the agrarian should be hurtful unto his country, it is
no less than my duty to give the best satisfaction I am able unto so
good a patriot, taking every one of his doubts in the order proposed; and first:
Whereas my lord, upon observation of the modern com-

monwealths, is of opinion that an agrarian is not necessary; it must be confessed that at the first sight of them there is some appearance favouring his assertion, but upon accidents of no precedents unto us. For the commonwealths of Switz and Holland (I mean of those leagues),[23] being situated in countries not alluring the inhabitants unto wantonness but obliging them unto universal industry, have an implicit agrarian in the nature of them and, being not obnoxious unto a growing nobility – which, as long as their former monarchies spread the wing over them, could either not at all be hatched, or was soon broken – are of no example unto us, whose experience in this point hath been unto the contrary. But what if even in these governments there be indeed an explicit agrarian? For when the law commands an equal, or near equal, distribution of a man's estate in land among his children, as in those countries, a nobility cannot grow, and so there needeth no agrarian, nor is one. And for the growth of the nobility in Venice (if so it be, for Machiavel observes in that republic, as a cause of it, a great mediocrity of estates),[24] it is not a point that she is to fear, but might study, seeing she consisteth of nothing else but nobility; by which whatever their estates suck from the people, especially if it come equally, is digested into the better blood of that commonwealth, which is all or the greatest benefit they can have by accumulation; for how unequal soever you will have them to be in their incomes, they have officers of the pomp, to bring them equal in expenses, or at least in the ostentation or show of them. And so unless the advantage of an estate consist more in the measure than in the use of it, the authority of Venice but enforceth our agrarian; nor shall a man evade or elude the prudence of it by the authority of any other commonwealth. For if a commonwealth have been introduced at once, as those of Israel and Lacedaemon, you are certain to find her underlaid with this as the main foundation; nor, if she have owed more unto fortune than prudence, hath she raised her head without musing upon this matter, as appeareth by that of Athens, which through her defect in this point, saith Aristotle, introduced her ostracism, as most of the democracies of Greece. *Ob hanc itaque causam civitates quae democratice administrantur*

---

[23] H is declining to treat the Swiss and Dutch confederacies as republics but as leagues on the Achaean or Aetolian pattern. He might have omitted 'of' before 'those leagues'.
[24] *Discorsi*, I, 55.

ostracismum instituunt.[25] But, not to restrain a fundamental of such latitude unto any one kind of government, do we not yet see that if there be a sole landlord of a vast territory, he is the Turk? That if a few landlords over-balance a populous country, they have store of servants? That if a people be in equal balance, they can have no lords? That no government can otherwise be erected than upon some one of these foundations? That no one of these foundations (each being else apt to change into some other) can give any security unto the government unless it be fixed? That through the want of this fixation, potent monarchies and commonwealths have fallen upon the heads of the people, and accompanied their own sad ruins with vast effusions of innocent blood? Let the fame, as was the merit, of the ancient nobility of this nation be equal unto, or above, what hath been already said or can be spoken, yet have we seen not only their glory, but that of a throne – the most indulgent to, and least invasive for so many ages upon, the liberty of a people that the world hath known – through the mere want of fixing her foot by a proportionable agrarian upon her proper foundation, to have fallen with such horror as hath been a spectacle of astonishment unto the whole earth. And were it well argued from one calamity that we ought not to prevent another? Nor is Aristotle so good a commonwealthsman for deriding the invention of Phaleas, as in recollecting himself, where he saith that democracies, when a lesser part of their citizens overtop the rest in wealth, degenerate into oligarchies and principalities; and, which comes nearer unto the present purpose, that the greater part of the nobility of Tarentum coming accidentally to be ruined, the government of the few came by consequence to be changed into that of the many.[26]

These things considered, I cannot see how an agrarian, as to the fixation or security of a government, can be less than necessary. And if a cure be necessary, it excuseth not the patient, his disease being otherwise desperate, that it is dangerous; which was the case of Rome, not so stated by Machiavel, where he saith that the strife about the agrarian caused the destruction of that commonwealth.

---

[25] 'Arist. Pol. I. 3. c. 9' – H's note. The figure I may be an error or the letter 'l'. Barker lists references to ostracism in the *Politics* at III, xiii, 15 (the probable source of the Latin above), 18 and 22; v, iii, 3 and v, viii, 12.
[26] 'Arist. Pol. l. (for *Lib.*) 5. c. 3.' – H's note. v, iii, 7, seems to be intended.

As if, when a senator was not rich (as Crassus held) except he could pay an army, that commonwealth could have done other than ruin; whether in strife about the agrarian, or without it. *Nuper divitiae avaritiam et abundantes voluptates desiderium per luxum atque libidinem pereundi perdendique omnia invexere.*[27] If the greatest security of a commonwealth consist in being provided with the proper antidote against this poison, her greatest danger must be from the absence of an agrarian, which is the whole truth of the Roman example. For the Laconic, I shall reserve the farther explication of it, as my lord also did, to another place; and first see whether an agrarian, proportioned unto a popular government, be sufficient to keep out monarchy. My lord is for the negative, and fortified by the people of Israel electing a king. To which I say that the action of the people, therein expressed, is a full answer unto the objection of that example. For the monarchy neither grew upon them, nor could by reason of the agrarian possibly have invaded them, if they had not pulled it upon themselves by the election of a king; which, being an accident the like whereof is not to be found in any other people so planted – nor in this till, as is manifest, they were given up by God unto infatuation; for, saith he to Samuel, *they have not rejected thee, but they have rejected me that I should not reign over them* – hath something in it which is apparent by what went before to have been besides the course of nature, and by what followed. For the king – having no other foundation than the calamities of the people, so often beaten by their enemies that, despairing of themselves, they were contented with any change – if he had peace as in the days of Solomon, left but a slippery throne unto his successor, as appeared by Rehoboam. And the agrarian, notwithstanding the monarchy thus introduced, so faithfully preserved the root of that commonwealth that it shot oftener forth, and by intervals continued longer than, any other government; as may be computed from the institution of the same by Joshua, one thousand four hundred and sixty-five years before Christ, unto the total dissolution of it, which happened in the reign of the Emperor Hadrian, one hundred and thirty-five years after the Incarnation. A people planted upon an equal agrarian and holding to it, if they part with their liberty, must do it upon good will, and make but a

---

[27] 'Liv. in praef.' – H's note.

bad title of their bounty. As to instance yet farther in that which is proposed by the present order to this nation, the standard whereof is at two thousand pounds a year: the whole territory of Oceana, being divided by this proportion, amounteth unto five thousand lots. So the lands of Oceana, being thus distributed, and bound unto this distribution, can never fall unto fewer than five thousand proprietors. But five thousand proprietors so seised will not agree to break the agrarian, for that were to agree to rob one another; nor to bring in a king, because they must maintain him and can have no benefit by him; nor to exclude the people, because they can have as little by that, and must spoil their militia. So the commonwealth, continuing upon the balance proposed, though it should come into five thousand hands, can never alter; and that it should ever come into five thousand hands, is as improbable as anything in the world that is not altogether impossible.

My lords, other considerations are more private: as that this order destroys families; which is as if one should lay the ruins of some ancient castle unto the herbs which do usually grow out of them, the destruction of those families being that indeed which naturally produced this order. For we do not now argue for that which we would have, but for that which we are already possessed of; as would appear, if a note were but taken of all such as have at this day above two thousand pounds a year in Oceana. If my lord should grant (and I will put it with the most) that they who are proprietors in land, exceeding the proportion, exceed not three hundred; with what brow can the interest of so few be balanced with that of the whole nation? Or rather, what interest have they to put in such a balance? They would live as they have been accustomed to do; who hinders them? They would enjoy their estates; who touches them? They would dispose of what they have according unto the interest of their families; it is that which we desire. A man hath one son; let him be called. Would he enjoy his father's estate? It is his, and his son's, and his son's son's after him. A man hath five sons; let them be called. Would they enjoy their father's estate? It is divided among them; for we have four votes for one in the same family, and therefore this must be the interest of the family; or the family knoweth not her own interest. If a man shall dispute otherwise, he must draw his arguments from custom and from greatness, which was the interest of the monarchy, not of the family; and we are now a commonwealth. If the monarchy could not bear with such divisions because they tended to be a commonwealth, neither can a commonwealth connive at such accumulations, because they tend to a monarchy. If the monarchy might make bold with so many for the good of one, we may make bold with one for the good of so many, nay, for the good of all. My lords, it cometh into my head that upon occasion of the variety of parties enumerated in our late civil wars, was said by a friend of mine coming home from his travels, about the latter end of these troubles, that he admired how it came to pass that younger brothers, especially being so many more in number than their elder, did not make one against a tyranny the like whereof hath not been exercised in any other nation. And truly, when I consider that our countrymen are none of the worst natured, I must confess I marvel much how it comes to pass that we should use our children as we do our puppies: take one, lay it in the lap, feed it with every good bit, and drown five! Nay, worse, for as much as the puppies are once drowned, whereas the children are left perpetually drowning. Really, my lords, it is a flinty custom! And all this for his cruel ambition that would raise himself a pillar, a golden pillar for his monument, though he have children, his own reviving flesh and a kind of immortality. And this is that interest of a family, for which we are to think ill of a government that will not endure it. But quiet yourselves. The land through which the river Nilus wanders in one stream is barren, but where he parts into seven, he multiplies his fertile shores by distributing, yet keeping and improving, such as property and nutrition as is a prudent agrarian unto a well ordered commonwealth.

Nor (to come unto the fifth assertion) is a political body rendered any fitter for industry, by having one gouty and another withered leg, than a natural. It tendeth not unto the improvement of merchandise that there be some who have no need of their trading, and others that are not able to follow it. If confinement discourage industry, an estate in money is not confined; and lest industry should want whereupon to work, land is not engrossed nor entailed upon any man, but remains at her devotion. I wonder whence the computation can arise, that this should discourage industry? Two thousand pounds a year a man may enjoy in Oceana, as much in Panopea, five hundred in Marpesia; there be other plantations, and the commonwealth will have more. Who knoweth how far the arms of our agrarian may extend themselves? And whether he that might have left a pillar, may not leave a temple or many pillars unto his more pious memory? Where there is some measure in riches, a man may be rich; but if you will have them to be infinite, there will be no end of starving himself, and wanting what he hath; and what pains does such an one take to be poor! Furthermore, if a man shall think that there may be an industry less greasy or more noble, and so cast his thoughts upon the commonwealth, he will have leisure for her, and she riches and honours for him; his sweat shall smell like Alexander's. My lord Philautus is a young man who, enjoying his ten thousand pounds a year, may keep a noble house in the old way, and have homely guests; and having but two, by the means proposed, may take the upper hand of his great ancestors, with reverence unto whom, I may say, there hath not been one of them would have disputed his place with a Roman consul. My lord, do not break my heart; the nobility shall go unto no other ploughs than those from which we call our consuls. But, saith he, it having been so with Lacedaemon that neither the city nor the citizens was capable of increase, a blow was given by that agrarian which ruined both. And what are we concerned with that agrarian or that blow, while our citizens and our city (and that by our agrarian) are both capable of increase? The Spartan, if he made a conquest, had not citizens to hold it; the Oceaner will have enow. The Spartan could have not trade; the Oceaner may have all. The agrarian in Laconia, that it might bind on knapsacks, forbidding all other arts but that of war, could not make an army of above thirty thousand citizens. The agrarian in Oceana, without interruption of traffic, provides us in the fifth part of the youth an annual source or fresh spring of one hundred thousand, besides our provincial auxiliaries, out of which to draw marching armies, and as many elders, not feeble, but men most of them in the flower of their age, and in arms for the defence of our territories. The agrarian in Laconia banished money; this multiplies it. That allowed a matter of twenty or thirty acres to a man; this two or three thousand. There is no comparison between them. And yet I differ so much from my lord, or his opinion that the agrarian was the ruin of Lacedaemon, that I hold it no less than demonstrable to have been her main support; for if, banishing all other diversions, it could not make an army of above thirty thousand, then, letting in all other diversions, it must have broken that army. Wherefore Lysander, bringing in the golden spoils of Athens, irrecoverably ruined that commonwealth, and is a warning to us that, in giving encouragement unto industry, we also remember that covetousness is the root of all evil. And our agrarian can never be the cause of those seditions threatened by my lord, but is the proper cure of them, as Lucan noteth well, in the state of Rome before the civil wars which happened through the want of such an antidote:

> *Hinc usura vorax, rapidumque in tempore foenus,*
> *Hinc concussa fides, et multis utile bellum.*[28]

Why then are we mistaken, as if we intended not equal advantages in our commonwealth unto either sex, because we would not have women's fortunes consist in that metal which exposeth them unto cut-purses? If a man cut my purse, I may have him by the heels or by the neck for it; whereas a man may cut a woman's purse and have her for his pains in fetters. How brutish, and much more than brutish, is that commonwealth which preferreth the earth before the fruits of her womb? If the people be her treasure, the staff by which she is sustained and comforted, with what justice can she suffer them by whom she is most enriched to be for that cause the most impoverished? And yet we see the gifts of God and the bounties of heaven in fruitful families, through this wretched custom of marrying for money, become their insupportable grief and poverty; nor falleth this so heavy upon the lower sort, being better able to shift for themselves, as upon the nobility or gentry. For what availeth it in this case from whence their veins have derive their blood, while they shall see the tallow of a chandler sooner converted into that beauty which is required in a bride? I appeal whether my lord Philautus or myself be the advocate of nobility, against which, in the case proposed by me, there would be nothing to hold the balance. And why is a woman, if she may have but fifteen hundred pounds, undone? If she be unmarried, what nobleman allows his daughter in that case a greater revenue than so much money may command? And if she marry, no nobleman

---

[28] Lucan, *De Bell. Civ.*, I, 158ff.; quoted in Bacon, 'Of Seditions and Troubles' (Liljegren).

can give his daughter a greater portion than she hath. Who is hurt in this case? Nay, who is not benefitted? If the agrarian give us the sweat of our brows without diminution, if it prepare our table, if it make our cup to overflow, and above all this, in providing for our children, anoint our heads with that oil which taketh away the greatest of worldly cares; what man that is not besotted with a covetousness as vain as endless can imagine such a constitution to be his poverty, seeing where no woman can be considerable for her portion, no portion will be considerable with a woman; and so his children will not only find better preferments without his brokage, but more freedom of their own affections. We are wonderful severe in laws that they shall not marry without our consent, as if it were care and tenderness over them; but is it not lest we should not have the other thousand pound with this son, or the other hundred pound a year more in jointure for that daughter? These when we are crossed in them are the sins for which we water our couch with tears, but not of penitence; seeing whereas it is a mischief beyond any that we can do unto our enemies, we persist to make nothing of breaking the affection of our children. But there is in this agrarian an homage unto pure and spotless love, the consequence whereof I will not give for all the romances. An alderman maketh not his daughter a countess till he have given her twenty thousand pounds, nor a romance a considerable mistress till she be a princess; these are characters of bastard love. But if our agrarian exclude ambition and covetousness, we shall at length have the care of our own breed, in which we have been curious as to that of our dogs and our horses. The marriage bed will be truly legitimate, and the race of the commonwealth not spurious.

But *impar magnanimis ausis imparque dolori*: I am hurled from all my hopes by my lord's last assertion of impossibility that the root, from whence we imagine these fruits, should be planted or thrive in this soil. And why? Because of the mixture of estates, and variety of tenures. Nevertheless there is yet extant in the exchequer an old survey of the whole nation, wherefore such a thing is not impossible. Now if a new survey were taken at the present rates, and the law made that no man should hold hereafter above so much land as is valued therein at two thousand pounds a year, it would amount unto a good and sufficient agrarian. It is true that there would remain some difficulty in the different kinds of rents, and that it is a matter requiring not only more leisure than we have, but an authority which may be better able to bow men unto a more general consent than is to be wrought out of them by such as are in our capacity; wherefore, as to the manner, it is necessary that we refer it unto the parliament, but as to the matter, they can no otherwise fix their government upon the right balance.

I shall conclude with a few words to some parts of the order which my lord hath omitted. As first to the consequences of the agrarian to be settled in Marpesia, which irreparably breaks the aristocracy of that nation: being of such a nature as, standing, it is not possible that you should govern. For while the people of that country are little better than the cattle of the nobility, you must not wonder if, according as these can make their markets with foreign princes, you find those to be driven upon your grounds. And if you be so tender, now you have it in your power, as not to hold an hand upon them that may prevent the slaughter that must otherwise ensue in like cases, the blood will lie at your door. But in holding such an hand upon them, you may settle the agrarian; and in settling the agrarian, you give the people not only liberty, but lands; which makes your protection necessary to their security, and their contribution due unto your protection, as to their own safety.

For the agrarian of Panopea, it allowing such proportions of so good land, men that conceive themselves straitened by this in Oceana will begin there to let themselves forth, where every citizen will in time have his villa. And there is no question but the improvement of that country by this means must be far greater than it hath been in the best of former times.

I have no more to say but that, in those ancient and heroical ages when men thought that to be necessary which was virtuous, the nobility of Athens, having the people so much engaged in their debt that there remained no other question among these than which of those should be king, no sooner heard Solon speak than they quitted their debts and restored the commonwealth, which ever after held a solemn and annual feast, called the *seisachtheia* or rescission, in memory of that action. Nor is this example the phoenix; for at the institution by Lycurgus, the nobility having estates (as ours here) in the lands of Laconia, upon no other valuable consideration than the commonwealth proposed by him, threw them up to be parcelled by his agrarian. But now, when no man is desired to throw up a farthing of his money or a shovelful of his earth, and that all we can do is but to make a virtue of necessity, we are disputing whether we should have peace or war. For peace you cannot have without some government, nor any government without the proper balance; wherefore, if you will not fix this which you have, the rest is blood, for without blood you can bring in no other.

By these speeches, made at the institution of the agrarian, you may perceive what were the grounds of it. The next is

> *The fourteenth order:* constituting the ballot of Venice, as it is fitted by several alterations, and appointed unto every assembly, to be the constant and only way of giving suffrage in this commonwealth.

This is the general order, whence those branches of the ballot, some whereof you have already seen, are derived; which with those that follow were all read and debated in this place at the institution; when my lord Epimonus de Garrula, being one of the councillors, and having no further patience (though the rules were composed by the agent of this commonwealth, residing for that purpose at Venice) than to hear the direction for the parishes, stood up and made way for himself in this manner:

> May it please your highness, my Lord Archon:
> Under correction of Mr Peregrine Spy, our very learned agent and intelligencer, I have seen the world a little; Venice, and (as gentlemen are permitted to do) the great council balloting. And truly I must needs say that it is for a dumb show the goodliest that I ever beheld with mine eyes. You should have some would take it ill, as if the noble Venetians thought themselves too good to speak to strangers; but they observed them not so narrowly. The truth is, they have nothing to say unto their acquaintance, or men that are in council sure would have tongues. For a council, and not a word spoken in it, is a contradiction. But there is such a pudder with their marching and counter-marching as, though never a one of them draw a sword, you would think they were training; which till I found that they did it only to entertain strangers, I came from among them as wise as I went thither. But in the parliament of

Oceana you had no balls nor dancing, but sober conversation; a man might know and be known, show his parts and improve 'em. And now, if you take the advice of this same fellow, you will spoil all with his whimsies. Mr Speaker – cry you mercy, my Lord Archon I mean – set the wisest man of your house in the great council of Venice, and you will not know him from a fool. Whereas nothing is more certain than that flat and dull fellows, in the judgment of all such as used to keep company with them before, upon election into our house, have immediately chitted like barley in the fat, where it acquires a new spirit, and flowed forth into language that, I am as confident as I am here, if there were not such as delight to abuse us, is far better than Tully's; or let anybody but translate one of his orations and speak it in the house, and see if everybody do not laugh at him. This is a great matter, Mr Speaker; they do not cant it with your book learning, your orbs, your centres, your prime magnitudes and your nebulones, things I profess that would make a sober man run stark mad to hear 'em; while we, who should be considering the honour of our country and that it goes now or never upon our hand whether it shall be ridiculous to all the world, are going to nine holes or trow-madam for our business, like your dumb Venetian whom this same Sir Politick your resident, that never saw him do anything but make faces, would insinuate into you at this distance to have the only knack of state. Whereas if you should take the pains, as I have done, to look a little nearer, you would find these same wonderful things to be nothing else but mere natural fopperies or *capriccios*, as they call them in Italian, even of the meanest of that nation; for put the case you be travelling in Italy, ask your *contadino*, that is the next country fellow you meet, some question, and presently he ballots you an answer with a nod, which is affirmative; or a shake with his head, which is the negative box; or a shrug with his shoulder, which is the *bossolo di non sinceri.*[29] Good! You will admire Sandys for telling you that *grotta di cane* is a miracle,[30] and I shall be laughed at for assuring you that it is nothing else but such

[29] The *non sinceri* in Venetian procedure were those ballots *che non dannano e non appruovano* (Giannotti, II, p. 96).
[30] George Sandys, *Travailes* (London, 1652), pp. 207–8, told a story of a grotto on Vesuvius whose air struck a dog momentarily dumb, until he was thrown into a lake and ran away barking.

a damp (continued by the neighbourhood of certain sulphur mines) as through accidental heat doth sometimes happen in our coal pits. But ingratitude must not discourage an honest man from doing good. There is not, I say, such a tongue-tied generation unto heaven as your Italian; that you should not wonder if he make signs. But our people must have something in their diurnals, we must ever and anon be telling 'em our minds; or if we be at it when we raise taxes like those gentlemen with the finger and the thumb, they will swear that we are cut-purses. Come, I know what I have heard 'em say, when some men had money that wrought hard enough for it; and do you conceive they will be better pleased when they shall be told that upon like occasions you are at mum-chance or stool-ball? I do not speak for myself; for though I shall always acknowledge that I got more by one year's sitting in the house than by my three years' travels, it was not of that kind. But I hate that this same Spy, for pretending to have played at billiards with the most serene commonwealth of Venice, should make such fools of us here, when I know that he must have had his intelligence from some corncutter upon the Rialto; for a noble Venetian would be hanged if he should keep such a fellow company. And yet if I do not think he hath made you all dote, never trust me; my Lord Archon is sometimes in such strange raptures. Why, good my lord, let me be heard, as well as your apple squire. She hath fresh blood in her cheeks, I must confess, but she is but an old lady; nor has he picked her cabinet; these he sends you are none of her receipts, I can assure you; he bought them for a julio at St Mark's of a mountebank. She hath no other wash, upon my knowledge, for that same envied complexion of hers but her marshes, being a little better scented, saving you presence, than a chamber pot. My lords, I know what I say. But you will never have done with it that neither the great Turk, nor any of those little Turks her neighbours, have been able to spoil her! Why, you may as well wonder that weasels do not suck eggs in swans' nests. Do you think that it hath lain in the devotion of her beads, which you that have puked so much at popery are now at length resolved shall consecrate Master Parson, and be dropped by everyone of his congregation, while those same whimsical intelligences your surveyors (you will break my heart) give the turn unto your *primum mobile*? And so I think they will, for you will find that money is *primum mobile*, and they will turn you thus out of some three or four hundred thousand pounds. A pretty sum for urns and balls, for boxes and pills, which these same quacksalvers are to administer unto the parishes; and for what disease, I marvel? Or how does it work? Out comes a constable, an overseer, and a churchwarden! Mr Speaker, I am amazed!

Never was there goose so stuck with lard as my lord Epimonus's speech with laughter, the Archon having much ado to recover himself in such manner as might enable him to return these thanks:

In your whole lives (my lords) were you never entertained with so much ingenuity; my lord Epimonus having at once mended all the faults of travellers. For first, whereas they are abominable liars, he hath not told you (except some malicious body have misinformed him concerning poor Spy) one syllable of falsehood. And secondly, whereas they never fail to give the upper hand in all their discourses unto foreign nations, still jostling their own into the kennel, he bears an honour unto his country that will not dissolve in Cephalonia, nor be corrupted with figs and melons; which I can assure you is no ordinary obligation, and therefore hold it a matter of public concernment that we be no occasion of quenching my lord's affections. Nor is there any such great matter between us, but might methinks be easily reconciled; for though that which my lord gained by sitting in the house, I steadfastly believe, as he can affirm, was gotten fairly; yet dare I not, nor do I, think that upon consideration he will promise so much for other gamesters, especially when they were at it so high as he intimates not only to have been in use, but to be like enough to come about again. Wherefore (say I) let them throw with boxes; for unless we will be below the politics of an ordinary, there is no such bar unto cogging. It is known unto his lordship that our game is 'most at a throw', and that every cast of our dice is in our suffrages; nor will he deny that partiality in a suffrage is downright cogging. Now, if the Venetian boxes be the most sovereign of all remedies against this same cogging, is it not a strange thing that they should be thrown first into the fire by a fair gamester? Men are naturally subject unto all kinds of passion; some you have that are not able to withstand the brow of an enemy, and others that make nothing of this are less of proof against that of a friend. So that if your suffrage be barefaced,

I dare say you shall not have one fair cast in twenty. But whatever a man's fortune be at the box, he neither knoweth whom to thank nor whom to challenge. Wherefore (that my lord may have a charitable opinion of the choice affection which I confess to have, above all other beauties, for that of incomparable Venice) there is in this way of suffrage no less than a demonstration that it is the most pure; and the purity of the suffrage in a popular government is the health if not the life of it, seeing the soul is no otherwise breathed into the sovereign power than by the suffrage of the people. Wherefore no wonder if Postellus[31] be of opinion that this use of the ball is the very same with that which was of the bean in Athens; or that others, by the text concerning Eldad and Medad, derive it from the commonwealth of Israel. There is another thing, though not so material unto us, that my lord will excuse me if I be not willing to yield, which is that Venice subsisteth only by her situation. It is true that a man in time of war may be more secure from his enemies by being in a citadel, but not from his diseases; wherefore the first cause, if he live long, is his good constitution, without which his citadel were to little purpose; and it is no otherwise with Venice.

With this speech of the Archon, I conclude the proof of the agrarian and of the ballot, being the fundamental laws of this commonwealth, and come now from the centre to the circumferences or orbs, whereof some have already been shown: as how the parishes annually pour themselves into the hundreds, the hundreds into the tribes, and the tribes into the galaxies, the annual galaxy of every tribe consisting of two knights and seven deputies, whereof the knights constitute the senate, the deputies the prerogative tribe, commonly called the people, and the senate and the people constitute the sovereign power or parliament of Oceana. Wherefore, to show what the parliament is, I must first open the senate, and then the people or prerogative tribe.

To begin with the senate, of which (as a man is differently represented by a picture drawer and by an anatomist) I shall first discover the face or aspect, and then the parts with the use of them. Every Monday morning, in the summer at seven and in the winter at

[31] Postellus, *De Republica Atheniensium*, III (Liljegren). I.e., Guillaume Postel, *De magistratibus Atheniensium liber* (1541).

eight, the great bell in the clock-house at the Pantheon beginneth, and continueth ringing for the space of one hour, in which time the magistrates of the senate, being attended according to their quality with a respective number of the ballotines,[32] doorkeepers and messengers, and having the ensigns of their magistracies borne before them – as the sword before the strategus, the mace before the orator, a mace with the seal before the commissioners of the chancery, the like with the purse before the commissioners of the treasury, and a silver wand, like those in use with the universities, before each of the censors (being chancellors of the same) – these, with the knights, in all three hundred, assemble in the house or hall of the senate.

The house or hall of the senate, being situated in the Pantheon or palace of justice, is a room consisting of a square and a half. In the middle of the lower end is the door; at the upper end hangeth a rich state,[33] overshadowing the greater part of a large throne, or half pace of two stages, the first ascended by two steps from the floor and the second, about the middle, rising two steps higher. Upon this stand two chairs; in that on the right hand sits the strategus, in the other the orator, adorned with scarlet robes, after the fashion that was used by the dukes in the aristocracy. At the right end of the upper stage stand three chairs, in which the three commissioners of the seal are placed, and at the other end sit the three commissioners of the treasury, every one in a robe or habit like that of the earls; of these magistrates of this upper stage consisteth the signory. At either end of the lower stage stands a little table, to which the secretaries of the senate are set, with their tufted sleeves in the habit of civil lawyers. Unto the four steps, whereby the two stages of the throne are ascended, answer four long benches which, successively deriving from every one of the steps, contain their respective height, and extend themselves by the side walls towards the lower end of the house, every bench being divided by numeral characters into the thirty-seven parts or places. Upon the upper benches sit the censors in the robes of barons; the first in the middle of the right-hand bench, and the second directly opposite unto him on the other side. Upon the rest of the benches sit the knights who, if they be called unto the urns, distributing themselves by the figures, come in equal files, either by the first seat, which consisteth of the two upper benches on either side, or by the second

---

[32] H's rendering of Italian *ballottini* (Giannotti, II, p. 102).
[33] I.e., a canopy of state.

seat, consisting of the two lower benches on either side, beginning also at the upper or at the lower ends of the same, according to the lot whereby they are called, for which end the benches are open and ascended at either end with easy stairs and large passages. The rest of the ballot is conformable unto that of the tribe, the censors of the house sitting at the side urns, and the youngest magistrate of the signory at the middle; the urns being placed before the throne, and prepared according unto the number of the magistrates to be at that time chosen by the rules already given unto the censors of the tribes. But before the benches of the knights on either side stands one being shorter; and at the upper end of this, sit the two tribunes of the horse, at the upper end of the other the two tribunes of the foot, in their arms; the rest of the benches being covered by the judges of the land in their robes; but these magistrates have no suffrage, neither the tribunes, though they derive their presence in the senate from the Romans, nor the judges, though they derive theirs from the ancient senate of Oceana. Every Monday, this assembly sits of course; at other times, if there be occasion, any magistrate of the house, by giving order for the bell, or by his lictor or ensign-bearer, calls a senate; and every magistrate or knight during his session hath the title, place and honour of a duke, earl, baron or knight respectively. And every one that hath borne the same magistracy *tertio*, by his third session, hath his respective place and title during the term of his life, which is all the honour conferred by this commonwealth, except upon the master of the ceremonies, the master of the horse and the king of the heralds, who are knights by their places. And thus you have the face of the senate, in which there is scarce any feature that is not Roman or Venetian; nor do the horns of this crescent extend themselves much unlike those of the Sanhedrim, on either hand of the prince and of the father of that senate. But upon beauty, in which every man hath his fancy, we will not otherwise philosophise than to remember that there is something more than decency in the robe of a judge that would not be well spared from the bench; and that the gravest magistrate unto whom you can commit the sword of justice will find a quickness in the spurs of honour which, if they be not laid unto virtue, will lay themselves unto that which may rout a commonwealth.

To come from the face of the senate unto the constitution and use of the parts, it is contained in the peculiar orders. And the orders which are peculiar unto the senate are either of election or instruction.

Elections in the senate are of three sorts, annual, biennial and extraordinary.

Annual elections are performed by the schedule called the tropic, and the tropic consisteth of two parts: the one containing the magistrates, and the other the councils, to be yearly elected. The schedule or tropic of the magistrates is as followeth in

The fifteenth order: requiring that upon every Monday next ensuing the last of March, the knights of the annual galaxies taking their places in the senate be called the first region of the same; and that the house, having dismissed the third region and received the first, proceed unto election of the magistrates contained in the first part of the tropic, by the ensuing schedule:

The lord strategus.	
The lord orator.	annual
The first censor.	magistrates.
The second censor.	
The third commissioner of the seal.	triennial
The third commissioner of the treasury.	magistrates.

The annual magistrates (provided that no one man bear above one of those honours during the term of one session) may be elected out of any region. But the triennial magistrates may not be elected out of any other than the third region only, lest the term of their session expire before that of their honour and (it being unlawful for any man to bear magistracy any longer than he is thereunto qualified by the election of the people) cause a fraction in the rotation of this commonwealth.

The strategus is first president of the senate, and general of the army if it be commanded to march; in which case there shall be a second strategus elected to be first president of the senate, and general of the second army: and if this also be commanded to march a third strategus shall be chosen, and so as long as the commonwealth sendeth forth armies.

The lord orator is second and more peculiar president of the senate, unto whom it appertaineth to keep the house unto orders.

The censors, whereof the first by consequence of his election is chancellor of the University of Clio and the second of that of Calliope, are presidents of the council for religion and magistrates, unto whom it belongeth to keep the house unto the order of the ballot. They are also inquisitors into the ways and means of acquiring magistracy, and have power to punish indirect proceeding in the same, by removing a knight or magistrate out of the house, under appeal unto the senate.

The commissioners of the seal, being three, whereof the third is annually chosen out of the third region, are judges in chancery.

The commissioners of the treasury, being three, whereof the third is annually chosen out of the third region, are judges in the exchequer; and every magistrate of this schedule hath right to propose unto the senate.

But the strategus with the six commissioners are the signory of this commonwealth, having right of session and suffrage in every council of the senate and power, either jointly or severally, to propose in all or any of them.

I have little in this order to observe or prove, but that the strategus is the same honour, both in name and thing, that was borne, among others, by Philopoemen and Aratus in the commonwealth of the Achaeans; the like having been in use also with the Aetolians (*quem ut Achaei strategon nominabant*, saith Emmius). The orator, called otherwise the speaker, is with small alteration the same that had been of former use in this nation. These two, if you will, may be compared unto the consuls in Rome, or the suffetes in Carthage, for their magistracy is scarce different.

The censors derive their power of removing a senator from those of Rome, the government of the ballot from those of Venice, and that of animadversion upon the *ambitus*, or canvass for magistracy, from both.

The signory, with the whole right and use of that magistracy, to be hereafter more fully explained, is almost purely Venetian.

The second part of the tropic is directed by

> *The sixteenth order:* whereby the constitution of the councils, being four, that is to say the council of state, the council of war, the council of religion, and the council of trade, is rendered conformable in their revolutions unto that of the senate. As first, by the annual election of five knights out of the third region of the senate into the council of state, consisting of fifteen knights, five in every region. Secondly, by the annual election of three knights out of the third region of the council of state, to be proposed by the provosts and elected by that council, into the council of war, consisting of nine knights, three in every region, not excluded by

this election from remaining members also of the council of state; the four tribunes of the people have right of sessions and suffrage in the council of war. Thirdly, by the annual election of four knights out of the third region of the senate into the council of religion, consisting of twelve knights, four in every region; of this council, the censors are presidents. Fourthly, by the annual election of four knights out of the third region of the senate into the council of trade, consisting of twelve knights, four in every region. And each region in every one of these councils thus constituted, shall weekly and interchangeably elect one provost, whose magistracy shall continue for one week, nor shall he be re-elected into the same till every knight of that region in the same council have once borne the same magistracy. And the provosts, being one in every region, three in every council, and twelve in all, besides their other capacities, shall assemble and be a council or rather an academy apart, to certain ends and purposes to be hereafter explained with those of the rest of the councils.

This order is of no other use than for the frame and turn of the councils, and yet of no small one; for in motion consisteth life, and the motion of a commonwealth will never be current, unless it be circular. Men that, like my lord Epimonus, not enduring the resemblance of this kind of government unto orbs and spheres, fall on physicking and purging of it, do no more than is necessary; for if it be not in rotation both as to persons and things, it will be very sick. The people of Rome, as to persons, if they had not been taken up by the wheel of magistracy, had overturned the chariot of the senate. And those of Lacedaemon, as to things, had not been so quiet when the senate trashed their business by encroaching upon the result, if by the institution of the ephors they had not brought it about again. So that if you allow not a commonwealth her rotation, in which consists her equality, you reduce her to a party, and then it is necessary that you be physicians indeed, or rather farriers; for you will have strong patients, and such as must be haltered and cast, or yourselves may need bone-setters. Wherefore the councils of this commonwealth, both in regard of their elections and, as will be shown, of their affairs, are uniform with the senate in their revolutions, not as whirl-pits to swallow, but to bite and, with the screws of their rotation, hold and turn a business, like the vice of a smith unto the hand of the workman; without engines of which nature it is not possible for the senate, much less for the people, to be perfect artificers in a political capacity. But I shall not hold you longer from

The *seventeenth order:* directing biennial elections or the constitution of the orb of ambassadors in ordinary, consisting of four residences, the revolution whereof is performed in eight years, and preserved through the election of one ambassador in two years by the ballot of the senate, to repair unto the court of France and reside there for the term of two years; and the term of two years being expired, to remove from thence unto the court of Spain, there to continue for the space of two years; and thence to remove unto the state of Venice and, after two years' residence in that city, to conclude with his residence at Constantinople, for a like term of time, and so to return. A knight of the senate or a deputy of the prerogative may not be elected ambassador in ordinary, because a knight or deputy so chosen must either lose his session, which would cause an unevenness in the motion of this commonwealth, or accumulate magistracy, which agreeth not with the equality of the same. Nor may any man be elected into this capacity that is above five and thirty years of age, lest the commonwealth lose the charge of his education by being deprived at his return of the fruit of it, or else enjoy it not long through the defects of nature.

This order is the perspective of the commonwealth whereby she foreseeth danger; or the traffic whereby she receiveth every two years the return of a statesman enriched with eight years' experience from the prime marts of negotiation in Europe. And so much for the elections in the senate that are ordinary; such as are extraordinary follow in

The *eighteenth order:* appointing all elections upon emergent occasions, except that of the dictator, to be made by the scrutiny, or that kind of election whereby a council comes to be a fifth order of electors. For example, if there be occasion of an ambassador extraordinary, the provosts of the council of state, or any two of them, shall propose unto the same, till one competitor be chosen by that council; and the council, having chosen a competitor, shall bring his name into the senate, which in the usual way shall choose four more competitors unto the same magistracy and put them, with the competitor of the council, unto the ballot of the house, by which he of the five that is chosen is said to be elected by the scrutiny of the council of state. A vice-admiral, a polemarch, or field officer shall be elected after the same manner, by the scrutiny of the council of war. A judge or sergeant-at-law by the scrutiny of the commissioners of the seal. A baron or considerable officer of the exchequer by the scrutiny of the commissioners of the treasury. Men in magistracy or out of it are equally capable of election by the scrutiny; but a magistrate or officer elected by the scrutiny unto a military employment, if he be neither a knight of the senate nor a deputy of the prerogative, ought to have his office confirmed by the prerogative, because the militia in a commonwealth where the people are sovereign is not lawful to be touched *injussu populi*.

The Romans were so curious that, though their consuls were elected *centuriatis*, they might not touch the militia except they were confirmed *curiatis comitiis*; for a magistrate not receiving his power from the people takes it from them, and to take away their power is to take away their liberty. As to the election by the scrutiny, it may be easily perceived to be Venetian, there being no such way to take in the knowledge, which in all reason must be best in every council, of such men as are most fit for their turns, and yet to keep them from the bias of particular affection or interest under that pretence. For the cause why the great council in Venice scarce ever elects any other than the name that is brought in by the scrutiny, is very probable to be that they may.[34] This election is the last of those appertaining unto the senate, the councils being chosen by the orders already shown. It remaineth that we come unto those whereby they are instructed, and the orders of instruction unto the councils are two: the first for the subject matter whereupon they are to proceed, and the second for the manner of their proceeding. The subject matter of the councils is distributed unto them by

The nineteenth order: distributing unto every council such businesses as are properly to belong unto their cognizance, whereof some they shall receive and determine, and others they shall receive, prepare and introduce into the house, as first:
The council of state is to receive all addresses, intelligences and letters of negotiation; to give audience to ambassadors sent unto, and to draw up instructions for such as shall be sent by, this

---

[34] There is a semi-colon after 'be' in C and P. The meaning seems to be that because they are free to choose, they normally choose the best candidate, and that he has emerged already.

commonwealth; to receive propositions from, and hold intelligence with, the provincial councils; to consider upon all laws to be enacted, amended or repealed, and upon all levies of men or money, war or peace, leagues or associations to be made by this commonwealth, so far forth as is conducible unto the orderly preparation of the same, to be introduced by them into the senate. Provided that all such affairs as (otherwise appertaining unto the council of state) are, for the good of the commonwealth, to be carried with greater secrecy, be managed by the council of war, with power to receive and send forth agents, spies, emissaries, intelligencers, frigates, and to manage affairs of that nature, if it be necessary, without communication unto the senate, till such time as it may be had without detriment unto the business. But they shall have no power to engage the commonwealth in a war, without the consent of the senate and the people. It appertaineth also unto this council to take charge of the fleet as admiral, and of all storehouses, armories, arsenals and magazines appertaining unto this commonwealth. They shall keep a diligent record of the military expeditions from time to time reported by him that was strategus or general, or one of the polemarchs, in that action, or at least so far forth as the experience of such commanders may tend unto the improvement of the military discipline, which they shall digest and introduce into the senate; and if the senate shall thereupon frame any article, they shall see that it be observed in the musters or education of the youth. And whereas the council of war is the sentinel or scout of this commonwealth, if any person or persons shall go about to introduce debate into any popular assembly of the same, or otherwise to alter the present government, or strike at the root of it, they shall apprehend, or cause to be apprehended, seized, imprisoned, and examine, arraign, acquit or condemn and cause to be executed any such person or persons, of their proper power and authority and without appeal.

The council of religion as the arbiter of this commonwealth in cases of conscience more peculiarly appertaining unto religion, Christian charity, and a pious life, shall have the care of the national religion and the protection of the liberty of conscience, with the cognizance of all causes relating unto either of them. And first as to the national religion: they shall cause all places or preferments of the best revenue in either of the universities to be conferred upon none other than such of the most learned and pious men as have dedicated themselves unto the study of theology. They shall also take an especial care that by such augmentations as be or shall hereafter be appointed by the senate, every benefice in this nation be improved at the least unto the value of one hundred pounds a year. And to the end that there be no interest at all whereby the divines or teachers of the national religion may be corrupted or corrupt religion, they shall be capable of no other kind of employment or preferment in this commonwealth. And whereas a directory for the administration of the national religion is to be prepared by this council, they shall in this and other debates of this nature proceed in manner following: a question arising in matter of religion shall be put and stated by the council in writing, which writing the censors shall send by their beadles (being proctors chosen to attend them), each unto the university whereof he is chancellor; and the vice-chancellor of the same, receiving the writing, shall call a convocation of all the divines of that university being above forty years of age. And the universities upon a point so proposed shall have no manner of intelligence or correspondence one with another until their debates be ended,[35] and they have made return of their answers unto the council of religion by two or three of their own members that may clear their sense, if any doubt should arise, unto the council; which done, they shall return and the council, having received such information, shall proceed according unto their own judgments in the preparation of the whole matter for the senate; that so, the interest of the learned being removed, there may be a right application of reason unto Scripture, which is the foundation of the national religion.

Secondly, this council, as to the protection of the liberty of conscience, shall suffer no coercive power in the matter of religion to be exercised in this nation; the teachers of the national religion being no other than such as voluntarily undertake that calling, and their auditors or hearers no other than are also voluntary. Nor shall any gathered congregation be molested or interrupted in their way of worship (being neither Jewish nor idolatrous) but vigilantly and vigorously protected and defended in the enjoyment, practice and profession of the same. And if there be officers or auditors appointed by any such congregation, for the introduction of causes into the council of religion, all such causes so introduced shall be received, heard and determined by the same (with recourse had if need be unto the senate).

[35] H evidently thought this provision necessary.

Thirdly, every petition addressed unto the senate, except that of a tribe, shall be received, examined and debated by this council; and such only as they upon such examination and debate had shall think fit may be introduced into the senate.

The council of trade, being the *vena porta* of this nation, shall hereafter receive instructions more at large. For the present, their experience attaining unto a right understanding of those trades and mysteries that feed the veins of this commonwealth, and a true distinction of them from those that suck or exhaust the same, they shall acquaint the senate with the conveniences and inconveniences, to the end that encouragement may be applied unto the one and remedy to the other.

The academy of the provosts, being the affability of the commonwealth, shall assemble every day towards the evening in a fair room, having certain withdrawing rooms thereunto belonging. And all sorts of company that will repair thither for conversation or discourse, so it be upon the matter of government, news or intelliegence, or to propose any thing unto the councils, shall be freely and affably received in the outer chamber and heard in the way of civil conversation, which is to be managed without any other awe or ceremony than thereunto is usually appertaining; to the end that every man may be free, and that what is proposed by one may be argued or discoursed upon by the rest, except the matter be of secrecy; in which case the provosts, or some of them, shall take such as desire audience into one of the withdrawing rooms. And the provosts are to give their minds that this academy be so governed, adorned and preserved, as may be most attractive unto men of parts and good affections unto the commonwealth, for the excellency of the conversation.[36]

Furthermore, if any man, not being able or willing to come in person, have any advice to give which he judgeth may be for the good of the commonwealth, he may write his mind unto the academy of the provosts, in a letter signed or not signed, which letter shall be left with the doorkeeper of the academy. Nor shall any person delivering such a letter be seized, molested or detained, though it should prove to be a libel. But the letters so delivered shall be presented unto the provosts; and in case they be so many that they cannot well be examined by the provosts

---

[36] This proposal, though one for verbal rather than written communication – itself typical of H's city-state view of the polity – might be compared with the proposals for an 'office of addresses' put forward by Samuel Hartlib in 1648 and Henry Robinson in 1650 (W. K. Jordan, *Men of Substance*, Chicago, 1942, pp. 250–2).

themselves, they shall distribute them as they please to be read by the gentlemen of the academy who, finding anything in them material, will find matters of discourse; or, if they happen upon a business that requires privacy, return it with a note upon it unto a provost. And the provosts by the secretaries attending shall cause such notes out of discourses or letters to be taken as they please, to the end that they may propose, as occasion serveth, what any two of them shall think fit, out of their notes so taken, unto their respective councils; to the end that not only the ear of the commonwealth be open unto all, but that, men of such education being in her eye, she may upon emergent elections or occasions be always provided of her choice of fit persons.

Every council, being adorned with a state[37] for the signory, shall be attended by two secretaries, two door-keepers and two messengers in ordinary, and have power to command more upon emergencies, as occasion requireth. And the academy shall be attended with two secretaries, two messengers and two door-keepers; this with the other councils being provided with their farther conveniences at the charge of the state.

But whereas it is incident unto commonwealths upon emergencies requiring extraordinary speed or secrecy, either through their natural delays or unnatural haste to incur equal danger, while holding unto the slow pace of their orders they come not in time to defend themselves from some sudden blow, or breaking them for the greater speed they but haste unto their own destruction; if the senate shall at any time make election of nine knights extraordinary to be added unto the council of war, as a *junta* for the term of three months, the council of war, with the *junta* so added, is for the term of the same dictator of Oceana, having power to levy men and money, to make war and peace, as also to enact laws which shall be good for the space of one year (if they be not sooner repealed by the senate and the people) and for no longer time, except they be confirmed by the senate and the people. And the whole administration of the commonwealth for the term of the said three months shall be in the dictator; provided that the dictator shall have no power to do anything that tendeth not unto his proper end and institution, but all unto the preservation of the commonwealth as it is established and for the sudden restitution of the same unto the natural channel and common course of government. And all acts, orders, decrees or

[37] See above, p. 119 n. 33.

laws of the council of war with the *junta*, being thus created, shall be signed: *Dictator Oceanae.*

This order of instructions unto the councils, being (as in a matter of tha nature is requisite) very large, I have used my best skill to abbreviate in such manner as might show no more of it than is necessary unto the understanding of the whole; though as to the parts or further duties of the councils, I have omitted many things of singular use in a commonwealth. But it was spoken to at the council by the Archon in this manner:

My lords the legislators:

Your councils (except the dictator only) are proper and native springs and sources, you see, which (hanging a few sticks and straws, that, as less considerable, would otherwise be more troublesome, upon the banks of their peculiar channels) derive the full stream of business into the senate; so pure, and so far from the possibility of being troubled, or stained (as will undeniably appear by the course contained in the ensuing order) with any kind of private interest or partiality, that it shall never be possible for any assembly, hearkening unto the advice or information of this or that worthy member – either instructed upon his pillow, or while he was making himself ready, or by the petition or ticket which he received at the door – to have half the security in his faith or advantage by his wisdom; such a senate or council being, through the uncertainty of the winds, like a wave of the sea, nor shall it otherwise mend the matter by flowing up into dry ditches, or referring business to be better examined by committees, than to go farther about with it to less purpose (if it do not ebb back again with the more mud in it). For in a case referred to an occasional committee, of which any member that is desirous may get himself named, and to which nobody will come but either for the sake of his friend or his own interest, it fareth little better as to the information of the senate, than if it had been referred unto the parties. Wherefore the Athenians, being distributed into four tribes, out of which by equal numbers they annually chose four hundred men called the senate of the bean (because the ballot at their election was performed by the use of beans), divided them by fifties into eight parts. And every fifty in their turn, for one eighth part of the year, was a council apart called the prytans; the prytans in their

distinct council, receiving all comers and giving ear unto every man
that had anything to propose concerning the commonwealth, had
power to debate and prepare all the businesses that were to be
introduced into the senate. The Achaeans had ten selected magistrates called the demiurges, constituting a council apart called the
synarchy, which with the strategus prepared all the business that
was introduced into their senate; but neither the senate of the
Athenians, nor of the Achaeans, but would have wondered if a
man should have told them that they had been to receive all
comers and discourses to the end that they might refer them
afterwards unto the prytans or the synarchy, much less unto an
occasional committee, exposed unto the catch-that-catch-may of
the parties interested. And yet Venice in this (as in most of her
orders,) excels them all by the constitution of her councils, that of
the college and the other of the *dieci*. The course of the college is
exactly described in the ensuing order; and for that of the *dieci* it so
little differs from what it hath bestowed upon our dictator that I
need not to make any particular description of it. But to dictatorian
power in general and the use of it, because it must needs be of
difficult digestion unto such as, puking still at ancient prudence,
show themselves to be in the nursery of mother-wit, it is no less
than necessary to say something. And first, in a commonwealth
that is not wrought up nor perfected, this power will be of very
frequent, if not continual use; wherefore it is said more than once
upon defects of the government in the Book of Judges that *in those
days there was no king in Israel*. Nor hath the translator (though for
no king, he should have said *no judge*) abused you so much; seeing
that the dictator (and such was the judge of Israel) or the dictatorian power, being in a single person, so little differs from
monarchy (which followed in that), that from the same cause there
hath been no other effect in any commonwealth, as in Rome was
manifest by Sulla and Caesar who, to make themselves absolute or
sovereign, had no more to do than to prolong their magistracy; for
dictatoris imperium quasi numen. Nevertheless, so it is that without
this power, which is so dangerous and subject to introduce
monarchy, a commonwealth cannot be safe from falling into the
like dissolution; for unless you have an expedient in this case of
your own, and bound up by your providence from recoiling,
expedients in some cases you must not only have, but be beholding

for them unto such whom you must trust at a pinch, when you have not leisure to stand with them for security; which will be a thousand times more dangerous. And there can never be a commonwealth otherwise than by the order in debate wrought up unto that perfection; but this necessity must sometimes happen in regard of her natural slowness and openness, and the suddenness of assaults that may be made upon her, as also the secrecy which in some cases may be of absolute necessity unto her affairs. Whence Machiavel concludes it positively, that a commonwealth unprovided of such a refuge must ruin; for her course is either broken by the blow, in one of those cases, or by herself while it startles her out of her orders. And indeed a commonwealth is like a greyhound which, having once coasted, will never after run fair, but grow slothful. And when she comes to make a common practice of taking nearer ways than her orders, she is dissolved; for the being of a commonwealth consists in her orders. Wherefore at this lift you will be exposed unto danger, if you have not provided beforehand for the safety of your report in like cases; nor is it sufficient that your resort be safe, unless it be as secret and quick, for if it be slow or open, your former inconveniences are not remedied. Now for our imitation in this part, there is nothing in experience like that of the council of ten in Venice; the benefit whereof would be too long to be shown in the whole piece, and therefore I shall take but a pattern out of Giannotti. In the war (saith he) which the Venetians had with Florence in Casentine, the Florentines, finding a necessity in their affairs, far from any other inclination in themselves, to ask their peace, sent ambassadors about it unto Venice, where they were no sooner heard than the bargain was struck up by the council of ten; and everybody admiring (seeing this commonwealth stood upon the higher ground) what should be the reason of such haste, the council upon the return of the ambassadors imparted letters unto the senate, whereby it appeared that the Turk had newly launched a formidable fleet against their state; which had it been known to the Florentines, it was well enough known they would have made no peace. Wherefore the service of the ten was highly applauded by the senate, and celebrated by the Venetians.[38] Whereby may

---

[38] Giannotti, II, pp. 120–1.

appear, not only in part what use there is of dictatorian power in that government, but that it is assumed at the discretion of that council; whereas in this of Oceana it is no otherwise entrusted than when the senate, in the election of nine knights extraordinary giveth at once the commission, and taketh security in a balance added unto the council of war, though securer before by the tribunes of the people than that of Venice, which yet never incurred jealousy. For if the younger nobility have been often girding at it, that happened not so much through the apprehension of danger in it unto the commonwealth, as through the awe of it upon themselves. Wherefore the graver have doubtlessly shown their prudence in the law whereby, the magistracy of these counsellors being to last until their successors be created, the council is established.

The instructions of the councils for their subject matter being shown, it remaineth that I show the instructions for the manner of their proceeding, as they follow in

> *The twentieth order:* containing the method of debate to be observed by the magistrates and the councils successively, in order to a decree of the senate.
>
> The magistrates of the signory, as counsellors of this commonwealth, shall take into their consideration all matters of state or of government; and, having right to propose in any council, may any one or more of them propose what business he or they please in that council whereunto it most properly belongeth. And that the councils may be held unto their duty, the said magistrates are superintendents and inspectors of the same, with right to propose unto the senate.
>
> The censors have equal power with these magistrates, but in relation unto the council of religion only.
>
> Any two of the three provosts in every council may propose to, and are the more peculiar proposers of, the same council; to the end that there be not only an inspection and superintendency of business in general, but that every work be also committed unto a peculiar hand.
>
> Any one or more of the magistrates, or any two of the provosts respectively having proposed, the council shall debate the business so proposed, to which they of the third region that are willing shall speak first in their order; they of the second, next; and they

of the first, last; and the opinions of those that proposed or spoke, as they shall be thought the most considerable by the council, shall be taken by the secretary of the same in writing, and each of them signed with the name of the author.

The opinions being thus prepared, any magistrate of the signory, censor, or any two of the provosts of that council, upon this occasion may assemble the senate.

The senate being assembled, the opinions (for example, if they be four) shall be read in their order, that is according unto the order or dignity of the magistrates or counsellors by which they were signed. And being read, if any of the council introducing them will speak, they, as best acquainted with the business, shall have precedence, and after them the senators shall speak according unto their regions, beginning by the third first, and so continuing till every man that will have spoken: and when the opinions have been sufficiently debated, they shall be put all together unto the ballot after this manner.

Four secretaries, carrying each of them one of the opinions in one hand, with a white box in the other, and each following another (according unto the order of the opinions), shall present his box, naming the author of his opinion unto every senator; and one secretary or ballotine with a green box shall follow the four white ones; and one secretary or ballotine with a red box shall follow the green one; and every senator shall put one ball into some one of these six boxes. The suffrage being gathered and opened before the signory, if the red box or non-sincere[39] had above half the suffrages, the opinions shall be all cast out, for the major part of the house is not clear in the business. If no one of the four opinions had above half the suffrages in the affirmative, that which had fewest shall be cast out, and the other three shall be ballotted again. If no one of the three had above half, that which had fewest shall be cast out, and the other two shall be ballotted again. If neither of the two had above half, that which had fewest shall be cast out, and the remaining opinion shall be ballotted again. And if the remaining opinion have not above half, it shall also be cast out. But the first of the opinions that arrives at most above half in the affirmative is the decree of the senate. The opinions being all of them cast out by the non-sincere may be reviewed (if occasion permit) by the council, and brought in again. If they be cast out by the negative, the case being of advice

[39] H's Anglicisation of *non sinceri* (p. 115, n. 29, above) has been retained.

only, the house approveth not, and there is an end of it; the case being necessary, and admitting delay, the council is to think again upon the business and to bring in new opinions, but the case being necessary, and not admitting delay, the senate forthwith, electing the junta, shall create the dictator. *Et videat dictator ne quid respublica detrimenti capiat.*

This in case the debate conclude not in a decree; but if a decree be passed, it is either in matter of state, or government according to law enacted already, and then it is good without going any farther; or it is in matter of law to be enacted, repealed or amended, and then the decree of the senate, especially if it be for a war, or for a levy of men or money, is invalid without the result of the commonwealth, which is in the prerogative tribe, or representative of the people.

The senate, having prepared a decree to be proposed unto the people, shall appoint their proposers; and no other may propose for the senate unto the people but the magistrates of the house: that is to say the three commissioners of the seal, or any two of them, the three of the treasury, or any two of them, or the two censors.

The senate, having appointed their proposers, shall require of the tribunes a muster of the people at a set time and place; and, the tribunes, or any two of them, having mustered the people accordingly, the proposers shall propose the sense or decree of the senate by clauses unto the people. And that which is proposed by the authority of the senate, and resolved by the command of the people, is the law of Oceana.

To this order, implicitly containing the sum very near of the whole civil part of the commonwealth, my Lord Archon spoke thus in council:

My dear lords:

There is a saying that a man must cut his coat according to his cloth. When I consider what God hath allowed or furnished unto our present work, I am amazed. You would have a popular government; he hath weighed it unto you in the present balance, as I may say, to a drachm; you have no more to do but to fix it. For the superstructures of such a government, they require a good aristocracy; you have, or have had, a nobility or a gentry the best studied, and the best writers, at least next that of Italy, in the whole world, nor have they been inferior, when so exercised, in the leading of armies. But the people are the main body of a commonwealth; show me *a Gadibus usque ad Auroram et Gangem*, from the treasuries of snow (as it is in Job) unto the burning zone, a people whose shoulders so universally and so exactly fit the corselet. Nevertheless it were convenient to be well provided with auxiliaries; there is Marpesia, through her fruitfulness inexhaustible of men, and men through her barrenness not only inured unto hardship, but bucked in your arms. It may be said that Venice, save only that she taketh not in the people, is the most incomparable situation of a commonwealth. You are Venice taking in your people and your auxiliaries too. My lords, the children of Israel were makers of brick, before they were builders of a commonwealth; but our brick is made, our mortar tempered, the cedars of Lebanon are hewed and squared unto our hands. Hath this been the work of man? or is it in man to withstand this work? *Shall he that contendeth with the Almighty instruct him? He that reproveth God, let him answer it.*[40] For our parts, everything is so laid that when we come to have use of it, it is the next at hand; and unless we can conceive that God and nature do anything in vain, there is no more for us to do but to dispatch. The piece which we have reached to us in the foregoing orders is the aristocracy. Athens, as hath been shown, was plainly lost through the want of a good aristocracy; but the sufficiency of an aristocracy goes demonstrably upon the hand of the nobility or gentry, for that the politics can be mastered without study, or that the people can have leisure to study, is a vain imagination; and what kind of aristocracy divines and lawyers would make, let their incurable run upon their own narrow bias and their perpetual invectives against Machiavel (though in some places justly reprovable, yet the only politician and incomparable patron of the people) serve for instruction. I will stand no more unto the judgment of lawyers and divines in this work than unto that of so many other tradesmen; but if the model chance to wander abroad, I recommend it unto the Roman *speculativi, garbatissimi signori*, the most complete gentlemen of this age, for their censure; or, with my lord Epimonus his leave, send three or four hundred copies unto your agent at Venice, to be presented unto the magistrates there, and when they have considered them, to be

[40] Job, 40: 1–2.

proposed unto the debate of the senate, the most competent judges under heaven, who though they have great affairs, will not refuse to return you the oracle of their ballot. The counsellors of princes I will not trust; they are but journeymen. 'The wisdom of these later times in princes' affairs', saith Verulamius, 'is rather fine deliveries and shiftings off dangers when they be near, than solid and grounded courses to keep them aloof.'[41] Their counsellors do not derive their proceedings from any sound root of government that may contain the demonstration and assure the success of them, but are expedient-mongers, givers of themselves to help a lame dog over a stile; else how cometh it to pass that the fame of Cardinal Richelieu hath been like thunder, whereof we hear the noise, but can make no demonstration of the reason? But to return, if neither the people, nor divines and lawyers, can be the aristocracy of a nation, there remains only the nobility, in which style, to avoid further repetition, I shall understand the gentry also, as the French do by the word *noblesse*.

Now to treat of the nobility, in such sort as may be less obnoxious unto mistake; it will be convenient and responsible unto the present occasion that I divide my discourse into four parts: the first treating of nobility, and the kinds of it; the second, of their capacity of the senate; the third, of the divers kinds of senates; the fourth, of the senate, according unto the foregoing orders.

Nobility may be defined divers ways, for it is either ancient riches, or ancient virtue, or title conferred by a prince or a commonwealth.

Nobility of the first kind may be subdivided into two other; such as hold an over-balance in dominion or property unto the whole people, or such as hold not an over-balance. In the former case a nobility (such was the Gothic, of which sufficient hath been spoken) is incompatible with popular government, for unto popular government it is essential that power should be in the people, but the over-balance of a nobility in dominion draweth the power unto themselves; wherefore in this sense it is that Machiavel is to be understood, where he saith *questi tali sono perniziosi in ogni repubblica ed in ogni provincia*,[42] that these are pernicious in a commonwealth, and of France, Spain, and Italy, that they are nations *le*

---

[41] Bacon, Essay XIX, 'Of Empire' (*Works*, ed. Spedding, vol. VI, London, 1890, p. 420).
[42] *Discorsi*, I, 55.

quali tutte insieme sono la corruttela del mondo, which for this cause
are the corruption of the world. For otherwise nobility may,
according unto his definition, which is 'that they are such as live
upon their own revenues in plenty, without engagement either
unto the tilling of their lands or other work for their livelihood',[43]
hold an under-balance unto the people; in which case they are not
only safe, but necessary unto the natural mixture of a well-ordered
commonwealth. For how else can you have a commonwealth that
is not altogether mechanic? Or what comparison is there of such
commonwealths as are or come nearest to mechanic, for example,
Athens, Switz, Holland, unto Lacedaemon, Rome, and Venice,
plumed with their aristocracies? Your mechanics, till they have first
feathered their nests – like the fowls of the air, whose whole
employment is to seek their food – are so busied in their private
concernments that they have neither leisure to study the public,
nor are safely to be trusted with it, *quia egestas haud facile habetur
sine damno*, because a man is not faithfully embarked in this kind of
ship if he have no share in the freight. But if his share be such as
gives him leisure, by his private advantage, to reflect upon that of
the public, what other name is there for this sort of men, being *à
leur aise*, but (as Machiavel you see calls them) nobility? Especially
when their families come to be such as are noted for their services
done unto the commonwealth, and so take into their ancient riches
ancient virtue, which is the second definition of nobility, but such
an one as is scarce possible in nature without the former. 'For as
the baggage', saith Verulamius, 'is to an army, so are riches to
virtue; they cannot be spared nor left behind, though they be
impedimenta, such as not only hinder the march, but sometimes
through the care of them lose or disturb the victory.'[44] Of this latter
sort is the nobility of Oceana; the best of all other, because they,
having no stamp whence to derive their price, can have it no
otherwise than by their intrinsic value. The third definition of
nobility is title, honour, or distinction from the people, conferred
or allowed by the prince or the commonwealth; and this may be in
two ways, either without any stamp or privilege as in Oceana, or
with such privileges as are inconsiderable, as in Athens after the

[43] *Ibid.* Machiavelli did not say that it was overbalancing nobilities which had made France
and the other countries named the corruption of the world.
[44] Bacon, Essay xxxiv, 'Of Riches' (*Works*, vi p. 460). Cf below, p. 141.

battle of Plataea, whence the nobility had no right as such but unto religious offices or inspection of the public games, whereunto they were also to be elected by the people; or with privileges and those considerable ones, as the nobility in Athens before the battle of Plataea, and the patricians in Rome, each of which had right, or claimed it, unto the senate and all the magistracies, wherein for some time they only by their stamp were current.

But to begin higher and speak more at large of nobility in their several capacities of the senate, *a Jove principium*: the phylarchs or princes of the tribes of Israel were the most renowned or, as the Latin, the most noble of the congregation (Numbers 1: 16), whereof by hereditary right they had the leading and judging. The patriarchs or princes of families, according as they declared their pedigrees (Numbers, 1: 18), had the like right as to their families, but neither in these nor the former was there any hereditary right unto the Sanhedrim, though there be little question but the 'wise men and understanding, and known among their tribes', which the people took or elected into those or other magistracies, and Moses made rulers over them (Deuteronomy, 1: 13), must have been of these, seeing these could not choose but be the most known among the tribes, and were likeliest by the advantages of education to be the most wise and understanding.

Solon, having found the Athenians neither locally nor genea-logically, but by their different ways of life, divided into four tribes, that is into the soldiery, the tradesmen, the husbandmen and the goat-herds, instituted a new distribution of them, according unto the cense or valuation of their estates, into four *classes*: the first, second and third consisting of such as were proprietors in land, distinguished by the rate of their freeholds, with that stamp upon them which, making them capable of honour unto their riches, that is to say of the senate and all the magistracies, excluded the fourth, being the body of the people and far greater in number than the former three, from other right as to those capacities than the election of these, who by this means became an hereditary aristocracy or senatorian order of nobility. This was that course which came afterwards to be the destruction of Rome, and had now ruined Athens – the nobility, according to the inevitable nature of such an one, having laid the plot how to divest the people of the result, and so to draw the whole power of the com-

monwealth unto themselves; which in all likelihood they had done
if the people, coming by mere chance to be victorious in the battle
of Plataea and famous for defending Greece against the Persian,
had not returned with such courage as irresistibly brake the *classes*
(unto which of old they had borne a white tooth), brought the
nobility unto equal terms, and the senate with the magistracies to
be common unto both; the magistracies by suffrage and the senate,
which was the mischief of it, as I shall show anon in that constitution, by lots only.

The Lacedaemonians were, in this manner and for the same
cause with the Venetians at this day, no other than nobility, even
according to the definition given of nobility by Machiavel, for they
neither exercised any trade nor laboured their lands or lots, which
was done by their helots; wherefore some nobility may be far from
pernicious in a commonwealth, by Machiavel's own testimony,
who is an admirer of this; though the servants thereof were more
than the citizens. To these servants I hold the answer of Lycurgus,
when he bade him who asked 'why he did not admit the people
unto the government of his commonwealth', go home and admit
his servants unto the government of his family, to relate; for
neither were the Lacedaemonians servants nor farther capable of
the government, unless, whereas the congregation had the result,
he should have given them the debate also; every one of these that
attained unto sixty years of age, and the major vote of the congregation, being equally capable of the senate.

The nobility of Rome, and their capacity of the senate, I have
already described by that of Athens before the battle of Plataea,
save only that the Athenian was never eligible into the senate
without the suffrage of the people till the introduction of the lot,
but the Roman nobility ever; for the patricians were elected into
the senate by the kings, by the consuls, or the censors; or, if a
plebeian happened to be conscribed, he and his posterity became
patrician. Nor, though the people had many disputes with the
nobility, did this ever come in controversy, which if there had been
nothing else might in my judgment have been enough to overturn
that commonwealth.

The Venetian nobility, but that they are richer and not military,
resemble at all other points the Lacedaemonian, as I have already
shown. These Machiavel excepts from his rule by saying that their

estates are rather personal than real, or of any great revenue in land,[45] which comes unto our account and shows that a nobility or party of the nobility, not over-balancing in dominion, is not dangerous but of necessary use in every commonwealth, provided that it be rightly ordered; for if it be so ordered as was that of Rome, though they do not over-balance in the beginning, as they did not there, it will not be long ere they do, as is clear both in reason and that experience towards the latter end. That the nobility be capable of the senate is there only not dangerous, where there be no other citizens; as in this government, and that of Lacedaemon.

The nobility of Holland and Switz, though but few, have privileges not only distinct from the people, but so great that in some sovereignties they have a negative voice; an example which I am far from commending, being such as, if those governments were not cantonised, divided and subdivided into many petty sovereignties that balance one another, and in which the nobility, except they had a prince at the head of them, can never join to make work, would be the most dangerous that ever was but the Gothic, of which it savours. For in ancient commonwealths you shall never find a nobility to have had a negative but by the poll, which, the people being far more in number, came to nothing; whereas these have it, be they never so few, by their stamp or order.

Ours of Oceana have nothing else but their education and their leisure for the public, furnished by their ease and competent riches, and their intrinsic value which, according as it comes to hold weight in the judgment or suffrage of the people, is their only way unto honour and preferment; wherefore I would have your lordships to look upon your children as such who, if they come to shake off some part of their baggage, shall make the more quick and glorious march; for it was nothing else but the baggage sordidly plundered by the nobility of Rome that lost the victory of the whole world in the midst of her triumph.

Having followed the nobility thus close, they bring us, according unto their natural course and divers kinds, unto the divers constitutions of the senate.

That of Israel (as was shown by my right noble lord Phosphorus

---

[45] *Discorsi*, I, 55. Does H mean that only a landed nobility can over-balance?

de Auge in the opening of the commonwealth) consisted of seventy elders, elected at the first by the people; but whereas they were for life, they ever after (though without any divine precept for it) substituted their successors by ordination, which ceremony was most usually performed by imposition of hands, and by this means a commonwealth of as popular institution as can be found became, as it is accounted by Josephus, aristocratical. From this ordination deriveth that which was introduced by the Apostles into the Christian church, for which cause I think it is that the presbyterians would have the government of the church to be aristocratical; albeit the Apostles, to the end, as I conceive, that they might give no occasion unto such a mistake, but show that they intended the government of the church to be popular, ordained elders (as hath been shown) by the holding up of hands (or free suffrage of the people) in every congregation or *ecclesia*. For that is the word in the original, being borrowed from the civil congregations of the people in Athens and Lacedaemon, which were so called. And the word for 'holding up of hands' in the text is also the very same which signified the suffrage of the people in Athens, χειροτονήσαντες; and the suffrage of the Athenians was given *per* χειροτονίαν, saith Emmius.

The council of the bean (as was shown by my lord Navarchus de Paralo in his full discourse), being the proposing senate of Athens (for that of the Areopagites was a judicatory), consisted of four, some say five hundred senators, elected annually, all at once, and by a mere lot without suffrage; wherefore albeit the senate, to correct the temerity of the lot, had power to cast out such as they should judge unworthy of that honour, this related to manners only, and was not sufficient to repair the commonwealth, which by such means became impotent and, for as much as her senate consisted not of the natural aristocracy, which in a commonwealth is the only spur and rein of the people, was cast headlong by the rashness of her demagogues or grandees into ruin; while her senate, like the Roman tribunes, *qui fere semper regebantur a multitudine magis quam regebant*,[46] proposed not unto the result only, but unto the debate also of the people, who were therefore called unto the pulpits, where some vomited and others drank poison.

[46] Livy, III, lxxi.

The senate of Lacedaemon (most truly discovered by my lord Laco de Scytale) consisted but of thirty for life, whereof the two kings, having but single votes, were hereditary, the rest elective by the free suffrage of the people, but out of such as were sixty years of age; these had the whole debate of the commonwealth in themselves, and proposed unto the result only of the people. And now the riddle, which I have heretofore found troublesome to unfold, is out: that is to say why, Athens and Lacedaemon consisting each of the senate and the people, the one should be held a democracy and the other an aristocracy or laudable oligarchy, as it is termed by Socrates (for that word is not, wherever you meet it, to be branded, seeing it is used also by Aristotle, Plutarch and others, sometimes in a good sense). The main difference was that the people in this had the result only, and in that the debate and result too. But for my part, where the people have the election of the senate, not bound unto a distinct order, and the result, which is the sovereign power, I hold them to have that share in the government (the senate being not for life) whereof, with the safety of the commonwealth, they are capable in nature, and such a government for that cause to be democracy; though I do not deny but in Lacedaemon, the paucity of the senators considered, it might be called oligarchy in comparison of Athens, or, if we look upon their continuance for life, though they had been more, aristocracy.

The senate of Rome (whose fame hath been heard to thunder in the eloquence of my lord Dolabella de Enyo), consisting of three hundred, was, in regard of the number, less oligarchical than that of Lacedaemon, but more in regard of the patricians who, having an hereditary capacity of the same, were not elected unto that honour by the people, but, being conscribed by the censors, enjoyed it for life; wherefore these, if they had had their wills, would have resolved as well as debated, which set the people at such variance with them as dissolved the commonwealth; whereas if the people had enjoyed the result, as well that about the agrarian as all other strife must of necessity have ceased.

The senates of Switz and Holland (as I have learned of my lords Alpester and Glaucus), being bound up, like the sheaf of arrows which this gives, by leagues, lie like those in their quivers. But arrows, when they come to be drawn, fly some this way and some that; and I am contented that these concern us not.

That of Venice (by the faithful testimony of my most excellent lord Linceus de Stella) hath obliged a world, sufficiently punished by its own blindness or ingratitude, to repent and be wiser; for whereas a commonwealth in which there is no senate, or where the senate is corrupt, cannot stand, the great council of Venice, like the statue of Nilus, leans upon an urn or water pot, which poureth forth the senate in so pure and perpetual a stream as, being unable to instagnate, is forever incapable of corruption. The fuller description of this senate is contained in that of Oceana; and that of Oceana in the foregoing orders. Unto every one of which, because something hath been already said, I shall not speak in particular. But in general, your senate (and the other assembly, or the prerogative, as I shall show in due place) are perpetual, not as lakes or puddles, but as the rivers of Eden; and are beds made, as you have seen, to receive the whole people, by a due and faithful vicissitude into their current. They are not, as in the later way, alternate. Alternate life in government is the alternate death of it.

Ut fratrem Pollux alterna morte redemit.[47]

This was the Gothic work, whereby the former government was not only a ship, but a gust too; could never open her sails, but in danger to overset herself; neither make any voyage, nor lie safe in her own harbour. The wars of later ages (saith Verulamius) seem to be made in the dark, in respect of the glory and honour which reflected upon men from the wars in ancient times.[48] Their shipping of this sort was for voyages; ours dare not launch, nor lie they safe at home. Your Gothic politicians seem unto me rather to have invented some new ammunition or gunpowder in their king and parliament (*duo fulmina belli*), than government. For what is become of the princes (a kind of people) in Germany? Blown up. Where are the estates, or the power of the people, in France? Blown up. Where is that of the people in Aragon, and the rest of the Spanish kingdoms? Blown up. On the other side, where is the king of Spain's power in Holland? Blown up. Where is that of the Austrian princes in Switz? Blown up. This perpetual peevishness and jealousy, under the alternate empire of the prince and of the

---

[47] *Aeneid*, VI, 121.
[48] Bacon, Essay XXIX, 'Of the True Greatness of Kingdoms and Estates' (*Works*, VI, p. 451).

people, is obnoxious unto every spark. Nor shall any man show a reason that will be holding in prudence why the people of Oceana have blown up their king, but that their kings did not first blow up them. The rest is discourse for ladies. Wherefore your parliaments are not henceforth to come out of the bag of Aeolus but, by the galaxies, to be the perpetual food of the fire of Vesta.

Your galaxies, which divide the house into so many regions, are three, one of which, constituting the third region, is annually chosen, but for the term of three years; which causeth the house, having blooms, fruit half ripe, and others dropping off in full maturity, to resemble an orange tree, such as is at the same time an education or spring, and an harvest too. For the people have made a very ill choice in the man who is not easily capable of the perfect knowledge in one year of the senatorian orders; which knowledge, allowing him for the first to have been a novice, brings him the second year unto practice, and time enough; for at this rate you must always have two hundred knowing men in the government, and thus the vicissitude of your senators is not perceivable in the steadiness and perpetuity of your senate, which, like that of Venice, being always changing, is forever the same. And though other politicians have not so well imitated their pattern, there is nothing more obvious in nature, seeing a man, who wears the same flesh but a short time, is nevertheless the same man and of the same genius; and whence is this but from the constancy of nature in holding a man unto her orders? Wherefore hold also unto your orders. But this is a mean request; your orders will be worth little if they do not hold you unto them; wherefore embark. They are like a ship; if you be once aboard, you do not carry them but they you. And see how Venice stands unto her tackling; you will no more forsake them than you will leap into the sea.

But they are very many, and difficult. O my lords, what seaman casts away his card because it hath four and twenty points of compass? And yet those are very near as many and as difficult as the orders in the whole circumference of your commonwealth. Consider how have we been tossed with every wind of doctrine, lost by the glib tongues of your demagogues and grandees in our own havens! A company of fiddlers that have disturbed your rest for your groat; two to one, three thousand pounds a year to another, hath been nothing, and for what? Is there one of them that yet knows what a commonwealth is?[49] And are you yet afraid of such a government in which these shall not dare to scrape, for fear of the statute? Themistocles could not fiddle, but could make of a small city a great commonwealth; these have fiddled, and for your money, till they have brought a great commonwealth to a small city.

It grieves me, while I consider how and from what causes imaginary difficulties will be aggravated, that the foregoing orders are not capable of any greater clearness in discourse or writing. But if a man should make a book describing every trick or passage, it would fare no otherwise with a game at cards; and this is no more, if a man play upon the square. 'There is a great difference', saith Verulamius, 'between a cunning man and a wise man' (between a demagogue and a legislator) 'not only in point of honesty, but in point of ability. As there be that can pack the cards, and yet cannot play well; so there be some that are good in canvasses and factions, that are otherwise weak men.' Allow me but these orders, and let them come with their cards in their sleeves, or pack if they can. Again, saith he: 'It is one thing to understand persons, and another to understand matters; for many are perfect in men's humours that are not greatly capable of the real part of business, which is the constitution of one that hath studied men more than books; but there is nothing more hurtful in a state than that cunning men pass for wise.'[50] His words are an oracle. As Dionysius, when he could no longer exercise his tyranny among men, turned schoolmaster that he might exercise it among boys; allow me but these orders and your grandees, so well skilled in the baits and palates of men, shall turn rat-catchers.

And whereas councils (as is discreetly observed by the same author in his time) 'are at this day in most places but familiar meetings' (somewhat like the academy of provosts) 'where matters are rather talked on than debated, and run too swift to order an act of council',[51] give me my orders, and see if I have not trashed your demagogues.

It is not so much my desire to return upon haunts, as theirs that will not be satisfied; wherefore if, notwithstanding what was said of

---

[49] This could be an allusion to the challenge thrown out by Cromwell to dissentient officers, reported in *The Examination of James Harrington* (Harrington: 1977, p. 859).

[50] This and the preceding quotation are from Essay XXII, 'Of Cunning' (*Works*, VI. p. 428).

[51] Essay XX, 'Of Counsel' (*Works*, VI, p. 426).

dividing and choosing in our preliminary discourses, men will yet be returning unto the question why the senate must be a council apart – though even in Athens, where it was of no other constitution than the popular assembly, the distinction of it from the other was never held less than necessary – this may be added unto the former reasons, that if the aristocracy be not for the debate it is for nothing, but if it be for the debate, it must have convenience for it; and what convenience is there for debate in a crowd, where there is nothing but jostling, treading upon one another and stirring of blood, than which in this case there is nothing more dangerous? Truly, it was not ill said of my lord Epimonus that Venice plays her game as it were at billiards or nine-holes, and so may your lordships, unless your ribs be so strong that you think better of football; for such sport is debate in a popular assembly as, notwithstanding the distinction of the senate, was the destruction of Athens.

This speech concluded the debate which happened at the institution of the senate; the next assembly is that of the people, or prerogative tribe.

The face or *mine*[52] of the prerogative tribe for the arms, the horses and the discipline, but more especially for the select men, is that of a very noble regiment, or rather of two; the one of horse, divided into three troops (besides that of the provinces, which will be shown hereafter), with their captains, cornets, and two tribunes of the horse at the head of them; the other of foot in three companies (besides that of the provinces) with their captains, ensigns, and two tribunes of the foot at the head of them. The first troop is called the Phoenix, the second the Pelican, and the third the Swallow. The first company the Cypress, the second the Myrtle, and the third the Spray. Of these again (not without a near resemblance of the Roman division of a tribe) the Phoenix and the Cypress constitute the first *classis*; the Pelican and the Myrtle the second; and the Swallow with the Spray the third, renewed every spring by

> *The one and twentieth order:* directing that upon every Monday next ensuing the last of March, the deputies of the annual galaxy, arriving at the pavilion in the Halo, and electing one captain and one cornet of the Swallow (triennial officers) by and out of the

---

[52] C and P have 'nime'; H's errata direct change to 'mine', presumably the French word.

cavalry at the horse urn, according unto the rules contained in the ballot of the hundred, and one captain with one ensign of the Spray (triennial officers) by and out of the infantry at the foot urn, after the same way of balloting, constitute and become the third *classis* of the prerogative tribe.

Seven deputies are annually returned by every tribe, whereof three are horse and four are foot, and there be fifty tribes; so the Swallow must consist of one hundred and fifty horse, the Spray of two hundred foot and, the rest of the *classes* being two, each of them in number equal, the whole prerogative (besides the provinces, that is, the knights and deputies of Marpesia and Panopea) must consist of one thousand and fifty deputies; it is right. And these troops and companies may as well be called centuries as those of the Romans, for the Romans related not, in so naming theirs, unto their number; and whereas they were distributed according unto the valuation of their estates, so are these, which by virtue of the last order are now accommodated with their triennial officers; but there be others appertaining unto this tribe whose election, being of far greater importance, is annual, as followeth in

The twenty-second order: whereby the first *classis*, having elected their triennial officers and made oath unto the old tribunes that 'they will neither introduce, cause nor to their power suffer debate to be introduced into any popular assembly of this government, but to their utmost be aiding and assisting to seize and deliver any person or persons in that way offending and striking at the root of this commonwealth unto the council of war', are to proceed with the other two *classes* of the prerogative tribe to election of the new tribunes, being four annual magistrates, whereof two are to be elected out of the cavalry at the horse urn, and two out of the infantry at the foot urn, according unto the common ballot of the tribes. And they may be promiscuously chosen out of any *classis*, provided that the same person shall not be capable of bearing the tribunician honour twice in the term of one galaxy. The tribunes thus chosen shall receive the tribe (in reference to the power of mustering and disciplining the same) as commanders in chief, and for the rest as magistrates, whose proper function is prescribed by the next order. The tribunes may give leave unto any number of the prerogative, not exceeding one hundred at a time, to be absent, so they be not magistrates nor officers, and return within three months. If a magistrate or officer have necessary occasion, he may also be absent for the space of one month; provided that there be not above three cornets or ensigns, two captains or one tribune so absent at one time.

To this the Archon spoke at the institution, after this manner:

My lords:
It is affirmed by Cicero in his oration for Flaccus that the commonwealths of Greece were all shaken or ruined by the intemperance of their *comitia*, or assemblies of the people.[53] The truth is, if good heed in this point be not taken, a commonwealth will have bad legs. But all the world knows he should have excepted Lacedaemon, where the people (as hath been shown by the oracle) had no power at all of debate, nor (till after Lysander, whose avarice opened a gulf that was not long ere it swallowed up his country) came it ever to be exercised by them. Whence that commonwealth stood longest and firmest of any other but this, in our days, of Venice, which having underlaid herself with the like institution, owes a great if not the greatest part of her steadiness unto the same principle; the great council, which is with her the people, by the authority of my lord Epimonus, never speaking a word. Nor shall any commonwealth where the people in their political capacity is talkative ever see half the days of one of these, but being carried away by vainglorious men (that, as Overbury says, piss more than they drink) swim down the sink; as did Athens, the most prating of these dames, when that same ranting fellow Alcibiades fell on demagoguing for the Sicilian war. But whereas debate, by the authority and experience of Lacedaemon and Venice, is not to be committed unto the people in a well-ordered government, it may be said that the order specified is but a slight bar in a matter of like danger; for so much as an oath, if there be no recourse upon the breach of it, is a weak tie for such hands as have the sword in them. Wherefore what should hinder the people of Oceana, if they happen not to regard an oath, from assuming debate, and making themselves as much an anarchy as those of Athens? To which I answer, take the common sort in a private capacity and, except they be injured, you shall find them to have *verecundiam patrum*, a bashfulness in the presence of the

---

[53] Cicero, *Pro. L. Flacco oratio*, IV, 9ff.; VII, 16.

better sort or wiser men; acknowledging their abilities by attention, and accounting it no mean honour to receive respect from them. But if they be injured by them, they hate them, and the more for being wise or great, because that makes it the greater injury. Nor refrain they in this case from any kind of intemperance of speech, if of action. It is no otherwise with a people in their political capacity. You shall never find that they have assumed debate for itself, but for something else; wherefore in Lacedaemon where there was, and in Venice where there is, nothing else for which they should assume it, they have never shown so much as an inclination to it. Nor was there any appearance of such a desire in the people of Rome (who from the time of Romulus had been very well contented with the power of result either *comitiis curiatis*, as it was settled upon them by him, or *centuriatis*, as it was altered in their regard for the worse by Servius Tullius) till news was brought some fifteen years after the exile of Tarquin their late king (during which time, the senate had governed passing well) that he was dead at the court of Aristodemus the tyrant of Cumae. *Eo nuntio erecti patres, erecta plebs. Sed patribus nimis luxuriosa ea fuit laetitia; plebi, cui ad eam diem summa ope inservitum erat, injuriae a primoribus fieri coepere.*[54] Whereupon the patricians or nobility began to let out the hitherto dissembled venom which is inherent in the root of oligarchy, and fell immediately upon injuring the people beyond all moderation. For whereas the people had served both gallantly and contentedly in arms, upon their own charges, and though joint purchasers by their swords of the conquered lands, had not participated in the same to above two acres a man, the rest being secretly usurped by the patricians; they, through the meanness of their support, and the greatness of their expense, being generally indebted, no sooner returned home with victory to lay down their arms, than they were snatched up by their creditors the nobility, to cram gaols. Whereupon (but with the greatest modesty that was ever known in the like case) they first fell upon debate. *Se foris pro libertate et imperio dimicantes, domi a civibus captos et oppressos esse; tutioremque in bello quam in pace, inter hostes quam inter cives, libertatem plebis esse.*[55] It is true that when they could not get the

[54] Livy, II, xxi.
[55] *Ibid.* The whole of the long narrative that follows is based on Livy, II, xxi–xxxiii.

senate (through fear, as was pretended by the patricians) to assemble and take their grievances into consideration, they grew so much warmer that it was glad to meet; where Appius Claudius, a fierce spirit, was of opinion that recourse should be had unto consular power whereby, some of the brands of sedition being taken off, the flame might be extinguished; Servilius, being of another temper, thought it better and safer to try if the people might be bowed, than broken. But this debate was interrupted by tumultuous news of the near approach of the Volsci, a case in which the senate had no recourse but to the people who, contrary unto their former custom upon like occasions, would not stir afoot, but fell on laughing and saying '*patres militarent, patres arma caperent, ut penes eosdem pericula belli, penes quos praemia, essent*'; let them fight that have something to fight for. The senate, that had purses and could not sing so well before the thief, being in great perplexity, found no possible way out of it but to beseech Servilius, one of a genius well known to be popular, that he would accept of the consulship and make some such use of it as might be helpful to the patrician interest. Servilius, accepting of the offer and making use of his interest with the people, persuaded them to hope well of the good intention of the fathers, whom it would little beseem to be forced unto those things which would lose their grace, and that in view of the enemy, if they came not freely; and withal published an edict that no man should withhold a citizen of Rome by imprisonment from giving his name (for that was the way, as I shall have opportunity hereafter to show more at large, whereby they drew out their armies), nor seize nor sell any man's goods or children that was in the camp. Whereupon the people with a mighty concourse immediately took arms, marched forth, and (which to them was as easy as to be put into the humour, and that as appears in this place was not hard) totally defeated the Volsci first, then the Sabines (for the neighbour nations, hoping to have had a good bargain of the discord in Rome, were up on all sides) and after the Sabines, the Aurunci. Whence returning victorious in three battles, they expected no less than that the senate would have made good their words; when Appius Claudius, the other consul, of his innate pride, and that he might frustrate the faith of his colleague, caused the soldiers (who being set at liberty had behaved themselves with such valour) to be restored at their return unto their creditors and their gaols. Great resort upon this was made by the people unto Servilius, showing him their wounds, calling him to witness how they had behaved themselves, and minding him of his promise. Poor Servilius was sorry, but so overawed with the headiness of his colleague and the obstinacy of the whole faction of the nobility that, not daring to do anything either way, he lost both parties, the fathers conceiving that he was ambitious, and the people that he was false; while the consul Claudius, continuing to countenance such as daily seized and imprisoned some of the indebted people, had still new and dangerous controversies with them; insomuch that the commonwealth was torn with horrid division, and the people (because they found it not so safe, or so effectual in public) minded nothing but laying their heads together in private conventicles. For this A. Virginius and Titus Vetusius, the new consuls, were reproved by the senate as slothful, and upbraided with the virtue of Appius Claudius. Whereupon the consuls, having desired the senate that they might know their pleasure, showed afterwards their readiness to obey it, by summoning the people according unto command, and requiring names whereby to draw forth an army for diversion; but no man would answer. Report hereof being made unto the senate, the younger sort of the fathers grew so hot with the consuls that they desired them to abdicate the magistracy, which they had not the courage to defend.

The consuls, though they conceived themselves to be roughly handled, made this soft answer: 'Fathers conscript, that you may please to take notice it was foretold some horrid sedition is at hand, we shall only desire that they whose valour in this place is so great may stand by us to see how we behave ourselves, and then be as resolute in your commands as you will. Your fatherhoods may know if we be wanting in the performance.'

At this, some of the hot bloods returned with the consuls unto the tribunal, before which the people were yet standing; and the consuls, having generally required names in vain, (to put it into something) required the name of one that was in their eye particularly, on whom, when he moved not, they commanded a lictor to lay hands. But the people, thronging about the party summoned, forbade the lictor, who durst not touch him; at which the hotspurs that came with the consuls, enraged by the affront, descended from the throne to the aid of the lictor, from whom, in so doing, they turned the indignation of the people upon themselves with such heat that the consuls, interposing, thought fit by remitting the assembly to appease the tumult; in which nevertheless there had been nothing but noise. Nor was there less in the senate, being suddenly rallied upon this occasion, where they that received the repulse, with others whose heads were as addled as their own, fell upon the business as if it had been to be determined by clamour, till the consuls, upbraiding the senate that it differed not from the market place, reduced the house unto orders; and the fathers having been consulted accordingly, there were three opinions. P. Virginius conceived that the consideration to be had upon the matter in question (or aid of the indebted and imprisoned people) was not to be farther extended than unto such as had engaged upon the promise made by Servilius; T. Largius, that it was no time to think it enough if men's merits were acknowledged, while the whole people, sunk under the weight of their debts, could not emerge without some common aid, which to restrain by putting some into a better condition than others, would rather more inflame the discord than extinguish it. Appius Claudius (still upon the old haunt) would have it that the people were rather wanton than fierce; it was not oppression that necessitated, but their power that invited them unto these freaks; the empire of the consuls, since the appeal unto the people (whereby a plebeian might ask his fellows if he were a thief), being but a mere scarecrow. 'Go to', says he, 'let us create the dictator, from whom there is no appeal, and then let me see more of this work; or him that shall forbid my lictor.' The advice of Appius was abhorred by many, and to introduce a general rescission of debts with Largius was to violate all faith. That of Virginius as the most moderate would have passed best, but that there were private interests (that same bane of the public) which withstood it; so they concluded with Appius, who also had been dictator, if the consuls and some of the graver sort had not thought it altogether unseasonable, at a time when the Volsci and the Sabines were up again, to venture so far upon alienation of the people; for which cause Valerius, being descended from the Publicolas, the most popular family, as also in his own person of a mild nature, was rather trusted with so rigid a magistracy. Whence it happened that the people, though they knew well enough against whom the dictator was created, feared nothing from Valerius, but, upon a new promise made to the same effect with that of Servilius, hoped better another time and, throwing away all disputes, gave their names roundly, went out and (to be brief) came home again as victorious as in the former action, the dictator entering the city in triumph. Nevertheless, when he came to press the senate to make good his promise and do something for the ease of the people, they regarded him no more as to that point than they had done Servilius. Whereupon the dictator, in disdain to be made a stale, abdicated his magistracy and went home. Here then was a victorious army without a captain, and a senate pulling it by the beard in their gowns. What is it (if you have read the story, for there is not such another) that must follow? Can any man imagine that such only should be the opportunity upon which this people could run away? Alas, poor men, the Aequi and the Volsci and the Sabines were nothing, but the fathers invincible! There they sat, some three hundred of them, armed all in robes and thundering with their tongues; no hopes in the earth to reduce them unto any tolerable conditions. Wherefore, not thinking to abide long so near them, away marches the army, and encamps in the fields. This retreat of the people is called the secession of Mount Aventine, where they lodged, very sad at their condition, but not letting fall so much as a word of murmur against the fathers. The senate by this time were great lords, had the whole city unto themselves; but certain neighbours were upon the way that might come to speak with them, not asking leave of the porter. Wherefore their minds became troubled, and an orator was posted unto the people to make as good conditions with them as he could but, whatever the terms were, to bring them home and with all speed. And here it was covenanted between the senate and the people that these should have the magistrates of their own election, called the tribunes; upon which they returned.

To hold you no longer, the senate, having done this upon necessity, made frequent attempts to retract it again; while the tribunes on the other side, to defend what they had gotten, instituted their *tributa comitia*, or council of the people, where they came in time, and as disputes increased, to make laws without the authority of the senate, called *plebiscita*. Now to conclude in the point at which I drive, such were the steps whereby the people of

Rome came to assume debate; nor is it in art or nature to debar a people of the like effect, where there is the like cause. For Romulus, having in the election of his senate squared out a nobility for the support of a throne, by making that of the patrician a distinct and hereditary order, planted the commonwealth upon two contrary interests or roots which, shooting forth in time, produced two commonwealths, the one oligarchical in the nobility, and the other a mere anarchy of the people, which thenceforth caused a perpetual feud and enmity between the senate and the people, even to death.

There is not a more noble or useful question in the politics than that which is started by Machiavel: whether means were to be found whereby the enmity that was between the senate and the people of Rome might have been removed.[56] Nor is there any other in which we, or the present occasion, are so much concerned, particularly in relation unto this author; for as much as, his judgment in the determination of the question standing, our commonwealth falleth. And he that will erect a commonwealth against the judgment of Machiavel is obliged to give such reasons for his enterprise as must not go on begging. Wherefore to repeat the politician very honestly but somewhat more briefly, he disputes thus:[57]

> There be two sorts of commonwealth: the one for preservation, as Lacedaemon and Venice; the other for increase, as Rome.
>
> Lacedaemon, being governed by a king and a small senate, could maintain itself a long time in that condition because the inhabitants, being few, having put a bar upon the reception of strangers, and living in strict observation of the laws of Lycurgus – which now had gotten reputation and taken away all occasion of tumults – might well continue long in tranquillity. For the laws of Lycurgus introduced a greater equality in estates, and a less equality in honours; whence there was equal poverty, and the plebeians were less ambitious because the

---

[56] *Discorsi*, I, 6.

[57] The paraphrase is essentially of *Discorsi*, I, 6, with a few elements of the preceding chapter. The effect of H's condensation is to make the whole study hang more directly upon the distinction between static commonwealths and commonwealths for increase, and to make the analysis of Venice follow that of Sparta, instead of preceding it and standing slightly outside the argument as it does in Machiavelli.

honours, or magistracies of the city, could extend but unto a few and were not communicable unto the people; nor did the nobility, by using them ill, ever give them a desire to participate of the same. This proceeded from the kings, whose principality, being placed in the midst of the nobility, had no greater means whereby to support itself than to shield the people from all injury; whence the people, not fearing empire,[58] desired it not. And so all occasion of enmity between the senate and the people was barred. But this union happened especially from two causes: the one that the inhabitants of Lacedaemon, being few, could be governed by the few. The other that, not receiving strangers into their commonwealth, they did not corrupt it, nor increase it unto such a proportion as was not governable by the few.

Venice hath not divided with her plebeians, but all are called gentlemen that be in administration of the government; for which government she is more beholding unto chance than the wisdom of her law-makers. For – many retiring unto those islands where that city is now built, from the inundations of barbarians that overwhelmed the Roman Empire – when they were increased unto such a number that to live together it was necessary to have laws, they ordained a form of government whereby, assembling often in council upon affairs and finding their number sufficient for government, they put a bar upon all such as, repairing afterwards to their city, should become inhabitants, excluding them from participation of power. Whence they that were included in the administration had right, and they that were excluded, coming afterwards and being received upon no other conditions to be inhabitants, had no wrong, and therefore had no occasions – nor were they trusted with arms, and therefore had no means – to be tumultuous. Wherefore this commonwealth might very well maintain herself in tranquillity.

These things considered, it is plain that the Roman legislators, to have introduced a quiet state, must have done one of these two things: either shut out strangers, as the Lacedaemonians; or, as the Venetians, not allowed the people to bear arms. But they did neither. By which means the people, having power and increase, were in perpetual tumult. Nor is this to be helped in a commonwealth for increase, seeing if Rome had cut off the occasion of her tumults, she

[58] 'Empire' is here, and frequently, used in the sense in which *imperium* means 'authority'.

must have cut off the means of her increase, and by consequence of her greatness.

Wherefore let a legislator consider with himself whether he would make his commonwealth for preservation, in which case she may be free from tumults; or for increase, in which case she must be infested with them.

If he make her for preservation she may be quiet at home, but will be in danger abroad. First, because her foundation must be narrow and therefore weak; as that of Lacedaemon, which lay but upon thirty thousand citizens, or that of Venice, which lies but upon three thousand. Secondly, such a commonwealth must either be in peace, or in war. If she be in peace, the few are soonest effeminated and corrupted, and so obnoxious also unto faction; if in war, succeeding ill, she is an easy prey, or, succeeding well, ruined by increase, a weight which her foundation is not able to bear. For Lacedaemon, when she had made herself mistress, upon the matter, of all Greece, through a slight accident – the rebellion of Thebes, occasioned by the conspiracy of Pelopidas, discovering this infirmity of her nature – the rest of her conquered cities immediately knocked off, and in the turn as it were of an hand reduced her from the fullest tide unto the lowest ebb of fortune. And Venice, having possessed herself of a great part of Italy by her purse, was no sooner, in defence of it, put unto the trial of her arms, than she lost all in one battle.

Whence I conclude that, in the ordination of a commonwealth, a legislator is to think upon that which is most honourable and, laying aside the models for preservation, to follow the example of Rome; conniving at and temporizing with the enmity between the senate and the people, as a necessary step unto the Roman greatness. For that any man should find out a balance that may take in the conveniences and shut out the inconveniences of both, I do not think it possible.

These are the words of the author, though the method be somewhat altered, to the end that I may the better turn them unto my hand.

My lords, I do not know how you hearken unto this sound, but to hear the greatest artist in the modern world giving sentence against our commonwealth is that with which I am nearly concerned. Wherefore, with the honour due unto the prince of politicians, let us examine his ratiocination, with the liberty which he hath asserted to be the right of a free people. But we shall never come up to him except, by taking the business a little lower, we descend from effects to their causes. The causes of commotion in a commonwealth are either external or internal. External are from enemies, from subjects, or from servants. To dispute then what was the cause why Rome was infested by the Italian or by the servile wars; why the slaves took the Capitol; why the Lacedaemonians were near as frequently troubled with their helots as Rome with all those; or why Venice, whose situation is not trusted unto the faith of men, hath as good or better quarter with them whom she governeth than Rome had with the Latins, were to dispute upon external causes. The question put by Machiavel is of internal causes: whether the enmity that was between the senate and the people of Rome might have been removed; and to determine otherwise of this question than he doth, I must lay down other principles than he hath. To which end I affirm, that a commonwealth internally considered is either equal, or unequal. A commonwealth that is internally equal hath no internal cause of commotion, and therefore can have no such effect but from without. A commonwealth internally unequal hath no internal cause of quiet, and therefore can have no such effect but by diversion.

To prove my assertions, I shall at this time make use of no other than his examples. Lacedaemon was externally unquiet because she was externally unequal, that is as to her helots, and she was internally at rest because she was equal in herself, both in root and branch; in the root by her agrarian, and in branch by the senate, inasmuch as no man was thereunto qualified but by election of the people. Which institution of Lycurgus is mentioned by Aristotle, where he saith that, rendering his citizens emulous (not careless) of that honour, he designed unto the people the election of the senate.[59] Wherefore Machiavel, in this as in other places, having his eye upon the division of patrician and plebeian families as they were in Rome, hath quite mistaken the orders of this commonwealth, where there was no such thing. Nor did the quiet of it derive from the power of the kings, who were so far from shielding

[59] 'Arist. Pol. B. 2' – H's note. Perhaps II, ix, 28.

the people from injury of the nobility, of which there was none in his sense but the senate, that one declared end of the senate at the institution was to shield the people from the kings, who thenceforth had but single votes. Neither did it proceed from the straitness of the senate, or their keeping the people aloof from the government, that they were quiet, but from the equality of their administrations; seeing the senate (as is plain by the oracle, their fundamental law) had no more than the debate, and the result of the commonwealth belonged unto the people. Wherefore when Theopompus and Polydore, kings of Lacedaemon, would have kept the people aloof from the government by adding unto the ancient law this clause, *si prave populus rogassit, senatui regibusque retractandi jus esto* (if the determination of the people be faulty, it shall be lawful for the senate to resume the debate), the people immediately became unquiet and resumed that debate, which ended not till they had set up their ephors and caused that magistracy to be confirmed by their kings.

Theopompo Spartanorum regi moderationis testimonium reddamus. Nam cum primus instituisset ut ephori Lacedaemone crearentur, ita futuri regiae potestati oppositi, quemadmodum Romae tribuni plebis consulari imperio sunt objecti; atque illi uxor dixisset, id egisse illum ut filiis minorem potestatem relinqueret; relinquam, inquit, sed diuturniorem. Optime quidem. Ea enim demum tuta est potentia, quae viribus suis modum imponit. Theopompus igitur legitimis regnum vinculis constringendo, quo longius a licentia retraxit, hoc propius ad benevolentiam civium admovit.[60]

By which it may appear that a commonwealth for preservation, if she come to be unequal, is as obnoxious unto enmity between the senate and the people as a commonwealth for increase; and that the tranquillity of Lacedaemon derived from no other cause than her equality.

For Venice, to say that she is quiet because she disarms her subjects is to forget that Lacedaemon disarmed her helots, and yet could not in their regard be quiet; wherefore, if Venice be defended from external causes of commotion, it is first through her situation, in which respect her subjects have no hope (and this indeed may be attributed unto her fortune) and secondly, through her exquisite justice, whence they have no will to invade her. But

---

[60] Valerius Maximus, *Facta et Dicta Memorabilia*, IV, i, 8.

this can be attributed to no other cause than her prudence, which will appear to be greater as we look nearer; for the effects that proceed from fortune (if there be any such thing) are like their cause, unconstant; but there never happened unto any other commonwealth, so undisturbed and constant a tranquillity and peace in herself, as in that of Venice; wherefore this must proceed from some other cause than chance. And we see that as she is of all others the most quiet, so the most equal commonwealth. Her body consists of one order, and her senate is like a rolling stone (as was said) which never did nor, while it continues upon that rotation, ever shall gather the moss of a divided or ambitious interest; much less such an one as that which grasped the people of Rome in the talons of their own eagles. And if Machiavel, averse from doing this commonwealth right, had considered her orders (as his reader shall easily perceive he never did), he must have been so far from attributing the prudence of them unto chance that he would have touched up his admirable work unto that perfection which, as to the civil part, hath no pattern in the universal world but this of Venice.

Rome, secure by her potent and victorious arms from all external causes of commotion, was either beholding for her peace at home unto her enemies abroad, or could never rest her head. My lords, you that are parents of a commonwealth, and so freer agents than such as are mere natural, have a care. For, as no man shall show me a commonwealth born straight that ever became crooked, so no man shall show me a commonwealth born crooked that ever became straight. Rome was crooked in her birth, or rather prodigious; her twins the patricians and plebeian orders came, as was shown by the foregoing story, into the world one body but two heads, or rather two bellies; for, notwithstanding the fable out of Aesop whereby Menenius Agrippa, the orator that was sent from the senate unto the people at Mount Aventine, showed the fathers to be the belly and the people to be the arms and the legs, which except that, how slothful soever it might seem, were nourished, not these but the whole body must languish and be dissolved; it is plain that the fathers were a distinct belly, such an one as took the meat indeed out of the people's mouths but, abhorring the agrarian, returning it not in the due and necessary nutrition of a commonwealth. Nevertheless, as the people that live about the cataracts of Nilus are said not to hear the noise, so neither the Roman writers, nor Machiavel the most conversant with them, seem among so many of the tribunician storms to hear their natural voice; for though they could not miss of it so far as to attribute them unto the strife of the people for participation in magistracy or, in which Machiavel more particularly joins, unto that about the agrarian, this was to take the business short, and the remedy for the disease. *Cujus levamen mali, plebes, nisi suis in summo imperio locatis nullum speraret.*[61]

A people, when they are reduced unto misery and despair, become their own politicians, as certain beasts when they are sick become their own physicians and are carried by a natural instinct unto the desire of such herbs as are their proper cure; but the people, for the greater part, are beneath the beasts in the use of them. Thus the people of Rome, though in their misery they had recourse, by instinct as it were, unto the two main fundamentals of a commonwealth, participation of magistracy and the agrarian, did but taste and spit at them, not (which is necessary in physic) drink down the potion and in that their healths. For when they had obtained participation of magistracy, it was but lamely, not to a full and equal rotation in all elections; nor did they greatly regard it in so much as they had gotten. And when they had attained unto the agrarian, they neglected it so far as to suffer the law to grow obsolete. But if you do not take the due dose of your medicines (as there be slight tastes which a man may have of philosophy that incline unto atheism), it may chance to be poison; there being a like taste of the politics that inclines to confusion, as appears in the institution of the Roman tribunes, by which magistracy, and no more, the people were so far from attaining unto peace that they, in getting but so much, got but heads for eternal feud; whereas if they had attained in perfection either unto the agrarian, they had introduced the equality and calm of Lacedaemon, or unto rotation, they had introduced that of Venice. And so there could have been no more enmity between the senate and the people of Rome than there was between those orders in Lacedaemon or is in Venice.

[61] Livy, VI, xxxv.

Wherefore Machiavel seemeth unto me, in attributing the peace of Venice more unto her luck than her prudence, of the whole stable to have saddled the wrong horse, for thought Rome

> *quae non imitabile fulmen*
> *Aere, et cornupedum cursu similarat equorum*[62]

in her military part could beat it better, beyond all comparison, upon the sounding hoof, Venice, for the civil, hath plainly had the wings of Pegasus.

The whole question then will come upon this point: whether the people of Rome could have obtained these orders. And first, to say that they could not have obtained them without altering the commonwealth is no argument; seeing neither could they, without altering the commonwealth, have obtained their tribunes, which nevertheless were obtained. And if a man consider the posture that the people were in when they obtained their tribunes, they might as well and with as great ease (for as much as the reason why the nobility yielded unto the tribunes was no other than that there was no remedy) have obtained anything else. And for experience, it was in the like case that the Lacedaemonians set up their ephors, and the Athenians after the battle of Plataea bowed the senate (so hard a thing it is for a commonwealth that was born crooked to become straight) as much the other way. Nor, if it be objected that this must have ruined the nobility, and in that deprived the commonwealth of the greatness which she acquired by them, is this opinion holding, but confuted by the sequel of the story, showing plainly that the nobility through the defect of such orders (that is to say, of rotation and the agrarian) came to eat up the people, and battening themselves in luxury, to be as Sallust speaketh of them: *inertissimi nobiles, in quibus sicut in statua, praeter nomen, nihil erat additamenti*;[63] to bring so mighty a commonwealth, so huge a glory, unto so deplorable an end. Wherefore means might have been found, whereby the enmity that was between the senate and the people of Rome might have been removed.

My lords, if I have argued well, I have given you the comfort and assurance that, notwithstanding the judgment of Machiavel, your

---

[62] *Aeneid*, VI, 590f.

[63] Sallust, *Ad Caesarem Senem de Re Publica Epistula* (ascription of authorship doubtful), IX, 4.

commonwealth is both safe and sound; but if I have not argued well, then take the comfort and assurance which he gives you, while he is firm that a legislator is to lay aside all other examples and follow that of Rome only, conniving and temporising with the enmity between the senate and the people as a necessary step unto the Roman greatness. Whence it follows that your commonwealth at the worst is that which he hath given you his word is the best.

I have held your lordships long, but upon an account of no small importance, which I can now sum up in these few words: where there is a liquorishness in a popular assembly to debate, it proceedeth not from the constitution of the people, but of the commonwealth. Now that the commonwealth is of such constitution as is naturally free from this kind of intemperance, is that, which to make good, I must divide the remainder of my discourse into two parts: the first, showing the several constitutions of the assemblies of the people in other commonwealths; the second, comparing of our assembly of the people with theirs, and showing how it excludeth the inconveniences and embraceth the conveniences of them all.

In the beginning of the first part I must take notice that among the popular error of our days it is no small one that men imagine the ancient governments of this kind to have consisted for the most part of one city, that is, of one town; whereas by what we have learned of my lords that opened them, it appears that there was not any considerable one of such a constitution but Carthage, till this in our days of Venice.

For to begin with Israel, it consisted of the twelve tribes, locally spread or quartered throughout the whole territory; these, being called together by trumpets, constituted the church or assembly of the people. The vastness of this weight, as also the slowness thence inavoidable, became a great cause (as hath been shown at large by my lord Phosphorus) of the breaking that commonwealth; not withstanding that the temple, and those religious ceremonies for which the people were at least annually obliged to repair thither, were no small ligament of the tribes, otherwise but slightly tacked together.

Athens consisted of four tribes, taking in the whole people both of the city and of the territory, not so gathered by Theseus into one town as to exclude the country, but to the end that there might be some capital of the commonwealth; though true it be that the congregation, consisting of the inhabitants within the walls, was sufficient to all intents and purposes, without those of the country. These also, being exceeding numerous, became burdensome unto themselves and dangerous unto the commonwealth; the more for their ill education, as is observed by Xenophon and Polybius, who compare them unto mariners, that in a calm are perpetually disputing and swaggering one with another, and never lay their hands unto the common tackling or safety till they be all endangered by some storm. Which caused Thucydides, when he saw this people, through the purchase of their misery, become so much wiser as to reduce their *comitia* or assemblies unto five thousand, to say, as in his eighth book; 'and now (at least in my time) the Athenians seem to have ordered their state aright; consisting of a moderate temper both of the few (by which he means the senate of the bean) and of the many, or the five thousand'; and he doth not only give you his judgment, but the best proof of it, for 'this', saith he, 'was the first thing that after so many misfortunes passed, made the city again to raise her head'.[64] The place I would desire your lordships to note, as the first example that I find, or think is to be found, of a popular assembly by way of representative.

Lacedaemon consisted of thirty thousand citizens dispersed throughout Laconia, one of the greatest provinces in all Greece, and divided (as by some authors is probable) into six tribes. Of the whole body of these, being gathered, consisted the great church or assembly, which had the legislative power; the little church, gathered sometimes for matters of concernment within the city, consisted of the Spartans only. These happened like that of Venice to be good constitutions of a congregation, but from an ill cause: the infirmity of a commonwealth which through her paucity was oligarchical.

Wherefore, go which way you will, it should seem that, without a representative of the people, your commonwealth consisting of an whole nation can never avoid falling either into oligarchy or confusion.

This was seen by the Romans, whose rustic tribes, extending themselves from the river Arno unto the Vulturnus, that is from

---

[64] Thucydides, VIII, 97, in Hobbes's translation.

Fesulae or Florence unto Capua, invented a way of representative by lots; the tribe upon which the first fell being the prerogative, and some two or three more that had the rest, the *jure vocatae*. These gave the suffrage of the commonwealth *binis comitiis*; the prerogative at the first assembly, and the *jure vocatae* at a second.

Now, to make the parallel, all the inconveniences that you have observed in these assemblies are shut out, and all the conveniences taken in, to your prerogative; for first, it is that for which Athens, shaking off the blame of Xenophon and Polybius, came to deserve the praise of Thucydides, a representative; and secondly, not – as I suspect in that of Athens, and is past suspicion in this of Rome – by lot, but by suffrage, as was also the late house of commons, by which means in the prerogatives all the tribes of Oceana are *jure vocatae*. And if a man shall except against the paucity of the standing number, it is a wheel which in the revolution of a few years turneth every hand that is fit, or fitteth every hand that it turns, unto the public work. Moreover, I am deceived if, upon due consideration, it do not fetch your tribes with greater equality and ease unto themselves and unto the government, from the frontiers of Marpesia, than Rome ever brought any one of hers out of her *pomoeria*, or the nearest parts of her adjoining territories. To this you may add that, whereas a commonwealth, which in regard of the people is not of facility in execution, were sure enough in this nation to be cast off through impatience, your musters and galaxies are given unto the people as milk unto babes, whereby, when they are brought up through four days' election in an whole year (one at the parish, one at the hundred, and two at the tribe) unto their strongest meat, it is of no harder digestion than to give their negative or affirmative as they see cause. There be gallant men among us that laugh at such appeal or umpire, but I refer it, whether you be more inclining to pardon them or me, who I confess have been this day laughing at a sober man, but without meaning him any harm; and that is Petrus Cunaeus,[65] where speaking of the nature of the people, he saith that 'taking them apart, they are very simple, but yet in their assemblies they see and know something', and so runs away without troubling himself with

---

[65] Petrus Cunaeus, *De Republica Hebraeorum* (Leyden, 1631), I, 12. Liljegren doubted whether H used the English translation of 1653. One might ask why Cunaeus is derided for a simple adaptation of Aristotle, *Politics*, III, xi, 2–3.

what that something is. Whereas the people, taken apart, are but so many private interests, but if you take them together they are the public interest; the public interest of a commonwealth (as hath been shown) is nearest that of mankind, and that of mankind is right reason. But with the aristocracy, whose reason or interest, when they are all together, as appeared by the patricians, is but that of a party, it is quite contrary; for, as taken apart they are far wiser than the people, considered in that manner, so, being put together, they are such fools that by deposing the people, as did those of Rome, they will saw off the branch whereupon they sit, or rather destroy the root of their own greatness. Wherefore Machiavel, following Aristotle, and yet going before him, may well assert *che la multitudine è più savia e più costante che un principe*:[66] the prerogative of popular government for wisdom. And hence it is that the prerogative of your commonwealth, as for wisdom, so for power, is in the people; which (albeit I am not ignorant, that the Roman prerogative was so called *a praerogando*, because their suffrage was first asked) gives the denomination unto your prerogative tribe.

The elections, whether annual or triennial, being shown by the twenty-second, that which comes in the next place to be considered is

The twenty-third order: showing the power, function, and manner of proceeding of the prerogative tribe.

The power or function of the prerogative is of two parts: the one of result, in which it is the legislative power, the other of judicature, in which regard it is the highest court and the last appeal in this commonwealth.

For the former part, the people by this constitution being not obliged by any law that is not of their own making or confirmation by the result of the prerogative, their equal representative, it shall not be lawful for the senate to require obedience from the people, nor for the people to give due obedience unto the senate, in or by any law that hath not been promulgated or printed and published for the space of six weeks and afterwards proposed by the authority of the senate unto the prerogative tribe, and resolved by the major vote of the same in the affirmative. Nor shall the senate have any power to levy war, men or money, otherwise than by the consent of the people so given, or by a law so enacted, except in

[66] *Discorsi*, I, 58.

166

cases of exigence, in which it is agreed that the power, both of the senate and the people, shall be in the dictator, so qualified and for such a term of time as is according unto that constitution already prescribed. While a law is in promulgation the censors shall animadvert upon the senate, and the tribunes upon the people, that there be no laying of heads together, conventicles or canvassing to carry on or oppose anything, but that all may be done in a free and open way.

For the latter part of the power of the prerogative, or that whereby they are the supreme judicatory of this nation, and of the provinces of the same, the cognizance of crimes against the majesty of the people, as high treason, as also of peculation, that is robbery of the treasury or defraudation of the commonwealth, appertaineth unto this tribe, and if any person or persons, provincials or citizens, shall appeal unto the people, it belongeth unto the prerogative to judge and determine the case; provided that if the appeal be from any court of justice in this nation or the provinces, the appellant shall first deposit one hundred pounds in the court from which he appealeth, to be forfeited unto the same if he be cast in his suit by the people. But the power of the council of war, being the expedition of this commonwealth, and the martial law of the strategus in the field, are those only from which there shall lie no appeal unto the people.

The proceeding of the prerogative, in case of a proposition, is to be thus ordered: the magistrates, proposing by authority of the senate, shall rehearse the whole matter and expound it unto the people; which done, they shall put the whole together unto the suffrage with three boxes, the negative, the affirmative, and the non-sincere, and the suffrage being returned unto the tribunes, and numbered in the presence of the proposers, if the major vote be in the non-sincere, the proposers shall desist and the senate shall resume the debate. If the major vote be in the negative, the proposers shall desist, and the senate too. But if the major vote be in the affirmative, then the tribe is clear, and the proposers shall begin and put the whole matter, with the negative and the affirmative (leaving out the non-sincere) by clauses; and the suffrages, being taken and numbered by the tribunes in the presence of the proposers, shall be written and reported by the tribunes unto the senate; and that which is proposed by the authority of the senate, and confirmed by the command of the people, is the law of Oceana.

The proceeding of the prerogative in a case of judicature is to be thus ordered. The tribunes, being auditors of all causes appertaining unto the cognizance of the people, shall have notice of the suit or trial, whether of appeal or otherwise, that is to be commenced, and if any one of them shall accept of the same it appertaineth unto him to introduce it. A cause being introduced and the people mustered or assembled for the decision of the same, the tribunes are presidents of the court, having power to keep it unto orders, and shall be seated upon a scaffold erected in the middle of the tribe; upon the right hand shall stand a seat or large pulpit, assigned unto the plaintiff or the accuser, and upon the left another for the defendant, each if they please with his counsel. And the tribunes, being attended upon such occasions with so many ballotines, secretaries, door-keepers and messengers of the senate as shall be requisite, one of them shall turn up a glass of the nature of an hour-glass, but such an one as is to be of an hour and a half's running; which being turned up, the party or counsel on the right hand may begin to speak to the people. If there be papers to be read, or witnesses to be examined, the officer shall lay the glass sideways until the papers be read and the witnesses examined, and then turn it up again; and so long as the glass is running the party on the right hand hath liberty to speak, and no longer. The party on the right hand having had his time, the like shall be done in every respect for the party on the left. And the cause being thus heard, the tribunes shall put the question unto the tribe with a white, a black and a red box (or non-sincere): whether guilty, or not guilty. And if, the suffrage being taken, the major vote be in the non-sincere, the cause shall be reheard upon the next juridical day following and put unto the question in the same manner. If the major vote come the second time in the non-sincere, the cause shall be heard again upon the third day; but at the third hearing the question shall be put without the non-sincere. Upon the first of the three days in which the major vote comes in the white box, the party accused is absolved; and upon the first of them in which it comes in the black box, the party accused is condemned. The party accused being condemned, the tribunes, if the case be criminal, shall put with the white and the black box these questions, or such of them as, regard had unto the case, they shall conceive most proper:

1. Whether he shall have a writ of ease.
2. Whether he shall be fined so much, or so much.
3. Whether he shall be confiscated.
4. Whether he shall be rendered incapable of magistracy.

5. Whether he shall be banished.
6. Whether he shall be put to death.

These or any three of these questions, whether simple or such as shall be thought fitly mixed, being put by the tribunes, that which hath most above half the votes in the black box is the sentence of the people, which the troop of the third *classis* is to see executed accordingly.

But whereas by the constitution of this commonwealth it may appear that neither the propositions of the senate, nor the judicature of the people, will be so frequent as to hold the prerogative in continual employment; the senate, a main part of whose office it is to teach and instruct the people, shall duly (if they have no greater affairs to divert them) cause an oration to be made unto the prerogative by some knight or magistrate of the senate, to be chosen out of the ablest men, and from time to time appointed by the orator of the house, in the great hall of the Pantheon while the parliament resideth in the town; or in some grove or sweet place in the field, while the parliament for the heat of the year shall reside in the country; upon every Tuesday morning or afternoon.

And the orator appointed *pro tempore* unto this office shall first repeat the orders of the commonwealth with all possible brevity, and then, making choice of one, or some part of it, discourse thereof unto the people. An oration or discourse of this nature, being afterward perused by the council of state, may as they see cause be printed and published.

The Archon's comment upon this order I find to have been of this sense:

My lords:

To crave pardon for a word or two in further explanation of what was read, I shall briefly show how the constitution of this tribe or assembly answers unto their function, and how their function, which is of two parts, the former in the result or legislative power, the latter in the supreme judicature of the commonwealth, answers unto their constitution. Machiavel hath a discourse,[67] where he puts the question, whether the guard of liberty be with more security to be committed unto the nobility, or to the people. Which doubt of his ariseth through the want of explaining his

---

[67] *Discorsi,* I, 5.

term, for 'the guard of liberty' can signify nothing else but the result of the commonwealth; so that to say that the guard of liberty may be committed unto the nobility is to say that the result may be committed unto the senate, in which case the people signify nothing. Now to show it was a mistake to affirm it to have been thus in Lacedaemon, sufficient hath been spoken; and whereas he will have it to be so in Venice also, '*quello*', saith Contarini, '*appresso il quale è la somma autorità di tutta la città e dalle leggi e decreti dei quali pende l'autorità così del senato come ancora di tutti i magistrati, è il consiglio grande*'.[68] It is institutively in the great council by the judgment of all that know that commonwealth, though for the reasons shown it be sometimes exercised by the senate. Nor need I run over the commonwealths in this place for the proof of a thing so doubtless, and such as hath been already made so apparent, as that the result of each was in the popular part of it. The popular part of yours, or the prerogative tribe, consisteth of seven deputies (whereof three are of the horse) annually elected out of every tribe of Oceana, which being fifty, amounteth unto one hundred and fifty horse and two hundred foot; and the prerogative, consisting of three of these lists, consisteth of four hundred and fifty horse, and six hundred foot (besides those of the provinces to be hereafter mentioned), by which means, the over-balance in the suffrage remaining unto the foot by one hundred and fifty votes, you have, unto the support of a true and natural aristocracy, the deepest root of a democracy that hath been planted. Wherefore there is nothing in art or nature better qualified for the result than this assembly. It is noted out of Cicero by Machiavel that the people, albeit they are not so prone to find out the truth of themselves, as to follow custom or run into error, yet, if they be shown truth, they not only acknowledge and embrace it very suddenly, but are the most constant and faithful guardians and conservators of it.[69] It is your duty and office, whereunto you are also qualified by the orders of this commonwealth, to have the people, as you have your hawks and greyhounds, in leases and slips, to range the fields and beat the bushes for them. For they are of a nature that is never good at this sport; but when you spring or start their proper quarry, think not that they will stand to ask you what it is, or less know it than the

---

[68] Contarini, p. ix *bis*, slightly misquoted.   [69] *Discorsi*, I, 4.

hawks and greyhounds do theirs, but forthwith make such a flight
or course that a huntsman may as well undertake to run with his
dogs, or a falconer to fly with his hawk, as an aristocracy at this
game to compare with the people. The people of Rome were
seized upon no less prey than the empire of the world, when the
nobility turned tails and perched among daws upon the tower of
monarchy. For though they did not all of them intend the thing,
they would none of them endure the remedy, which was the
agrarian.

But the prerogative tribe hath not only the result, but is the
supreme judicature and the ultimate appeal in this commonwealth.
For the popular government that makes account to be of any
standing must make sure in the first place of the appeal unto the
people. *Ante omnes de provocatione adversus magistratus ad populum,
sacrandoque cum bonis capite ejus, qui regni occupandi concilia inesset.*[70]
As an estate in trust becomes a man's own if he be not answerable
for it, so, the power of a magistracy not accountable unto the
people from whom it was received becoming of private use, the
commonwealth loses her liberty. Wherefore the right of supreme
judicature in the people (without which there can be no such thing
as popular government) is confirmed by the constant practice of all
commonwealths, as that of Israel in the cases of Achan and of the
tribe of Benjamin, adjudged by the congregation. The *dicasterion*
or court called the Heliaia in Athens, which (the *comitia* of that
commonwealth consisting of the whole people, and so being too
numerous to be a judicatory) was constituted sometimes of five
hundred, at others of one thousand or, according to the greatness
of the cause, of fifteen hundred, elected by the lot out of the whole
body of the people, and had, with the nine archons that were
presidents, the cognisance of such causes as were of highest
importance in that state. The five ephors in Lacedaemon, which
were popular magistrates, might question their kings; as appears
by the cases of Pausanias and of Agis, who, being upon his trial in
this court, was cried unto by his mother to appeal unto the people,
as Plutarch hath it in his life. The tribunes of the people of Rome –
like, in their nature of their magistracy and for some time in
number, unto the ephors (as being, according unto Halicarnassus

[70] Livy, II, viii.

and Plutarch, instituted in imitation of them) – had power *diem dicere*, to summon any man, his magistracy at least being expired (for from the dictator there lay no appeal), to answer for himself unto the people. As in the case of Coriolanus, which was going about to force the people, by withholding corn from them in a famine, to relinquish the magistracy of the tribunes; in that of Sp. Cassius for affecting tyranny; of M. Sergius for running away at Veii; of C. Lucretius for spoiling his province; of Junius Silanus for making war against the Cimbri *injussu populi*; with divers others. And the crimes of this nature were called *laesae majestatis*. Examples of such as were arraigned, or tried for peculation or defraudation of the commonwealth, were M. Curius, for intercepting the money of the Samnites; Salinator, for the unequal division of spoils unto his soldiers; M. Posthumius, for cheating the commonwealth by a feigned shipwreck. Causes of these two kinds were of more public nature, but the like power upon appeals was also exercised by the people in private matters, even during the time of the kings, as in the case of Horatius. Nor is it otherwise with Venice, where Doge Loredano was sentenced by the great council, and Antonio Grimani, afterwards Doge, questioned for that he, being admiral, had suffered the Turk to take Lepanto in view of his fleet.

Nevertheless, there lay no appeal from the Roman dictator unto the people, which if there had, might have cost the commonwealth dear, when Sp. Melius, affecting empire, circumvented and debauched the tribunes; whereupon T. Quintius Cincinnatus was created dictator, who, having chosen Servilius Ahala to be his lieutenant or *magister equitum*, sent him to apprehend Melius, whom, while he disputed the commands of the dictator and implored the aid of the people, Ahala cut off upon the place. By which example you may see in what cases the dictator may prevent the blow, which is ready sometimes to fall ere the people be aware of the danger. Wherefore there lies no appeal from the *dieci* in Venice unto the great council, or from our council of war to the people. For the way of proceeding of this tribe, or the ballot, it is, as was once said for all, Venetian.

This discourse *de judiciis* whereupon we are fallen bringeth us, rather naturally than of design, from the two general orders of every commonwealth – that is to say, from the debating part, or the senate, and the resolving part, or the people – to the third, which is the executive part, or the magistracy, whereupon I shall have no need to dwell. For the executive magistrates of this commonwealth are the strategus in arms, the signory in their several courts (as the chancery, the exchequer), as also the councils in divers cases within their instructions, the censors, as well in their proper magistracy as in the council of religion, the tribunes in the government of the prerogative, and that judicatory, and the judges with their courts; of all which so much is already said or known as may suffice.

The Tuesday lectures or orations unto the people will be of great benefit unto the senate, the prerogative and the whole nation. Unto the senate, because they will not only teach your senators elocution, but keep the system of the government in their memories. Elocution is of great use unto your senators; for if they do not understand rhetoric (giving it at this time for granted, that the art were not otherwise good), and come to treat with or vindicate the cause of the commonwealth against some other nation that is good at it, the advantage will be subject to remain upon the merit of the art, and not upon the merit of the cause. Furthermore, the genius or soul of this government being in the whole and in every part, they will never be of ability in determination upon any particular, unless at the same time they have an idea of the whole. That this therefore must be, in that regard, of equal benefit unto the prerogative, is plain; though these have a greater concernment in it. For this commonwealth is the estate of the people, and a man (you know) though he be virtuous, yet, if he do not understand his estate, may run out or be cheated of it. Last of all, the treasures of the politics will by this means be so opened, rifled, and dispersed that this nation will as soon dote like the Indians upon glass beads, as disturb your government with whimsies and freaks of mother-wit, or suffer themselves to be stuttered[71] out of their liberties. There is not any reason why your grandees, your wise men of this age, that laugh out and openly at a commonwealth as the most ridiculous thing, do not appear to be, as in this regard they are, mere idiots, but that the people have not eyes.

There remaineth no more pertaining unto the senate and the people, than

---

[71] This might be 'fluttered'; but *sic* in both C and P.

The twenty-fourth order: whereby it is lawful for the province of Marpesia to have thirty knights of their own election continually present in the senate of Oceana together with sixty deputies of horse and one hundred and twenty of foot in the prerogative tribe, endowed with equal power (respect had unto their quality and number) in the debate and result of this commonwealth. Provided that they observe the course or rotation of the same by the annual return of ten knights, twenty deputies of the horse and forty of the foot. The like in all respects is lawful for Panopea; and the horse of both the provinces amounting unto one troop and the foot unto one company, one captain and one cornet of the horse shall be annually chosen by Marpesia, and one captain and one ensign of the foot shall be annually chosen by Panopea.

The orb of the prerogative, being thus complete, is not unnaturally compared unto that of the moon; either in consideration of the light, borrowed from the senate as from the sun, or of the ebbs and floods of the people, which are marked by the negative or affirmative of this tribe. And the constitution of the senate and the people being shown, you have that of the parliament of Oceana, consisting of the senate proposing and of the people resolving, which amounts unto an act of parliament. So the parliament is the heart which, consisting of two ventricles, the one greater and replenished with a grosser store, the other less and full of a purer, sucketh in and gusheth forth the life blood of Oceana by a perpetual circulation.

Wherefore the life of this government is no more unnatural, or obnoxious for this unto dissolution, than that of a man, nor unto giddiness than the world (seeing the earth, whether it be itself or the heavens that are in rotation, is so far from being giddy that it could not subsist without the motion). But why should not this government be much rather capable of duration and steadiness by a motion? than which God hath ordained no other unto the universal commonwealth of mankind, seeing one generation cometh and another goeth, but the earth remaineth firm for ever;[72] that is, in her proper situation or place, whether she be moved or not moved upon her proper centre. The senate, the people and the magistracy, or the parliament so constituted (as you have seen), is the guardian of this commonwealth, and the husband of such a wife as is elegantly described by Solomon. *She is like the merchant's ship; she bringeth her food from far. She con-*

---

[72] Ecclesiastes, 1: 3; not as in the Authorised Version.

sidereth a field and buyeth it; with the fruit of her hands she planteth a vineyard; she conceiveth that her merchandise is good; she stretcheth forth her hands to the poor; she is not afraid of the snow for her household, for all her household are clothed with scarlet; she maketh herself coverings of her tapestry; her clothing is silk and purple; her husband is known by his robes in the gates, when he sitteth amongst the senators of the land.[73] The gates, or inferior courts, were branches, as it were, of the Sanhedrim or senate of Israel. Nor is our commonwealth a worse housewife, or hath she less regard unto her magistrates; as may appear by:

The twenty-fifth order: that, whereas the public revenue is through the late civil wars dilapidated, the excise, being improved or improveable to the revenue of one million, be applied for the space of eleven years to come unto the reparation of the same, and the present maintenance of the magistrates, knights, deputies and other officers who, according unto their several dignities and functions, shall annually receive towards the support of the same, as followeth:

The lord strategus, marching,[74] is upon another account to have field pay as general.

	£ per annum
The lord strategus sitting	2,000
The lord orator	2,000
The three commissioners of the seal	4,500
The three commissioners of the treasury	4,500
The two censors	3,000
The 290 knights, at 500£ a man	145,000
The 4 ambassadors in ordinary	12,000
The council of war for intelligence	3,000
The master of the ceremonies	500
The master of the horse	500
His substitute	150
The 12 ballotines for their winter liveries	240
For their summer liveries	120
For their board-wages	480
For the keeping of three coaches of state, 24 coach-horses with coachmen, and postillions	1,500

---

[73] Proverbs, 31. The words 'by his robes' are not in the Authorised Version and there are other variants, e.g. 'senators' for 'elders'.

[74] I.e. 'in the field'. Cf. the distinction between a 'marching' and a 'standing' army, pp. 288, 303, 316, in Harrington: 1977.

£ per annum

For the grooms and keeping of 16 great horses for the master of the horse; and for the ballotines whom he is to govern and instruct in the art of riding	480
The 20 secretaries of the parliament	2,000
The 20 door-keepers who are to attend with pole-axes, for their coats	200
For their board-wages	1,000
The 20 messengers, which are trumpeters: for their coats	200
For their board-wages	1,000
For ornament of the musters of the youth	5,000

Sum   189,370

Out of the personal estates of every man who at his death bequeatheth not above forty shillings unto the muster of that hundred wherein it lies, shall be levied one per cent, until the solid revenue unto the muster of the hundred amount unto fifty pounds per annum, for the prizes of the youth.

The twelve ballotines are to be divided into three regions according unto the course of the senate, the four of the first region to be elected at the tropic out of such children as the knights of the same shall offer, not being under eleven years of age nor above thirteen. And their election shall be made by the lot at an urn set by the sergeant of the horse for that purpose in the hall of the Pantheon. The livery of the commonwealth, for the fashion or the colour, may be changed at the election of the strategus according unto his fancy. But every knight during his session shall be bound to give unto his footman, or some one of his footmen, the livery of the commonwealth.

The prerogative tribe shall receive as followeth:

£ by the week

The 2 tribunes of the horse	14
The 2 tribunes of the foot	12
The 3 captains of horse	15
The 3 cornets	9
The 3 captains of foot	12
The 3 ensigns	7

The 442 horse at £2 a man	884
The 592 foot at £1 10s. a man	888
The 6 trumpeters	7–10s.
The three drummers	2–5s.

Sum by the week	1,850–15s.

Sum by the year	96,239–0s.

The total of the senate, the
people and the magistracy   287,459–15s.[75]

The dignity of the commonwealth, and aids of the several magistracies and offices thereunto belonging, being provided for as aforesaid, the overplus of the excise with the product of the sum arising shall be carefully managed by the senate and the people through the diligence of the officers of the exchequer, till it amount unto eight millions, or to the purchase of about four hundred thousand pounds solid revenue. At which time, the term of eleven years being expired, the excise (except if it be otherwise ordered by the senate and the people) shall be totally remitted and abolished forever.

At this institution the taxes (as will better appear in the Corollary) were abated about one half, which made the order, when it came to be tasted, to be of good relish with the people in the very beginning, though the advantages then were nowise comparable unto the consequences to be hereafter shown. Nevertheless, my lord Epimonus, who with much ado had been held till now, found it midsummer moon, and broke out of bedlam in this mood:

My lord Archon:
I have a singing in my head like that of a cartwheel, my brains are upon a rotation, and some are so merry that a man cannot speak his griefs; but if your high-shod prerogative, and those same slouching fellows your tribunes, do not take my lord strategus's and my lord orator's heads, and jole them together under the canopy, then let me be ridiculous unto all posterity. For here is a

---

[75] This figure is arrived at by adding together the annual sum given on p. 288, the weekly *and* the yearly figures calculated as due the prerogative tribe. It is difficult to see how this can be justified.

commonwealth to which, if a man should take that of the prentices
in their ancient administration of justice at Shrove-tide, it were an
aristocracy. You have set the very rabble with truncheons in their
hands, and the gentry of this nation like cocks with scarlet gills,
and the golden combs of their salaries to boot, lest they should not
be thrown at.

Not a night can I sleep for some horrid apparition or other. One
while these myrmidons are measuring silks by their quarter-staves;
another stuffing their greasy pouches with my lord high treasurer's
jacobuses. For they are above a thousand in arms to three hundred, which, their gowns being pulled over their ears, are but in
their doublets and hose. But what do I speak of a thousand?
There be two thousand in every tribe, that is an hundred thousand
in the whole nation, not only in the posture of an army, but in a
civil capacity sufficient to give us what laws they please. Now
everybody knows that the lower sort of people regard nothing but
money; and you say it is the duty of a legislator to presume all men
to be wicked, wherefore they must fall upon the richer, as they are
an army; or, lest their minds should misgive them in such a villany,
you have given them encouragement that they have a nearer way,
seeing it may be done every whit as well by the overbalancing
power which they have in elections. There is a fair which is annually kept in the centre of these territories, at Kiberton, a town
famous for ale, and frequented by good fellows; where there is a
solemnity of the piper and fiddlers of this nation (I know not
whether Lacedaemon, where the senate kept account of the stops
of the flutes and of the fiddlestrings of that commonwealth, had
any such custom) called the Bull-running; and he that catcheth
and holdeth the bull is the annual and supreme magistrate of that
comitia or congregation, called King Piper, without whose license it
is not lawful for any of those citizens to enjoy the liberty of his
calling, nor is he otherwise legitimately qualified (or *civitate
donatus*) to lead apes or bears in any perambulation of the same.
Mine host of the Bear, in Kiberton, the father of ale and patron of
good football and cudgel-players, hath any time since I can
remember been grand chancellor of this order. Now, say I, seeing
great things arise from small beginnings, what should hinder the
people, prone to their own advantage and loving money, from
having intelligence conveyed unto them by this same King Piper

and his chancellor, with their loyal subjects the minstrels and bearwards, masters of ceremonies, unto which there is great recourse in their respective perambulations, and which they will commission and instruct with directions unto all the tribes, willing and commanding them that, as they wish their own goods, they choose none other into the next *primum mobile* but of the ablest cudgel and football players; which done as soon as said, your *primum mobile*, consisting of no other stuff, must of necessity be drawn forth into your nebulones and your gallimaufries; and so, the silken purses of your senate and prerogative being made of sows' ears, most of them blacksmiths, they will strike while the iron is hot and beat your estates into hobnails, mine host of the Bear being strategus and King Piper lord orator. Well, my lords, it might have been otherwise expressed, but this is well enough a conscience.[76] In your way, the wit of man shall not prevent this or the like inconvenience, but if this (for I have conferred with artists) be a mathematical demonstration, I could kneel to you that, ere it be too late, we might return unto some kind of sobriety.

If we empty our purses with these pomps, salaries, coaches, lacquies and pages, what can the people say less than that we have dressed a senate and a prerogative to nothing but to go unto the park with the ladies?

My Lord Archon, whose meekness resembled that of Moses, vouchsafed this answer:

My lords:
For all this, I can see my lord Epimonus every night in the park, and with ladies; nor do I blame this in a young man, or the respect which is and ought to be given unto a sex that is one half of the commonwealth of mankind, and without which the other would be none. Howbeit, our magistrates, I doubt, may be somewhat with the oldest to perform this part with much acceptation; and *servire e non gradire è cosa da morire*. Wherefore we will lay no certain obligation upon them in this point, but leave them (if it please you) unto their own fate or discretion. But this, for I know my lord Epimonus loves me (and though I can never get his esteem) I will

---

[76] Perhaps 'o' conscience'; 'in all conscience'.

say, if he had a mistress should use him so, he would find it a sad life; or I appeal unto your lordships, how I can resent it from such a friend that he puts King Piper's politics in the balance with mine. King Piper, I deny not, may teach his bears to dance, but they have the worst ear of all creatures. Now how he should make them keep time in fifty several tribes, and that two years together – for else it will be to no purpose – may be a small matter with my lord to promise, but it seemeth unto me of impossible performance, first through the nature of the beast, and secondly through that of the ballot; or what he hath hitherto thought so hard is now come to be easy. But he may think that for expedition they will eat up these balls like apples. However, there is so much more in their way by the constitution of this, than is to be found in that of any other commonwealth, that I am reconciled; it now appearing plainly that the points of my lord's arrows are directed at no other white than to show the excellency of our government above others. Which as he proceeds further is yet plainer, while he makes it appear that there can be no other elected by the people but smiths:

Brontesque Steropesque et nudus membra Pyraemon.[77]

Othniel, Ehud, Gideon, Jephtha, Samson, as in Israel; Miltiades, Aristides, Themistocles, Cimon, Pericles, as in Athens; Papirius, Cincinnatus, Camillus, Fabius, Scipio, as in Rome: smiths of the fortune of the commonwealth, not such as forged hobnails but thunderbolts. Popular elections are of that kind that all the rest of the world is not able either in number or glory to equal those of these three commonwealths. These indeed were the ablest cudgel and football players; bright arms were their cudgels, and the world was the ball that lay at their feet. Wherefore we are not so to understand the maxim of legislators which holdeth all men to be wicked, as if it related to mankind or a commonwealth, the interests whereof are the only straight lines that they have whereby to reform the crooked, but as it relates unto every man or party, under what colour soever he or they pretend to be trusted apart, with or by the whole.[78] Hence then it is derived, which is made good in all experience, that the aristocracy is ravenous, and not the people. Your highwaymen are not such as have trades or

[77] *Aeneid*, VIII, 425.　　[78] *Sic*, including punctuation.

have been brought up unto industry, but such whose education hath pretended unto that of gentlemen. My lord is so honest, he doth not know the maxims that are of absolute necessity unto the arts of wickedness; for it is most certain, if there be not more purses than thieves, that the thieves themselves must be forced to turn honest, because they cannot thrive of their trade; but now if the people should turn thieves, who sees not that there would be more thieves than purses? Wherefore that an whole people should turn robbers or levellers is as impossible in the end as in the means. But that I do not think your artist mentioned, astronomer or arithmetician which he be, can tell me how many barley corns would reach unto the sun, I could be content he were called unto the account, with which I shall conclude this point; when, by the way, I have chidden my lords the legislators, who, as if they doubted my tackling would not hold, leave me to flag in a perpetual calm, but for my lord Epimonus, who breathes now and then into my sails and stirs the waters. A ship maketh not her way so briskly as when she is handsomely brushed by the waves, and tumbles over those that seem to tumble against her; in which case I have perceived in the dark that light hath been stricken even out of the sea, as in this place, where my lord Epimonus, feigning to give us a demonstration of one thing, hath given it of another and of a better. For the people of this nation, if they amount in each tribe unto two thousand elders and two thousand youth upon the annual roll, holding a fifth unto the whole tribe; then the whole of a tribe (not accounting women and children) must amount unto twenty thousand, and so the whole of all the tribes, being fifty, unto one million. Now you have ten thousand parishes and, reckoning these, one with another, each at one thousand pounds a year dry rent, the rent or revenue of the nation, as it is or might be let to farm, amounteth unto ten millions; and ten millions in revenue, divided equally unto one million of men, comes but to ten pounds a year unto each, whereupon to maintain himself, his wife and children. But he that hath a cow upon the common and earns his shilling by the day at his labour, hath twice as much already as this would come unto for his share, because, if the land were thus divided, there would be nobody to set him on work. My lord Epimonus's footman, who costs him thrice as much as one of these could thus get, would lose by this bargain. What should we speak of those

innumerable trades whereupon men live not only better than
others upon good shares of lands, but become also purchasers of
greater estates? Is not this the demonstration which my lord meant,
that the revenue of industry in a nation, at the least in this, is three-
or four-fold greater than that of the mere rent? If the people then
obstruct industry, they obstruct their own livelihood; but if they
make a war, they obstruct industry. Take the bread out of the
people's mouths, as did the Roman patricians, and you are sure
enough of a war, in which case they may be levellers; but our
agrarian causeth their industry to flow with milk and honey. It may
be answered:

> *O fortunati nimium, bona si sua norint*
> *Agricolae:*[79]

that this is true, if the people were given to understand their own
happiness; but where do they that? Let me answer with the like
question: where do they not? They do not know their happiness, it
should seem, in France, Spain and Italy; teach them what it is, and
try whose sense is the truer. But as to the late wars in Germany, it
hath been affirmed unto me there that the princes could never
make the people to take arms while they had bread, and have
therefore suffered countries now and then to be wasted that they
might get soldiers. This you will find to be the certain pulse and
temper of the people; and if they have been already proved to be
the most wise and constant order of a government, why should we
think, when no man can produce one example of the common
soldiery in an army mutinying because they had not captain's pay,
that the prerogative should jole the heads of the senate together, in
regard that these have the better salaries? While it must be as
obnoxious[80] unto the people in a nation as to the soldiery in an
army, that it is no more possible their emoluments of this kind
should be afforded by any commonwealth in the world to be made
equal with those of the senate, than that the common soldier's
should be equal with the captain's; it is enough to the common
soldier that his virtue may bring him to be a captain, and more unto
the prerogative that each of them is nearer to be a senator.

---

[79] *Georgics*, II, 458.

[80] H is using 'obnoxious' to mean 'obvious' or 'evident'; the commonest meaning in this
period was 'vulnerable'.

If my lord think our salaries too great, and that the commonwealth is not housewife enough; whether it is better housewifery that she should keep her family from the snow, or suffer them to burn her house that they may warm themselves? For one of these will be; do you think that she came off at a cheaper rate when men had their rewards by a thousand, two thousand pounds a year in land of inheritance? If you say that they will be more godly than they have been, it may be ill taken; and if you cannot promise that, it is time we find out some way of stinting at least, if not curing them, of that same *sacra fames*. On the other side, if a poor man (as such an one may save a city) give his sweat unto the public, with what conscience can you suffer his family in the meantime to starve? But he that lays his hand unto this plough shall not lose by taking it off from his own; and a commonwealth that will mend this shall be penny-wise. The Sanhedrim of Israel, being the supreme, and a constant, court of judicature, could not choose but to be gainful. The senate of the bean in Athens, because it was but annual, was moderately salariated, but that of the Areopagites, being for life, bountifully; what advantage the senators of Lacedaemon had, where there was little money or use of it, was in honour for life. The patricians, having no profit, took all; Venice being a situation where a man goes but to the door for his employment, the honour is great and the reward very little; but in Holland a counsellor of state hath fifteen hundred Flemish pounds a year, besides other accommodations. The states general have more. And that commonwealth looketh nearer her penny than ours need to do.

For the revenue of this nation, besides that of her industry, amounts, as hath been shown, unto ten millions, and the salaries in the whole come not unto three hundred thousand pounds a year; the beauty they will add unto the commonwealth will be exceedingly great, and the people delight in the beauty of their commonwealth; the encouragement they will give unto the study of the public very profitable, the accommodation they will afford unto your magistrates very honourable and easy. And the sum, when it or twice as much was spent on hunting and housekeeping, was never any grievance unto the people. I am ashamed to stand huckling upon this point; it is sordid. Your magistrates are rather to be provided with farther accommodations. For what if there should be sickness? Whither will you have them to remove? And this city in the soundest times, for the heat of the year, is no wholesome abode; have a care of their healths unto whom you commit your own. I would have the senate and the people, except they see cause to the contrary, every first of June, to remove into the country air, for the space of three months. You are better fitted with summer houses for them, than if you had built them to that purpose; there is some twelve miles distant the Convallium upon the river Halcionia for the tribunes and the prerogative, a palace capable of a thousand men, and at twenty miles distant you have Mount Celia,[81] reverend as well for the antiquity as state of a castle, completely capable of the senate; the proposers having lodgings in the Convallium, and the tribunes in Celia, it holds the correspondence between the senate and the people exactly. And it is a small matter for the proposers, being attended with the coaches and officers of state, besides other conveniences of their own, to go a matter of five or ten miles (those seats are not much farther distant) to meet the people upon any heath or field that shall be pointed; where, having dispatched their business, they may hunt their own venison (for I would have the great walled park upon the Halcionia to belong to the signory, and those about the Convallium unto the tribunes) and so go to supper. Pray, my lords, see that they do not pull down these houses to sell the lead of them; for when you have considered on it, they cannot be spared. The founders of the school in Hiera provided that the boys should have a summer seat.[82] You should have as much care of these magistrates. But there is such a selling, such a Jewish humour in our republicans, that I cannot tell what to say to it, only this: any man that knows what belongs to a commonwealth, or how diligent every nation in that case hath been to preserve her ornaments, and shall see waste lately made – the woods adjoining unto this city, which served for the delight and health of it, cut down to be sold for three pence – will tell you that they who did such things would never have made a commonwealth. The like may be said of the ruin or damage done upon our cathedrals, ornaments in which this nation excels all others; nor shall this ever be excused upon the score of religion, for though true it be that God dwelleth not in

[81] The equivalents here are Hampton Court, the Thames and Windsor.
[82] Hiera is Westminster.

houses made with hands, yet you cannot hold your assemblies but in such houses, and these are of the best that have been made with hands. Nor is it well argued that they are pompous and therefore profane, or less proper for divine service, seeing that the Christians in the primitive church chose to meet with one accord in the temple; so far were they from any inclination to pull it down.

The orders of this commonwealth, so far or near so far forth as they concern the elders, together with the several speeches at the institution, which may serve unto the better understanding of them as so many commentaries, being shown, I should now come from the elders unto the youth, or from the civil constitution of this government unto the military, but that I judge this the fittest place whereinto by the way to insert the government of the city, though for the present but perfunctorily.[83]

The metropolis or capital city of Oceana is commonly called Emporium, though it consist of two cities distinct, as well in name as in government, whereof the other is called Hiera. For which cause I shall treat of each apart, beginning with Emporium.

Emporium with the liberties is under a twofold division, the one regarding the national and the other urban or city government. It is divided in regard of the national government into three tribes, and in respect of the urban into twenty-six, which for distinction sake are called wards; being contained under the three tribes but unequally, wherefore the first tribe, containing ten wards, is called Scazon, the second, containing eight, Metoche, and the third, containing as many, Telicouta; the bearing of which names in mind concerns the better understanding of the government.

Every ward hath her wardmote, court or inquest, consisting of all that are of the clothing or liveries of companies residing within the same.

Such are of the livery or clothing as have obtained unto the dignity to wear gowns and parti-coloured hoods or tippets, according unto the rules and ancient customs of their respective companies.

A company is a brotherhood of tradesmen professing the same art, governed, according unto their charter, by a master and wardens. Of these there be a matter of sixty, whereof twelve are of greater dignity

---

[83] The following section (to p. 189, n. 84) is italicised, somewhat as if it were an 'order', but seems to belong in the text.

than the rest: that is to say the mercers, grocers, drapers, fishmongers, goldsmiths, skinners, merchant-tailors, haberdashers, salters, ironmongers, vintners, cloth-workers; which with most of the rest have common halls, divers of them being of ancient and magnificent structure, wherein they have frequent meetings at the summons of their masters or wardens, for the managing and regulation of their respective trades and mysteries. These companies, as I shall show, are the roots of the whole government of the city; for the liveries that reside in the same ward, meeting at the wardmote inquest, unto which it belongeth to take cognizance of all sorts of nuisances and violations of the customs and orders of the city, and to present them unto the court of aldermen, have also power to make election of two sorts of magistrates or officers: the first of elders or aldermen of the ward, the second of deputies of the same, otherwise called common-council men.

The wards in these elections, because they do not elect all at once, but some one year and some another, observe the distinction of the three tribes; for example, the Scazon, consisting of ten tribes, maketh election the first year of ten aldermen, one in each ward, and of one hundred and fifty deputies, fifteen in each ward; all which are triennial magistrates or officers; that is to say, are to bear their dignity for the space of three years.

The second year, the Metoche, consisting of eight wards, electeth eight aldermen, one in each ward, and an hundred and twenty deputies, fifteen in each ward; being also triennial magistrates.

The third year, Telicouta, consisting of a like number of wards, electeth an equal number of like magistrates for a like term. So that the whole number of the aldermen, according unto that of the wards, amounteth unto twenty-six, and the whole number of the deputies unto three hundred and ninety.

The aldermen thus elected have divers capacities; for first, they are justices of the peace, for the term and by consequence of their election; secondly, they are presidents of the wardmote, and governors each of that ward whereby he was elected; and last of all, these magistrates, being assembled together, constitute the senate of the city, otherwise called the court of aldermen. But no man is capable of this election that is not worth ten thousand pounds; this court upon every new election maketh choice of censors out of their own number.

The deputies in like manner, being assembled together, constitute the prerogative tribe of the city, otherwise called the common council; by which means the senate and the people of the city were caught in, as it were, by the rapture of the national government, to the same wheel of annual, triennial, and perpetual revolution.

But the liveries, over and above the right of these elections, by their divisions mentioned, being assembled all together at the guild of the city, constitute another assembly called the common hall.

The common hall hath right of two other elections: the one of the lord mayor, and the other of the two sheriffs, being annual magistrates. The lord mayor can be elected out of no other than one of the twelve companies of the first ranks, and the common hall agreeth by the plurality of suffrages upon two names, which being preferred unto the lord mayor for the time being, and the court of aldermen, they elect one by their scrutiny, for so they call it, though it differ from that of the commonwealth. The orator, or assistant unto the lord mayor in the holding of his courts, is some able lawyer elected by the court of aldermen, and called the recorder of Emporium.

The lord mayor, being thus elected, hath two capacities, the one regarding the nation, the other the city; in that which regards the city, he is president of the court of aldermen, having power to assemble the same or any other council of the city, as the common council or common hall, at his will and pleasure; and in that which regards the nation, he is commander-in-chief of the three tribes, whereinto the city is divided, one of which he is to bring up in person at the national muster unto the ballot; as his *vice-comites* or high sheriffs are to do by the other two, each at their distinct pavilion, where the nine aldermen elected censors are to officiate by three in each tribe, according unto the rules and orders already given unto the censors of the rustic tribes. And the tribes of the city have no other than one common phylarch, which is the court of aldermen and the common council; for which cause they elect not at their muster the first list called the prime magnitude.

The conveniences of this alteration of the city government, besides the bent of it unto conformity with that of the nation, were many, whereof I shall mention but a few, as first: whereas men under the former administration, when the burden of some of these magistrates lay for life, were oftentimes chosen not for their fitness, but rather unfitness or at least unwillingness, to undergo such a weight, whereby they were put at great rates to sign for their ease; a man might now take his share in magistracy with that equity which is due unto the public, and without any great inconvenience unto his private affairs. Secondly, whereas the city, inasmuch as the acts of the aristocracy, or court of aldermen, in their former way of proceeding, were rather impositions than propositions, was frequently disquieted, with the inevitable consequence in the power of debate exercised by the popular part or common council; the right of debate being henceforth established in the court of aldermen and that of result in the common council, killed the branches of division in the root, which for the present may suffice to have been said of the city of Emporium.

That of Hiera consisteth, as to the national government, of two tribes, the first called Agoraea, the second Propola; but as to the peculiar policy, of twelve maniples or wards, divided into three cohorts, each cohort containing four wards, whereof the wards of the first cohort elect for the first year four burgesses, one in each ward; the wards of the second cohort for the second year, four burgesses, one in each ward; and the wards of the third cohort for the third year, four burgesses, one in each ward, all triennial magistrates; by which the twelve burgesses, making one court for the government of this city, according unto their instructions by act of parliament, fall likewise into an annual, triennial and perpetual revolution.

This court, being thus constituted, maketh election of diverse magistrates: as first of an high steward, who is commonly some person of quality, and this magistracy is elected in the senate by the scrutiny of this court; unto him they choose some able lawyer to be his deputy, and to hold the court; and last of all they elect out of their own number six censors.

The high steward is commander-in-chief of the two tribes, whereof he in person bringeth up the one at the national muster unto the ballot, and his deputy the other at a distinct pavilion; the six censors chosen by the court officiating by three in each tribe at the urns, and these tribes have no other phylarch but this court.

As for the manner of elections and suffrage, both in Emporium and Hiera, it may be said once for all that they are performed by the ballot, and according unto the respective rules already given.

There be other cities and corporations throughout the territory, whose policy, being much of this kind, would be tedious and not worth the labour to insert, nor dare I stay. *Juvenum manus emicat ardens.*[84]

I return with the method of the commonwealth, unto the remaining part of her orbs, which are military and provincial: the military, except the strategus and the polemarchs or field officers, consisting of the youth only, and the provincial consisting of a mixture both of the elders and of the youth.

To begin with the youth, or the military orbs, they are circles unto which the commonwealth must have a care to keep close. A man is a spirit raised up by the magic of nature; if she do not stand safe and so that she may set him to some good and useful work, he spits fire and blows up castles; for where there is life, there must be motion or work, and the work of idleness is mischief (*non omnibus dormit*), but the work of industry is health. To set men unto this, the commonwealth must begin early with them, or it will be too late; and the means whereby she sets them unto it is education, the plastic art of government. But it is as frequent as sad in experience, whether through negligence or, which in the consequence is all one or worse, overfondness in domestic performance of this duty, that innumerable children come to owe their utter perdition unto their own parents; in each of which, the commonwealth loseth a citizen. Wherefore the laws of a government, how wholesome so ever in themselves, being such as if men by a congruity in their education be not brought up to find a relish in them, they will spit at; the education of a man's children is not wholly to be committed or trusted unto himself. You find in Livy the children of Brutus, having been bred under monarchy, making faces at the commonwealth of Rome. 'A king', say they, 'is a man; you may prevail with him when you have need there should be law, or when you have need there should be no law. He hath favours in the right, and he frowns not in the wrong place; he knows his friends from his enemies. But laws are deaf inexorable things, such as make no difference between a gentleman and an ordinary fellow; a man can never be merry for them, for to trust altogether to his own innocence is a sad life.'[85] Unhappy wantons! Scipio (on the other side), when he was but a boy (some two or three

---

[84] *Aeneid*, VI, 5. This concludes the italicised section on the government of Emporium.
[85] Livy, II, iii.

and twenty), being informed that certain patricians or Roman gentlemen, through a qualm upon the defeat which Hannibal had given them at Cannae, were laying their heads together and contriving their flight with the transportation of their goods out of Rome, drew his sword and, setting himself at the door of the chamber where they were at council, protested that who did not immediately swear not to desert the commonwealth, he would make his soul to desert his body. Let men argue as they please for monarchy, or against a commonwealth, the world shall never see any man so sottish or wicked as (in cool blood) to prefer the education of the sons of Brutus before that of Scipio; and of this mould, except a Melius or a Manlius, was the whole youth of that commonwealth, though not ordinarily so well cast. Now the health of a government and the education of the youth being of the same pulse, no wonder if it have been the constant practice of well ordered commonwealths to commit the care and feeling[86] of it unto public magistrates; a duty that was performed in such manner by the Areopagites as is elegantly praised by Isocrates. The Athenians, saith he, write not their laws upon dead walls, nor content themselves with having ordained punishments for crimes, but provide in such manner by the education of their youth that there be no crimes for punishment;[87] he speaks of those laws which regarded manners, not of those orders which concerned the administration of the commonwealth, lest you should think he contradicts Xenophon and Polybius. The children of Lacedaemon, at the seventh year of their age, were delivered unto the *paedonomi* – schoolmasters, not mercenary but magistrates of the commonwealth, unto which they were accountable for their charge. By these at the age of fourteen they were presented unto other magistrates called the *beidiaei*, having the inspection of the games and exercises, among which that of the *platanista* was famous; a kind of fight in squadrons, but somewhat too fierce. When they came to be of military age, they were listed of the *mora*, and so continued in readiness for public service under the discipline of the polemarchs. But the Roman education and discipline by the centuries and *classes* is that unto which the commonwealth of Oceana hath had a more concerned eye in her three essays, being certain degrees by which the youth commence as it were in arms for magistracy, as appears by

[86] *Sic*, but 'feeding'?   [87] Isocrates, *Areopagiticus*, 39ff.

The twenty-sixth order: instituting that if a parent have but one son, the education of that one son shall be wholly at the disposing of that parent, but whereas there be free schools erected and endowed, or to be erected and endowed in every tribe of this nation, to a sufficient proportion for the education of the children of the same; which schools, to the end that there be no detriment or hindrance unto the scholars upon case of removing from one unto another, are every of them to be governed by the strict inspection of the censors of the tribes, both upon the schoolmasters, their manner of life and teaching, and the proficiency of the children, after the rules and method of that in Hiera. If a parent have more sons than one, the censors of the tribe shall animadvert upon and punish him that sendeth not his sons within the ninth year of their age unto some one of the schools of a tribe, there to be kept and taught if he be able at his charges, and if he be not able gratis, till they arrive at the age of fifteen years. And a parent may dispose of his sons at the fifteenth year of their age, according unto his choice or ability, whether it be unto service in the way of apprentices unto some trade or otherwise, or unto farther study, as by sending them unto the Inns of Court, of Chancery, or unto one of the universities of this nation. But he that taketh not upon him some one of the professions proper unto some one of those places, shall not continue longer in any of them till they have [*sic*] attained unto the age of eighteen years; and every man having not at that age of eighteen years taken upon him, or addicted himself unto, the profession of the law, theology or physic, and being no servant, shall be capable of the essay of the youth, and no other person whatsoever; except a man, having taken upon him such a profession, happen to lay it by ere he arrive at three or four and twenty years of age, and be admitted unto this capacity by the respective phylarch, being satisfied that he kept not out so long with any design to evade the service of the commonwealth, but that being no sooner at his own disposing it was no sooner at his own choice to come in. And if any youth or other person of this nation have a desire to travel into foreign countries upon occasion of business, delight or farther improvement of his education, the same shall be lawful for him upon a pass obtained from the censors in parliament, putting a convenient limit unto the time and recommending him unto the ambassadors, by whom he shall be assisted and unto whom he shall yield honour and obedience in their respective residences. Every youth at his return from his travel is to present the censors with a paper of his own writing, containing the interest of state or form of government of the countries or some one of the countries where he hath been; and if it be good, the censors shall cause it to be printed and published, prefixing a line in commendation of the author.

Every Wednesday next ensuing the last of December, the whole youth of every parish, that is to say every man (not excepted by the foregoing part of the order) being from eighteen years of age to thirty, shall repair at the sound of the bell unto the respective church, and being there assembled in presence of the overseers who are to govern the ballot, and the constable who is to officiate at the urn, shall after the manner of the elders elect every fifth man of their whole number (provided that they choose not above one of two brothers at one election, nor above half if they be four or upward) to be a stratiot or deputy of the youth; and the list of the stratiots so elected, being taken by the overseers, shall be entered in the parish book and diligently preserved as a record, called the essay. They whose estates by the law are able, or whose friends are willing, to mount them shall be of the horse, the rest are of the foot. And he who hath been one year of this list is not capable of being re-elected till after one year's interval.

Every Wednesday next ensuing the last of January, the stratiots, being mustered at the rendezvous of their respective hundred, shall in the presence of the jurymen who are overseers of that ballot, and of the high constable who is to officiate at the urn, elect out of the horse of their troop or company one captain and one ensign or cornet, unto the command of the same; and, the jurymen having entered the list of the hundred into a record to be diligently kept at the rendezvous of the same, the first public game of this commonwealth shall begin and be performed in this manner. Whereas there is to be at every rendezvous of an hundred one cannon, culverin or saker, the prize arms, being forged by sworn armourers of this commonwealth, and for their proof, besides their beauty, viewed and tried at the Tower of Emporium, shall be exposed by the justice of peace appertaining unto that hundred, the said justice with the jurymen being judge of the game. And the judges shall deliver unto the horseman that gains the prize at the career one suit of arms being of the value of twenty pounds; unto the pikeman that gains the prize at throwing the bullet one suit of arms of the value of ten pounds; unto the musketeer that gains the prize at the park with his musket one suit of arms of the value of ten pounds; and unto the cannoneer that gains the prize at the mark with the cannon, culverin or saker, one chain of silver being of the value of ten pounds. Provided that no one man at the same muster play above one of the prizes. Whosoever gaineth a prize is bound to wear it (if it be his lot) upon service; and no man shall sell or give away an armour thus won, except he have lawfully attained unto two or more of them at the games.

The games being ended and the muster dismissed, the captain of the troop or company shall repair with a copy of the list unto the lord lieutenant of the tribe, and the high constable with a duplicate of the same unto the custos rotulorum or muster-master-general, to be also communicated with the censors; in each of which the jurymen, giving a note upon every name of an only son, shall certify that the list is without subterfuge or evasion or, if it be not, upon whom the evasion or subterfuge lieth, unto the end that the phylarch or the censors may animadvert accordingly.

And every Wednesday next ensuing the last of February, the lord lieutenant, custos rotulorum, the censors and the conductor shall receive the whole muster of the youth of that tribe at the rendezvous of the same, distributing the horse and foot with their officers according unto the directions given in the like case for the distribution of the elders; and, the whole squadron being put by that means in battalia, the second game of this commonwealth shall begin by the exercise of the youth in all the parts of their military discipline according unto the orders of parliament, or direction of the council of war in that case. And the hundred pounds allowed by the parliament for the ornament of the muster in every tribe shall be expended by the phylarch upon such artificial castles, citadels, or like devices as may make the best and most profitable sport for the youth and their spectators. Which being ended, the censors having prepared the urns by putting into the horse-urn two hundred and twenty gold balls, whereof ten are to be marked with the letter M and other ten with the letter P, into the foot-urn seven hundred gold balls, whereof fifty are to be marked with the letter M and fifty with the letter P, and made up the gold balls in each urn by the addition of silver balls unto the same, in number equal with the horse and foot of the stratiots, the lord lieutenant shall call the stratiots unto their urns; where they that draw the silver balls shall return unto their places and they that draw the gold balls shall fall off to the pavilion, where for the space of one hour they may chop and change their balls, according as one can agree with another whose lot he likes better; but the hour being out, the conductor, separating them whose gold balls have no letter from those whose balls are marked, shall cause the crier to call the alphabet, as first A: whereupon all they whose gold balls are not marked and whose surnames begin with the letter A shall repair unto a clerk appertaining unto the custos rotulorum, who shall first take the names of that letter, then those of B, and so forth till all the names be alphabetically enrolled. And the youth of this list, being six hundred in a tribe foot, that is thirty thousand foot in all the tribes, and two hundred in a tribe horse, that is ten thousand horse in all the tribes, are the second essay of the stratiots and the standing army of this commonwealth, to be always ready upon command to march. They whose balls are marked with M, amounting by twenty horse and fifty foot in a tribe unto two thousand five hundred foot and five hundred horse in all the tribes, and they whose balls are marked with P, in every point correspondent, are parts of the third essay; they of M being forthwith to march for Marpesia and they of P for Panopea, to the ends and according to the further directions following in the order for the provincial orbs.

If the polemarchs or field officers be elected by the scrutiny of the council of war, and the strategus commanded by the parliament or the dictator to march, the lords lieutenants (who have power to muster and discipline the youth so often as they receive orders for the same from the council of war) are to deliver the second essay, or so many of them as shall be commanded, unto the conductors, who shall present them unto the lord strategus at the time and place appointed by his excellency to be the general rendezvous of Oceana; where the council of war shall have the accommodation of horses and arms for his men in readiness, and the lord strategus, having armed, mounted, and distributed them, whether according unto the recommendation of their prize arms or otherwise, shall lead them away unto his shipping, being also ready and provided with victuals, ammunition, artillery and all other necessaries, commanding them and disposing of the whole conduct of the war by his sole power and authority. And this is the third essay of the stratiots, which being shipped or marched out of their tribes, the lords lieutenants shall re-elect the second essay out of the remaining part of the first, and the senate another strategus.

If any veteran or veterans of this nation, the term of whose youth or militia is expired, having a desire to be entertained in the further service of the commonwealth, shall present him or themselves at the rendezvous of Oceana unto the strategus, it is in his power to take on such and so many of them as shall be consented unto by the polemarchs, and to send back an equal number of the stratiots.

And for the better managing of the proper forces of this nation, the lord strategus by appointment of the council of war, and out of such levies as they shall have made in either or both of the provinces unto that end, shall receive auxiliaries at sea or elsewhere at some certain place, not exceeding his proper arms in number.

And whosoever shall refuse any one of his three essays, except upon cause shown he be dispensed withal by the phylarch or, if the phylarch be not assembled, by the censors of his tribe, shall be deemed an helot or public servant, pay one fifth of his yearly revenue besides all other taxes unto the commonwealth for his protection, and be incapable of bearing magistracy except such as is proper to the law. Nevertheless, if a man have but two sons, the lord lieutenant shall not suffer above one of them to come unto the urn at one election of the second essay; and though he have above two sons, there shall not come above half the brothers at one election; and if a man have but one son, he shall not come unto the urn at all without the consent of his parents or his guardians, nor shall it be any reproach unto him or impediment unto his bearing of magistracy.

This, for expeditions that are foreign, will be proved and explained together with

The twenty-seventh order: providing in case of invasion apprehended that the lords high sheriffs of the tribes, upon commands received from the parliament or the dictator, distribute the bands of the elders into divisions after the nature of the essays of the youth, and that the second division or essay of the elders, being made and consisting of thirty thousand foot and ten thousand horse, be ready to march with the second essay of the youth, and be brought also by the conductors unto the strategus.

The second essay of the elders and youth being marched out of their tribes, the lords high sheriffs and lieutenants shall have the remaining part of the annual bands, both of elders and youth, in readiness, which, if the beacons be fired, shall march unto the rendezvous to be in that case appointed by the parliament or the dictator; and, the beacons being fired, the *curiata comitia* or parochial congregations shall elect a fourth, both of elders and youth, to be immediately upon the guard of the tribes and, dividing themselves as aforesaid, to march also in their divisions according unto orders, which method in case of extremity shall proceed unto the election of a third, or the levy of a second or of the last man in the nation, by the power of the lords high sheriffs; to the end that the commonwealth in her utmost pressure may show her trust that God in his justice will remember mercy, by humbling herself and yet preserving her courage, discipline and constancy, even unto the last drop of her blood and the utmost farthing.

The services performed by the youth or by the elders, in case of invasion and according unto this order, shall be at their proper cost and charges that are any ways able to endure it; but if there be such as are known in their parishes to be so indigent that they cannot march out of their tribes, nor undergo the burden in this case incumbent, the congregations of their parishes shall furnish them with sufficient sums of money, to be repaid upon the certificate of the same by the parliament when the action shall be over. And of that which is respectively enjoined by this order, any tribe, parish, magistrate, or person that shall fail, is to answer for it at the council of war, as a deserter of his country.

The Archon, being the greatest captain of his (if not of any) age, added much unto the glory of this commonwealth, by interweaving the militia with more art and lustre than any legislator from, or before, the time of Servius Tullius. But as the bones or skeleton of a man, though the greatest part of his beauty be contained in their proportion or symmetry, yet shown without flesh, are a spectacle that is rather horrid; so without discourses, the orders of a commonwealth which, if she go forth in that manner, may complain of her friends that they stand mute and staring upon her. Wherefore this order was thus fleshed by the Archon:

My lords:

Diogenes, seeing a young fellow drunk, told him that his father was drunk when he begot him. For this in natural, I must confess I see no reason; but in political generation, it is right: the vices of the people are from their governors; those of their governors from their laws or orders; and those of their laws or orders from their legislators. *Ut male posuimus initia, sic caetera sequuntur.*[88] What ever was in the womb imperfect as to her proper work, comes very rarely or not at all to perfection; and the formation of a citizen in the womb of the commonwealth is his education.

Education by the first of the foregoing orders is of six kinds: at the school, in the mechanics, at the universities, at the inns of court or chancery, in travels, and in military discipline; some of which I shall touch, and some I shall handle.

That which is proposed for the erecting and endowing of schools throughout the tribes, capable of all the children of the same and able to give unto the poor the education of theirs gratis, is only matter of direction in a case of very great charity, as easing the needy of the charge of their children from the ninth to the fifteenth year of their age, during which time their work cannot be profitable, and restoring them when they may be of use, furnished with tools whereof there be advantages to be made in every work, seeing he that can read and use his pen hath some convenience by it in the meanest vocation; and it cannot be conceived but that which comes (though in small parcels) to the advantage of every man in his vocation must amount unto the advantage of every vocation, and so unto that of the commonwealth. Wherefore this is commended unto the charity of every wise-hearted and well-minded man to be done in time, and as God shall stir him up or enable him; there being such provision already in the case as may give us leave to proceed without obstruction.

Parents (under animadversion of the censors) are to dispose of their children at the fifteenth year of their age unto something; but what, is left, according to their abilities or inclination, in their own choice. This, with the many, must be unto the mechanics: that is to say, unto agriculture or husbandry, unto manufactures, or unto merchandise.

Agriculture is the bread of the nation; we are hung upon it by the teeth; it is a mighty nursery of strength, the best army and the most assured knapsack; it is managed with the least turbulent or ambitious, and the most innocent hands of all other arts. Wherefore I am of Aristotle's opinion, that a commonwealth of husbandmen (and such is ours) must be the best of all others. Certainly, my

---

[88] Cicero, *Ep. ad Att.*, x, xviii, 2.

lords, you have no measure of what ought to be, but what can be done for the encouragement of this profession; I could wish I were husband good enough to direct something to this end; but racking of rents is a vile thing in the richer sort, an uncharitable one to the poorer, a mark of slavery, and nips your commonwealth in the fairest blossom. On the other side, if there should be too much ease given in this kind, it would occasion sloth, and so destroy industry, the nerve of a commonwealth. But if ought might be done to hold the balance even between these two, it would be a work in this nation equal unto that for which Fabius was called Maximus by the Romans.

In manufactures and merchandise the Hollander hath gotten the start of us; but at the long run it will be found that a people working upon a foreign commodity doth but farm the manufacture, and that it is entailed upon them only where the growth of it is native; as also that it is one thing to have the carriage of other men's goods, and another for a man to bring his own unto the best market. Wherefore, nature having provided encouragement for these arts in this nation above others where, the people growing, they of necessity must also increase, it cannot but establish them upon a far more sure and effectual foundation than that of the Hollanders. But their educations are in order unto the first things or necessities of nature: as husbandry unto the food, manufacture unto the clothing, and merchandise unto the purse of the commonwealth.

There be other things in nature which, being second as to their order, for their dignity and value are first, and such to which the other are but accommodations. Of this sort are especially these: religion, justice, courage, wisdom.

The education that answers unto religion in our government is that of the universities. Moses the divine legislator was not only learned in all the learning of the Egyptians, but took into the fabric of his commonwealth the learning of the Midianites in the advice of Jethro, and his foundation of an university, laid in the Tabernacle and finished in the Temple, became that pinnacle from whence all the learning in the world hath taken wing; as the philosophy of the Stoics from the Pharisees, that of the Epicureans from the Sadducees, and from the learning of the Jews, so often quoted by our Saviour and fulfilled in him, the Christian religion.

Athens was the most famous university in her days and her senators, that is to say the Areopagites, were all philosophers. Lacedaemon (to speak truth), though she could write and read, was not very bookish. But who disputeth hence against universities, disputeth in the same argument against agriculture, manufacture and merchandise, every one of these having been equally forbidden by Lycurgus, not for itself (for if he had not been learned in all the learning of Crete, and well travelled in the knowledge of other governments, he had never made his commonwealth), but for the diversion which they must have given his citizens from their arms, who, being but few, if they had minded anything else, must have deserted the commonwealth. For Rome, she had *ingenium par imperio*, was as learned as great, and held her college of augurs in much reverence. Venice hath taken her religion upon trust; Holland cannot tend it to be very studious; nor doth Switz mind it much; yet are they all addicted unto their universities. We cut down trees to build houses, but I would have somebody show me by what reason or experience the cutting down of an university should tend unto the setting up of a commonwealth. Of this I am sure, the perfection of a commonwealth is not to be attained unto without the knowledge of ancient prudence, nor the knowledge of ancient prudence without learning, nor learning without schools of good literature; and these are such as we call universities. Now though mere university learning of itself, be that which (to speak the words of Verulamius), 'crafty men condemn and simple men only admire, yet is it such as wise men have use of; for studies do not teach their own use, but that is a wisdom without and above them, won by observation. Expert men may execute, and perhaps judge of particulars one by one; but the general counsels, and the plots, and the marshalling of affairs, come best from those that are learned.'[89] Wherefore, if you would have your children to be statesmen, let them drink by all means of these fountains, where perhaps there was never any. But what though the water a man drinks be not nourishment? It is the *vehiculum* without which he cannot be nourished. Nor is religion less concerned in this point than government; for take away your universities, and in a few years you lose it.

---

[89] Bacon, Essay L, 'Of Studies' (*Works*, VI, p. 497; a composite quotation).

The Holy Scriptures are written in Hebrew and in Greek; they that have neither of these languages may think light of both, but find me a man that hath one in perfection, the study of whose whole life it hath not been. Again this is apparent to us in daily conversation: that if four or five persons that have lived together be talking, another speaking the same language may come in and yet understand very little of their discourse, in that it relateth unto circumstances, persons, things, times and places which he knoweth not. It is no otherwise with a man having no insight of the times in which they were written and the circumstances unto which they relate, in the reading of ancient books, whether they be divine or humane. For example, when we fall upon the discourse about baptism and regeneration that was between our Saviour and Nicodemus, where Christ reproacheth him of his ignorance in this manner: *Art thou a doctor in Israel, and understandest not these things?* what shall we think of it? Or wherefore should a doctor in Israel have understood these things more than another, but that both baptism and regeneration (as was showed at large by my lord Phosphorus) were doctrines held in Israel? Instance in one place of a hundred, which he that hath not mastered the circumstances unto which they relate cannot understand. Wherefore to the understanding of the Scripture, it is necessary to have ancient languages and the knowledge of ancient times, or the aid of them who have such knowledge; and to have such as may be always able and ready to give such aid (unless you would borrow it of another nation, which would not only be base, but deceitful), it is necessary unto a commonwealth that she have schools of good literature, or universities, of her own. We are commanded (as hath been said more than once) to search the Scriptures; and whether do they search the Scriptures that take this pains in ancient languages and learning, or they that will not, but trusting unto translations only, and to words as they sound unto present circumstances (than which nothing is more fallible or certain to lose the true sense of Scriptures), pretend to be above human understanding, for no other cause than that they are below it? But in searching the Scriptures by the proper use of our universities, we have been heretofore blessed with greater victories and trophies against the purple hosts and golden standards of the Romish hierarchy, than any nation; and therefore, why we should relinquish this, upon the presumption of some that because there is a greater light they have it, I do not know. There is a greater light than the sun, but it doth not extinguish the sun; nor doth any light of God's giving extinguish that of nature, but increase and sanctify it. Wherefore neither the honour borne by the Israelite, Roman or any other commonwealth that I have shown, unto their ecclesiastics, consisted in being governed by them, but in consulting them in matter of religion; upon whose *responsa*, or oracles, they did afterwards as they thought fit.[90] Nor would I be mistaken as if, by affirming the universities to be, in order both unto religion and government, of absolute necessity, I declared them or the ministry in any wise fit to be trusted so far as to exercise any power not derived from the civil magistrate, in the administration of either. If the Jewish religion were directed and established by Moses, it was directed and established by the civil magistrate; or if Moses exercised this administration as a prophet, the same prophet did invest with the same administration the Sanhedrim and not the priests; and so doth our commonwealth the senate and not the clergy. They who had the supreme administration or government of the national religion in Athen were the first archon, the *rex sacrificulus*[91] or high priest, and a polemarch; which magistrates were ordained or elected *per χειροτονίαν*, by the holding up of hands, in the church, congregation or *comitia* of the people. The religion of Lacedaemon was governed by the kings, who were also high priests and officiated at the sacrifice; these had power to substitute their *Pythii*, ambassadors or nuncios, by which, not without concurrence of the senate, they held intelligence with the oracle of Apollo at Delphos. And the ecclesiastical part of the commonwealth of Rome was governed by the *pontifex maximus*, the *rex sacrificulus* and the *flamines*, all ordained or elected by the people; the *pontifex tributis*, the king *centuriatis*, and the *flamines*, or parish priests, *curiatis comitiis*. I do not mind you of these things as if, for the matter, there were any parallel to be drawn out of their superstitions to our religion, but to show that, for the manner, ancient prudence is as well a rule in divine as human things; nay, and such an one as the apostles themselves, ordaining elders by the holding up of hands in every congregation, have exactly followed, for some of the congre-

[90] The criticism of 'enthusiasm' has led to a Machiavellian conclusion.
[91] H is using the Roman term by mistake for the Attic *archon basileus*.

gations where they thus ordained elders were those of Antioch, Iconium, Lystra, Derbe, the country of Lycaonia, Pisidia, Pamphylia, Perga, with Attalia. Now that these cities and countries, when the Romans propagated their empire into Asia, were found most of them commonwealths, and that many of the rest were indued with like power, so that the people, living under the protection of the Roman emperors, continued to elect their own magistrates, is so known a thing that I wonder whence it is men, quite contrary unto the universal proof of these examples, will have ecclesiastical government to be necessarily distinct from civil power; when the right of the elders, ordained by the holding up of hands in every congregation, to teach the people was plainly derived from the same civil power by which they ordained the rest of their magistrates. And it is no otherwise in our commonwealth where the parochial congregation electeth or ordaineth her pastor. To object the commonwealth of Venice in this place were to show us that it hath been no otherwise, but where the civil power hath lost the liberty of her conscience by embracing of popery; as also that to take away the liberty of conscience in this administration from the civil power were a proceeding which hath no other precedent than such as is popish. Wherefore your religion is thus settled: the universities are the seminaries of that part which is national, by which means others withal safely may be permitted to follow the liberty of their consciences, in regard that however they behave themselves, the ignorance of the unlearned in this case cannot lose the religion nor disturb the government, which otherwise it would most certainly do. And the universities with their emoluments, as also the benefices of the whole nation, are to be improved by such augmentations as may make a very decent and comfortable subsistence for the ministry, which is neither to be allowed synods nor assemblies (but upon the occasion shown in the universities, they are consulted by the council for religion), suffered to meddle with affairs of state nor to be capable of any other public preferment whatsoever; by which means the interest of the learned can never come to corrupt your religion nor disturb your government, which otherwise it would most certainly do. Venice, though she do not see or cannot help the corruption of her religion, is yet so circumspect to avoid disturbance in this kind of her government that her council proceeds not unto election of

magistrates, till it be proclaimed *'fuora papalini'*; by which words
such as have consanguinity with red hats, or relation unto the court
of Rome, are warned to withdraw. If a minister in Holland meddle
with matter of state, the magistrate sendeth him a pair of shoes;
whereupon if he do not go, he is driven away from his charge. I
wonder why ministers of all men should be perpetually tampering
with government; first because they as well as others have it in
express charge to submit themselves unto the ordinances of men,
and secondly because these ordinances of men must go upon such
political principles as they of all others (by anything that can be
found in their writings or actions) least understand; whence you
have the suffrage of all nations unto this sense: 'An ounce of
wisdom is worth a pound of clergy.' Your greatest clerks are not
your wisest men; and when some foul absurdity in state is committed, it is common with the French and even the Italians to call it *pas
de clerc*, or *governo da prete*. They may bear with men that will be
preaching without study, while they will be governing without
prudence. My lords, if you know not how to rule your clergy, you
will most certainly be like a man that cannot rule his wife; have
neither quiet at home nor honour abroad. Their honest vocation is
to teach your children at the schools and the universities, and the
people in the parishes; and yours is concerned to see that they do
not play the shrews. Of which parts consists the education of your
commonwealth, so far forth as it regards religion.

To justice, or that part of it which is commonly executive,
answers the education of the Inns of Court or Chancery. Upon
which to philosophise requires a peculiar kind of learning that I
have not. But they who take upon them any profession proper unto
the educations mentioned, that is, theology, physic, law, are not at
leisure for the essays. Wherefore, the essays being degrees
whereby the youth commence for all magistracies, offices and
honours in the parish, hundred, tribe, senate or prerogative,
divines, physicians and lawyers, not taking these degrees, exclude
themselves from all such magistracies, offices and honours. And
whereas lawyers are likest to exact farthest reason for this; they,
growing up from the most gainful art at the bar unto those
magistracies upon the bench which are continually appropriated to
themselves, and not only endowed with the greatest revenues but
held for life, have the least reason of all the rest to pretend unto

any other; especially in an equal commonwealth, where accumulation of magistracy, or to take a person engaged by his profit unto the laws as they stand into the power which is legislative, and should keep them unto what they were or ought to be, were a solecism in prudence. It is true that the legislative power may have need of advice and assistance from the executive magistracy or such as are learned in the law; for which cause the judges are (as they have heretofore been) assistants in the senate. Nor, however it came about, can I see any reason why a judge, being but an assistant, a lawyer, should be a member of a legislative council.[92]

I deny not that the Roman patricians were all patrons and that the whole people were clients, some unto one family and some unto another, by which means they had their causes pleaded and defended in some appearance gratis; for the patron took no money, though, if he had a daughter to marry, his clients were to pay her portion, nor was this so much. But if the client accused his patron, gave testimony or suffrage against him, it was a crime of such nature that any man might lawfully kill him as a traitor; and this, as being the nerve of the optimacy, was a great cause of ruin unto that commonwealth, for when the people would carry anything that pleased not the senate, the senators were ill provided if they could not intercede, that is, oppose it by their clients, with whom to vote otherwise than they pleased was so high a crime. The observation of this bond till the time of the Gracchi (that is to say, till it was too late, or to no purpose, to break it) was the cause why, in all the former heats and disputes that had happened between the senate and the people, it never came to blows, which was good; but withal, the people could have no remedy, which was evil.[93] Wherefore I am of opinion that a senator ought not to be a patron or advocate, nor a patron or advocate to be a senator; for if his practice be gratis it debaucheth the people, and if it be mercenary it debaucheth himself. Take it which way you will, when he should be making of laws, he will be knitting of nets.

Lycurgus, as I said, by being a traveller became a legislator; but in times when prudence was another thing. Nevertheless we may not shut out this part of education, in a commonwealth which will

---

[92] Punctuation as in original.

[93] H has travelled some distance from Machiavelli (*Discorsi*, 1, 4), who had given liberty and *virtù* as the cause why these disputes were bloodless.

be herself a traveller, for those of this make have seen the world; especially because this (though it be not regarded in our times, when things being left to take their chance, it fares with us accordingly) is certain: no man can be a politician, except he be first an historian or a traveller; for except he can see what must be, or what may be, he is no politician. Now, if he have no knowledge in story, he cannot tell what hath been; and if he hath not been a traveller, he cannot tell what is; but he that neither knoweth what hath been, nor what is, can never tell what must be or what may be. Furthermore, the embassies in ordinary, by our constitution, are the prizes of young men, more especially such as have been travellers. Wherefore they of these inclinations, having leave of the censors, owe them account of their time, and cannot choose but lay it out with some ambition of praise or reward, where both are open; whence you will have eyes abroad and better choice of public ministers, your gallants showing themselves not more unto the ladies at their balls, than unto your commonwealth at her academy, when they return from their travels.

But this commonwealth, being constituted more especially of two elements, arms and councils, driveth by a natural instinct at courage and wisdom, which he who hath attained is arrived at the perfection of human nature. It is true that these virtues must have some natural root in him that is capable of them; but this amounteth not unto so great a matter as some will have it. For if poverty make an industrious, a moderate estate a temperate, and a lavish fortune a wanton man, and this be the common course of things; wisdom is rather of necessity than inclination. And that an army which was meditating upon flight hath been brought by despair to win the field, is so far from being strange that like causes will evermore produce like effects. Wherefore this commonwealth driveth her citizens like wedges: there is no way with them but through, nor end but that glory whereof man is capable by art or nature. That the genius of the Roman families preserved itself throughout the line, as (to instance in some) that the Manlii were still severe, the Publicolae lovers and the Appii haters of the people, is attributed by Machiavel unto their education;[94] nor, if interest might add unto the reason why the genius of a patrician

<hr>

[94] *Discorsi*, III, 22.

was one thing and that of a plebeian another, is the like so apparent between different nations who, according unto their different educations, have yet as different manners. It was anciently noted and long confirmed by the French, that in their first assaults their courage was more than that of men, and for the rest less than that of women; which nevertheless, through the amendment of their discipline, we see to be otherwise. I will not say but that some man or nation, upon equal improvement of this kind, may be lighter than some other, but certainaly education is the scale without which no man or nation can truly know his or her own weight or value. By our histories we can tell when one Marpesian would have beaten ten Oceaners, and when one Oceaner would have beaten ten Marpesians. Mark Antony was a Roman, but how did that appear in the embraces of Cleopatra? You must have some other education for your youth; or they, like that passage, will show better in romance than true story.

The custom of the commonwealth of Rome, in distributing her magistracies without respect of age, happened to do well in Corvinus and Scipio, for which cause Machiavel (with whom that which was done by Rome, and that which is well done, is for the most part all one) commendeth this course.[95] Yet how much it did work at other times is obvious in Pompey and Caesar; examples by which Boccalini illustrateth the prudence of Venice in her contrary practice, affirming it to have been no small step unto the ruin of the Roman liberty that these, having tasted in their youth of the supreme honours, had no greater in their age to hope for, but by perpetuating of the same in themselves, which came to blood, and ended in tyranny.[96] The opinion of Verulamius is safe: 'the errors', saith he, 'of young men are the ruin of business; whereas the errors of aged men amount but to this, that more might have been done or sooner.'[97] But though their wisdom be little, their courage is great. Wherefore (to come unto the main education of this commonwealth) the militia of Oceana is the province of youth.

The distribution of this province by the essays is so fully described in the order that I need repeat nothing, the order itself being but a repetition or copy of that original which in ancient

---

[95] *Discorsi*, I, 60.
[96] Boccalini, *The New-founde Politicke* (London, 1626), III, 10 (p. 197).
[97] Bacon, Essay XLII, 'Of Youth and Age (*Works*, VI, p. 477).

prudence is, of all other, the fairest; as that from whence the commonwealth of Rome more especially derived the empire of the world. And there is much more reason in this age, when governments are universally broken or swerved from their foundations, and the people groan under tyranny, that the same causes (which could not be withstood when the world was full of popular governments) should have the like effect.

The causes in the commonwealth of Rome, whereof the empire of the world was not any miraculous, but a natural (nay, I may safely say necessary) consequence, are contained in that part of her discipline which was domestic, and in that which she exercised in her provinces or conquests. Of the latter I shall have better occasion to speak when we come unto our provincial orbs. The former divided the whole people by tribes, amounting, as Livy shows, at their full growth unto thirty-five, and every tribe, by the cense or valuation of estates, into five classes; for the sixth, being proletary, that is the nursery, or such as through their poverty contributed nothing to the commonwealth but children, was not reckoned nor used in arms. And this is the first point of the militia, in which modern prudence is quite contrary unto the ancient; for whereas we, excusing the rich and arming the poor, become the vassals of our servants, they, by excusing the poor and arming such as were rich enough to be freemen, became lords of the earth. The nobility and gentry of this nation, who understand so little what it is to be lords of the earth that they have not been able to keep their lands, will think it a strange education for their children to be common soldiers and obliged unto all the duties of arms; nevertheless it is not for four shillings a week, but to be capable of being the best man in the field or in the city, the latter part of which consideration makes the common soldier in this a better man than the general of any monarchical army. And whereas it may be thought that this would drink deep of noble blood, I dare boldly say: take the Roman nobility in the heat of their fiercest wars, and you shall not find such a shambles of them as hath been made of ours by mere luxury and slothfulness, which, killing the body, *animasque in vulnere ponunt,*[98] kill the soul also; whereas common right is that which who stands in the vindication of, hath used that sword of

---

[98] *Georgics*, IV, 237–8.

justice for which he receiveth the purple of magistracy. The glory of a man on earth can go no higher, and if he fall he riseth, and comes sooner unto that reward which is so much higher as heaven is above earth. To return unto the Roman example. Every *classis* was divided (as hath been more than once shown) into centuries, and every century was equally divided into youth and elders; the youth for foreign service, and the elders for the guard of the territory. In the first *classis* were a matter of eighteen centuries of horse, being those which by the institution of Servius were first called unto the suffrage *centuriatis*. But the *delectus* or levy of an army (which is the present business) proceeded, according to Polybius, in this manner.

Upon a war decreed, the consuls elected four and twenty military tribunes or colonels; whereof ten, being such as had merited their tenth stipend, were younger officers. The tribunes being chosen, the consuls appointed the day unto the tribes, when those in them of military age were to appear at the capital. The day being come and the youth assembled accordingly, the consuls ascended their tribunal, and the younger tribunes were forthwith divided into four parts after this manner: four were assigned unto the first legion (a legion at the most consisted of six thousand foot and three hundred horse), three unto the second, four unto the third and three unto the fourth; the younger tribunes being thus distributed, two of the elder were assigned unto the first legion, three unto the second, two unto the third and three unto the fourth. And the officers of each legion thus assigned having drawn the tribes by lots, and being seated according unto their divisions at a convenient distance from each other, the tribe of the first lot was called; whereupon they that were of it, knowing the business and being prepared, presently bolted out four of their number, in the choice whereof such care was taken that they offered none that was not a citizen, no citizen that was not of the youth, no youth that was not of some one of the five *classes*, nor any one of the five *classes* that was not expert at his exercises. Moreover, they used such diligence in matching them for age and stature, that the officers of the legions, except they happened to be acquainted with the youths so bolted, were forced to put themselves upon fortune, while they of the first legion chose one, they of the second the next, they of the third another, and the fourth youth fell to the last legion; and thus was the election (the legions and the tribes varying according unto their lots) carried on till the foot were complete. The like course with little alteration was taken by horse officers till the horse also were complete. This was called giving of names (which the children of Israel did also by lot), and if any man refused to give his name he was sold for a slave, or his estate confiscated to the commonwealth. *Marcus Curius consul cum subitum delectum edicere coactus esset et juniorum nemo respondisset conjectis in sortem omnibus, Polliae* (it is the name of a tribe) *quae proxima exierat, primum nomen urna extractum citari jussit, neque eo respondente, bona adolescentis hasta subjecit;*[99] which was conformable unto the law in Israel, according whereunto Saul took a yoke of oxen, and hewed them in pieces, and sent them throughout the tribes, saying *whosoever cometh not forth* (unto battle) *after Saul and Samuel, so shall it be done unto his oxen.*[100] By which you may observe also that they who had no cattle were not of the militia in Israel. But the age of the Roman youth (*lege Tullia*) determined at thirty, and by the law (though it should seem by Machiavel and others that this was not well observed) a man could not stand for magistracy till he was *miles emeritus*, had fulfilled the full term of his militia, which was complete in his tenth stipend or service; nor was he thenceforth obliged under any penalty to give his name, except the commonwealth were invaded, in which case the elders were as well obliged as the youth. (*Quod per magnos tumultus fieri solitum erat, justitio indicto, delectus sine vacationibus habitus est.*)[101] The consul might also levy *milites evocatos*, commanded men out of such as had served their term, and this at his discretion. The legions, being thus complete, were divided by two unto each consul; and in these no man had right to serve but a Roman citizen. Now because two legions made but a small army, the Romans added unto every one of their armies an equal number of foot and a double number of horse, levied among their Latin or Italian associates; so a consular army with the legions and auxiliaries amounted to about thirty thousand, and whereas they commonly levied two such armies together, these being joined made a matter of sixty thousand.

The steps whereby our militia follows the greatest captain are

---

[99] Valerius Maximus, VI, iii, 4. Liljegren (p. 351) remarks: 'I have been unable to find one (edition) which accounts for all corruptions in H's quotation.'
[100] I Samuel, 11: 7.   [101] Livy, VII, xxviii.

the three essays: the first elected by a fifth man *curiatis*, in the parishes, amounting in the whole unto one hundred thousand, choosing their officers *centuriatis*, and the hundreds, where they fall also unto their games or exercises, invited by handsome prizes, such as for themselves and the honour of them will be coveted; such as in the space of ten years will harness you thirty thousand men, horse and foot, with such arms, for their forge, proof and beauty, as (notwithstanding the *argyraspides*, or silver shields of Alexander's guard) were never worn by so many; such as will present marks of virtue and direction unto your general or strategus in the distribution of his army, which doubles the value of them unto the proprietors, who are bound to wear them, and easeth the commonwealth of so much charge, so many being armed already. But here will be the objection now. How shall such a revenue be compassed? Fifty pounds a year in every hundred is a great deal, not so easily raised; men will not part with their money; nor would the sum, as it is proposed by the order of pomp, rise in many years. These are difficulties that fit our genius exactly. And yet a thousand pounds in each hundred, once levied, establisheth the revenue for ever. Now the hundreds, one with another, are worth ten thousand pounds a year dry rent, over and above personal estates which bring it unto twice the value. So a twentieth part of one year's revenue of the hundred does it. If you cannot afford this while you pay taxes, though from henceforth they will be but small ones, do it when you pay none; if it be then too much for one year, do it in two; if it be too much for two years, do it in four. What husbands have we hitherto been? What is become of greater sums? My lords, if you should thus cast your bread upon the waters, after many days you would find it; stand not huckling, when you are offered corn and your money again in the mouth of the sack.

But to proceed: the first essay, being officered at the hundreds, and mustered *tributis*, at the tribes, where they are entertained with other sports which will be very fine ones, proceed unto the election of the second essay, or standing army of this nation, consisting of thirty thousand foot and ten thousand horse; and these (upon a war decreed), being delivered at the rendezvous of Oceana unto the strategus, are the third essay, which answereth unto the Roman legions. But you may observe, that whereas the consuls elected the military tribunes, and raised commanded men out of the veterans at their own discretion, our polemarchs or field officers are elected by the scrutiny of the council of war, and our veterans not otherwise taken on than as volunteers, and with the consent of the polemarchs, which may serve for the removal of certain scruples which might otherwise be incident in this place, though without encouragement by the Roman way of proceeding, much less that which is proposed. But whereas the Roman legions in all amounted not in one army to above thirty thousand men, or little more, you have here forty thousand; and whereas they added auxiliaries, in this regard it is that Marpesia will be of greater revenue unto you than if you had the Indies, for whereas heretofore she hath brought you forth nothing but her native thistle, ploughing out the rankness of her aristocracy by your agrarian, you will find her an inexhaustible magazine of men, and to her own advantage, who will make a far better account by the arms, than by the pins of Poland.[102] Wherefore, as a consular army consisted of about an equal number of auxiliaries added unto their legions by their Latin or Italian associates, you may add unto a parliamentary army an equal number of Marpesians or Panopeans, as that colony shall hereafter be able to supply you. By which means the commonwealth will be able to go forth to battle with fourscore thousand men. To make wars with small forces is no husbandry, but a waste, a disease, a lingering and painful consumption of men and money; the Romans, making theirs thick, made them short, and had little regard unto money, as that which they who have men enough can command where it is fittest that it should be levied.[103] All the ancient monarchies by this means got on wing and attained unto vast riches; whereas your modern princes, being dear purchasers of small parcels, have but empty pockets. But it may be that some will accuse the order of rashness, in that it committeth the sole conduct of the war unto the general, and the custom of Venice by her *proveditori*, or checks upon her commanders in chief, may seem to be of greater prudence; but in this part of our government neither Venice, nor any nation that maketh use of mercenary forces, is for our instruction. A mercenary army, with a standing

---

[102] Attempts such as Liljegren's (p. 354) to associate 'the pin[e]s of Poland' with the thistles of Scotland or the 'staddles' of Bacon's essay (p. 2 n. 2, above) are not very satisfying.

[103] *Discorsi*, III, 6, and 8.

general, is like the fatal sister that spins; but proper forces, with an annual magistrate, are like her that cuts the thread. Their interests are quite contrary, and yet you have a better *proveditore* than the Venetian, another strategus sitting with an army standing by him; whereupon that which is marching, if there were any probability it should, would find as little possibility that it could recoil, as a foreign enemy to invade you. These things considered, a war will appear to be of a contrary nature unto that of all other reckonings, in as much as of this you must never look to have a good account if you be strict in imposing checks. Let a council of huntsmen assembled beforehand tell you which way the stag shall run, where you shall cast about at the fault, and how you shall ride to be in at the chase all the day; but these may as well do that, as a council of war direct a general. The hours, that have painted wings and of different colours, are his counsel: he must be like the eye, that maketh not the scene, but hath it so soon as it changes. That 'in many counsellors there is strength' is spoken of civil administrations; as to those that are military, there is nothing more certain than that in many counsellors there is weakness. Joint commissions in military affairs are like hunting your hounds in their couples. In the Attic war, Cleomenes and Demaratus, kings of Lacedaemon, being thus coupled, tugged one against another and, while they should have joined against the Persian, were the cause of the calamity; whereupon that commonwealth took better counsel, and made a law whereby from thenceforth there went at once but one of her kings unto battle.

The Fidenati being in rebellion, and having slain the colony of the Romans, four tribunes with consular power were created by the people of Rome, whereof one being left for the guard of the city, the other three were sent against the Fidenati, who through the division that happened among them, brought nothing home but dishonour, whereupon the Romans created the dictator; and Livy gives his judgment in these words: *Tres tribuni, potestate consulari, documento fuere, quam plurimum imperium bello inutile esset; tendendo ad sua quisque consilia, cum alii aliud videretur, aperuerunt ad occasionem locum hosti.*[104] When the consuls, Quinctius and Agrippa, were sent against the Aequi, Agrippa for this reason

[104] Livy, IV, xxxi.

refused to go forth with his colleague, saying *saluberrimum in administratione magnarum rerum, summum imperii apud unum esse.*[105] And if the ruin of modern armies were well considered, most of it would be found to have fallen upon this point; it being in this case far safer to trust unto any one man of common prudence, than to any two or more together of the greatest parts. The consuls indeed, being equal in power, while one was present with the senate and the other in the field with the army, made a good balance; and this with us is exactly followed by the election of a new strategus upon the march of the old one.

The seven and twentieth order, whereby the elders in case of invasion are obliged unto equal duty with the youth, and each upon their own charge, is suitable unto reason (for every man defends his own estate) and unto our copy, as in the war with the Samnites and Tuscans. *Senatus justitium indici, delectum omnis generis hominum haberi jussit; nec ingenui modo, et juniores sacramento adacti sunt, sed senorium etiam cohortes factae.*[106] This nation of all others is the least obnoxious unto invasion. Oceana, saith a French politician, is a beast that cannot be devoured but by herself.[107] Nevertheless, that government is not perfect which is not provided at all points, and in this *ad triarios res rediit*; the elders being such as in a martial state must be veterans, the commonwealth invaded gathers strength (like Antaeus) by her fall, whilst the whole number of the elders consisting of five hundred thousand, and the youth of as many (being brought up according unto the order), give twelve successive battles, each battle consisting of eighty thousand men, half elders, and half youth. And the commonwealth, whose constitution can be no stranger unto any of those virtues which are to be acquired in human life, grows familiar with death ere she die. If the hand of God be upon her for her transgressions, she shall mourn for her sins and lie in the dust for her iniquities, without losing of her manhood.

> *Si fractus illabatur orbis*
> *Impavidam ferient ruinae.*[108]

---

[105] Livy, III, lxix (paraphrased). [106] Livy, X, xxi.

[107] Liljegren (pp. 355–6) gave two Italian versions of this dictum, and might as well have cited the closing speech of Shakespeare's *King John*. Many versions were current; the 'French politician' is probably Henri, Duc de Rohan.

[108] Horace, *Carmina*, III.

The remaining part, being the constitution of the provincial orb, is partly civil, or consisting of the elders, and partly military, or consisting of the youth. The civil part of the provincial orb is directed by:

> *The twenty-eighth order:* whereby the council of a province, being constituted of twelve knights, divided by four into three regions (for their term and revolution conformable unto the parliament), is perpetuated by the annual election at the tropic of four knights (being triennial magistrates) out of the region of the senate whose term expireth, and of one knight out of the same region to be strategus or general of the province, which magistracy is annual. The strategus or magistrate thus chosen shall be as well president of the provincial council, with power to propose unto the same as general of the army. The council for the rest shall elect weekly provosts, having any two of them also right to propose, after the manner of the senatorian councils of Oceana. And whereas all provincial councils are members of the council of state, they may and ought to keep diligent correspondence with the same, which is to be done after this manner: any opinion or opinions legitimately proposed and debated at a provincial council, being thereupon signed by the strategus or any two of the provosts, may be transmitted unto the council of state in Oceana. And the council of state, proceeding upon the same in their natural course (whether by their own power if it be a matter within their instructions, or by authority of the senate thereupon consulted if it be a matter of state which is not in their instructions, or by authority of the senate and command of the people if it be a matter of law, as for the levies of men or money upon common use and safety), shall return such answers, advice or orders, as in any of the ways mentioned shall be determined upon the case. The provincial councils of Marpesia and Panopea respectively shall take especial care that the agrarian laws, as also all other laws that be or shall from time to time be enacted by the parliament of Oceana for either of them, be duly put in execution. They shall manage and receive the customs of either nation for the shipping of Oceana, being the common guard; they shall have a care that moderate and sufficient pay upon the respective province be duly raised for the purport and maintenance of the officers and soldiers, or army of the same, in the most effectual, constant and convenient way. They shall receive the *regalia*, or public revenues of those nations, out of which every counsellor shall have, for his term and unto his proper use, the sum of five hundred pounds *per annum*, and the

strategus five hundred pounds as president, besides his pay as general, which shall be one thousand pounds; the remainder to go unto the use of the knights and deputies of the respective provinces, to be paid, if it will reach according unto the rates of Oceana; if not, by an equal distribution, respectively; or the over-plus, if there be any, to be returned unto the treasury of Oceana. They shall manage the lands (if there be any such) holden in either of the provinces by the commonwealth of Oceana in dominion, and return the rents into the exchequer. If the commonwealth come to be possessed of richer provinces, the pay of the general or strategus, and of the councils, may be respectively increased. The people for the rest shall elect ther own magistrates, and be governed by their own laws having power also to appeal from their native or provincial magistrates, if they please, unto the people of Oceana. And whereas there may be such as, receiving injury, are not able to prosecute their appeals at so great a distance, eight serjeants at law, being sworn by the commissioners of the seal, shall be sent by four into each province once in two years, who, dividing the same by circuits, shall hear such causes, and having gathered and introduced them shall return unto the several appellants, gratis, the determinations and decrees of the people in their several cases.

The term of a knight in a provincial orb, as to domestic magistracies, shall be esteemed a vacation and no bar unto present election into any other honour, his provincial magistracy being expired.

The quorum of a provincial council, as also of every other council or assembly in Oceana, shall in time of health consist of two parts in three of the whole number proper unto that council or assembly; and in a time of sickness of one part in three. But of the senate there can be no quorum without three of the signory nor of a council without two of the provosts.

The civil part of the provincial orb being declared by the foregoing order, the military part of the same is constituted by:

The twenty-ninth order: whereby the stratiots of the third essay, having drawn the gold balls marked with the letter M, and being ten horse and fifty foot in a tribe, that is to say five hundred horse and two thousand five hundred foot in all, the tribes shall be delivered by the respective conductors unto the provincial strategus or general, at such a time and place or rendezvous as he shall appoint by order and certificate of his election; and the strategus, having received the horse and foot mentioned, which are the third *classis* of his provincial guard or army, shall forthwith lead them away unto Marpesia, where, the army consisting of three *classes*, each *classis* containing three thousand men, whereof five hundred are horse, and receiving the new strategus with the third *classis*, the old strategus with the first *classis*, the old strategus with the first *classis* shall be dismissed by the provincial council. The same method with the stratiots of the letter P is to be observed for the provincial orb of Panopea; and, the commonwealth coming to acquire new provinces, the senate and the people may erect new orbs in like manner, consisting of greater or less numbers according as is required by the respective occasion. If a stratiot have once served his term in a provincial orb, and happen afterwards to draw the letter of a province at the election of the second essay, he may refuse his lot; and if he refuse it, the censor of that urn shall cause the files balloting at the same to make an halt, and if the stratiot produce the certificate of his strategus or general that he hath served his time accordingly, the censor, throwing the ball that he drew into the urn again and taking out a blank, shall dismiss the youth and cause the ballot to proceed.

To perfect the whole structure of this commonwealth, some directions are given unto the third essay, or army marching in:

The thirtieth order:

> *When thou goest to battle against thine enemy, and seest horses and chariots, and a people more than thou, be not afraid of them, for the Lord thy God is he that goeth with thee to fight for thee against thine enemies: and when thou dividest the spoil, it shall be as a statute and an ordinance unto thee that as his part is that goeth down to the battle, so shall his part be that tarryeth by the stuff.*[109]

That is, as to the commonwealth of Oceana: the spoil taken of the enemy (except clothes, arms, horses, ammunition and victual, to be divided unto the soldiery by the strategus and the polemarchs upon the place according unto their discretion) shall be delivered unto four commissaries of the spoils, elected and sworn by the council of war, which commissaries shall be allowed shipping by the state and convoys according as occasion shall require by the strategus, to the end that, having a bill of lading signed by three or more of the polemarchs, they may ship and bring or cause such spoils to be brought unto the prize office in Oceana, where they

---

[109] This is a conflation of Deuteronomy, 20: 1 and 1 Samuel (H in error says 11) 30: 24.

shall be sold and the profit arising by such spoils shall be divided into three parts, whereof one shall go unto the treasury, another shall be paid to the soldiery of this nation, a third unto the auxiliaries at their return from their service, provided that the said auxiliaries be equal in number unto the proper forces of this nation; otherwise their share shall be so much less as they are fewer in number; the rest of the two-thirds to go unto the officers and soldiers of the proper forces; and the spoils so divided unto the proper forces shall be subdivided into three equal parts, whereof one shall go unto the officers and two unto the common soldiers, the like for the auxiliaries; and the share allotted unto the officers shall be divided into four equal parts, whereof one shall go to the strategus, another unto the polemarchs, a third unto the colonels and a fourth unto the captains, cornets, ensigns and under officers, receiving their share of the spoil as common soldiers. The like for the auxiliaries; and this upon pain, in the case of failure, of what the people of Oceana, unto whom the cognizance of peculation or crimes of this nature is properly appertaining, shall adjudge or decree.[110]

Upon these three last orders the Archon seemed to be haranguing at the head of his army, in this manner:

My dear lords and excellent patriots:
A government of this make is a commonwealth for increase. Of those for preservation, the inconveniences and frailties have been shown; their roots are narrow, such as do not run, have no fivers,[111] their tops weak and dangerously exposed unto the weather; except you chance to find one (as Venice) planted in a flowerpot, and if she grow, she grows top-heavy and falls too. But you cannot plant an oak in a flowerpot; she must have earth for her root, and heaven for her branches.

Imperium Oceano famamque terminet astris.[112]

Rome was said *mole sua ruere*, to be broken by her own weight, but poetically. For that weight, by which she was pretended to be ruined, was supported in her emperors by a far slighter foundation. And in the common experience of good architecture, there is

---

[10] This is the point at which the break in pagination occurs, apparently occasioned by the 'spaniel questing'; see Harrington: 1977, p. 6.
[11] I.e., fibres (*OED*).   [112] *Aeneid*, I, 287.

nothing more known than that buildings stand the firmer and the longer for their own weight, nor ever swerve through any other internal cause than that their materials are corruptible; but the people never die nor, as a political body, are subject unto any other corruption than that which deriveth from their government. Unless a man will deny the chain of causes, in which he denies God, he must also acknowledge the chain of effects; wherefore there can be no effect in nature that is not from the first cause, and those successive links of the chain without which it could not have been. Now, except a man can show the contrary in a commonwealth, if there be no cause of corruption in the first make of it, there can never be any such effect. Let no man's superstition impose profaneness upon this assertion; for as man is sinful, but yet the world is perfect, so may the citizen be sinful and yet the commonwealth be perfect. And as man, seeing the world is perfect, can never commit any such sin as can render it imperfect or bring it unto a natural dissolution, so the citizen, where the commonwealth is perfect, can never commit any such crime as can render it imperfect or bring it unto a natural dissolution. To come unto experience, Venice, notwithstanding that we have found some flaws in it, is the only commonwealth in the make whereof no man can find a cause of dissolution; for which reason we behold her (albeit she consist of men that are not without sin) at this day with one thousand years upon her back, for any internal cause as young, as fresh and free from decay or any appearance of it, as she was born. But whatever in nature is not sensible of decay by the course of a thousand years is capable of the whole age of nature; by which calculation, for any check that I am able to give myself, a commonwealth rightly ordered may for any internal causes be as immortal, or long-lived, as the world. But if this be true, those commonwealths that are naturally fallen must have derived their ruin from the rise of them. Israel and Athens died not natural, but violent deaths; in this manner the world is to die. We are speaking of those causes of dissolution which are natural unto government, and they are but two: either contradiction or inequality. If a commonwealth be a contradiction she must needs destroy herself; and if she be unequal, it tends to strife, and strife to ruin. By the former of these fell Lacedaemon, by the latter Rome. Lacedaemon being made altogether for war and yet not for increase, her natural progress became her natural dissolution, and the building of her own victorious hand too heavy for her foundation; so she indeed fell by her own weight. But Rome through her native inequality; which how it inveterated the bosoms of the senate and the people against other and even unto death, hath been shown at large.

Look well unto it, my lords, for if there be a contradiction or inequality in your commonwealth, it must fall; but if it have neither of these, it hath no principle of mortality. Do not think me impudent; if this be truth, I should commit a gross indiscretion in concealing it. Sure I am that Machiavel is for the immortality of a commonwealth upon far weaker principles. 'If a commonwealth', saith he, 'were so happy as to be provided often with men that, when she is swerving from her principles, should reduce her unto her institution, she would be immortal.'[113] But a commonwealth, as we have demonstrated, swerveth not from her principles, but by and through her institution; if she brought no bias into the world with her, her course for any internal cause must be straight forward, as we see is that of Venice; she cannot turn unto the right hand nor to the left, but by some rubs, which is not an internal but an external cause; against such she can be no way fortified but through her situation, as in Venice, or through her militia, as was Rome; by which examples a commonwealth may be secure of those also. Think me not vain, for I cannot hold;[114] a commonwealth that is rightly instituted can never swerve, nor one that is not rightly instituted be secured from swerving by reduction unto her principles; wherefore it is no less apparent in this place that Machiavel understood not a commonwealth as to the whole piece. As where having told you 'that a tribune, or any other citizen of Rome, might propose a law unto the people, and debate it with them', he adds: 'this order was good while the people were good, but when the people became evil, it became most pernicious';[115] as if this order, through which, with the like, the people most apparently became evil, could ever have been good; or that the people or the commonwealth could ever have become good, by being reduced unto such principles as were the original of their evil. The disease of Rome was, as hath been shown, from the

---

[113] *Discorsi*, III, 22. H also cites II, 29, without apparent warrant, but neglects III, 1, where the subject is treated at length.
[114] Toland amended this to: 'I cannot conceal my opinion here.'   [115] *Discorsi*, I, 18.

native inequality of her balance, and no otherwise from the empire of the world, which then as this falling into one scale, that of the nobility (an evil in such a fabric inevitable) kicked out the people, wherefore a man that could have made her to throw away the empire of the world might in that have reduced her unto her principles, and yet have been so far from rendering her immortal that going no farther he should never have cured her. But your commonwealth[116] is founded upon an equal agrarian; and if the earth be given unto the sons of men, this balance is the balance of justice, such an one as, in having due regard unto the different industry of different men, yet *faithfully judgeth the poor. And the king that faithfully judgeth the poor, his throne shall be established forever.*[117] Much more the commonwealth; seeing that equality, which is the necessary dissolution of monarchy, is the generation, the very life and soul of a commonwealth. And now, if ever, I may be excusable, seeing that 'the throne of a commonwealth may be established for ever' is consonant unto the holy Scriptures.

The balance of a commonwealth that is equal is of such nature that whatever falleth into her empire must fall equally, and if the whole earth fall into your scales it must fall equally; and so you may be a greater people and yet not swerve from your principles one hair. Nay, you will be so far from that, that you must bring the world in such a case unto your balance, even unto the balance of justice. But hearken, my lords, are we on earth? do we see the sun? or are we visiting those shady places which are feigned by the poets?

Continuo audita voces, vagitus et ingens.[118]

These Gothic empires that are yet in the world were at the first, though they had legs of their own, but an heavy and unwieldy burden; but, their foundations being now broken, the iron of them entereth even into the souls of the oppressed; and hear the voice of their comforters: *My father hath chastised you with whips, but I will chastise you with scorpions.*[119] Hearken, I say; if thy brother cry unto thee in affliction, wilt thou not hear him? This is a commonwealth of the fabric that hath an open ear and a public concernment; she is not made for herself only, but given as a magistrate of God unto

---

[116] 'C.W.' in original.   [117] Proverbs, 29: 14.
[118] *Aeneid*, VI, 426.   [119] I Kings, 12: 11 and 14; II Chronicles, 10: 11 and 14.

mankind, for the vindication of common right and the law of nature. Wherefore saith Cicero of the like, that of the Romans, '*nos magis patronatum orbis terrarum suscepimus, quam imperium*'; we have rather undertaken the patronage than the empire of the world.[120] If you, not regarding this example – like some other nations that are upon the point to smart for it – shall, having attained unto your own liberty, bear the sword of your common magistracy in vain, sit still and fold your arms, or which is worse, let out the blood of your people unto tyrants, to be shed in the defence of their yokes like water, and so not only *turn the grace of God into wantonness*, but his *justice into wormwood*, you are not now making a commonwealth, *but heaping coals of fire upon your own heads.*[121] A commonwealth, I say, of this make is a minister of God upon earth, to the end that the world may be governed with righteousness. For which cause (that I may come at length unto our present business), the orders last rehearsed are buds of empire, such as, with the blessing of God, may spread the arms of your commonwealth like an holy asylum unto the distressed world, and give the earth her sabbath of years or rest from her labours, under the shadow of your wings. It is upon this point where the writings of Machiavel, having for the rest excelled all other authors, come as far to excel themselves.

'Commonwealths', saith he, 'have had three ways of propagating themselves'; one, after the manner of monarchies, 'by imposing the yoke, which was the way of Athens and towards the latter times of Lacedaemon; another by equal leagues, which is the way of Switz' (I shall add of Holland though since his time); 'a third by unequal leagues, which, to the shame of the world, was never practiced', nay not so much as seen or minded, 'by any other commonwealth, but that only of Rome.'[122] They will each of them, either for caution or imitation, be worthy to be well weighed, which is the proper work of this place. Athens and Lacedaemon have been the occasion of great scandal to the world in two, or at least one of two, regards. The first their emulation, which involved Greece in perpetual wars; the second their way of propagation which, by imposing yokes upon others, was plainly contradictory to their own principles.

For the first, governments, be they of what kind soever, if they

---

[120] Cicero, *De Officiis*, II, 27; 'patronatum' should be 'patrocinium'.
[121] Proverbs, 25: 22.   [122] *Discorsi*, II, 4.

be planted too close, are like trees that, impatient in their growth to have it hindered, eat out one another. It was not unknown unto these in contemplation, or (if you read the story of Agesilaus) in action, that either of them with thirty thousand men might have mastered the East; and certainly, if the one had not stood in the other's light, Alexander had come too late to that end, which was the means (and would be if they were to live again) of ruin at the least unto one of them; wherefore with any man that understandeth the nature of government, this is excusable. So it was between Oceana and Marpesia; so it is between France and Spain (though less excusable); and so it ever will be in like cases. But to come unto the second occasion of scandal by them given, which was in the way of their propagation, it is not excusable, for they brought their confederates under bondage; by which means Athens gave occasion of the Peloponnesian war, the wound of which she died stinking, when Lacedaemon, taking the same infection from her carcass, soon followed.

Wherefore, my lords, let these be warnings unto you not to make that liberty which God hath given you a snare unto others, in using this kind of enlargement of yourselves.

The second way of propagation or enlargement used by commonwealths is that of Switz and Holland, equal leagues. This, though it be not otherwise mischievous, is useless to the world and dangerous unto themselves; useless unto the world, for, as the former governments were storks, these are blocks, have no sense of honour, or concernment in the sufferings of others, but, as the Aetolians, a state of the like fabric, were reproached by Philip of Macedon, prostrate[123] themselves by letting out their arms unto the lusts of others; while they have their own liberty barren, and without legitimate issue. I do not defame the people; the Switz for valour have no superior, the Hollander for industry no equal; but themselves in the meantime shall so much the less excuse their governments, seeing that unto the Switz it is well enough known that the ensigns of his commonwealth have no other motto than *in te converte manus*, and that of the Hollander, though he sweat more gold than the Spaniard digs, lets him languish in debt, for she herself lives upon charity. These are dangerous unto themselves,

---

[123] *Sic*; but 'prostitute'?

precarious governments, such as do not command but beg their bread from province to province; coats that, being patched up of all colours, are of none. That their cantons and provinces are so many arrows is good; but they are so many bows too, which is naught.

Like unto these was the commonwealth of the ancient Tuscans, hung together like bobbins without an hand to weave with them; therefore easily overcome by the Romans, though at that time for number a far less considerable people. If your liberty be not a root that grows, it will be a branch that withers; which consideration brings me unto the paragon, the commonwealth of Rome.

The ways and means whereby the Romans acquired the patronage and in that the empire of the world, were different according unto the different condition of their commonwealth, in her rise and in her growth; in her rise she proceeded rather by colonies, in her growth by unequal leagues. Colonies without the bounds of Italy she planted none (such dispersion of the Roman citizen as to plant him in foreign parts, till the contrary interest of the emperors brought in that practice, was unlawful), nor did she ever demolish any city within that compass, or divest it of liberty; but whereas the most of them were commonwealths, stirred up by emulation of her great felicity to war against her, if she overcame any, she confiscated some part of their lands that were the greatest incendiaries or causes of the trouble, upon which she planted colonies of her own people, preserving the lands and liberties for the rest unto the natives or inhabitants. By this way of proceeding (that I may be brief as is possible) she did many and great things. For in confirming of liberty, she propagated her empire; in holding the inhabitants from rebellion, she put a curb upon the incursion of enemies; in exonerating herself of the poorer sort, she multiplied her citizens; in rewarding her veterans, she rendered the rest less seditious; and in acquiring unto herself the reverence of the common parent, she from time to time became the mother of new-born cities.

In her farther growth, the way of her propagation went more upon leagues, which for the first division were of two kinds, social and provincial. Again, social leagues, or leagues of society, were of two kinds, the first called Latinity or Latin, the second Italian right.

The league between the Romans and the Latins, or Latin right, approached nearest unto *jus Quiritium*, the right of a native Roman. The man or the city that was honoured with this right was *civitate donatus cum suffragio*, adopted a citizen of Rome, with the right of giving suffrage with the people in some cases, as those of confirmation of law, or determination in judicature (if both the consuls were agreed, not otherwise), wherefore, that coming to little, the greatest and most peculiar part of this privilege was that who had born magistracy, at least that of aedile or quaestor, in any Latin city, was by consequence of the same a citizen of Rome at all points.

Italian right was also donation of the city, but without suffrage; they who were in either of these leagues were governed by their own laws and magistrates, having all the rights as to liberty of citizens of Rome, yielding and paying to the commonwealth, as head of the league and having the conduct of all affairs appertaining to the common cause, such aid of men and monies as were particularly agreed upon the merit of the cause, and specified in their respective leagues; whence such leagues came to be called equal or unequal accordingly.

Provincial leagues were of different extension, according unto the merit and capacity of a conquered people, but of one kind; for every province was governed by Roman magistrates, as a praetor or a consul, according to the dignity of the province, for the civil administration and conduct of the provincial army; and a quaestor for the gathering of the public revenue, from which magistrates a province might appeal unto Rome.

For the better understanding of these particulars, I shall exemplify in as many of them as is needful; and first, in Macedon. The Macedonians were thrice conquered by the Romans, first under the conduct of T. Quintus Flaminius, secondly under that of L. Aemilius Paulus, and thirdly, under that of Q. Caecilius Metellus, thence called Macedonicus.

For the first time, *pax petenti Philippo data, Graeciae libertas.*[124] Philip of Macedon who, possessed of Acrocorinthus, boasted, no less than was true, that he had Greece in fetters, being overcome by Flaminius, had his kingdom restored unto him upon condition that he should forthwith set all the cities which he held in Greece

---

[124] The story of the 'liberation' of Greece is from Livy, XXXIII, xxx–xxxiii.

and in Asia at liberty; and that he should not make war out of Macedon, but by leave of the senate of Rome; which Philip (having no other way to save anything) agreed should be done accordingly.

The Grecians being at this time assembled at the Isthmian games, where the concourse was mighty great, a crier, appointed unto the office by Flaminius, was heard among them proclaiming all Greece to be free; to which the people, being amazed at so hopeless a thing, gave little credit, till they received such testimony of the truth as put it past all doubt; whereupon they fell immediately on running unto the pro-consul, with flowers and garlands and such violent expressions of their admiration and joy, as if Flaminius, a young man (about some thirty-three), had not also been very strong, he must have died of no other death than their kindness, while, everyone striving to touch his hand, they bore him up and down the field with an unruly throng, full of such ejaculations as these: 'How! Is there a people in the world that at their own charge, at their own peril, will fight for the liberty of another? Did they live at the next door unto this fire? Or what kind of men are these, whose business it is to pass seas that the world may be governed with righteousness? The cities of Greece and of Asia shake off their iron fetters at the voice of a crier! Was it madness to imagine such a thing, and is it done? O virtue! O felicity! O fame!'

In this example your lordships have a donation of liberty, or of Italian right, unto a people, by restitution to what they had formerly enjoyed, and some particular men, families, or cities, according unto their merit of the Romans, if not upon like occasions, were gratified with Latinity.

But Philip's share by this means did not please him, wherefore the league was broken by his son Perseus; and the Macedonians thereupon for the second time conquered by Aemilius Paulus, their king taken, and they, sometime after the victory, summoned unto the tribunal of the general, where, remembering how little hope they ought to have of pardon, they expected some dreadful sentence; when Aemilius in the first place declared the Macedonians to be free, in the full possession of their lands, goods, and laws, with right to elect annual magistrates, yielding and paying unto the people of Rome one half of the tribute which they were accustomed to pay unto their own kings. This done, he went on, making so skillful a division of the country, in order to the methodizing of the people and casting them into a form of popular government, that the Macedonians, being first surprised with the virtue of the Romans, began now to alter the scene of their admiration, that a stranger to them should do such things for them in their own country, and with full facility as they had never so much as once imagined to be possible. Nor was this all, for Aemilius, as if not dictating to conquered enemies but to some well-deserving friends, gave them in the last place laws so suitable, and contrived with such care and prudence, that long use and experience (the only correctress of works of this nature) could never find a fault in them.

In this example you have a donation of liberty, or of Italian right, unto a people that had not tasted it before, but were now taught how to use it.

My lords, the royalists should compare what we are doing, and what hitherto we have done for them, with this example. It is a shame that while we are boasting up ourselves above all, we should be so far from imitating such examples as these that we do not so much as understand that if government be the parent of manners, where there be no heroical virtues there is no heroical government.

But the Macedonians, rebelling (at the name of a false Philip) the third time against the Romans, were by them judged incapable of liberty, and reduced by Metellus into a province.

Now whereas it remains that I explain the nature of a province, I shall rather choose that of Sicily, because, having been the first that the Romans made, the descriptions of the rest relate to it.

'We have so received the Sicilian cities into amity', saith Cicero, 'that they enjoy their ancient laws, and upon no other condition than of the same obedience unto the people of Rome, which they formerly yielded unto their own princes or superiors.'[125] So the Sicilians, whereas they had been parcelled forth unto divers princes and into divers states, the cause of perpetual wars whereby, hewing one another down, they became sacrifices unto the ambition of their neighbours or of some invader, were now received at the old rate unto a new protection, which could hold them and in which no enemy durst touch them; nor was it possible (as the case

[125] Liljegren (pp. 360–1) thought that H took the quotation from Sigonius, *De antiquo jure provinciarum*, I, 3.

stood with such) for the Sicilians to receive, or for the Romans to give more.

A Roman province is defined by Sigonius, *a region having provincial right.*[126] Provincial right in general was to be governed by a Roman praetor or consul, in matter at least of state and of the militia; and by a quaestor, whose office it was to receive the public's revenue. Provincial right in particular was different, according unto the different leagues or agreements between the commonwealth and the people reduced unto a province.

> *Siculi hoc jure sunt, ut quod vivis cum cive agat, domi certet suis legibus, quod Siculus cum Siculo non ejusdem civitatis, ut de eo praeter judices, ex P. Rupilii decreto, sortiatur. Quod privatus a populo petit, aut populus a privato, senatus ex aliqua civitate, qui judicet, datur, cui alterna civitates rejecta sunt. Quod civis Romanus a Siculo petit, Siculus judex datur; quod Siculus a cive Romano, civis Romanus datur. Ceterarum rerum selecti judices ex civium Romanorum conventu proponi solent. Inter aratores et decumanos lege frumentaria, quam Hieronicam appellant, judicia fiunt.*[127]

Because the rest would oblige me into a discourse too large for this place, it shall suffice that I have shown you how it was in Sicily.

My lords, upon the fabric of your provincial orb I shall not hold you, because it is sufficiently described in the order, and I cannot believe that you think it inferior to the way of a praetor and a quaestor. But whereas the provincial way of the Roman commonwealths was that whereby she held the empire of the world, and your orbs are intended to be capable at the least of the like use, there may arise many controversies. As whether such a course be lawful, whether it be feasible and, seeing that the Romans ruined upon that point, whether it would not be unto the destruction of the commonwealth.

For the first, if the empire of a commonwealth be patronage, to ask whether it be lawful for a commonwealth to aspire unto the empire of the world is to ask whether it be lawful for her to do her duty, or to put the world into a better condition than it was before.

And to ask whether this be feasible is to ask why the Oceaner, being under the like administration of government, may not do as

---

[126] Sigonius, I, 1.

[127] Cicero, *In Verrem*, II, 13 (cf. Liljegren, pp. 361–2).

227

much with two hundred men as the Roman did with one hundred; for comparing their commonwealths in their rise, the difference is yet greater. Now that Rome, *seris avaritia luxuriaque*, through the natural thirst of her constitution, came at length, with the fullness of her provinces, to burst herself, this is no otherwise to be understood than as when a man, that from his own evil constitution had contracted the dropsy, dies with drinking; it being apparent that, in case her agrarian had held, she could never have been thus ruined. And I have already demonstrated that your agrarian, being once poised, can never break or swerve.

Wherefore, to draw towards some conclusion of this discourse, let me inculcate the use, by selecting a few considerations out of many. The regard had in this place unto the empire of the world appertaineth to a well-ordered commonwealth, more especially for two reasons.

1. The facility of this great enterprise, by a government of the model proposed.
2. The danger that you would run, in the omission of such government.

The facility of this enterprise, upon the grounds already laid, must needs be great, for as much as the empire of the world hath been, both in reason and experience, the necessary consequence of a commonwealth of this nature only; for, though it have been given unto all kinds to drive at it, inasmuch as that of Athens or Lacedaemon, if the one had not hung in the other's light, might have gained it, yet could neither of them have held it; not Athens, through the manner of her propagation which, being by downright tyranny, could not preserve what she had; nor Lacedaemon, because she was overthrown by the weight of a less conquest. The facility then of this great enterprise being peculiar unto popular government, I shall consider it, first in gaining, and secondly in holding.

For the former, *volenti non fit injuria*; it is said of the people under Eumenes that they would not have changed their subjection for liberty, wherefore the Romans gave them no disturbance.

If a people be contented with their government, it is a certain sign that it is good, and much good do them with it. The sword of your magistracy is for a terror unto them that do evil.

Eumenes had the fear of God, or of the Romans, before his eyes; concerning such he hath given you no commission. But[128] till we can say 'here are the Romans', where is Eumenes? Do not think that the late appearances of God unto you have been altogether for yourselves; *he hath surely seen the affliction* of your brethren, *and heard their cry by reason of their task-masters.*[129] For to believe otherwise is not only to be mindless of his ways, but altogether deaf. If you have ears to hear, this is the way in which you will assuredly be called upon; for if while there is no stock of liberty, no sanctuary of the afflicted, it be a common object to behold a people casting themselves out of the pan of one prince into the fire of another, what can you think but if the world should see the Roman eagle again, she would renew her age and her flight? Nor ever did she spread her wing with better omen than will be read in your ensigns, which, if called in by an oppressed people, they interpose between them and their yoke. The people themselves must either do nothing in the meantime, or have no more pains to take for their wished fruit than to gather it, if that be not done for them. Wherefore this must needs be easy, and yet you have a greater facility than is in the arm of flesh; for if the cause of mankind be the cause of God, the Lord of Hosts will be your captain, and you shall be a praise unto the earth.

The facility of holding is in the way of your propagation; if you take that of Athens and Lacedaemon, you shall rain snares, but either catch or hold nothing. Lying lips are an abomination unto the Lord; if setting up for liberty you impose yokes, he will assuredly destroy you. On the other side, to go about a work of this nature by a league without an head is to abdicate that magistracy, wherewithal he hath not only indued you but whereof he will require an account of you; for *cursed is he that doth the work of the Lord negligently.*[130] Wherefore you are to take the course of Rome. If you have subdued a nation that is capable of liberty, you shall make them a present of it, as did Flaminius unto Greece and Aemilius unto Macedon, reserving unto yourselves some part of that revenue which was legally paid unto the former government, together with the right of being head of the league, which

[128] There is a paragraph break between 'commission' and 'But' in both C and P (pp. 267–8).
[129] Exodus, 3: 7.
[130] Jeremiah, 48: 16 ('deceitfully' in A.V.).

includeth such levies of men and money as shall be necessary for the carrying on of the public work; for if a people have by your means attained unto freedom, they owe both unto the cause and you such aid as may propagate the like fruit unto the rest of the world. But whereas every nation is not capable of her liberty unto this degree; lest you be put to doing and undoing of things, as the Romans were in Macedon, you shall diligently observe what nation is fit for her liberty unto this degree, and what not; which is to be done by two marks, the first if she be willing to *help the Lord against the mighty*,[131] for if she have no care of the liberty of mankind, she deserveth not her own. But because in this you may be deceived by pretences which, continuing for a while specious, may afterwards vanish, the other is more certain, and that is if she be capable of an equal agrarian; which that it was not observed by excellent Aemilius, in his donation of liberty and introduction of a popular state among the Macedonians, I am more than moved to believe, for two reasons; the first because at the same time the agrarian was odious unto the Roman patricians; the second, that the pseudo-Philip could afterwards so easily recover Macedon, which could not have happened but by the nobility, and their impatience, having great estates, to be equalled with the people; for that the people should otherwise, at the mere sound of a name, have thrown away their liberty, is incredible. Wherefore be assured that the nation where you cannot establish an equal agrarian is incapable of her liberty, as to this kind of donation. For example, except the aristocracy in Marpesia be dissolved, neither can that people have their liberty there, nor you govern at home; for they continuing still liable to be sold by their lords unto foreign princes, there will never (especially in a country of which there is no other profit to be made) be want of such merchants and drovers, while you must be the market where they are to receive their second payment.

Nor can the aristocracy there be dissolved but by your means, in relation whereunto you are provided with your provincial orb which, being proportioned unto the measure of the nation that you have vindicated or conquered, will easily hold it; for there is not a people in the world more difficult to be held than the Marpesians, which, though by themselves it be given unto their own nature, is

[131] Judges, 5: 23. The curse of Meroz, famous in Civil War rhetoric, is upon those who are not willing.

truly to be attributed unto that of their country. Nevertheless, you having nine thousand men upon the continual guard of it that, threatened by any sudden insurrection, have places of retreat, and an army of forty thousand men upon a day's warning ready to march unto their rescue, it is not to be rationally shown which way they can possibly slip out of your hands; and if a man shall think that upon a province more remote, and divided by sea, you have not the like hold, he hath not so well considered your wings as your talons, your shipping being of such nature as maketh the descent of your armies almost of equal facility in any country, so that what you take you hold, both because your militia, being already populous, will be of great growth in itself, and through the confederates by whom, in taking and holding, you are still more enabled to take and hold.

Nor shall you easilier hold than the people under your empire or patronage be held. My lords, I would not go unto the door, to see whether it be *rimarum plena*, close shut; this is no under-board dealing, nor game at which he shall have any advantage against you that sees your cards, but to the contrary the advantage shall be your own; for with eighteen thousand men (which number I put because it circulates your orb by the annual charge of six thousand), having set the matters in the order shown, you will be able to hold the greatest province; and eighteen thousand men, allowing them greater pay than any prince ever gave, will not stand the province in one million revenue.[132] In consideration whereof, they shall have their own estates free unto themselves, be governed by their own laws and magistrates; which if the revenue of the province be in dry rent (as there may be some that are four times as big in Oceana) forty millions, will bring it with that of industry (to speak with the least) unto twice the value, so that the people there, who at this day are so oppressed that they have nothing at all whereupon to live, shall for one million paid unto you receive at the least seventy-nine unto their proper use. In which place I appeal unto any man whether the empire described can be other than the patronage of the world.

Now if you add unto the propagation of civil liberty, what is so natural unto this commonwealth that it cannot be omitted, the

---

[132] 'This by the pay of a Parliamentary army, is demonstrated in the Corollary' – H's note. See p. 261 below.

propagation of the liberty of conscience, this empire, this
patronage of the world, is the kingdom of Christ. For as the
kingdom of God the Father was a commonwealth, so shall be the
kingdom of God the Son; *the people shall be willing in the day of his
power.*[133]

Having showed you in this and other places some of those
inestimable benefits of this kind of government, together with the
natural and facile emanation of them from their fountain, I come
(lest God, who hath appeared unto you, for he is the God of
nature, in the glorious constellation of these subordinate causes
whereof we have hitherto been taking the true elevation, should
shake off the dust of his feet against you) to warn you of your
dangers, which you, not taking the opportunity, will run by
omission.

Machiavel, speaking of the defect of Venice, through her want
of proper arms, cries out '*Questo tagliogli le gambe da montar in
cielo*';[134] this cut her wings and spoiled her mount unto heaven. If
you lay your commonwealth upon any other foundation than the
people, you frustrate yourself of proper arms and so lose the
empire of the world; nor is this all, but some other nation will have
it.

Columbus offered gold unto one of your kings, through whose
happy incredulity another prince hath drunk the poison, even unto
the consumption of his people; but I do not offer you a nerve of
war that is made of purse-strings, such an one as hath drawn the
face of the earth into convulsions, but such an one as is natural
unto her health and beauty. Look you to it, where there is tumbling
and tossing upon the bed of sickness, it must end in death or
recovery. Though the people of the world, in the dregs of the
Gothic empire, be yet tumbling and tossing upon the bed of sickness, they cannot die, nor is there any means of recovery for them
but by ancient prudence, whence of necessity it must come to pass
that this drug be better known. If France, Italy and Spain were not
all sick, all corrupted together, there would be none of them so, for
the sick would not be able to withstand the sound, nor the sound to
preserve her health without curing of the sick. The first of these
nations (which, if you stay her leisure, will in my mind be France)

[133] Psalms, 110: 3 – H's note; 'his' substituted for 'thy'.
[134] *Discorsi*, I, 6.

that recovers the health of ancient prudence shall assuredly govern the world, for what did Italy when she had it? And as you were in that, so shall you in the like case be reduced unto a province; I do not speak at random. Italy, *L. Aemilio Papo, C. Attilio Regulo cos.*, armed, upon the Gallic tumult that then happened, of herself and without the aid of foreign auxiliaries, seventy thousand horse and seven hundred thousand foot; but as Italy is the least of those three countries in extent, so is France the greatest in population.

I decus, i nostrum, melioribus utere fatis.[135]

My dear lords, Oceana *is as the rose of Sharon; and the lily of the valley. As the lily among thorns, such is my love among the daughters. She is comely as the tents of Kedar, and terrible as an army with banners. Her neck is as the tower of David, builded for an armoury, whereon there hang a thousand bucklers and shields of mighty men. Let me hear thy voice in the morning, whom my soul loveth. The south hath dropped and the west is breathing upon thy garden of spices. Arise, queen of the earth; arise, holy spouse of Jesus. For lo, the winter is past, the rain is over and gone. The flowers appear on the earth, the time of singing of birds is come, and the voice of the turtle is heard in our land. Arise, I say, come forth, and do not tarry; ah! wherefore should mine eyes behold thee by the rivers of Babylon, hanging thy harps upon the willows, thou fairest among women?*[136]

Excellent patriots, if the people be sovereign, here is that which establish their prerogative. If we be sincere, here is that which disburdeneth our souls, maketh good all our engagements. If we be charitable, here is that which embraceth all parties. If we would be settled, here is that which will stand.

If our religion be anything else but a vain boast, scratching and defacing human nature or reason, which, being the image of God, makes it a kind of murder, here is that empire whence *justice shall run down like a river, and judgment like a mighty stream.*[137] Who is it then that calls us? or what is in our way, a lion? is it not *the dragon, that old serpent?* for what wretched shifts are these? Here is a great

---

[135] *Aeneid*, VI, 546.
[136] The Archon's rhapsody is a composite of Song of Solomon, 3: 1–2; 1: 5; 6: 4; 4: 4; 5: 3; 4: 16; 2: 10–12; Psalms, 137: 1–2.
[137] Amos, 5: 24 – H's note in text; 'like a river' is 'as waters' in the Authorised Version.

deal; might we not have some of this at one time, and some at another?

My lords, permit me to give you the sum or brief

EPITOME OF THE WHOLE COMMONWEALTH

The centre or fundamental laws are, first, the agrarian, proportioned at two thousand pounds a year in land, lying and being within the proper territory of Oceana, and so stating property in land at such a balance that the power can never swerve out of the hands of the many.

Secondly the ballot, conveying this equal sap from the root, by an equal election or rotation, unto the branches of magistracy or sovereign power.

The orbs of this commonwealth, being civil, military or provincial, are as it were cast upon this mould or centre, by the divisions of the people, first, into citizens and servants; secondly, into youth and elders; thirdly, into such as have one hundred pound a year in lands, goods or monies, who are of the horse, and such as have under, who are of the foot. Fourthly, by their usual residence into parishes, hundreds, and tribes.

The civil orbs consist of the elders, and are thus created: every Monday next ensuing the last of December, the elders in every parish elect the fifth man to be a deputy, half a day's work; every Monday next ensuing the last of January, the deputies meet at their respective hundred and elect out of their number one justice of the peace, one juryman, one coroner, and one high constable of the foot; one day's work.

Every Monday next ensuing the last of February, the hundreds meet at their respective tribe, and there elect the lords high sheriff, lieutenant, custos rotulorum, the conductor, the two censors, out of the horse; the magistrates of the tribe and of the hundreds, with the jurymen, constituting the phylarch, assist in their respective offices at the assizes, hold the quarter sessions, etc. The day following the tribe elects the annual galaxy, consisting of two knights and three deputies out of the horse with four deputies of the foot, thereby indued with power as magistrates of the whole nation for the term of three years; an officer chosen at the hundred may not be elected a magistrate of the tribe, but a magistrate or officer, either of the hundred or of the tribe, being elected into the galaxy, may substitute any one of his own order unto his magistracy or office in the hundred or in the tribe. This of the muster is two days' work; so the body of the people is annually at the charge of three days' work and an half, in their own tribes, for the perpetuation of their power, receiving over and above the magistracies so divided among them.

Every Monday next ensuing the last of March, the knights, being an hundred in all the tribes, take their places in the senate. The knights, having taken their places in the senate, make the third region of the same, and the house proceeds unto the senatorian elections. Senatorian elections are annual, biennial, or emergent.

The annual are performed by the tropic.

The tropic is a schedule consisting of two parts, the first by which the senatorian magistrates are elected, the second by which the senatorian councils are perpetuated.

The first part is of this tenor.

The lord strategus	Annual magistrates, and there-
The lord orator	fore such as may be elected out
The first censor	of any region; the term of every
The second censor	region having at the tropic one
	year at the least unexpired.
The third commis-	Triennial magistrates, and there-
sioner of the seal	fore such as can be chosen out of
The third commis-	the third region only, as that
sioner of the treasury	alone which hath the term of
	three years unexpired.

The strategus and the orator sitting are consuls, or presidents of the senate.

The strategus marching is general of the army, in which case a new strategus is elected to sit in his room.

The strategus sitting with the six commissioners, being counsellors of the nation, are the signory of the commonwealth.

The censors are magistrates of the ballot, presidents of the council for religion, and chancellors of the universities.

The second part of the tropic perpetuateth the council of state by the election of five knights out of the first region of the senate, to be the first region of that council, consisting of fifteen knights, five in every region.

The like is done by the election of four into the council of religion, and four into the council of trade, out of the same

235

region in the senate, each of these councils consisting of twelve knights, four in every region.

But the council of war, consisting of nine knights, three in every region, is elected by and out of the council of state, as the other councils are elected by and out of the senate. And if the senate add a junta of nine knights more, elected out of their own number, for the term of three months, the council of war, by virtue of that addition, is dictator of Oceana for the said term.

The signory jointly or severally hath right of session and suffrage in every senatorian council, and to propose either unto the senate or any of them. And, every region in a council electing one weekly provost, any two of those provosts have power also to propose unto their respective council, as the proper and peculiar proposers of the same; for which cause they hold an academy, where any man, either by word of mouth or writing, may propose unto the proposers.

Next unto the elections of the tropic is the biennial election of one ambassador in ordinary, by the ballot of the house, unto the residence of France, at which time the resident of France removes to Spain, he of Spain to Venice, he of Venice to Constantinople, and he of Constantinople returns. So the orb of the residents is wheeled about in eight years, by the biennial election of one ambassador in ordinary.

The last kind of election is emergent. Emergent elections are made by the scrutiny. Election by scrutiny is when, a competitor being made by a council and brought into the senate, the senate chooseth four more competitors unto him and, putting all the five unto the ballot, he who hath most above half the suffrages is the magistrate. The polemarchs, or field officers, are chosen by the scrutiny of the council of war, an ambassador extraordinary by the scrutiny of the council of state, the judges and serjeants at law by the scrutiny of the seal, and the barons and prime officers of the exchequer by the scrutiny of the treasury.

The opinion or opinions that are legitimately proposed unto any council must be debated by the same, and so many as are resolved upon the debate are introduced into the senate, where they are debated and resolved or rejected by the whole house; that which is resolved by the senate is a decree which is good in matter of state, but no law except it be proposed unto and resolved by the prerogative.

The deputies of the galaxy, being three horse and four foot in a tribe, amount in all the tribes unto one hundred and fifty horse and two hundred foot, which, having entered the prerogative and chosen their captains, cornet and ensign (triennial officers), make the third *classis*, consisting of one troop and one company, and so, joining with the whole prerogative, elect four annual magistrates called tribunes, whereof two are of the horse and two of the foot; these have the command of the prerogative sessions and suffrage in the council of war, and sessions without suffrage in the senate.

The senate having passed a decree which they would propose unto the people, cause it to be printed and published, or promulgated, for the space of six weeks, which being ordered, they choose their proposers. The proposers must be magistrates, that is the commissioners of the seal, those of the treasury, or the censors. These being chosen desire the muster of the tribunes, and appoint the day. The people being assembled at the day appointed and the decree proposed, that which is proposed by authority of the senate and commanded by the people is the law of Oceana, or an act of parliament.

So the parliament of Oceana consisteth of the senate proposing, and the people resolving.

The people, or prerogative, are also the supreme judicatory of this nation, having power of hearing and determining all causes of appeal from all magistrates or courts provincial or domestic, as also to question any magistrate, the term of his magistracy being expired, if the case be introduced by the tribunes or any of them.

The military orbs consist of the youth, that is, such as are from eighteen to thirty years of age, and are thus created.

Every Wednesday next ensuing the last of December, the youth of every parish, assembling, elect the fifth of their number to be their deputies; the deputies of the youth are called stratiots, and this is the first essay.

Every Wednesday next ensuing the last of January, the stratiots, assembling at the hundred, elect their captain and their ensign, and fall to their game.

Every Wednesday next ensuing the last of February, the stratiots are received by the lord lieutenant their commander-in-chief, with the conductors and the censors; and having been disciplined and entertained with other games, are called unto the urns, where they elect the second essay, consisting of two hundred horse and six hundred foot in a tribe, that is, of ten thousand horse and thirty thousand foot in all the tribes, which is the standing army of this nation, to march at any warning. They also elect at the same time a part of the third essay, by the mixture of balls marked with the letter M and the letter P, for Marpesia and Panopea, they of either mark being ten horse and fifty foot in a tribe, that is five hundred horse and two thousand foot in all the tribes, which are forthwith to march to their respective provinces.

But the third essay of this nation, more properly so called, is when the strategus with the polemarchs (the senate and the people, or the dictator, having decreed a war) receive in return of his warrants the second essay from the hands of the conductors at the rendezvous of Oceana, which army marching, with all accommodations provided by the council of war, the senate elects a new strategus, and lords lieutenants a new second essay.

A youth, except he be an only son, refusing any one of his three essays without sufficient cause shown unto the phylarch or the censors, is incapable of magistracy, and is fined a fifth part of his yearly rent, or of his estate, for protection. In case of invasion the elders are obliged unto like duty with the youth, and upon their own charge.

The provincial orb, consisting in part of the elders and in part of the youth, is thus created.

Four knights, out of the first region falling, are elected in the senate to be the first region of the provincial orb of Marpesia; these, being triennial magistrates, take their places in the provincial council, consisting of twelve knights, four in every region, each region choosing their weekly provosts; of the council thus constituted, one knight more, chosen out of the same region in the senate, being an annual magistrate, is president with power to propose; and the opinions proposed by the president, or any two of the provosts, are debated by the council and, if occasion be of farther power or instruction than they yet have, transmitted into the council of state, with which the provincial is to hold intelligence.

The president of this council is also strategus or general of the provincial army, wherefore the conductors, upon notice of his election and appointment of his rendezvous, deliver unto him the stratiots of his letter, which he takes with him into his province; and, the provincial army having received the new strategus with the third *classis*, the council dismisseth the old strategus with the first *classis*. The like is done for Panopea, or any other province.

But whereas the term of every other magistracy, or election in this commonwealth, whether annual or triennial, requireth an equal vacation, the term of a provincial councillor or magistrate requireth no vacation at all. The quorum of a provincial, as also that of every other council and assembly, requireth two thirds in a time of health, and one third in a time of sickness.

> *Insula portum*
> *Efficit objectu laterum, geminique minantur*
> *In coelum scopuli, quorum suo vertice late*
> *Aequora tuta silent.*[138]

I think I have omitted nothing but the props and scaffolds, which are not of use but in building. And how much is here? Show me another commonwealth in this compass. How many things? Show me another entire government consisting but of thirty orders. If you go to suit, there lie unto some of your courts two hundred original writs; if you stir your hand, there go more nerves and bones unto the motion; if you play, you have more cards in the pack; nay, you could not sit with your ease in that chair, if it consisted not of more parts. Will you not allow unto your legislator what you can afford your upholsterer; unto the throne, what is necessary to a chair?

My lords, if you will have fewer orders in a commonwealth, you will have more, for where she is not perfect at first, every day, every hour, will produce a new order, the end whereof is to have no order at all, but to grind with the clack of some demagogue. Is he providing already for his golden thumb? Lift up your heads; away with ambition, that fulsome complexion of a statesman, tempered like Sulla's *luto cum sanguine*, with blood and muck. *And the Lord give unto his senators wisdom, and make our faces to shine, that we may be a light unto them that sit in darkness and the shadow of death, to guide their feet in the way of peace.*[139] . . . In the name of God, what's the matter?

[138] *Aeneid*, I, 159–64.
[139] From Psalms, 105: 35 and Luke, I: 78f.

Philadelphus, the secretary of the council, having performed his task in reading the several orders as you have seen, upon the receipt of a packet (it should seem from his correspondent Boccalini, secretary of Parnassus), in reading one of the letters, burst forth into such a violent passion of weeping and downright howling that, your legislators being startled with the apprehension of some horrid news, one of them had no sooner snatched the letter out of his hand, than the rest crying 'read, read', he obeyed in this manner:

The third instant, his Phoebean majesty – having taken the nature of free states into his royal consideration, and being steadily persuaded that the laws in such governments are incomparably better and more assuredly directed unto the good of mankind than in any other, that the courage of such a people is the aptest tinder unto noble fire, that the genius of such a soil is that wherein the roots of good literature are least worm-eaten with pedantism, and where their fruits have ever come unto the greatest maturity and highest relish – conceived such a loathing of their ambition and tyranny who, usurping the liberty of their native countries, become slaves to themselves, in as much as be it never so contrary unto their own nature or consciences, they have taken the earnest of sin and are engaged to persecute all men that are good (for *nemo unquam imperium flagitio quaesitum bonis artibus exercuit*)[140] with the same or greater rigour than is ordained by laws for the wicked, that he[141] assembled all the senators residing in the learned court at the theatre of Melpomene, where he caused Caesar the dictator to come upon the stage, and his sister Actia, his nephew Augustus, Julia his daughter with the children which she had by Marcus Agrippa, Lucius and Caius Caesar, Agrippa Posthumus, Julia and Agrippina, with the numerous progeny which she bare unto her renowned husband Germanicus, to enter. A miserable scene in any, but most deplorable in the eyes of Caesar, thus beholding what havoc his prodigious ambition, not satisfied with his own bloody ghost, had made upon his more innocent remains, even unto the total extinction of his family. For it is (seeing where there is any humanity, there must be some compassion) not to be spoken without tears that of the full branches deriving from Octavia the elder sister, and Julia the daughter, of Augustus, there should not be one fruit or blossom that was not cut off or blasted, by the sword, famine or poison.

[140] Tacitus, *Histories*, I, 30.   [141] 'that he' inserted.

Now might the great soul of Caesar have been full; and yet that which poured in as much or more was to behold that execrable race of the Claudii, having hunted and sucked his blood with the thirst of tigers, to be rewarded with the Roman empire and remain in full possession of the famous patrimony; a spectacle to pollute the light of heaven. Nevertheless, as if Caesar had not yet enough, his Phoebean majesty caused to be introduced, on the other side of the theatre, the most illustrious and happy prince Andrea Doria, with his dear posterity, embraced by the soft and constant arms of the city Genoa, into whose bosom, ever fruitful in her gratitude, he had dropped her fair liberty like the dew of heaven; which when the Roman tyrant beheld, and how much more fresh that laurel was worn, with a root in the hearts of the people, than that which he had torn off, he fell into such horrid distortion of limbs and countenance that the senators, who had thought themselves steel and flint at such an object, having hitherto stood in their reverent snow like thawing Alps, now covered their faces with their large sleeves.[142]

My lords (said the Archon, rising), witty Philadelphus hath given us a grave admonition in a dreadful tragedy. *Discite justitiam moniti, et non temnere divos.* Great and glorious Caesar, the highest character of flesh, yet could not rule but by that part of man which is the beast; but a commonwealth is a monarchy, where God is king, in as much as reason, his dictate, is her sovereign power.

Which said, he adjourned the council. And the model being soon after promulgated, *quod bonum felix faustumque sit huic reipublicae, agite quirites, censuere patres, jubeat populus. The sea roared, and the floods clapped their hands.*[143]

LIBERTAS

The Proclamation of his Highness the Lord Archon of Oceana,
upon Promulgation of the Model

Whereas his highness and the council, in the framing of the model promulgated, had not had any private interest or ambition, but the fear of God and the good of this people before their eyes, and it remains their desire that this great work may be carried on accordingly, this present greeting is to inform the good people of

---

[142] Boccalini, *Ragguagli di Parnasso*, I, 21: freely rendered.
[143] The Latin phrases are several times found in Livy (I, xxviii; III, xxxiv, liv; X, viii; XXIV, vii). The scriptural passage is Psalms, 98: 7.

this land that as the council of prytans sat, during the framing of the model, to receive from time to time such propositions as should be offered by any wise-hearted or public spirited man towards the institution of a well-ordered commonwealth, so the said council is to sit[144] as formerly in the great hall of the Pantheon during promulgation, which is to continue for the space of three months, to receive, weigh, and as there shall be occasion transmit unto the council of legislators all such objections as shall be made against the said model, whether in the whole or in any part. Wherefore that nothing be done rashly, or without consent of the people, such of what party soever with whom there may remain any doubts or difficulties are desired with all convenient speed to address themselves into the said prytans, where if such objections, doubts or difficulties receive solution unto the satisfaction of the auditory, they shall have public thanks, but if the said objections, doubts, or difficulties receive no solution unto the satisfaction of the auditory, then the model promulgated shall be reviewed, and the party that was the occasion of the review shall receive public thanks, together with the best horse in his highness's stable, and be one of the council of legislators. And so God have you in keeping.

I should now write the same council of the prytans, but for two reasons, the one that, having had but a small time for that which is already done, I am over-laboured; the other, that there may be new objections. Wherefore, if my reader have any such as to the model, I entreat him to address himself by way of oration, as it were unto the prytans, that when this rough draft comes to be a work,[145] his speech, being faithfully inserted in this place, may give or receive correction unto amendment. For what is written will be weighed, but conversation in these days is a game, at which they are best provided that have light gold.

It is like the sport of women that make flowers of straws, which must be stuck up but may not be touched. Nor, which is worse, is this the fault of conversation only. But to the examiner I say, if to invent method and to teach an art be all one, let him show that this method is not truly invented, or this art is faithfully taught.

I cannot conclude a circle (and such is this commonwealth) without

---

[144] 'See the course of the Decemvirs in the promulgation of the first ten of their twelve Tables in Livy' – H's marginal note to this passage. Livy, III, xxxiii–xxxv.
[145] Cf. p. 70, n. 4, above.

turning the end into the beginning. The time of promulgation being expired, the surveyors were sent down, who having in due season made report that their work was perfect, the orators followed, under the administration of which officers and magistrates the commonwealth was ratified and established by the whole body of the people, *curiatis, centuriatis* and *tributis comitiis*. And the orators, being by virtue of their scrolls or lots members of their respective tribes, were elected each first knight of the third list or galaxy; wherefore, having at their return assisted the Archon in putting the senate and the people or prerogative into motion, they abdicated the magistracy both of orators and legislators.

The Corollary

For the rest (says Plutarch,[1] closing up the story of Lycurgus), when he saw that his government had taken root and was in the very plantation strong enough to stand by itself, he conceived such a delight within him, as God is described by Plato to have done, when he had finished the creation of the world, and saw his own orbs move below him. For in the art of man, being the imitation of nature which is the art of God,[2] there is nothing so like the first call of beautiful order out of chaos and confusion as the architecture of a well-ordered commonwealth. Wherefore Lycurgus, seeing in effect that his orders were good, fell into deep contemplation how he might render them, so far forth as is in human providence, unalterable and immortal. To which end he assembled the people and remonstrated unto them that for aught he could perceive their policy was already such, and so well established, as was sufficient to entail upon them and theirs that virtue and felicity whereof human life is capable.

Nevertheless, there being another thing of greater concernment than all the rest, whereof he was not yet provided to give them a perfect account, nor could till he had consulted the oracle of Apollo, he desired that they would observe his laws, without any change or alteration whatsoever, till his return from Delphos; unto which all the people cheerfully and unanimously engaged themselves by promise, desiring him that he would make as much haste as he could. But Lycurgus, before he went, began with the kings and the senators, and

[1] Plutarch, *Lycurgus*, XXIX, 1–11.
[2] 'Hobbes' – H's note. The allusion will be to the opening sentence of *Leviathan*. It is the only mention in *Oceana* of the author of *Leviathan* by name.

thence, taking the whole people in order, made them all swear unto that which they had promised, and then took his journey. Being arrived at Delphos, he sacrificed unto Apollo, and afterwards inquired if the policy which he had established were good and sufficient for a virtuous and an happy life. (It hath been a maxim with legislators not to give checks unto the present superstition, but to make the best use of it, as that which is always the most powerful with the people; otherwise, though Plutarch, being a priest, was interested in the cause, there is nothing plainer than Cicero in his book *De Divinatione* hath showed it, that there was never any such thing as an oracle, except in the art of the priests. But to be civil unto the author.) The god answered Lycurgus that his policy was exquisite and that his city, holding unto the strict observation of his form of government, should attain unto the height of fame and glory. Which oracle Lycurgus causing to be written, failed not to send unto his Lacedaemon. This done, that his citizens might be for ever inviolably bound by their oath that they would alter nothing till his return, he took so firm a resolution to die in the place that, from thenceforward receiving no manner of food, he soon after performed it accordingly. Nor was he deceived in the consequence, for his city became the first in glory and excellency of government in the whole world. And so much for Lycurgus according to Plutarch.

My Lord Archon, when he beheld not only the rapture of motion, but of joy and harmony, into which his spheres without any manner of obstruction or interfering, but as it had been naturally, were cast, conceived not less of exultation in his spirit, but saw no more necessity or reason why he should administer an oath unto the senate and the people that they would observe his institutions, than unto a man in perfect health and felicity of constitution that he would not kill himself. Nevertheless whereas Christianity, though it forbid violent hands, consisteth no less in self-denial than any other religion, he resolved that all carnal concupiscence should die in the place, to which end, that no manner of food might be left unto ambition, he entered into the senate with an unanimous applause and, having spoken of his government as Lycurgus did when he assembled the people, abdicated the magistracy of Archon. The senate, as stricken with astonishment, continued silent, men upon so sudden an accident being altogether unprovided of what to say; till, the Archon withdrawing and being almost at the door, divers of the knights flew from their places, offering as it were to lay violent hands on him; while he escaping left the senate with the tears in their eyes of children that had lost their father, and to rid himself of all farther importunity, retired unto a country house of his, being remote and very private, in so much that no man could tell for some time what was become of him. Thus the lawmaker happened to be the first object and reflection of the law made; for as liberty of all things is the most welcome unto a people, so is there nothing more abhorrent from their nature than ingratitude. We, accusing the Roman people of this crime against some of their greatest benefactors, as Camillus, heap mistake upon mistake, for being not so competent judges of what belongs unto liberty as they were, we take upon us to be more competent judges of virtue. But whereas virtue, for being a vulgar thing among them, was of no less rate than jewels are with such as wear the most, we are selling this stone, which we have ignorantly raked out of the Roman ruders,[3] at such a rate as the Switz did that which they took in the baggage of Charles of Burgundy. For that Camillus had stood more firm against the ruin of Rome than her capitol, was acknowledged; but on the other side, that he stood as firm for the patricians against the liberty of the people was as plain; wherefore he never wanted of the people that would die at his foot in the field, nor that would withstand him to his beard in the city. An example in which they that think that Camillus had wrong neither do themselves right nor the people of Rome, who in this signify no less than that they had a scorn of slavery beyond the fear of ruin, which is the height of magnanimity. The like might be shown by other examples objected against this and other popular government, as in the banishment of Aristides the Just from Athens by the ostracism, which first was no punishment nor ever understood for so much as a disparagement, but tended only to the security of the commonwealth, through the removal of a citizen, whose riches or power with a party was suspected, out of harm's way for the space of ten years, neither to the diminution of his estate or honour. And next, though the virtue of Aristides might in itself be unquestioned, yet for him under the name of the Just to become universal umpire of the people in all cases, even to the neglect of the legal ways and orders of the commonwealth, approached so much unto the prince that the Athenians, doing Aristides no wrong, did

---

[3] I.e., 'ruins', from the Latin *rudera*. Toland substituted the more familiar word.

their government no more than right in removing him, which therefore is not so probable to have come to pass, as Plutarch presumeth,
through the envy of Themistocles; seeing Aristides was far more
popular than Themistocles, who soon after took the same walk upon a
worse occasion. Wherefore, as Machiavel for anything since alleged
hath irrefragably proved that popular governments are of all other the
least ungrateful, so the obscurity (I say), into which my Lord Archon
had now withdrawn himself, caused an universal sadness and cloud in
the minds of men upon the glory of his rising commonwealth.

Much had been ventilated in private discourse, and the people (for
the nation was divided into parties that had not yet lost their animosities), being troubled, bent their eyes upon the senate, when, after
some time spent in devotion and the solemn action of thanksgiving,
his excellency Navarchus de Paralo in the tribe of Dorean, lord
strategus of Oceana (though in a new commonwealth, a very prudent
magistrate) proposed his part or opinion in such manner unto the
council of state that, passing the ballot of the same (with great
unanimity and applause, it was introduced into the senate, where it
passed with greater. Wherefore, the decree being forthwith printed
and published, copies were returned by the secretaries unto the
phylarchs (which is the manner of promulgation) and the commissioners of the seal, that is to say, the right honourable Phosphorus de
Auge in the tribe of Eudia, Dolabella de Enyo in the tribe of Turmae,
and Linceus de Stella in the tribe of Nubia, being elected proposers
pro tempore, bespoke of the tribunes a muster of the people to be held
that day six weeks, which was the time allowed for promulgation, at
the Halo.

The satisfaction, which the people throughout the tribes received
upon promulgation of the decree, loaded the carriers with weekly
letters between friend and friend, whether magistrates or private
persons. But the day for proposition being come, and the prerogative
upon the place appointed in discipline, Sanguine de Ringwood in the
tribe of Saltum, captain of the phoenix, marched by order of the
tribunes with his troop unto the piazza of the Pantheon, where his
trumpets, entering into the great hall, by their blazon gave notice of
his arrival, at which the sergeant of the house came down and, returning, informed the proposers, who, descending, were received at the
foot of the stairs by the captain and attended unto the coaches of state,
with which Calcar de Gilvo in the tribe of Phalera, master of the

horse, and the ballotines upon their great horses stood waiting at the gate.

The proposers being in their coaches, the train being for the pomp the same that is used at the reception of ambassadors, proceeded in this order. In the front marched the troop, with the cornet in the van and the captain in the rear; next the troop came the twenty messengers or trumpets; the, ballotines upon the curvet, with their usher in the van and the master of the horse in the rear; next the ballotines, Bronchus de Rauco in the tribe of Bestia, king of the heralds, with his fraternity in their coat of arms; and next unto Sir Bronchus, Boristenes de Holiwater in the tribe of Ave, master of the ceremonies. The mace and the seal of the chancery went immediately before the coaches, and on either side the doorkeepers or guard of the senate with their pole-axes, accompanied with some three or four hundred footmen belonging unto the knights or senators; the trumpeters, ballotines, guards, postilions, coachmen and footmen being very gallant in the liveries of the commonwealth, but all except the ballotines without hats, in lieu whereof they wore black velvet calots being pointed with a little peak at the forehead. After the proposers came a long file of coaches full of such gentlemen as use to grace the commonwealth upon like occasions. In this posture they moved slowly through the streets, affording in the gravity of the pomp and the welcomeness of the end, a most reverent and acceptable prospect unto the people, from the Pantheon to the Halo, being about half a mile, arrived at the Halo, where they found the prerogative in a close body environed with scaffolds that were covered with spectators. The tribunes received the proposers and conducted them into a seat placed in front of the tribe, like a pulpit but that it was of some length, and well adorned by the heralds with all manner of birds and beasts, save that they were ill painted and never a one of his natural colour. The tribunes were placed at a table that stood below the long seat, those of the horse in the middle and those of the foot at either end, with each of them a bowl or basin before him, that on the right hand being white, and the other green; in the middle of the table stood a third which was red. And the housekeeper of the pavilion, who had already delivered a proportion of linen balls or pellets unto every one of the tribe, now presented boxes unto the ballotines. But the proposers, as they entered the gallery or long seat, having put off their hats by way of salutation, were answered by the people with a shout, whereupon the younger commissioners seated themselves at either end and the first, standing in the middle, spake after this manner:

My lords, the people of Oceana.

While I find in myself what a felicity it is to salute you by this name, and in every face anointed as it were with the oil of gladness, a full and sufficient testimony of the like sense, to go about to feast you with words, who are already filled with that food of the mind which, being of pleasing and wholesome digestion, taketh in the definition of true joy, were a needless enterprise. I shall rather remember you of that thankfulness which is due, than puff you up with anything that might seem vain. Is it from the arms of flesh that we derive these blessings? Behold the commonwealth of Rome falling upon her own victorious sword. Or is it from our own wisdom, whose counsels had brought it even to that pass that we began to repent ourselves of victory? Far be it from us (my lords) to sacrifice unto your own nets, which we ourselves have so narrowly escaped; let us rather lay our mouths in the dust, and look up (as was taught the other day when we were better instructed in this lesson) unto the hills with our gratitude. Nevertheless, seeing we read how God upon neglect of his prophets hath been provoked unto wrath, it must needs follow that he expecteth honour should be given unto them by whom he hath chosen to work as his instruments. For which cause, nothing doubting of my warrant, I shall proceed unto that which more particularly concerneth the present occasion, the discovery of my Lord Archon's virtues and merit, to be ever placed by this nation in their true meridian.

My lords, I am not upon a subject which persuadeth me to balk, but necessitateth me to seek out the greatest examples. To begin with Alexander, erecting trophies common with his sword and the pestilence, to what good of mankind did he infect the air with his heaps of carcasses? The sword of war, if it be any otherwise used than as the sword of magistracy for the fear and punishment of those that do evil, is as guilty in the sight of God as the sword of a murderer; nay more, for if the blood of Abel, of one innocent man, cried in the ears of the Lord for vengeance, what shall the blood of an innocent nation? Of this kind of empire, the throne of ambition, the quarry of a mighty hunter, it hath been truly said that it is but a great robbery. But if Alexander had restored the liberty of Greece, and propagated it unto mankind, he had done like my Lord Archon, and might have been truly called the Great. Alexander cared not to steal a victory that would be given. But my Lord Archon hath torn away a victory, which had been stolen while we were tamely yielding up obedience unto a nation reaping in our fields, whose fields he hath subjected unto our empire, and nailed them with his victorious sword unto their native Caucasus.[4]

Machiavel gives an handsome caveat: Let no man (saith he) be circumvented with the glory of Caesar, from the false reflection of their pens who, through the longer continuance of his empire in the name than in the family, changed their freedom for flattery. But if a man would know truly what the Romans thought of Caesar, let him observe what they said of Catiline.

And yet by how much he who hath perpetrated some heinous crime is more execrable than he who did but attempt it, by so much is Caesar more execrable than Catiline. To the contrary, let him that would know what ancient and heroical times, what the Greeks and Romans would both have thought and said of my Lord Archon, observe what they thought and said of Solon, Lycurgus, Brutus and Publicola. And yet, by how much his virtue, that is crowned with the perfection of his work, is beyond theirs who were either inferior in their aim or in their performance, by so much is my Lord Archon to be preferred before Solon, Lycurgus, Brutus and Publicola.

Nor will we shun the most illustrious example of Scipio; this hero, though never so little less, yet was he not the founder of a commonwealth; and for the rest, allowing his hue to have been of the most untainted ray, in what did it outshine this of my Lord Archon? But if, dazzling the eyes of the magistrates, it over-awed liberty, Rome might be allowed some excuse that she did not like it, and I if I admit not of this comparison. For where is my Lord Archon? Is there a genius, how free soever, which in his presence would not find itself to be under power? He is shrunk into clouds, he seeks obscurity in a nation that sees by his light. He is impatient of his own glory, lest it should stand between you and your liberty.

Liberty! What is that, if we may not be grateful? And if we may, we have none: for who hath anything he doth not owe? My lords,

---

[4] Clearly the Scots.

there be some hard conditions of virtue. If this debt were exacted, it were not due; whereas, being cancelled, we are all entered into bonds. On the other side, if we make such payment as will not stand with a free people, we do not enrich my Lord Archon, but rob him of his whole estate and of his immense glory.

These particulars had in due deliberation and mature debate, according unto the orders of this commonwealth, it is proposed by authority of the senate to you, my lords the people of Oceana:

I. That the dignity and office of Archon or protector of the commonwealth of Oceana be and is hereby conferred by the senate and the people of Oceana upon the most illustrious prince and sole legislator of this commonwealth, Olphaus Megaletor (*Pater Patriae*), whom God preserve, for the term of his natural life.

II. That three hundred and fifty thousand pounds per annum, yet remaining of the ancient revenue, be estated upon the said illustrious prince or Lord Archon, for the said term and to the proper and peculiar use of his highness.

III. That the Lord Archon have the reception of all foreign ambassadors, by and with the council of state, according unto the orders of this commonwealth.

IV. That the Lord Archon have a standing army of twelve thousand men, defrayed upon a monthly tax during the term of three years, for the protection of this commonwealth against dissenting parties, to be governed, directed and commanded by and with the advice of the council of war, according unto the orders of this commonwealth.

V. That this commonwealth make no distinction of persons or parties, but every man being elected and sworn according unto the orders of the same, shall be equally capable of magistracy; or not elected, shall be equally capable of liberty, and the enjoyment of his estate free from all other than common taxes.

VI. That a man putting a distinction upon himself, refusing the oath upon election, or declaring himself of a party not conformable to the civil government, may, within any time of the three years standing of the army, transport himself and his estate without molestation or impediment into any other nation.

VII. That in case there remain any distinction of parties not conforming unto the civil government of this commonwealth after the three years of the standing army be expired, and the commonwealth be thereby forced to prolong the term of the said army, the pay from thenceforth of the said army shall be levied upon the estates of such parties so remaining unconformable unto the civil government.

The proposer having ended his oration, the trumpets sounded, and the tribunes of the horse, being mounted to view the ballot, caused the tribe, which, thronging up to the speech, came almost round the gallery, to retreat a matter of twenty paces, when Linceus de Stella, receiving the propositions, repaired, with Bronchus de Rauco the herald, unto a little scaffold erected in the middle of the tribe, where he seated himself, the herald standing bare upon his right hand. The ballotines, having their boxes ready, stood before the gallery, and at the command of the tribune marched one unto every troop on horseback and one unto every company on foot, each of them being followed by other children that bore red boxes (this is putting the question whether the question should be put). And the suffrage being very suddenly returned unto the tribunes of the table and numbered in the view of the proposers, the votes were all in the affirmative whereupon the red or doubtful boxes were laid aside, it appearing that the tribe, whether for the negative or affirmative, was clear in the matter. Wherefore the herald began, from the scaffold in the middle of the tribe, to pronounce the first proposition, and the ballotines marching with the negative and affirmative only, Bronchus, with his voice like thunder, continued to repeat the proposition over and over again so long as it was in balloting. The like was done for every clause, till the ballot was finished and the tribunes, assembling, had signed the points, that is to say, the number of every suffrage, as it was taken by the secretary upon the tale of the tribunes and in the sight of the proposers; for this may not be omitted, it is the pulse of the people. Now whereas it appertaineth unto the tribunes to report the suffrage of the people unto the senate, they cast the lot for this office with three silver balls and one gold one, and it fell upon the right worshipful Argus de Crookhorne, in the tribe of Pascua, first tribune of the foot. Argus, being a good sufficient man in his own country, was yet of the mind that he should make but a bad spokesman and therefore became something blank at his luck, till his colleagues persuaded him that it was no such great matter, if he could but read, having his paper before him. The proposers, taking coach, received a volley upon the field and returned in the same order, save that, being accompanied with the tribunes, they were also attended by the whole prerogative unto the piazza of the Pantheon, where with another volley they took their leaves. Argus, who had not thought upon his wife and children all the way, went very gravely up, and everyone being seated, the senate by their silence seemed to call for the report, which Argus standing up, delivered in this wise.

Right honourable lords and fathers assembled in parliament,
So it is, that it hath fallen unto my lot to report unto your excellencies the votes of the people, taken upon the third instant, in the first year of this commonwealth, at the Halo; the right honourable Phosphorus de Auge, in the tribe of Eudia, Dolabella de Enyo, in the tribe of Turmae, and Linceus de Stella, in the tribe of Nubia, lords commissioners of the great seal of Oceana, and proposers *pro temporibus*, together with my brethren the tribunes and myself, being present. Wherefore these are to certify unto your fatherhoods that the said votes of the people were as followeth; that is to say:
Unto the first proposition, *nemine contradicente.*
Unto the second, *nemine contradicente.*
Unto the third, the like.
Unto the fourth, 211 above half.
Unto the fifth, 201 above half.
Unto the sixth, 150 above half in the affirmative.
Unto the seventh, *nemine* again, and so forth.
My lords, it is a language that is out of my prayers, and if I be out at it, no harm.
But as concerning my Lord Archon (as I was saying), these are to signify unto you the true-heartedness and goodwill which is in the people, seeing by joining with you as one man, they confess that all they have to give is too little for his highness. For truly, fathers, if he who is able to do harm and doth none may well be called honest, what shall we say unto my Lord Archon's highness,

who, having had it in his power to have done us the greatest mischief that ever befell a poor nation, so willing to trust such as they thought well of, hath done us so much good as we should never have known how to do ourselves? Which was so sweetly delivered by my lord chancellor Phosphorus unto the people that I dare say there was never an one of them could forbear to do as I do. . . . An't please your fatherhoods, they be tears of joy. Ah, my Lord Archon shall walk the streets (as it be for his ease I mean) with a switch, while the people run after him, and pray for him; he shall not wet his foot, they will strew flowers in his way; he shall sit higher in their hearts, and in the judgment of all good men, than the kings that go up stairs unto their seats, and one of these had as good pull two or three of his fellows out of the great chairs as wrong him or meddle with him; he has two or three hundred thousand men that, when you say the word, shall sell themselves unto their shirts for him and die at his foot. His pillow is of down, and his grave shall be as soft, over which they that are alive shall wring their hands. And to come unto your fatherhoods, most truly so called, as being the loving parents of the people; truly you do not know what a feeling they have of your kindness, seeing you are so bound up, that if there come any harm, they may thank themselves. And (alas! poor fools) they see that they are given to be of so many minds that, though they always mean well, yet if there come any good they may thank them that teach them better. Wherefore there was never such a thing as this invented; they do verily believe that it is none other than the same which they always had in their very heads, if they could have but told how to bring it out; as now for a sample, my lords the proposers had no sooner said your minds than they found it to be that which heart could wish. And your fatherhoods may comfort yourselves that there is not a people in the world more willing to learn what is for their own goods, nor more apt to see it, when you have shown it them. Wherefore they do love you as they do their own selves, honour you as fathers, resolve to give you as it were obedience forever; and so thanking you for your most good and excellent laws, they do pray for you as the very worthies of the land, right honourable lords and fathers assembled in parliament.

Argus came off beyond his own expectation, for thinking right and speaking as he thought, it was apparent by the house and the thanks they gave him that they esteemed him to be absolutely of the best sort of orators, upon which, having a mind that till then misgave him, he became very crounse,[5] and much delighted with that which might go down the next week in print unto his wife and his neighbours. Livy makes the Roman tribunes to speak in the same style with the consuls, which could not be, and therefore, for aught in him to the contrary, Volero and Canuleius might have spoken no otherwise forth their style than Argus. However, they were not created the first year of the commonwealth; and the tribunes of Oceana are since become better orators than were needful. But the laws being enacted had the preamble annexed and were delivered unto Bronchus, who loved nothing in the earth so much as to go staring and bellowing up and down the town like a stag in a forest, as he now did, with his fraternity in their coats of arms and I know not how many trumpets, proclaiming the act of parliament, when, meeting my Lord Archon (who from a retreat that was without affectation, as being for devotion only, and to implore a blessing by prayer and fasting upon his labours, now newly arrived in town) the herald of the tribe of Bestia set up his throat, and, having chanted out his lesson, passed as haughtily by him as if his own had been the better office; which in this place was very well taken, though Bronchus for his high mind happened afterwards upon some disasters (too long to tell) that spoiled much of his embroidery.[6]

My Lord Archon's arrival being known, the signory, accompanied by the tribunes, repaired unto him with the news he had already heard by the herald; to which my lord strategus added that his highness could not doubt, upon the demonstrations given, but the minds of men were firm in the opinion that he could be no seeker of himself in the way of earthly pomp and glory; and that the gratitude of the senate and the people could not therefore be understood to have any such reflection upon him. But so it was that, in regard of dangers abroad and parties at home, they durst not trust themselves without a standing army, nor a standing army in any man's hands but those of his highness.

The Archon made answer that he ever expected this would be the

<hr/>

[5] The *Oxford English Dictionary* does not give this as a variant of 'crouse . . . Sc. and north dial. . . . 2. Bold, audacious, daring, hardy. . . . 3. In somewhat high or lively spirits. . .' Cf. *English Dialect Dictionary* and *Scottish National Dictionary*.
[6] H seems to have conceived a dislike of heralds.

sense of the senate and the people, and this being their sense, he should have been sorry they had made choice of any other than himself for a standing general; first, because it could not have been more unto their own safety and, secondly, because so long as they should have need of a standing army, his work was not done. That he would not dispute against the judgment of the senate and the people, nor ought that to be. Nevertheless, he made little doubt but experience would show every party their own interest in this government, and that better improved than they could expect from any other; that men's animosities should overbalance their interest for any time was impossible, that humour could never be lasting nor, through the constitution of the government, of any effect at the first charge. For supposing the worst, and that the people had chosen none other into the senate and the prerogative than royalists, a matter of fourteen hundred men must have taken their oaths at their election, with an intention to go quite contrary, not only to their oaths so taken but to their own interest; for being estated in the sovereign power, they must have decreed it from themselves (such an example as for which there was never any experience, nor can be any reason) or, holding it, it must have done in their hands as well every whit as in any other. Furthermore, they must have removed the government from a foundation that apparently would hold, to set it upon another which apparently would not hold, which things, if they could not come to pass, the senate and the people consisting wholly of royalists, much less by a parcel of them elected. But if the fear of the senate and of the people derived from a party without, such an one as would not be elected nor engage themselves unto the commonwealth by any oath, this again must be so large as would go quite contrary to your own interest, they being as free and as fully estated in their liberty as any other, or so narrow that they could do no hurt; while, the people being in arms and at the beck of the strategus, every tribe would at any time make a better army than such a party, and there being no parties at home, fears from abroad would vanish. But seeing it was otherwise determined by the senate and the people, the best course was to take that which they held the safest, in which, with his humble thanks for their great bounty, he was resolved to serve them with all duty and obedience.

A very short time after, the royalists, now equal citizens, made good the Archon's judgment, there being no other that found anything near so great a sweet in the government. For he who hath not been acquainted with affliction (saith Seneca) knoweth but half the things of this world. Moreover they saw plainly that to restore the ancient government, they must cast up their estates into the hands of three hundred men; wherefore in case the senate and the prerogative, consisting of thirteen hundred men, had been all royalists, there must of necessity have been, and be for ever, one thousand against this or any such vote.

But the senate, being informed by the signory that the Archon had accepted of his dignity and office, caused a third chair to be set for his highness, between those of the strategus and the orator in the house, the like at every council; to which he repaired, not of necessity, but at his pleasure, being the best, and as Argus not vainly said, the greatest prince in the world; for in the pomp of his court he was not inferior unto any, and in the field he was followed with a force that was formidable unto all. Nor was there a cause in the nature of this constitution to put him unto the charge of guards, spoil his stomach or his sleep; insomuch as being handsomely disputed by the wits of the academy whether my Lord Archon, if he had been ambitious, could have made himself so great, it was carried clear in the negative; not only for the reasons drawn from the present balance, which was popular, but putting the case the balance had been monarchical. For there be some nations (whereof this is one) that will bear a prince in a commonwealth, far higher than it is possible for them to bear a monarch. Spain looked upon the prince of Orange as her most formidable enemy, but if ever there be a monarch in that country, he will be her best friend. For whereas a prince in a commonwealth deriveth his greatness from the root of the people, a monarch deriveth his from one of those balances which nip them in the root; by which means the Low Countries under a monarch were poor and inconsiderable, but in bearing a prince, could grow unto a miraculous height and give the glory of his actions by far the upper hand of the greatest king in Christendom. There are kings in Europe to whom a king of Oceana would be but a petty companion. But the prince of this commonwealth is the terror and the judge of them all.

That which my Lord Archon now minded most was the agrarian, upon which debate he incessantly thrust the senate and the council of state, to the end it might be planted upon some firm root, as the main point and basis of perpetuity unto the commonwealth.

And these are some of the most remarkable passages that happened in the first year of this government. About the latter end of the second, the army was disbanded, but the taxes continued at thirty thousand pounds a month for three years and an half. By which means a piece of artillery was planted, and a portion of land to the value of fifty pounds a year purchased, for the maintenance of the games and of the prize-arms forever, in each hundred.

With the eleventh year of the commonwealth, the term of the excise, allotted for the maintenance of the senate and the people and for the raising of a public revenue, expired. By which time the exchequer, over and above the annual salaries, amounting unto three hundred thousand pounds, accumulating every year out of one million income, seven hundred thousand pounds *in banco*, brought it, with the product of the sum, rising to about eight millions in the whole, whereby at several times they had purchased unto the senate and the people four hundred thousand pounds *per annum* solid revenue; which, besides the lands holden in Panopea, together with the perquisites of either province, was held sufficient for a public revenue. Nevertheless, taxes being now wholly taken off, the excise of no great burden, and many specious advantages not vainly proposed in the heightening of the public revenue, the excise was very cheerfully established by the senate and the people for the term of ten years longer; and the same course being taken, the public revenue was found in the one and twentieth of the commonwealth to be worth one million in good land. Whereupon the excise was so abolished for the present, as withal resolved to be the best, the most fruitful and easy way of raising taxes, according unto future exigencies. But the revenue, now such as was able to be a yearly purchaser, gave a jealousy that by this means the balance of the commonwealth, consisting in private fortunes, might be eaten out; whence this year is famous for that law whereby the senate and the people, forbidding any farther purchase of lands unto the public within the dominions of Oceana and the adjacent provinces, put the agrarian upon the commonwealth herself. These increases are things which men addicted unto monarchy deride as impossible, whereby they unwarily urge a strong argument against that which they would defend. For having their eyes fixed upon the pomp and expense, by which not only every child of a king being a prince, exhausteth his father's coffers, but favourites and servile spirits, devoted unto the flattery of those princes, grow insolent and profuse, returning a fit gratitude unto their masters, whom, while they hold it honourable to deceive, they suck and keep eternally poor, it follows that they do not see how it should be possible for a commonwealth to clothe herself in purple, and thrive so strangely upon that which would make a prince's hair grow through his hood, and not afford him bread. As if it were a miracle that a careless and prodigal man should bring ten thousand pounds a year to nothing, or that an industrious and frugal man brings a little unto ten thousand pounds a year. But the fruit of a man's industry and frugality can never be like that of a commonwealth, first because the greatness of the increase follows the greatness of the stock or principal, and secondly because a frugal father is for the most part succeeded by a lavish son, whereas a commonwealth is her own heir.

This year a part was proposed by the right honourable Aureus de Woolsacke in the tribe of Pecus, first commissioner of the treasury, unto the council of state, which soon after passed the ballot of the senate and the people, by which the lands of the public revenue, amounting unto one million, were equally divided into five thousand lots, entered by their names and parcels into a lot-book preserved in the exchequer; and if any orphan, being a maid, should cast her estate into the exchequer for fourteen hundred pounds, the treasury was bound by the law to pay her quarterly two hundred pounds a year, free from taxes for her life, and to assign her a lot for her security. If she married, her husband was neither to take out the principal without her consent (acknowledged by herself unto one of the commissioners of the treasury who, according as he found it to be free or forced, was to allow or disallow of it) nor any other way engage it than to her proper use. But if the principal were taken out, the treasury was not bound to repay any more of it than one thousand pounds; nor might be repaid at any time, save within the first year of the marriage: the like was to be done by a half or quarter lot respectively.

This was found to be a great charity unto the weaker sex, and, as some say who are more skilful in like affairs than myself, of good profit to the commonwealth.

Now began the native spleen of Oceana to be much purged, and men not to affect sullenness and pedantism. The elders could remember that they had been youth. Wit and gallantry were so far from being thought crimes in themselves that care was taken to preserve their innocence. For which cause it was proposed unto the council for religion, by the right honourable Cadiscus de Clero, in the tribe of Stamnum, first censor, that such women as, living in gallantry and view about the town, were of evil fame and could not show that they were maintained by their own estates or industry, or such as, having estates of their own, were yet wasteful in their way of life unto others, should be obnoxious unto the animadversion of the council of religion, or of the censors. In which the proceeding should be after this manner. Notice should be first given of the scandal unto the party offending, in private; if there were no amendment within the space of six months, she should be summoned and rebuked before the said council or censors; and if after other six months it were found that neither this availed, she should be censured not to appear at any public meetings, games or recreations, upon penalty of being taken up by the doorkeepers or guards of the senate, and by them to be detained until for every such offence five pounds were duly paid for her enlargement.

Furthermore, if any common strumpet should be found, or any scurrility or profaneness represented at either of the theatres, the prelates for every such offence should be fined twenty pounds by the said council, and the poet for every such offence on his part should be whipped. This law relates unto another, which also was enacted the same year upon this occasion.

The youth and wits of the academy, having put the business so home in the defence of comedies that the provosts had nothing but the consequences provided against by the foregoing law to object, prevailed so far that two of the provosts of the council of state joined in a proposition, which after much ado came to a law, whereby one hundred thousand pounds was allotted for the building of two theatres, one on each side of the piazza of the Halo, and two annual magistrates called prelates chosen out of the knights, were added unto the tropic, the one called the prelate of the buskin, for inspection of the tragic scene called Melpomene, and the other the prelate of the sock, for the comic called Thalia, which magistrates had each of them five hundred pounds a year allowed out of the profits of the theatres, the rest (except eight hundred pounds a year to four poets) payable into the exchequer. A poet laureate, created in one of these theatres by the strategus, receives a wreath of five hundred pounds in gold, paid out of the said profits. But no man is capable of this creation that had not two parts in three of the suffrages at the academy, assembled after six weeks warning and upon that occasion.

These things among us are sure enough to be censured, but by such only as do not know the nature of a commonwealth; for to tell men that they are free, and yet to curb the genius of a people in a lawful recreation unto which they are naturally inclined, is to tell a tale of a tub. I have heard the Protestant ministers in France, by men that were wise and of their own profession, much blamed in that they forbade dancing, a recreation to which the genius of that air is so inclining that they lost many who would not lose that; nor do they less than blame the former determination of rashness, who now gently connive at that which they had so roughly forbidden. These sports in Oceana are so governed that they are pleasing for private diversion and profitable unto the public; for the theatres soon defrayed their own charge, and now bring in a good revenue. All this so far from the detriment of virtue that it is to the improvement of it, seeing women that heretofore made havoc of their honours that they might have their pleasures, are now incapable of their pleasures if they lose their honours.

About the one and fortieth year of the commonwealth, the censors, according unto their annual custom, reported the pillar of Nilus, by which it was found that the people were increased very near one third. Whereupon the council of war was appointed by the senate to bring in a state of war, and the treasurers the state of the treasury. The state of war, or pay and charge of an army, was soon after exhibited by the council in this account.

The Field Pay of a Parliamentary Army

	£ per annum
The lord strategus marching	10,000
Polemarchs { General of the horse	2,000
Lieutenant general	2,000
General of the artillery	1,000
Commissary general	1,000
Major general	1,000
Quarter-master general	1,000
Two adjutants to the major general	1,000
Forty colonels	40,000
100 captains of horse, at £500 a man	50,000
300 captains of foot, at £300 a man	90,000
100 cornets, at £100 a man	10,000

(*cont.*)

		£ per annum
300 ensigns, at £50 a man		15,000
800 quarter-masters, sergeants, trumpeters, drummers		20,000
10,000 horse, at 2s. 6d. a day each		470,000
30,000 foot, each at 1s. a day		500,000
Surgeons		400
	Sum	1,114,400
40,000 auxiliaries, amounting unto (within a little as much)		1,100,000
The charge of mounting 20,000 horse		300,000
The training of artillery, holding a third to the whole		900,000
	Summa totalis	3,414,400

Arms and ammunition are not reckoned, as those which are furnished out of the store or arsenal of Emporium. Nor wastage, as that which goes upon the account of the fleet maintained by the customs, which customs, through the care of the council for trade and growth of traffic, were long since improved unto about a million revenue. The house being informed of a state of war, the commissioners brought in

The state of the treasury this present year, being the one and fortieth of the commonwealth

	£
Received from the one and twentieth of this commonwealth, by £700,000 a year in bank, with the product of the sum rising	16,000,000

Expended from the one and twentieth of this commonwealth

Imprimis, for the addition of arms for 100,000 men, unto the arsenal or Tower of Emporium	1,000,000
For the storing of the same with artillery	300,000
For the storing of the same with ammunition	200,000

For beautifying the cities, parks, gardens, public walks and places for recreation of Emporium and Hiera, with public buildings, aquaducts, statues and fountains, etc.	1,500,000
Extraordinary embassies	150,000
Sum	3,150,000
Remaining in the treasury, the salaries of the exchequer being defaulked	12,000,000

By comparison of which accounts, if a war with an army of 80,000 men were to be made by the penny, yet was the commonwealth able to maintain such an one above for three years without levying a tax. But it is against all experience, sense and reason, that such an army should not be soon broken, or make a great progress; in either of which cases the charge ceaseth, or rather, if a right course be taken in the latter, profit comes in, for the Romans had no other considerable way but victory whereby to fill their treasury, which nevertheless was seldom empty. Alexander did not consult his purse upon his design for Persia. It is observed by Machiavel that Livy, arguing what the event in reason must have been, had that king invaded Rome, and diligently measuring what on each side was necessary unto such a war, never speaks a word of money. No man imagines that the Gauls, Goths, Vandals, Huns, Lombards, Saxons, Normans, made their inroads or conquests by the strength of their purse; and if it be thought enough, according unto the dialect of our age, to say in answer unto these things that those times are past and gone, what money did the late Gustavus, the most victorious of modern princes, bring out of Sweden with him into Germany? An army that goes upon a golden leg will be as lame as if it were a wooden one; but proper horses have nerves and muscles in them, such for which, having four or five millions, a sum easy with a revenue like this of Oceana to be had at any time in readiness, you need never or very rarely charge the people with taxes. What influence the commonwealth by such arms hath had upon the world, I leave unto historians, whose custom it hath been of old to be as diligent observers of foreign actions as careless of those domestic revolutions, which (less pleasant it may be, as not partaking so much of the romance) are unto statesmen of far greater profit; and this fault, if it be not mine, is so much more frequent with modern writers as hath caused me to undertake this work, on which to give my own judgment, it is performed as much above the time I have been about it as below the dignity of the matter.

But I cannot depart out of this country till I have taken leave of my Lord Archon, a prince of immense felicity, who having built as high with his counsels as he digged deep with this sword, had now been fifty years measured with his own unerring orbs.

Timoleon, so great a hater of tyrants that, not able to dissuade his brother Timophanes to relinquish the tyranny of Corinth, he slew him, was afterwards elected by the people (the Sicilians groaning unto them from under the like burden) to be sent unto their relief. Whereupon Teleclides, the man at that time of most authority in the commonwealth of Corinth, stood up and, giving an exhortation unto Timoleon how he should behave himself in his expedition, told him that if he restored the Sicilians unto liberty, it would be acknowledged that he had destroyed a tyrant; if otherwise, he must expect to hear that he had murdered a king. Timoleon, taking his leave with a very small provision for so great a design, pursued it with a courage not inferior to, and a felicity beyond, any that had been known unto that day in mortal flesh, having in the space of eight years utterly rooted out of all Sicily those weeds of tyranny, through the distraction whereof men fled in such abundance from their native country that whole cities were left desolate; and brought it unto such a pass that others, through the fame of his virtues and the excellency of the soil, flocked as fast from all quarters unto it as to the garden of the world. While he, being presented by the people of Syracuse with his town house and his country retreat, the sweetest places in either, lived with his wife and children a most quiet, happy, and holy life; for he attributed no part of his success unto himself, but all unto the blessing and providence of the gods. As he passed his time in this manner, admired and honoured by mankind, Laphystius, an envious demagogue, going to summon him upon some pretence or other to answer for himself before the assembly, the people fell into such a mutiny as could not be appeased but by Timoleon who, understanding the matter, reproved them by repeating the pains and travail which he had gone through, unto no other end than that every man might have the free use of the laws. Wherefore when Demaenetus, another demagogue, had brought the same design about again, and blamed him impertinently unto the people for things which he did when he was

general, Timoleon answered nothing but, raising up his hands, gave
the gods thanks for their return unto his frequent prayers, that he
might but live to see the Syracusans so free that they might question
whom they pleased.

Not long after, being old, through some natural imperfection he fell
blind, but the Syracusans by their perpetual visits held him, though he
could not see, the greatest object; if there arrived strangers, they
brought them to see this sight. Whatever came in debate at the
assembly, if it were of small consequence, they determined it themselves, but if of importance, they always sent for Timoleon, who being
brought by his servants in a chair and set in the middle of the theatre,
there ever followed a great shout after which some time was allowed
for the benedictions of the people; and then the matter proposed,
when Timoleon had spoken of it, was put to the suffrage, which given,
his servants bore him back in his chair, accompanied by the people,
clapping their hands and making all expressions of joy and applause,
till, leaving him at his house, they returned unto the dispatch of their
business. And this was the life of Timoleon, till he died of age and
dropped like a mature fruit, while the eyes of the people were as the
showers of autumn.

The life and death of my Lord Archon, save that he had his senses
unto the last, and that his character, being not the restorer but the
founder of a commonwealth, was greater, is so exactly the same again,
that (seeing by men wholly ignorant of antiquity, I am accused of
writing romance) I shall repeat nothing, but tell you that this year the
whole nation of Oceana, even unto the women and children, was in
mourning, where so great or sad a pomp of funeral had never been
seen or known. Sometime after the performance of the exequies, a
colossus, mounted upon a brazen horse, of excellent fabric, was erected in the piazza of the Pantheon, engraved with this inscription on
the eastern side of the pedestal.

HIS
NAME
IS AS
PRECIOUS OINTMENT

And on the western, with this.

Grata Patria
Piae et perpetuae memoriae
D. D.
Olphaus Megaletor
Lord Archon and sole Legislator
of
OCEANA
Pater Patriae.

Invincible in the Field.
Inviolable in his Faith.
Unfeigned in his Zeal.
Immortal in his Fame.

The Greatest of Captains.
The Best of Princes.
The Happiest of Legislators.
The Most Sincere of Christians.

Who, setting the Kingdoms of the Earth at Liberty,
Took the Kingdom of the Heavens by Violence.

Aetat. suae. 116.

Anno

Hujus Reipub. 50.[7]

---

[7] Cromwell was 56 in 1656, not 66; if this is the implication.

A
System of Politics
Delineated in short and easy
APHORISMS
Published from the Author's own Manuscript

Chap. I
Of government

1. A people is either under a state of civil government, or in a state of civil war; or neither under a state of civil government, nor in a state of civil war.
2. Civil government is an art whereby a people rule themselves, or are ruled by others.
3. The art of civil government in general is twofold: national or provincial.
4. National government is that by which a nation is governed independently, or within itself.
5. Provincial government is that by which a province is governed dependently, or by some foreign prince or state.
6. A people is neither governed by themselves, nor by others, but[1] by reason of some external principle thereto forcing them.
7. Force is of two kinds, natural and unnatural.
8. Natural force consists in the vigour of principles, and their natural necessary operations.
9. Unnatural force is an external or adventitious opposition to the vigour of principles and their necessary working, which, from a violation of nature, is called violence.
10. National government is an effect of natural force, or vigour.
11. Provincial government is an effect of unnatural force, or violence.
12. The natural force which works or produces national government (of which only I shall speak hereafter) consists in riches.
13. The man that cannot live upon his own must be a servant; but he that can live upon his own may be a freeman.

[1] I.e., 'except'.

14. Where a people cannot live upon their own, the government is either monarchy or aristocracy; where a people can live upon their own, the government may be democracy.

15. A man that could live upon his own may yet, to spare his own and live upon another, be a servant; but a people that can live upon their own cannot spare their own and live upon another, but (except they be no servants, that is, except they come to a democracy) they must waste their own by maintaining their masters,[2] or by having others to live upon them.

16. Where a people that can live upon their own imagine that they can be governed by others, and not lived upon by such governors, it is not the genius of the people; it is the mistake of the people.

17. Where a people that can live upon their own will not be governed by others lest they be lived upon by others, it is not the mistake of the people; it is the genius of the people.

18. Of government there are three principles: matter, privation, and form.

Chap. II
Of the matter of government

1. That which is the matter of government is what we call an estate, be it in lands, goods or money.

2. If the estate be more in money than in land, the port or garb of the owner goes more upon his monies than his lands; which with private men is ordinary, but with nations (except such only as live more upon their trade than upon their territory) is not to be found; for which cause overbalance of riches in money or goods, as to the sequel of these aphorisms, is altogether omitted.

3. If the estate be more in land than in goods or money, the garb and port of the owner (whether as man or a nation) goes more if not altogether upon his land.

4. If a man has some estate, he may have some servants or a family, and consequently some government, or something to govern; if he has no estate, he can have no government.

5. Where the eldest of many brothers has all, or so much that the rest for their livelihood stand in need of him, that brother is as it were prince in that family.

[2] Toland has 'master's'.

6. Where of many brothers the eldest has but an equal share, or not so inequal as to make the rest to stand in need of him for their livelihood, that family is as it were a commonwealth.

7. Distribution of shares in land as to the three grand interests, the king, the nobility and the people, must be equal or inequal.

8. Equal distribution of land, as if one man or a few men have one half of the territory and the people have the other half, causes privation of government, and a state of civil war; for, the lord or lords on the one side being able to assert their pretension or right to rule, and the people on the other their pretension or right to liberty, that nation can never come under any form of government till that question be decided; and, property being not by any law to be violated or moved, any such question cannot be decided but by the sword only.

9. Inequal distribution of shares in land as to the three grand interests, or the whole land in any one of these, is that which causes one of these three to be the predominant interest.

10. All government is interest, and the predominant interest gives the matter or foundation of the government.

11. If one man has the whole, or two parts in three of the whole land or territory, the interest of one man is the predominant interest, and causes absolute monarchy.

12. If a few men have the whole, or two parts in three, of the whole land or territory, the interest of the few or of the nobility is the predominant interest; and, were there any such thing in nature, would cause a pure aristocracy.

13. It being so that pure aristocracy, or the nobility having the whole, or two parts in three, of the whole land or territory without a moderator or prince to balance them, is a state of war, in which everyone, as he grows eminent or potent, aspires to monarchy; and that not any nobility can have peace or can reign without having such a moderator or prince as, on the one side, they may balance or hold in from being absolute, and on the other side may balance or hold them and their factions from flying out into arms; it follows that if a few men have the whole, or two parts in three, of the whole land or territory, the interest of the nobility, being the predominant interest, must of necessity produce regulated monarchy.

14. If the many or the people have the whole, or two parts in three, of

the whole land or territory, the interest of the many or of the people is the predominant interest, and causes democracy.

15. A people neither under absolute or under regulated monarchy, nor yet under democracy, are under a privation of government.

Chap. III
Of the privation of government

1. Where a people are not in a state of civil government, but in a state of civil war, or where a people are neither under a state of civil government, nor under a state of civil war, there the people are under privation of government.

2. Where one man, not having the whole, or two parts in three, of the whole land or territory, yet assumes to himself the whole power, there the people are under privation of government, and this privation is called tyranny.

3. Where a few men, not having the whole, or about two parts in three, of the whole land or territory, yet assume to themselves the whole power, there the people are under privation of government, and this privation is called oligarchy.

4. Where the many or the people, not having the whole, or two parts in three, of the whole land or territory, yet assume to themselves the whole power, there the people are under privation of government, and this privation is called anarchy.

5. Where the tyranny, the oligarchy or the anarchy, not having in the land or territory such a full share as may amount to the truth of government, have nevertheless such a share in it as may maintain an army, there the people are under privation of government, and this privation is a state of civil war.

6. Where the tyranny, the oligarchy or the anarchy have not any such share in the land or territory as may maintain an army, there the people are in privation of government, which privation is neither a state of civil government, nor a state of civil war.

7. Where the people are neither in a state of civil government, nor in a state of civil war, there the tyranny, the oligarchy or the anarchy cannot stand by any force of nature, because it is void of any natural foundation, nor by any force of arms, because it is not able to maintain an army; and so must fall away of itself through the want of a foundation, or be blown up by some tumult; and in

this kind of privation the matter or foundation of a good orderly government is ready and in being, and there wants nothing to the perfection of the same but proper superstructures or form.

Chap. IV
Of the form of government

1. That which gives the being, the action and the denomination to a creature or thing, is the form of that creature or thing.
2. There is in form something that is not elementary but divine.
3. The contemplation of form is astonishing to man, and has a kind of trouble or impulse accompanying it, that exalts his soul to God.
4. As the form of a man is the image of God, so the form of a government is the image of man.
5. Man is both a sensual and a philosophical creature.
6. Sensuality in a man is when he is led only as are the beasts, that is, no otherwise than by appetite.
7. Philosophy is the knowledge of divine and human things.
8. To preserve and defend himself against violence is natural to man as he is a sensual creature.
9. To have an impulse, or to be raised upon contemplation of natural things, to the adoration or worship of God, is natural to man as he is a philosophical creature.
10. Formation of government is the creation of a political creature after the image of a philosophical creature, or it is an infusion of the soul or faculties of a man into the body of a multitude.
11. The more the soul or faculties of a man (in the manner of their being infused into the body of a multitude) are refined or made incapable of passion, the more perfect is the form of government.
12. Not the refined spirit of a man, or of some men, is a good form of government; but a good form of government is the refined spirit of a nation.
13. The spirit of a nation (whether refined or not refined) can neither be wholly saint nor atheist: not saint, because the far greater part of the people is never able in matters of religion to be their own leaders; nor atheist, because religion is every whit as indelible a character in man's nature as reason.
14. Language is not a more natural intercourse between the soul of

one man and another, than religion is between God and the soul of a man.

15. As not this language, nor that language, but some language; so not this religion, nor that religion, yet some religion is natural to every nation.

16. The soul of government, as the true and perfect image of the soul of man, is every whit as necessarily religious as rational.

17. The body of a government, as consisting of the sensual part of man, is every whit as preservative and defensive of itself as sensual creatures are of themselves.

18. The body of a man, not actuated or led by the soul, is a dead thing out of pain and misery; but the body of a people, not actuated or led by the soul of government, is a living thing in pain and misery.

19. The body of a people, not led by the reason of the government, is not a people, but a herd; not led by the religion of the government, is at an inquiet and an uncomfortable loss in itself; not disciplined by the conduct of the government, is not an army for defence of itself, but a rout; not directed by the laws of the government, has not any rule of right; and without recourse to the justice or judicatories of the government, has no remedy of wrongs.

20. In contemplation of, and in conformity to the soul of man, as also for supply of those his necessities which are not otherwise supplied or to be supplied by nature, form of government consists necessarily of these five parts: the civil, which is the reason of the people; the religious, which is the comfort of the people; the military, which is the captain of the people; the laws, which are the rights of the people; and the judicatories, which are the avengers of their wrongs.

21. The parts of form in government are as the offices in a house; and the orders of a form of government are as the orders of a house or family.

22. Good orders make evil men good, and bad orders make good men evil.

23. Oligarchists (to the end they may keep all others out of the government) pretending themselves to be saints, do also pretend that they in whom lust reigns are not fit for reign or for government. But *libido dominandi*, the lust of government, is the greatest

lust, whch also reigns most in those that have least right, as in oligarchists; for many a king and many a people have and had unquestionable right, but an oligarchist never; whence from their own argument, the lust of government reigning most in oligarchists, it undeniably follows that oligarchists of all men are least fit for government.

24. As in houses not differing in the kinds of their offices, the orders of the families differ much; so the difference of form in different governments consists not in the kinds or number of the parts, which in every one is alike, but in the different ways of ordering those parts. And as the different orders of a house arise for the most part from the quantity and quality of the estate by which it is defrayed or maintained, according as it is in one or more of the family as proprietors, so it is also in a government.

25. The orders of the form, which are the manners of the mind of the government, follow the temperament of the body, or the distribution of the lands or territories, and the interests thence arising.

26. The interest of arbitrary monarchy is the absoluteness of the monarch; the interest of regulated monarchy is the greatness of the nobility; the interest of democracy is the felicity of the people; for in democracy the government is for the use of the people, and in monarchy the people are for the use of the government, that is, of one lord or more.

27. The use of a horse without his provender, or of the people without some regard had to the necessities of human nature, can be none at all; nor are those necessities of nature in any form whatsoever to be otherwise provided for than by those five parts already mentioned; for which cause every government consists of five parts: the civil, the religious, the military, the laws, and the judicatories.

Chap. V
Of form in the civil parts

1. Those naturalists that have best written of generation do observe that all things proceed from an egg, and that there is in every egg a *punctum saliens*, or a part first moved, as the purple speck observed in those of hens; from the working whereof the other

organs or fit members are delineated, distinguished and wrought into one organical body.

2. A nation without government, or fallen into privation of form, is like an egg unhatched; and the *punctum saliens*, or first mover from the corruption of the former to the generation of the succeeding form, is either a sole legislator or a council.

3. A sole legislator, proceeding according to art or knowledge, produces government in the whole piece at once and in perfection. But a council (proceeding not according to art, or what in a new case is necessary or fit for them, but, according to that which they call the genius of the people, still hankering after the things they have been used to, or their old customs, how plain soever it be made in reason that they can no longer fit them) make patching work, and are ages about that which is very seldom or never brought by them to any perfection; but commonly comes by the way to ruin, leaving the noblest attempts under reproach, and the authors of them exposed to the greatest miseries while they live, if not their memories when they are dead and gone to the greatest infamy.

4. If the *punctum saliens*, or first mover in generation of the form be a sole legislator, his proceeding is not only according to nature, but according to art also, and begins with the delineation of distinct orders or members.

5. Delineation of distinct organs or members (as to the form of government) is a division of the territory into fit precincts once stated for all, and a formation of them to their proper offices and functions, according to the nature or truth of the form to be introduced.

6. Precincts in absolute monarchy are commonly called provinces; and as to the delineation or stating of them, they may be equal or inequal. Precincts in regulated monarchy, where the lords or nobility as to their titles or estates ought not to be equal, but to differ as one star differs from another in glory, are commonly called counties, and ought to be inequal. Precincts in democracy, where without equality in the electors there will hardly be any equality in the elected, or where, without equality in the precincts, it is almost if not altogether impossible there should be equality in the commonwealth, are properly called tribes, and ought by all means to be equal.

7. Equality or parity has been represented an odious thing, and made to imply the levelling of men's estates; but if a nobility, how inequal soever in their estates or titles, yet, to come to the truth of aristocracy, must as to their votes or participation in the government be *pares regni*, that is to say peers or in parity among themselves; as well likewise the people, to attain to the truth of democracy, may be peers or in parity among themselves, and yet not as to their estates be obliged to levelling.

8. Industry of all things is the most accumulative, and accumulation of all things hates levelling; the revenue therefore of the people being the revenue of industry, though some nobility (as that of Israel, or that of Lacedaemon) may be found to have been levellers, yet not any people in the world.[1]

9. Precincts, being stated, are in the next place to be formed to their proper offices and functions, according to the truth of the form to be introduced; which in general is to form them as it were into distinct governments, and to endow them with distinct governors.

10. Governments or governors are either supreme or subordinate. For absolute monarchy to admit in its precincts any government or governors, that are not subordinate but supreme, were a plain contradiction. But that regulated monarchy, and that democracy, may do it is seen in the princes of Germany and in the cantons of Switzerland; nevertheless, these being governments that have derived this not from the wisdom of any legislator, but from accident, and an ill disposition of the matter, whereby they are not only incapable of greatness but even of any perfect state of health, they come not under the consideration of art, from which they derive not; but of chance, to which we leave them. And, to speak according to art, we pronounce that, as well in democracy and in regulated as in absolute monarchy, governors and governments in the several divisions ought not to be sovereignties, but subordinate to one common sovereign.

11. Subordinate governors are at will, or for life, or upon rotation or changes.

12. In absolute monarchy the governors of provinces must either be at will or upon rotation, or else the monarch cannot be absolute. In regulated monarchy the governors of the counties may be for

---

[1] Arguably the most 'bourgeois' utterance to be found anywhere in H's works.

life or hereditary, as in counts or lords, or for some certain term and upon rotation, as in viscounts or sheriffs. In democracy the people are servants to their governors for life, and so cannot be free;[1] or the governors of the tribes must be upon rotation and for some certain term, excluding the party that have borne the magistracy for that term from being elected into the like again, till an equal interval or vacation be expired.

13. The term in which a man may administer government to the good of it, and not attempt upon it to the harm of it, is the fittest term of bearing magistracy; and three years in a magistracy, described by the law under which a man has lived, and which he has known by the carriage or practice of it in others, is a term in which he cannot attempt upon his government for the hurt of it, but may administer it for the good of it, though such a magistracy or government should consist of divers functions.

14. Governors in subordinate precincts have commonly three functions: the one civil, the other judicial, and the third military.

15. In absolute monarchy the government of a province consists of one *beglerbeg*, or governor for three years, with his council or divan for civil matters, and his guard of janissaries and spahis, that is, of horse and foot, with power to levy and command the timariots or military farmers.

16. In regulated monarchy the government of a county consists of one count or lord for life, or of one viscount or sheriff for some limited term, with power in certain civil and judicial matters, and to levy and command the *posse comitatus*.

17. In democracy the government of a tribe consists of one council or court, in one third part elected annually by the people of that tribe for the civil, for the judicial and for the military government of the same; as also to preside at the election of deputies in that tribe towards the annual supply in one third part of the common and sovereign assemblies of the whole commonwealth, that is to say, of the senate and of the popular assembly; in which two these tribes, thus delineated and distinguished into proper organs or fit members to be actuated by those sovereign assemblies, are wrought up again by connection into one entire and organical body.

---

[1] H means that rotation of office is necessary to a democracy.

18. A parliament of physicians would never have found out the circulation of the blood, nor could a parliament of poets have written Virgil's *Aeneis*; of this kind therefore in the formation of government is the proceeding of a sole legislator. But if the people, without a legislator, set upon such work by a certain instinct that is in them, they never go further than to choose a council; not considering that the formation of government is as well a work of invention as of judgment, and that a council, though in matters laid before them they may excel in judgment, yet invention is as contrary to the nature of a council as it is to musicians in consort, who can play and judge of any air that is laid before them, though to invent a part of music they can never well agree.

19. In councils there are three ways of result, and every way of result makes a different form. A council with the result in the prince makes absolute monarchy. A council with the result in the nobility, or where without the nobility there can be no result, makes aristocracy, or regulated monarchy. A council with the result in the people makes democracy. There is a fourth kind of result or council which amounts not to any form, but to privation of government: that is, a council not consisting of a nobility, and yet with the result in itself, which is rank oligarchy; so the people, seldom or never going any further than to elect a council without any result but itself, instead of democracy introduce oligarchy.

20. The ultimate result in every form is the sovereign power. If the ultimate result be wholly and only in the monarch, that monarchy is absolute. If the ultimate result be not wholly and only in the monarch, that monarchy is regulated. If the result be wholly and only in the people, the people are in liberty, or the form of the government is democracy.

21. It may happen that a monarchy founded upon aristocracy, and so as to the foundation regulated, may yet come by certain expedients or intrusions (as at this day in France and in Spain) as to the administration of it to appear or be called absolute; of which I shall treat more at large when I come to speak of reason of state, or of administration.

22. The ultimate result in the whole body of the people, if the commonwealth be of any considerable extent, is altogether impracticable; and if the ultimate result be but in a part of the people, the rest are not in liberty, nor is the government democracy.

23. As a whole army cannot charge at one and the same time, yet is so ordered that every one in his turn comes up to give the charge of the whole army; so, though the whole people cannot give the result at one and the same, yet may they be so ordered that every one in his turn may come up to give the result of the whole people.

24. A popular assembly, rightly ordered, brings up everyone in his turn to give the result of the whole people.

25. If the popular assembly consists of one thousand or more, annually changeable in one third part by new elections made in the tribes by the people, it is rightly ordered; that is to say, so constituted that such an assembly can have no other interest whereupon to give the result than that only which is the interest of the whole people.

26. But in vain is result where there is no matter to resolve upon; and where maturity of debate has not preceded, there is not yet matter to resolve upon.

27. Debate, to be mature, cannot be managed by a multitude; and result, to be popular, cannot be given by a few.

28. If a council capable of debate has also the result, it is oligarchy. If an assembly capable of the result has debate also, it is anarchy. Debate in a council not capable of result, and result in an assembly not capable of debate, is democracy.

29. It is not more natural to a people in their own affairs to be their own choosers, than upon that occasion to be provided of their learned council; insomuch that the saying of Pacuvius, that either a people is governed by a king or counselled by a senate, is universally approved.

30. Where the senate has no distinct interest, there the people are counsellable, and venture not upon debate; where the senate has any distinct interest, there the people are not counsellable, but fall into debate among themselves, and so into confusion.

31. Of senates there are three kinds: first, a senate eligible out of the nobility only, as that of Rome, which will not be contented to be merely the council of the people, but will be contending that they are lords of the people, never quitting their pretensions till they have ruined the commonwealth. Secondly, a senate elected for life, as that of Sparta, which will be a species of nobility, and will

have a kind of Spartan king; and a senate upon rotation,[1] which, being rightly constituted, is quiet, and never pretends more than to be the learned council of the people.

32. Thirdly, three hundred senators, for example, changeable in one third part of them annually by new elections in the tribes, and constituted a senate to debate upon all civil matters, to promulgate to the whole nation what they have debated – this promulgation to be made some such convenient time before the matters by them debated are to be proposed, that they may be commonly known and well understood, and then to propose the same to the result of the popular assembly, which only is to be the test of every public act – is a senate rightly ordered.

Form of government (as to the civil part), being thus completed, is summed up in the three following aphorisms:

33. Absolute monarchy (for the civil part of the form) consists of distinct provinces under distinct governors, equally subordinate to a grand signor or sole lord, with his council or divan debating and proposing, and the result wholly and only in himself.

34. Regulated monarchy (for the civil part of the form) consists of distinct principalities or counties under distinct lords or governors, which if rightly constituted are equally subordinate to the king and his peerage, or to the king and his estates assembled in parliament, without whose consent the king can do nothing.

35. Democracy (for the civil part of the form), if rightly constituted, consists of distinct tribes under the government of distinct magistrates, courts or councils, regularly changeable in one third part upon annual elections, and subordinate to a senate consisting of not above three hundred senators, and to a popular assembly consisting of not under a thousand deputies; each of these also regularly changeable in one third part upon annual elections in the tribes, the senate having the debate, and the popular assembly the result of the whole commonwealth.

---

[1] This appears misplaced; it should be part of no. 32.

Chap. VI
Of form in the religious part

1. Form for the religious part either admits of liberty of conscience in the whole or in part, or does not admit of liberty of conscience at all.

2. Liberty of conscience entire, or in the whole, is where a man according to the dictates of his own conscience may have the free exercise of his religion, without impediment to his preferment or employment in the state.

3. Liberty of conscience in part is where a man according to the dictates of his conscience may have the free exercise of his religion; but if it be not the national religion, he is thereby incapable of preferment or employment in the state.

4. Where the form admits not of the free exercise of any other religion except that only which is national, there is no liberty of conscience.

5. Men who have the means to assert liberty of conscience have the means to assert civil liberty; and will do it if they are oppressed in their consciences.

6. Men participating in property, or in employment civil or military, have the means to assert liberty of conscience.

7. Absolute monarchy, being sole proprietor, may admit of liberty of conscience to such as are not capable of civil or military employment, and yet not admit of the means to assert civil liberty; as the Greek Christians under the Turk, who, though they enjoy liberty of conscience, cannot assert civil liberty, because they have neither property nor any civil or military employments.

8. Regulated monarchy, being not sole proprietor, may not admit naturally of liberty of conscience, lest it admit of the means to assert civil liberty, as was lately seen in England by pulling down the bishops, who, for the most part, are one half of the foundation of regulated monarchy.

9. Democracy, being nothing but entire liberty – and liberty of conscience without civil liberty, or civil liberty without liberty of conscience, being but liberty by halves – must admit of liberty of conscience both as to the perfection of its present being, and as to its future security; as to the perfection of its present being, for the reasons already shown, or that she do not enjoy liberty by halves;

and for future security, because this excludes absolute monarchy, which cannot stand with liberty of conscience in the whole, and regulated monarchy, which cannot stand safely with it in any part.

10. If it be said that in France there is liberty of conscience in part, it is also plain that while the hierarchy is standing this liberty is falling, and that if ever it comes to pull down the hierarchy, it pulls down that monarchy also; wherefore the monarchy or hierarchy will be beforehand with it, if they see their true interest.

11. The ultimate result in monarchy being that of one man, or of a few men, the national religion in monarchy may happen not to be the religion of the major part of the people; but the result in democracy being in the major part of the people, it cannot happen but that the national religion must be that of the major part of the people.

12. The major part of the people, being in matters of religion enabled to be their own leaders, will in such cases therefore have a public leading; or, being debarred of their will in that particular, are debarred of their liberty of conscience.

13. Where the major part of the people is debarred of their liberty by the minor, there is neither liberty of conscience nor democracy, but spiritual or civil oligarchy.

14. Where the major part is not debarred of their liberty of conscience by the minor, there is a national religion.

15. National religion is either coercive, or not coercive.

16. Religion is not naturally subservient to any corrupt or worldly interest, for which cause, to bring it into subjection to interest, it must be coercive.

17. Where religion is coercive, or in subjection to interest, there it is not, or will not long continue to be the true religion.

18. Where religion is not coercive, nor under subjection to any interest, there it either is, or has no obstruction why it may not come to be, the true religion.

19. Absolute monarchy pretends to infallibility in matters of religion, employs not any that is not of its own faith, and punishes its apostates by death without mercy.

20. Regulated monarchy comes not much short of the same pretence, but, consisting of proprietors, and such as if they dissent have oftentimes the means to defend themselves, it does not therefore always attain to the exercise of the like power.

21. Democracy pretends not to infallibility, but is in matters of religion no more than a seeker, not taking away from its people their liberty of conscience, but educating them, or so many of them as shall like of it, in such a manner or knowledge in divine things as may render them best able to make use of their liberty of conscience, which it performs by the national religion.

22. National religion, to be such, must have a national ministry or clergy.

23. The clergy is either a landed or a stipendiated clergy.

24. A landed clergy attaining to one third of the territory, is aristocracy; and therefore equally incompatible with absolute monarchy and with democracy; but to regulated monarchy for the most part is such a supporter, as in that case it may be truly enough said, that *no bishop, no king.*[1]

25. The sovereignty of the prince in absolute monarchy, and of the people in democracy, admitting not of any counterpoise, in each of these the clergy ought not to be landed; the labourer nevertheless being worthy of his hire, they ought to be stipendiated.

26. A clergy well landed is to regulated monarchy a very great glory; and a clergy not well stipendiated is to absolute monarchy or to democracy as great an infamy.

27. A clergy, whether landed or stipendiated, is either hierarchical or popular.

28. A hierarchical clergy is a monarchical ordination; a popular clergy receives ordination from election by the people.

Form of government (as to the religious part), being thus completed, is summed up in the three following aphorisms:

29. Absolute monarchy (for the religious part of the form) consists of a hierarchical clergy and of an *alcoran* (or some book received in the nature of Scripture) interpretable by the prince only and his clergy, willingly permitting to them that are not capable of employments a liberty of conscience.

30. Regulated monarchy (for the religious part of the form) consists of an aristocratical hierarchy, of the liturgy and of the holy Scriptures (or some such book received for a rule of faith) interpret-

[1]Capitalised in Toland.

able only by the clergy, not admitting liberty of conscience, except through mere necessity.

31. Democracy (for the religious part of the form) consists of a popular clergy, of the Scriptures (or some other book acknowledged divine), with a directory, for the national religion, and a council for the equal maintenance both of the national religion and of the liberty of conscience.

Chap. VII
Of form in the military part

1. A man may perish by the sword; yet no man draws the sword to perish, but to live by it.
2. So many ways as there are of living by the sword, so many ways there are of a militia.
3. If a prince be lord of the whole, or of two parts in three, of the whole territory, and divides it into military farms at will and without rent, upon condition of service at their own charge in arms whenever he commands them, it is the sword of an absolute monarchy.
4. If the nobility, being lords of the whole or of two parts in three of the whole territory, let their lands by good pennyworths to tenants at will, or by their leases bound at their commands by whom they live to serve in arms upon pay, it is the sword of a regulated monarchy.
5. In countries that have no infantry, or militia of free commoners, as in France and Poland, the nobility themselves are a vast body of horse and the sword of that monarchy.
6. If a people, where there neither is lord nor lords of the whole, nor of two parts in three of the whole territory, for the common defence of their liberty and of their livelihood, take their turns upon the guard or in arms, it is the sword of democracy.
7. There is a fourth kind of militia, or of men living more immediately by the sword, which are soldiers of fortune or a mercenary army.
8. Absolute monarchy must be very well provided with court guards or a mercenary army; otherwise, its military farmers having no bar

from becoming proprietors, the monarchy itself has no bar from
changing into democracy.

*Form of government (as to the military part), being thus completed, is
summed up in the three following aphorisms:*

9. In a regulated monarchy where there is an infantry, there needs
not any mercenary army; and there the people live tolerably well.
10. In a regulated monarchy where there is no infantry, but the
nobility themselves are a vast body of horse, there must also be a
mercenary infantry, and there the people are peasants or slaves.
11. There is no such thing in nature as any monarchy (whether
absolute or regulated) subsisting merely by a mercenary army,
and without an infantry or cavalry planted upon the lands of the
monarch, or of his whole nobility.

Chap. VIII
Of form in the legal part

1. If justice be not the interest of a government, the interest of that
government will be its justice.
2. Let equity or justice be what it will, yet if a man be to judge or
resolve in his own case, he resolves upon his own interest.
3. Every government, being not obnoxious to any superior, resolves
in her own case.
4. The ultimate result in every government is the law in that
government.
5. In absolute monarchy, the ultimate result is in the monarch.
6. In aristocracy, or regulated monarchy, the ultimate result is in the
lords or peers, or not without them.
7. In democracy the ultimate result is in the people.
8. Law in absolute monarchy holds such a disproportion to natural
equity, as the interest of one man to the interest of all mankind.
9. Law in aristocracy holds such a disproportion to natural equity, as
the interest of a few men to the interest of all mankind.
10. Law in democracy holds such a disproportion to natural equity,
as the interest of a nation to the interest of all mankind.
11. One government has much nearer approaches to natural equity
than another; but in case natural equity and self-preservation

286

come in competition, so natural is self-preservation to every creature, that in that case no one government has any more regard to natural equity than another.

12. A man may devote himself to death or destruction to save a nation, but no nation will devote itself to death or destruction to save mankind.

13. Machiavel is decried for saying that 'no consideration is to be had of what is just or unjust, of what is merciful or cruel, of what is honourable or ignominious, in case it be to save a state, or to preserve liberty';[1] which as to the manner of expression is crudely spoken. But to imagine that a nation will devote itself to death or destruction any more upon faith given or an engagement thereto tending, than if there had been no such engagement made or faith given, were not piety but folly.

14. Wheresoever the power of making law is, there only is the power of interpreting the law so made.

15. God, who has given his law to the soul of that man who shall voluntarily receive it, is the only interpreter of his law to that soul; such at least is the judgment of democracy. With absolute monarchy, and with aristocracy, it is an innate maxim that the people are to be deceived in two things, their religion and their law; or that the church or themselves are interpreters of all Scripture, as the priests were anciently of the sibyl's books.

Form of government (as to the legal part), being thus completed, is summed up in the three following aphorisms:

16. Absolute monarchy (for the legal part of the form) consists of such laws as it pretends God has delivered or given the king and priests power to interpret; or it consists of such laws as the monarch shall choose[2] or has chosen.

17. Aristocracy (for the legal part of the form) consists of such laws as the nobility shall choose or have chosen; or of such as the people shall choose or have chosen, provided they be agreed to by their lords, or by the king and their lords.

[1] 'perchè dove si delibera al tutto della salute della patria, non vi debbe cadere alcuna considerazione nè di giusto, nè d'ingiusto; nè di pietoso, nè di crudele; nè di laudabile, nè d'ignominioso; anzi, posposto ogni altro rispetto, seguire al tutto quel partito che le salvi la vita, e mantenghile la libertà'. *Discorsi*, III, 41.

[2] 'Choose' inserted; omitted by Toland.

18. Democracy (for the legal part of the form) consists of such laws as the people, with the advice of their council, or of the senate, shall choose or have chosen.

Chap. IX
Of form in the judicial part

1. Multiplicity of laws, being a multiplicity of snares for the people, causes corruption of government.
2. Paucity of laws requires arbitrary power in courts, or judicatories.
3. Arbitrary power (in reference to laws) is of three kinds: (1) in making, altering, abrogating or interpreting of laws, which belong to the sovereign power; (2) in applying laws to cases which are never any one like another; (3) in reconciling the laws among themselves.
4. There is no difficulty at all in judging of any case whatsoever according to natural equity.
5. Arbitrary power makes any man a competent judge for his knowledge but, leaving him to his own interest, which oftentimes is contrary to justice, makes him also an incompetent judge, in regard that he may be partial.
6. A partiality is the cause why laws pretend to abhor arbitrary power; nevertheless, seeing that not one case is altogether like another, there must in every judicatory be some arbitrary power.
7. Paucity of laws causes arbitrary power in applying them; and multiplicity of laws causes arbitrary power in reconciling and applying them too.
8. Arbitrary power, where it can do no wrong, does the greatest right; because no law can ever be so framed but that without arbitrary power it may do wrong.
9. Arbitrary power, going upon the interest of one or of a few, makes not a just judicatory.
10. Arbitrary power, going upon the interest of the whole people, makes a just judicatory.
11. All judicatories and laws, which have been made by arbitrary power, allow of the interpretation of arbitrary power, and acknowledge an appeal from themselves to it.
12. That law which leaves the least arbitrary power to the judge or judicatory, is the most perfect law.

13. Laws that are the fewest, plainest, and briefest, leave the least arbitrary power to the judge or judicatory; and, being a light to the people, make the most incorrupt government.

14. Laws that are perplexed, intricate, tedious and voluminous, leave the greatest arbitrary power to the judge or judicatory; and, raining snares on the people, make the most corrupt government.

15. Seeing no law can be so perfect as not to leave arbitrary power to the judicatory, that is the best constitution of a judicatory where arbitrary power can do the least hurt, and the worst constitution of a judicatory is where arbitrary power can do the most ill.

16. Arbitrary power in one judge does the most, in a few judges does less, and in a multitude of judges does the least hurt.

17. The ultimate appeal from all inferior judicatories is to some sovereign judge or judicatory.

18. The ultimate result in every government (as in absolute monarchy, the monarch; in aristocracy, or aristocratical monarchy, the peers; in democracy, the popular assembly) is a sovereign judge or judicatory that is arbitrary.

19. Arbitrary power in judicatories is not such as makes no use of the law, but such by which there is a right use to be made of the laws.

20. That judicatory where the judge or judges are not obnoxious to partiality or private interest cannot make a wrong use of power.

21. That judicatory that cannot make a wrong use of power must make a right use of law.

22. Every judicatory consists of a judge or some judges without a jury, or of a jury on the bench without any other judge or judges, or of a judge or judges on the bench with a jury at the bar.

Form of government (as to the judicial part), being thus completed, is summed up in the three following aphorisms:

23. Absolute monarchy (for the judicial part of the form) admits not of any jury, but is of some such kind as a *cadi* or judge in a city, or as we say in a hundred, with an appeal to a *cadaliskar* or a judge in a province, from whom also there lies an appeal to the *mufti*, who is at the devotion of the grand signor or of the monarch.

24. Aristocracy or aristocratical monarchy (for the judicial part of the form) may admit of a jury, so it be at the bar only, and consists of some such kind as delegates or ordinary judges, with an appeal to

a house of peers; or some such court as the parliament at Paris, which was, at the institution in the reign of Hugh Capet, a parliament of sovereign princes.

25. Democracy (for the judicial part of the form) is of some such kind as a jury on the bench in every tribe, consisting of thirty persons or more annually eligible in one third part by the people of that tribe, with an appeal from thence to a judicatory residing in the capital city of the like constitution, annually eligible in one third part out of the senate or the popular assembly, or out of both; from which also there lies an appeal to the people, that is to the popular assembly.

Chap. X
Of administration of government, or reason of state

1. As the matter of a ship or of a house is one thing, the form of a ship or of a house is another thing, and the administration or reason of a ship or of the house is a third thing; so the matter of a government or of a state is one thing, the form of a government or of a state is another, and the administration of a government (which is what's properly and truly called reason of state) is a third thing.

2. There are those who can play, and yet cannot pack the cards, and there are who can pack the cards, and yet cannot play.

3. Administration of government, or reason of state, to such as propose to themselves to play upon the square is one thing; and to such as propose to themselves to pack the cards is another.[1]

4. Reason of state is that in a kingdom or a commonwealth which in a family is called the main chance.

5. The master of a family, that either keeps himself up to his ancient bounds or increases his stock, looks very well to the main chance, at least if his play be upon the square: that is, upon his own abilities, or good fortune, or the laws; but if it were not upon the square, yet an estate, however gotten, is not for that a less estate in itself, nor less descending by the law to his successors.

6. If a people through their own industry, or the prodigality of their

---

[1] To 'pack the cards' might mean to do it fairly, or unfairly. The antithesis with 'on the square' in no. 3 suggests the latter significance, which does not however seem obligatory in no. 2.

lords, come to acquire liberty; if a few by their industry, or through the folly or slothfulness of the people, come to eat them out and make themselves lords; if one lord by his power or his virtue, or through their necessity, their wisdom, or their folly, can overtop the rest of these lords and make himself king; all this was fair play and upon the square.

7. Reason of state, if we speak of it as fair play, is foreign or domestic.

8. Reason of state which is foreign consists in balancing foreign princes and states in such a manner as you may gain upon them, or at least that they may not gain upon you.

9. Reason of state which is domestic is the administration of a government (being not usurped) according to the foundation and superstructures of the same if they be good, or so as, not being good, that they may be mended, or so as, being good or bad, they may be altered; or, the government being usurped, the reason of state then is the way and means whereby such usurpation may be made good or maintained.

10. Reason of state, in a democracy which is rightly founded and rightly ordered, is a thing of great facility, whether in a foreign or in a domestic relation. In a foreign, because one good democracy, weighing two or three of the greatest princes, will easily give the balance abroad at its pleasure; in a domestic, because it consists not of any more than giving such a stop in accumulation that the state comes not to be monarchical; which one reason of state being made good, all the rest goes well; and which one reason of state being neglected, all the rest comes in time to infallible ruin.

11. Reason of state, in a democracy which is not right in its foundations, may flourish abroad and be one; but at home will languish or be two reasons of state: that is, the reason of the state or orders of[1] the nobility, which is to lord it over the people, and the reason of the popular state or order, which is to bring the commonwealth to equality; which two reasons of state, being irreconcilable, will exercise themselves against one another, first by disputes, then by plots, till it comes at last to open violence and so to the utter ruin of the commonwealth, as it happened in Rome.

12. Reason of state in an absolute monarchy (whether foreign or

[1] It is unclear why the plural 'orders' should be used. Note that 'state' here has the meaning of 'estate'.

domestic) is but threefold: as first, to keep its military farmers or timariots to the first institution; next, to cut him that grows anything above his due stature, or lifts up his head above the rest, by so much the shorter; and last of all, to keep its arms in exercise.

13. In aristocratical monarchy reason of state (as to the whole) is but one thing, that is, to preserve the counterpoise of the king and the two, or the three, or the four estates; for in some counties, as in Poland, there are but two estates, the clergy and the nobility; in others, as in Sweden, there are four, the nobility, the gentry, the clergy and the commons;[1] in most others there are but three, the lords spiritual, the lords temporal and the commons.

14. In aristocratical monarchy reason of state (as to the parts) is a multifarious thing, every state having its peculiar reason of state, and the king also his reason of state; with the king it is to balance the nobility, that he may hold them under; reason of state with the nobility is to balance the king, lest he should grow absolute; reason of state both with the king and the nobility is to keep down the people; and reason of state with the people is to drive at their liberty.

15. In forms that are pure, or in governments that have no more than an absolute prince or one state, as absolute monarchy and equal or pure democracy, there is but one reason of state, and that is to preserve the form entire. In forms that are mixed (as in an inequal commonwealth where there are two estates, and in aristocratical monarchy where there is a king and two if not three estates), there are so many reasons of state to break the form, that there has not been any inequal commonwealth which either the people have not brought to democracy, or the nobility to monarchy. And scarce was there any aristocratical monarchy, where (to omit the wars of the nobility with their king, or among themselves) the people have not driven out their king, or where the king has not brought the people into slavery. Aristocratical monarchy is the true theatre of expedient-mongers and state-empirics, or the deep waters wherein that Leviathan the minister of state takes his pastime.[2]

16. The complaint that the wisdom of all these latter times in princes'

---

[1] Incorrect: nobles, clergy, burghers and peasants.
[2] H would be very wrong if he thought that this shaft would pierce Hobbes, but it need not even have been aimed at him.

affairs consists rather in fine deliveries and shiftings of dangers or mischiefs when they are near, than in solid and grounded courses to keep them off, is a complaint in the streets of aristocratical monarchy; and not to be remedied, because, the nobility being not broken, the king is in danger, and the nobility being broken, the monarchy is ruined.

17. An absurdity in the form of the government (as that in a monarchy there may be two monarchs) shoots out into a mischief in the administration or some wickedness in the reason of state, as in Romulus's killing of Remus and the monstrous assassinations of the Roman emperors.

18. Usurpation of government is a surfeit that converts the best arts into the worst; *nemo unquam imperium flagitio acquisitum bonis artibus exercuit.*

19. As in the privation of virtue and in beggary, men are sharks or robbers, and the reason of their way of living is quite contrary to those of thrift; so in the privation of government, as in anarchy, oligarchy or tyranny, that which is reason of state with them is directly opposite to that which is truly so; whence are all those black maxims set down by some politicians, particularly Machiavel in his *Prince*, and which are condemned to the fire even by them who, if they lived otherwise, might blow their fingers.

20. Where the government from a true foundation rises up into proper superstructures or form, the reason of state is right and straight; but give our politician peace when you lease, if your house stands awry, your props do not stand upright.

21. Take a juggler and commend his tricks never so much, yet if in so doing you show his tricks, you spoil him; which has been and is to be confessed of Machiavel.

22. Corruption in government is to be read and considered in Machiavel, as diseases in a man's body are to be read and considered in Hippocrates.

23. Neither Hippocrates nor Machiavel introduced diseases into man's body, nor corruption into government, which were before their times; and seeing they do but discover them, it must be confessed that so much as they have done tends not to the increase but the cure of them, which is the truth of these two authors.

Index

Cambridge Texts in the History of Political Thought

Titles published in the series thus far

Dante *Monarchy* (edited by Prue Shaw)
0 521 56781 5 paperback
Diderot *Political Writings* (edited by John Hope Mason and Robert Wokler)
0 521 36911 8 paperback
The Dutch Revolt (edited by Martin van Gelderen)
0 521 39809 6 paperback
Early Greek Political Thought from Homer to the Sophists
(edited by Michael Gagarin and Paul Woodruff)
0 521 43768 7 paperback
The Early Political Writings of the German Romantics
(edited by Frederick C. Beiser)
0 521 44951 0 paperback
The English Levellers (edited by Andrew Sharp)
0 521 62511 4 paperback
Erasmus *The Education of a Christian Prince* (edited by Lisa Jardine)
0 521 58811 1 paperback
Fenelon *Telemachus* (edited by Patrick Riley)
0 521 45662 2 paperback
Ferguson *An Essay on the History of Civil Society* (edited by Fania Oz-Salzberger)
0 521 44736 4 paperback
Filmer *Patriarcha and Other Writings* (edited by Johann P. Sommerville)
0 521 39903 3 paperback
Fletcher *Political Works* (edited by John Robertson)
0 521 43994 9 paperback
Sir John Fortescue *On the Laws and Governance of England*
(edited by Shelley Lockwood)
0 521 58996 7 paperback
Fourier *The Theory of the Four Movements* (edited by Gareth Stedman Jones and
Ian Patterson)
0 521 35693 8 paperback
Gramsci *Pre-Prison Writings* (edited by Richard Bellamy)
0 521 42307 4 paperback
Guicciardini *Dialogue on the Government of Florence* (edited by Alison Brown)
0 521 45623 1 paperback
Harrington *The Commonwealth of Oceana* and *A System of Politics*
(edited by J. G. A. Pocock)
0 521 42329 5 paperback
Hegel *Elements of the Philosophy of Right* (edited by Allen W. Wood and
H. B. Nisbet)
0 521 34888 9 paperback
Hegel *Political Writings* (edited by Laurence Dickey and H. B. Nisbet)
0 521 45979 3 paperback
Hobbes *On the Citizen* (edited by Michael Silverthorne and Richard Tuck)
0 521 43780 6 paperback
Hobbes *Leviathan* (edited by Richard Tuck)
0 521 56797 1 paperback
Hobhouse *Liberalism and Other Writings* (edited by James Meadowcroft)
0 521 43726 1 paperback
Hooker *Of the Laws of Ecclesiastical Polity* (edited by A. S. McGrade)
0 521 37908 3 paperback
Hume *Political Essays* (edited by Knud Haakonssen)
0 521 46639 3 paperback

King James VI and I *Political Writings* (edited by Johann P. Sommerville)
    0 521 44729 1 paperback
Jefferson *Political Writings* (edited by Joyce Appleby and Terence Ball)
    0 521 64841 6 paperback
John of Salisbury *Policraticus* (edited by Cary Nederman)
    0 521 36701 8 paperback
Kant *Political Writings* (edited by H. S. Reiss and H. B. Nisbet)
    0 521 39837 1 paperback
Knox *On Rebellion* (edited by Roger A. Mason)
    0 521 39988 2 paperback
Kropotkin *The Conquest of Bread and other writings* (edited by Marshall Shatz)
    0 521 45990 7 paperback
Lawson *Politica sacra et civilis* (edited by Conal Condren)
    0 521 39248 9 paperback
Leibniz *Political Writings* (edited by Patrick Riley)
    0 521 35899 x paperback
The Levellers (edited by Andrew Sharp)
    0 521 62511 4 paperback
Locke *Political Essays* (edited by Mark Goldie)
    0 521 47861 8 paperback
Locke *Two Treatises of Government* (edited by Peter Laslett)
    0 521 35730 6 paperback
Loyseau *A Treatise of Orders and Plain Dignities* (edited by Howell A. Lloyd)
    0 521 45624 x paperback
Luther and Calvin on Secular Authority (edited by Harro Höpfl)
    0 521 34986 9 paperback
Machiavelli *The Prince* (edited by Quentin Skinner and Russell Price)
    0 521 34993 1 paperback
de Maistre *Considerations on France* (edited by Isaiah Berlin and Richard Lebrun)
    0 521 46628 8 paperback
Malthus *An Essay on the Principle of Population* (edited by Donald Winch)
    0 521 42972 2 paperback
Marsiglio of Padua *Defensor minor* and *De translatione Imperii*
(edited by Cary Nederman)
    0 521 40846 6 paperback
Marx *Early Political Writings* (edited by Joseph O'Malley)
    0 521 34994 x paperback
Marx *Later Political Writings* (edited by Terrell Carver)
    0 521 36739 5 paperback
James Mill *Political Writings* (edited by Terence Ball)
    0 521 38748 5 paperback
J. S. Mill *On Liberty, with The Subjection of Women* and *Chapters on Socialism*
(edited by Stefan Collini)
    0 521 37917 2 paperback
Milton *Political Writings* (edited by Martin Dzelzainis)
    0 521 34866 8 paperback
Montesquieu *The Spirit of the Laws* (edited by Anne M. Cohler,
Basia Carolyn Miller and Harold Samuel Stone)
    0 521 36974 6 paperback
More *Utopia* (edited by George M. Logan and Robert M. Adams)
    0 521 40318 9 paperback

Morris *News from Nowhere* (edited by Krishan Kumar)
  0 521 42233 7 paperback
Nicholas of Cusa *The Catholic Concordance* (edited by Paul E. Sigmund)
  0 521 56773 4 paperback
Nietzsche *On the Genealogy of Morality* (edited by Keith Ansell-Pearson)
  0 521 40610 2 paperback
Paine *Political Writings* (edited by Bruce Kuklick)
  0 521 66799 2 paperback
Plato *The Republic* (edited by G. R. F. Ferrari and Tom Griffith)
  0 521 48443 x paperback
Plato *Statesman* (edited by Julia Annas and Robin Waterfield)
  0 521 44778 x paperback
Price *Political Writings* (edited by D. O. Thomas)
  0 521 40969 1 paperback
Priestley *Political Writings* (edited by Peter Miller)
  0 521 42561 1 paperback
Proudhon *What is Property?* (edited by Donald R. Kelley and
Bonnie G. Smith)
  0 521 40556 4 paperback
Pufendorf *On the Duty of Man and Citizen according to Natural Law*
(edited by James Tully)
  0 521 35980 5 paperback
The Radical Reformation (edited by Michael G. Baylor)
  0 521 37948 2 paperback
Rousseau *The Discourses and other early political writings*
(edited by Victor Gourevitch)
  0 521 42445 3 paperback
Rousseau *The Social Contract and other later political writings*
(edited by Victor Gourevitch)
  0 521 42446 1 paperback
Seneca *Moral and Political Essays* (edited by John Cooper and John Procope)
  0 521 34818 8 paperback
Sidney *Court Maxims* (edited by Hans W. Blom, Eco Haitsma Mulier and
Ronald Janse)
  0 521 46736 5 paperback
Sorel *Reflections on Violence* (edited by Jeremy Jennings)
  0 521 55910 3 paperback
Spencer *The Man versus the State* and *The Proper Sphere of Government*
(edited by John Offer)
  0 521 43740 7 paperback
Stirner *The Ego and Its Own* (edited by David Leopold)
  0 521 45647 9 paperback
Thoreau *Political Writings* (edited by Nancy Rosenblum)
  0 521 47675 5 paperback
Utopias of the British Enlightenment (edited by Gregory Claeys)
  0 521 45590 1 paperback
Vitoria *Political Writings* (edited by Anthony Pagden and Jeremy Lawrance)
  0 521 36714 x paperback
Voltaire *Political Writings* (edited by David Williams)
  0 521 43727 x paperback

Weber *Political Writings* (edited by Peter Lassman and Ronald Speirs)
   0 521 39719 7 paperback
William of Ockham *A Short Discourse on Tyrannical Government*
(edited by A. S. McGrade and John Kilcullen)
   0 521 35803 5 paperback
William of Ockham *A Letter to the Friars Minor and other writings*
(edited by A. S. McGrade and John Kilcullen)
   0 521 35804 3 paperback
Wollstonecraft *A Vindication of the Rights of Men* and *A Vindication of the Rights
of Woman* (edited by Sylvana Tomaselli)
   0 521 43633 8 paperback